Algorithms, Collusion and Competition Law

Algorithms, Collusion and Competition Law

A Comparative Approach

Edited by

Steven Van Uytsel

Professor of International Business Law, Faculty of Law, Kyushu University, Japan

Salil K. Mehra

James E. Beasley Professor of Law, Beasley School of Law, Temple University, USA

Yoshiteru Uemura

Professor of Competition Law, Faculty of Economics, Hannan University, Japan

Cheltenham, UK • Northampton, MA, USA

Published by
Edward Elgar Publishing Limited
The Lypiatts
15 Lansdown Road
Cheltenham
Glos GL50 2JA
UK

Edward Elgar Publishing, Inc.
William Pratt House
9 Dewey Court
Northampton
Massachusetts 01060
USA

A catalogue record for this book
is available from the British Library

Library of Congress Control Number: 2023931501

This book is available electronically in the **Elgar**online
Law subject collection
http://dx.doi.org/10.4337/9781802203042

ISBN 978 1 80220 303 5 (cased)
ISBN 978 1 80220 304 2 (eBook)

Printed and bound by CPI Group (UK) Ltd, Croydon, CR0 4YY

Contents

Figures

Tables

Contributors

Baskaran Balasingham is an Assistant Professor at Utrecht University in the Netherlands.

Jan Blockx is an Assistant Professor at the University of Antwerp in Belgium.

Ai Deng is an Associate Director of NERA Economic Consulting and a Lecturer at Johns Hopkins University in the United States of America.

Yajie Gao is a Ph.D. student at Queen Mary University of London.

Wei Han is an Associate Professor and Executive Director of the Competition Research Center at the University of the Chinese Academy of Social Sciences.

Nikita Koradia is an Assistant Professor at the Institute of Law of Nirma University, Ahmedabad, Gujarat, India.

Cassey Lee is a Senior Fellow and Coordinator of the Regional Economic Studies Programme at ISEAS, Yusof Ishak Institute (Singapore).

Gloria Lin is a Research Assistant at the Institute of Policy Studies, National University of Singapore.

Kiran Manokaran is associated with Lakshmikumaran and Sridharan Attorneys (Chennai) as a Senior Associate and also with Nishimura and Asahi (Tokyo) as a Foreign Attorney.

Zara Saeed is a Contract Review Specialist at the Association of International Certified Professional Accountants in London, United Kingdom.

Yoshiteru Uemura is a Professor of Competition Law at Hannan University in Osaka, Japan.

Steven Van Uytsel is a Professor of International Business Law at the Faculty of Law of Kyushu University, Japan.

Thomas Weck is Professor of Public, Regulatory and Comparative Law at Frankfurt School of Finance and Management, Germany.

Preface

Salil K. Mehra

What is algorithmic collusion? The chapters in this volume tackle this important question for competition law. Critically, they do so from different directions, including theoretical, empirical and doctrinal – the latter frequently from a comparative perspective.

Early in the past decade, this question would have seemed purely academic, or possibly even science-fictional. The initial work on algorithmic collusion, including that of the author of this preface, was long on theory, but had relatively few real-world examples to point to.[1] But experience gathered since then has shown that competition law enforcers are right to be concerned about the adoption of price monitoring and setting algorithms and their impact on consumers.

The chapter collected in this volume are a welcome addition to the literature on algorithms and competition law. The chapters by Van Uytsel and Weck respectively (specifically "The Algorithmic Collusion Debate: A Focus on (Autonomous) Tacit Collusion" and "Algorithms and the Limits of Antitrust") stress the likely competitive effects of automated price monitoring and response, whether by pricing algorithms, or perhaps down the road, artificial intelligence. While it would be wrong to call these chapters doctrine free, they provide a robust discussion of the theory by which algorithmic pricing can become a competitive concern, as well as overlapping but interestingly nuanced takes on algorithmic collusion as a phenomenon.

Valuably, the chapters in this volume go beyond the focus on the theory that characterized initial discussions of algorithmic collusion. The contributions by Lee and Lin, and by Van Uytsel (specifically "Pricing in Online Grocery Markets: Challenges in Monitoring Competition" and "Algorithms

---

[1]   *See, e.g.*, Salil K. Mehra, 'De-Humanizing Antitrust' (16 October 2014) Colum. L. Sch. Blue Sky Blog, available at https://clsbluesky.law.columbia.edu/2014/10/16/de-humanizing-antitrustthe-rise-of-the-machines-and-the-regulation-of-competition/ (linking to draft of article later published as Salil K. Mehra, 'Antitrust and the Robo-Seller: Competition in the Time of Algorithms' (2016) 100 Minn. L. Rev. 1323, 1327 (2016) (working through implications of robo-selling for the Cournot model of interdependent pricing).

Unravelled: Observations on the Audit of Uber and Amazon Marketplace Algorithms"), dive into data on pricing algorithms' actual behavior to achieve a better understanding of the implications for competition and consumers. And the chapters by Koradia, Manokaran and Saeed; Han, Gao and Deng; Van Uytsel and Uemura (specifically "Tackling Algorithmic Collusion: The Scope of the Indian Competition Act", "Challenges Brought by and in Response to Algorithms: the Perspective of China's Anti-Monopoly Law", and "Algorithmic Collusion and the Japanese Antimonopoly Act"); as well as the individual chapters by Balasingham, Blockx and Uemura provide thorough understandings of how algorithmic collusion might interact with doctrine under several different competition law regimes. Helpfully, even where these chapters are not explicitly comparative, reading them as a collection in this volume provides implicit comparative insight.

As mentioned, these chapters flow from a meeting at Kyushu University held in-person shortly before the COVID-19 pandemic made such gatherings impossible for a time, and are a reminder of the importance of active scholarly give-and-take at in-person academic meetings. Let us hope that the COVID-19 shutdowns are over or soon will be, and that we have developed a new appreciation for the scholarly engagement that events like this provide.

July 2022
Salil K. Mehra
Temple University
James E. Beasley School of Law
Philadelphia, USA

Acknowledgements

This volume benefitted from a Grants-in-Aid of the Japan Society for the Promotion of Science, titled Artificial Intelligence, Price Setting Strategies and Antitrust Law: Towards a Regulatory Framework (N. 18K01300) and the Progress 100 – Research Hub for Humanities, Social Sciences and Interdisciplinary Knowledge (RINK) Grant of Kyushu University.

The editors owe a word of gratitude to Yuko Matsumura and Oliver Posani for their assistance with the editing of this volume. We would like to show gratitude to Ben Booth, Amber Watts and their colleagues at Edward Elgar for their endless support in bringing this book to fruition. We further like to acknowledge the decision of two anonymous referees who approved this volume.

1 August 2022
Steven Van Uystel, Fukuoka, Japan
Yoshiteru Uemura, Osaka, Japan
Salil K. Mehra, Philadelphia, United States of America

1. The algorithmic collusion debate: a focus on (autonomous) tacit collusion

Steven Van Uytsel[1]

1   INTRODUCTION

Ariel Ezrachi and Maurice E. Stucke have given the competition law community a taxonomy to converse about algorithmic collusion.[2] Despite their recognition of four models of algorithmic collusion ("Messenger, Hub and Spoke, Predicable Agent and Digital Eye"),[3] the debate mainly developed around the last scenarios, which presupposes the capacity of the algorithm to reach autonomously a colluded outcome. The centre of the debate was on the question of whether algorithms could collude autonomously and how competition law can or should respond. The former question tells to the technological debate, while the latter recounts the legal debate.

One could expect that the technological debate would be fairly straightforward and seek an answer to the question of what kind of algorithms can collude under what kind of circumstances. However, the debate is more complex than that. Of course, there is already considerable research on these two questions and this body of research is still growing.[4] The fact none of these

---

[1]   This chapter is a reworked and updated version of an earlier publication, Steven Van Uytsel, 'Artificial Intelligence and Collusion: A Literature Overview' in Marcelo Corrales, Mark Fenwick, Nikolaus Forgó (eds), *Robotics, AI and the Future of Law* (Springer 2018). The author has a license from Springer to re-use a part of the content.

[2]   Ariel Ezrachi and Maurice E. Stucke, *Virtual Competition: The Promise and Perils of the Algorithm-Driven Economy* (Harvard University Press 2016).

[3]   ibid., 35–81.

[4]   See, e.g., Matthias Hettich, 'Algorithmic Collusion: Insights from Deep Learning' (2021), available at https://papers.ssrn.com/sol3/papers.cfm?abstract_id= 3785966 (accessed 30 June 2022); Timo Klein, 'Autonomous Algorithmic Collusion: Q-learning under Sequential Pricing' (2021) 52(3) *RAND Journal of Economics* 538; Ibrahim Abada and Xavier Lambin, 'Artificial Intelligence: Can Seemingly Collusive Outcomes Be Avoided?' (2020), available at https://papers.ssrn.com/sol3/papers.cfm

studies have provided real-world results, have contributed to a wide variety of speculations. It was ventured that algorithms could result in pricing strategies other than algorithmic collusion.[5] More dramatically formulated, but in line with the previous view, is the suggestion that algorithms will never be able to collude in a real-world scenario.[6] To prevent speculation, a part of the debate has advocated the auditing of existing algorithms or testing algorithms before being released on the market.[7]

?abstract_id=3559308 (accessed 30 June 2020); Emilio Calvano, Giacomo Calzolari, Vincenzo Denicolò, and Sergio Pastorello, 'Artificial Intelligence, Algorithmic Pricing, and Collusion' (2020) 110(10) *American Economic Review* 3265; Ulrich Schwalbe, 'Algorithms, Machine Learning, and Collusion' (2018), available at https://papers.ssrn .com/sol3/papers.cfm?abstract_id=3232631 (accessed 30 June 2022); Ashwin Ittoo and Nicholas Petit, 'Algorithmic Pricing Agents and Tacit Collusion: A Technological Perspective' (2017), available at https://papers.ssrn.com/sol3/papers.cfm?abstract_id =3046405 (accessed 30 June 2022). A summary of the experimental debate is provided by Hans-Theo Normann and Martin Sternberg, 'Do Machines Collude Better than Humans?' (2021) 12(10) *Journal of European Competition Law & Practice* 765.

⁵ See, e.g., Ai Deng, 'An Antitrust Lawyer's Guide to Machine Learning' (2018) 32(2) *Antitrust* 82; Maurice Dolmans, 'Artificial Intelligence and the Future of Competition Law – Further Thoughts (Reaction to Prof. Ariel Ezrachi)' (GCLC Lunch Talk: "Algorithms and Markets: Virtual or Virtuous Competition?, 2017), available at www.coleurope.eu/sites/default/files/uploads/event/dolmans.pdf (accessed 30 June 2022).

⁶ See, e.g., Thibault Schrepel, 'The Fundamental Unimportance of Algorithmic Collusion for Antitrust Law' (2019) 33 *Harv. J.L. & Tech.* 117.

⁷ See, e.g., Ezrachi and Stucke (n. 2 above) at 230–31. On testing algorithms, see, e.g., Joseph E. Harrington, 'Developing Competition Law for Collusion by Autonomous Artificial Agents' (2018) 14(3) *Journal of Competition Law & Economics* 638; Joseph E. Harrington, Jr., 'Developing Competition Law for Collusion by Autonomous Price-Setting Agents' (2017), available at https://papers.ssrn.com/sol3/ papers.cfm?abstract_id=3037818 (accessed 30 June 2022). For actual auditing of algorithms, see, e.g., Marcel Wieting and Geza Sapi, 'Algorithms in the Marketplace: An Empirical Analysis of Automated Pricing in E-Commerce' (NET Institute Working Paper #21-06, 2021), available at https://papers.ssrn.com/sol3/papers.cfm?abstract_id =3945137 (accessed 30 June 2022); Stephanie Assad, Robert Clark, Daniel Ershov, and Lei Xu, 'Algorithmic Pricing and Competition: Empirical Evidence from the German Retail Gasoline Market' (CESifo Working Paper No. 8521, August 2020), available at https://papers.ssrn.com/sol3/papers.cfm?abstract_id=3682021 (accessed 30 June 2022); Le Chen, Alan Mislove, and Christo Wilson, 'Peeking Beneath the Hood of Uber' (Internet Measurement Conference, Tokyo, 28–30 October 2015), available at www.ccs.neu.edu/home/amislove/publications/Uber-IMC.pdf (accessed 30 June 2022); Le Chen, Alan Mislove, and Christo Wilson, 'An Empirical Analysis of Algorithmic Pricing on Amazon Marketplace' (25th International Conference on World Wide Web, Montréal, 11–15 April 2016), available at https://dl.acm.org/doi/10 .1145/2872427.2883089 (accessed 30 June 2022).

The legal debate has been characterized from the beginning by a big divide. On the one hand, there are scholars arguing that competition law is up to the task.[8] On the other hand, there are scholars maintaining that competition law needs to change. The call for change can be divided between re-interpreting existing concepts and introducing new concepts.[9] A more drastic option that has been suggested was to create regulatory instruments outside the traditional competition law framework.[10]

It is the purpose of this chapter to detail the above-mentioned debate. The chapter will first introduce the taxonomy of Ezrachi and Stucke and point out that this taxonomy has barely been questioned (Section 2). Subsequently, the chapter will elaborate the technological side of the debate (Section 3). The chapter will detail the legal side of the debate (Section 4), before introducing the book (Section 5).

---

[8] See, e.g., Luca Calzolari, 'The Misleading Consequences of Comparing Algorithmic and Tacit Collusion: Tackling Algorithmic Concerted Practices Under Art. 101 TFEU' (2021) 6(2) *European Papers – A Journal on Law and Integration* 1193; Pieter Van Cleynenbreugel, 'Article 101 TFEU's Association of Undertakings Notion and Its Surprising Potential to Help Distinguish Acceptable from Unacceptable Algorithmic Collusion' (2020) 65(3) *The Antitrust Bulletin* 423; Jan Blockx, 'Policing Price Bots: Algorithms and Collusion' (2018 ASCOLA Conference, 2018), available at www.law.nyu.edu/sites/default/files/upload_documents/Blockx.pdf (accessed 30 June 2022), Jan Blockx, 'Antitrust in Digital Markets in the EU: Policing Price Bots' (Radbound Economic Law Conference, 2017), available at https://papers.ssrn.com/sol3/papers.cfm?abstract_id=2987705 (accessed 30 June 2022). If only looking at the European law, see also Cento Veljanovski, 'Algorithmic Antitrust: A Critical Overview' in Aurelien Portuese (ed), *Algorithmic Antitrust* (Springer 2022) 39, 57.

[9] See, e.g., Michal Gal, 'Algorithms as Illegal Agreements' (2019) 34 *Berkeley Technology Law Journal* 67.

[10] See, e.g., Vasileios Tsoukalas, 'Should the New Competition Tool be Put Back on the Table to Remedy Algorithmic Tacit Collusion? A Comparative Analysis of the Possibilities under the Current Framework and under the NCT, Drawing on the UK Experience' (2022) 13(3) Journal of European Competition Law & Practice 234; Colm Hawkes, 'A Market Investigation Tool to Tackle Algorithmic Tacit Collusion: An Approach for the (Near) Future' (Research Papers in Law 3/2021, 2021), available at www.coleurope.eu/sites/default/files/research-paper/ResearchPaper_3_2021_Colm _Hawkes.pdf (accessed 30 June 2022); Ingrid Vandenborre and Michael J. Frese, 'Algorithmic Pricing: Candidate for the New Competition Tool?' (2020), available at https://globalcompetitionreview.com/guide/e-commerce-competition-enforcement -guide/third-edition/article/algorithmic-pricing-candidate-the-new-competition-tool (accessed 30 June 2022).

2   A TAXONOMY ON ALGORITHMIC COLLUSION

2.1   The Taxonomy of Ezrachi and Stucke and its Implication for Competition Law

Ezrachi and Stucke contend that collusion "reflects a concurrence of wills between the colluding companies' agents. Illegality is triggered when companies, through their directors, officers, employees, agents, or controlling shareholders, operate in concert to limit or distort competition."[11] With the arrival of algorithms, this human-centred cause of collusion may be coming to an end. Algorithms may take over the roles traditionally played by the companies' agents. Ezrachi and Stucke distinguish four different scenarios in which algorithms can contribute to collusion: Messenger, Hub and Spoke, Predicable Agent and Digital Eye.[12] These scenarios have been repeated in various official documents and scholarly writings, often with different terminology.[13]

---

[11]   Ariel Ezrachi and Maurice E. Stucke, 'Artificial Intelligence & Collusion: When Computers Inhibit Competition' (2017) 5(1) *University of Illinois Law Review* 1775, 1782. For a summary and examples, see Schwalbe (n. 4 above).

[12]   Ezrachi and Stucke (n. 2) at 35–71.

[13]   See, e.g., OECD, 'Algorithms and Collusion – Background Note by the Secretariat' (DAF/Comp(2017)4, 2018), available at https://one.oecd.org/document/DAF/COMP(2017)4/en/pdf (accessed 30 June 2022) at 24–32; Niccolò Colombo, 'Virtual Competition: Human Liability Vis-à-Vis Artificial Intelligence's Anticompetitive Behaviours' (2018) 2(1) *European Competition and Regulatory Law Review* 11, at 12–14. It can be stated that "[t]he Secretariat of the Organization for Economic Co-operation and Development (OECD) follows this categorization but uses different names. The OECD distinguished between monitoring algorithms, parallel algorithms, signaling algorithms, and self-learning algorithms. Niccolò Colombo terms these four categories as follows: classical digital cartel, inadvertent hub-and-spoke, tacit algorithmic collusion and dystopian virtual reality." See Steven Van Uytsel. 'Artificial Intelligence and Collusion: A Literature Overview' in Marcelo Corrales, Mark Fenwick, Nikolaus Forgó (eds), *Robotics, AI and the Future of Law* (Springer 2018) 155, 157. For the wide spread of the terminology, see also Ambroise Descamps, Timo Klein, and Gareth Shier, 'Algorithms and Competition: The Latest Theory and Evidence' (2021) 20(1) *Competition Law Journal* 32; Gintarė Surblytė-Namavičienė, *Competition and Regulation in the Data Economy: Does Artificial Intelligence Demand a New Balance?* (Edward Elgar 2020) 155–78; Aurelien Portuese, 'Prologue: Algorithmic Antitrust – A Primer' in Aurelien Portuese (ed), *Algorithmic Antitrust* (Springer 2022) 1; Aleksandra Lamontanaro, 'Bounty Hunters for Algorithmic Cartels: An Old Solution for a New Problem' (2020) 30 *Fordham Intell. Prop. Media & Ent. L.J.* 1259; Lorenz Marx, Christian Ritz, and Jonas Weller, 'Liability for Outsourced Algorithmic Collusion – A Practical Approximation' (2019) 2 *Concurrences* 1, available at www.concurrences.com/IMG/pdf/_08.concurrences_2-2019_legal _practices_marx_et_al.pdf?50150/0f71319df3abe8b18a7387586dc4488bc3713519 (accessed 30 June 2022); Nicolo Colombo, 'Virtual Competition: Human Liability

Messenger embodies a scenario in which an algorithm is put in place after humans have discussed and agreed to collude. The algorithm's main purpose is to implement, monitor, and police the cartel.[14] Hub and Spoke represents a scenario in which the same algorithm is used "to determine the market price charged by numerous users."[15] This model is based on the fact that retailers use pricing algorithms provided by the same third-party provider. Predictable Agent exemplifies a scenario in which an algorithm is designed to provide a specific outcome based on the market conditions it can observe.[16] These algorithms are implemented by firms independently from each other. Digital Eye is the most advanced scenario and is based on algorithms that operate with machine learning and deep learning technologies. The algorithm is given a goal to achieve, such as profit maximization. The algorithm itself will then determine the best pricing strategy to obtain that goal.[17]

Linking these scenarios to competition law, Ezrachi and Stucke draw the following conclusions. Messenger, Hub and Spoke, and Predictable Agent may not pose a problem for enforcement authorities. Digital Eye, to the contrary, may fall outside the scope of most competition law. The reasons are as follows.

Messenger is a scenario that operates based on a human-made agreement. Such agreements are perfectly within the scope of competition law. It is just important that the existence of the agreement can be proven.[18] Hub and Spoke is a scenario with a slightly more complex factual setting, since it involves both horizontal and vertical communication. However, Ezrachi and Stucke predict that, based upon the algorithm's collusion facilitating design, and this design was intended by the competing firms or the firms had at least knowledge about it, most competition laws would not have a problem to be applied.[19] Predictable Agent differs from the previous scenarios due to the absence of an agreement or concerted practice. Whether competition law will apply, will depend on the conceptualization of the competition law. Ezrachi and Stucke suggest that the United States competition laws have some flexibility because, next to the

---

Vis-à-Vis Artificial Intelligence's Anticompetitive Behaviours' (2018) 2(1) *European Competition and Regulatory Law Review* 11; Sebastian Felix Janka and Severin Benedict Uhsler, 'Antitrust 4.0 – The Rise of Artificial Intelligence and Emerging Challenges to Antitrust Law' 39(3) *E.C.L.R.* 112.

[14]   Ezrachi and Stucke (n. 11 above) at 1782.
[15]   ibid.
[16]   ibid.
[17]   ibid., 1795. See also OECD (n. 13 above) at 30.
[18]   Ezrachi and Stucke (n. 11 above) at 1782.
[19]   ibid.

Sherman Act, also the Federal Trade Act (FTA) exists.[20] The application of paragraph 5 of the FTA does not require an agreement, but just an unfair trade practice. This requires either an intent to bring about some anticompetitive effect or knowledge that an anticompetitive effects will be brought about.[21]

The Digital Eye scenario is similar to tacit collusion, thus neither based on an agreement nor an intent to implement an anticompetitive effect. In other words, this scenario falls outside the scope of competition law. The knowledge that competition law does not apply limits the motivation for the algorithm developers to alter the design of algorithms or competitors to diversify the algorithms they apply. This could contribute to an even more stable collusive outcome. The question is whether competition law and theory should accept a *status quo* in the law for the digital environment.[22]

2.2   Questioning the Taxonomy of Ezrachi and Stucke

The early literature on algorithmic collusion barely questioned the above-mentioned taxonomy. The structure of the taxonomy, albeit with different terminology, was heavily copied. The content, if it did not remain the

---

[20]   Ezrachi and Stucke (n. 2 above) at 68. For a reference how to deal with in the German context, see Janka and Uhsler (n. 13 above) at 119–20.

[21]   Ezrachi and Stucke (n. 11 above) at 1785, who hold that for the application of paragraph 5 of the Federal Trade Act, the following is required: "(1) evidence that defendants tacitly or expressly agreed to a facilitating device to avoid competition, or (2) oppressiveness, such as (a) evidence of defendants' anticompetitive intent or purpose or (b) the absence of an independent, legitimate business reason for defendants' conduct. Accordingly, in Category III, the defendants may be liable if, when developing the algorithms or in seeing the effects, they were: (1) motivated to achieve an anticompetitive outcome, or (2) aware of their actions' natural and probable anticompetitive consequences." Ibid.

[22]   "Here customers are harmed just as much as (if not more than) in our other collusion scenarios (given fewer episodes of retaliation). We therefore witness a new reality: an anticompetitive outcome which we may not readily perceive and with no one to blame. Any reduction in our welfare is 'merely' a side effect of the rise of the machines and their quest to optimize and serve." Ezrachi and Stucke (n. 11 above) at 1785; Ezrachi and Stucke (n. 2 above) at 79. It should be noted that several scholars have already questioned the theory of tacit collusion. See Richard Posner, *Antitrust Law: An Economic Perspective* (The University of Chicago Press 1976) (even though he withdrew from his critique, see Richard Posner, 'Review of Kaplow, Competition Policy and Price Fixing' (2014) 79 *Antitrust Law Journal* 761) and Louis Kaplow, *Competition Policy and Price Fixing* (Princeton University Press 2013). The early critique has been part of the current scholars debate to indicate that it is not the first time that the theory of tacit collusion has been questioned. See Gal (n. 9 above), at 27–8. See also Fransisco Beneke and Mark-Oliver Mackenrodt, 'Artificial Intelligence and Collusion' (2019) 50 *IIC – International Review of Intellectual Property and Competition Law* 109, 118–25.

same, was merely a fine-tuning of the basic typology. But, even in today's literature, the taxonomy remains influential. For example, the Study Group on Competition Policy in Digital Markets, commissioned by the Japan Fair Trade Commission, used the taxonomy in 2021 to elaborate whether the Japanese Antimonopoly Act could apply to the various scenarios of algorithmic collusion.[23]

The first critical voices towards the taxonomy were not related to the categorization into different scenarios. Uber, the often-cited example of algorithmic hub-and-spoke collusion,[24] has also been explored from a labour law perspective.[25] The focus of courts and scholars was on the degree of control Uber exerts over the drivers. Concluding that Uber has control over its drivers implies that the drivers are "false self-employed". This would mean that the relationship between Uber and its drivers falls outside of the scope of competition law. However, no unequivocal answer has been given, either by courts or by scholars, on this point.[26] Some hold that there are enough arguments to conclude that the drivers are employees of Uber.[27] Others consider that the "antagonistic relation between labour law and competition law"[28] is no longer tenable with the arrival of the platform economy and call for a recalibration of the relationship by reinterpreting some concepts within labour and competition law.[29] Still others have searched for qualifying the relationship within existing

---

[23] JFTC, 'Report on the Study Group on Competition Policy in Digital Markets "Algorithms/AI and Competition Policy"' (21 March 2021), available at www.jftc.go .jp/en/pressreleases/yearly-2021/March/210331004.pdf (accessed 30 June 2022).

[24] Ezrachi and Stucke (n. 2 above) at 50–55.

[25] Jorn Kloostra, 'Algorithmic Pricing: A Concern for Platform Workers?' (2021) *ELLJ* 1; Ioannis Lianos, Nicola Countouris, and Valerio De Stefano, 'Re-thinking the Competition Law/Labour Law Interaction: Promoting a Fairer Labour Market' (CLES Research Paper Series 3/2019, 2019), available at https://papers.ssrn.com/sol3/papers .cfm?abstract_id=3465996 (accessed 30 June 2022); Pieter-Jan Aerts, 'Uber and Autodelen' in Matthias E. Storme and Frederic Helsen (eds), *Innovatie en Disruptie in het Economisch Recht* (Intersentia 2017) 217, 257–65 and 269–72; Julian Nowag, 'The UBER-Cartel? UBER between Labour and Competition Law' (LundLawCompWP 1/2016, 2016), available at https://papers.ssrn.com/sol3/papers.cfm?abstract_id= 2826652 (accessed 30 June 2022).

[26] For an extensive discussion, see Christina Hießl, 'The Classification of Platform Workers in Case Law: A Cross-European Comparative Analysis' (2022) 41–58, available at https://papers.ssrn.com/sol3/papers.cfm?abstract_id=3839603 (accessed 30 June 2022), where the author maps out the dominant patterns across several European countries.

[27] Ibid., at least when it relates to ride-hailing, food, grocery, and parcel delivery. More uncertainty seems to exist when it concerns services offered to help in the household or in a business.

[28] Lianos, Countouris, and De Stefano (n. 25 above).

[29] ibid.

concepts of competition law. An agency relationship has been given particular attention.[30] But, just as within the labour law discussion, this qualification would also exclude the application of competition law.[31] This also led to the conclusion that it may be necessary to reconfigure competition law in order to grasp the economic reality of the platform economy.[32]

Aurelien Portuese and Cento Veljanovski are among the first scholars questioning a part of the taxonomy itself.

Portuese's focus is on Digital Eye.[33] This scenario may not belong in the taxonomy if the real economics of it are taken into consideration. If Digital Eye is a "technological innovation, a technical progress, a market improvement for which firms have allegedly spend lots of money researching, developing and commercializing,"[34] this scenario is rather an expression of real competition than a concern for competition law.

Veljanovski's emphasis is on all types of machine-based learning, potentially including both Predictable Agent and Digital Eye.[35] Besides his observation that there is no evidence that machines can autonomously collude, he assumes a potential contradiction in the observation that algorithms could facilitate both price discrimination and collusion. If algorithms offer different prices depending on the willingness of consumers to pay, there will be no stable environment to set up a cartel. If this assumption is correct, algorithmic collusion will only occur in markets not open to price discrimination. Whether these markets exist, is hard to establish according to Veljanovski.[36] He further points out that the proponents of algorithmic collusion have remained too vague on this issue of the industries and sectors that could face algorithmic collusion. This could imply that there may be some industries or sectors that are

---

[30]   See, e.g., Pinar Akman, 'Online Platforms, Agency, and Competition Law: Mind the Gap' (2019) 43 (2) *Fordham International Law Journal* 209. But see *Uber B.V. and Others v Mr Y Aslam and Others*, UKEAT/0056/17/DA, in which the UK Employment Tribunal rejected the label of agency – as was included in the contract between Uber and its drivers, and considered the drivers as employees.

[31]   Akman (n. 30 above) at 242–56. See also Julian Nowag, 'When Sharing Platforms Fix Sellers' Prices' (LundLawCompWP 1/2018, 2018) 17, available at https://papers .ssrn.com/sol3/papers.cfm?abstract_id=3217193 (accessed 30 June 2022).

[32]   Akman (n. 30 above) at 295–315.

[33]   See Portuese (n. 13 above) at 17–21.

[34]   ibid., 18.

[35]   Veljanovski (n. 8 above) at 54–7.

[36]   ibid., 55–6. Personalized pricing strategies may constitute an entry barrier. See Peter Georg Picht and Gaspare Tazio Loderer, 'Framing Algorithms: Competition Law and (Other) Regulatory Tools' (2019) 42(3) *World Competition* 391, 407, but the authors do not deny that algorithms may "put the traditional conditions for tacit collusion to their test."

rather prone towards price collusion rather than discrimination.[37] Veljanovski also speculates that there will not be many industries or sectors where algorithmic collusion can develop.[38] Salil K. Mehra, however, argues that the assumption may not be correct.[39] With an extensive reference to game theory, he shows that price discrimination allows for shift of wealth from consumers to the producers that is so essential that the gains of cooperating over a long time significantly outweigh the gains created by competing with each other. It is indicated in the conclusion that the idea of price-discrimination-driven algorithmic collusion is quite novel.[40]

3 TACIT ALGORITHMIC COLLUSION AND THE TURN TO TECHNOLOGY

Before the criticism on the taxonomy, a different type of scholarship developed. A part of the scholarship either wanted to prove whether algorithms could tacitly, whether or not autonomously, collude. Thus, it wanted to deliver proof for the Predictable Agent and Digital Eye scenarios. In response to the slow progress of this scholarship in terms of real-world examples, it was argued that algorithms could equally result in pricing strategies different than collusion, or that algorithmic collusion is not an issue for competition law. The opposite stance has also been defended, namely that algorithmic collusion will be realized at some point. With this as a starting point, this kind of scholarship investigated how technology should or could respond. Auditing and sandboxing algorithms or providing algorithms to consumers are the main trends in this scholarship.

3.1 Q-Learning and Beyond: The First Evidence of Tacit Algorithmic Collusion

The early literature on algorithmic collusion had little direct empirical evidence that algorithms could lead to collusive strategies. Mehra relied on a the-

---

[37] Veljanovski (n. 8 above) at 56.
[38] ibid.
[39] Salil K. Mehra, 'Price Discrimination-Driven Algorithmic Collusion: Platforms for Durable Cartels' (2021) 26 *Stan. J.L. Bus. & Fin.* 171. See also, Salil K. Mehra, 'Algorithmic Competition, Collusion, and Price Discrimination' in Woodrow Barfield (ed), *The Cambridge Handbook of the Law of Algorithms* (Cambridge University Press 2020) 199.
[40] Mehra (2021) (n. 39 above) at 217.

oretical model to explain that algorithms would collude.[41] Stucke and Ezrachi referred to examples of the retail gasoline market in Chile, Germany, and Perth (Australia) to make that point.[42] Because the evidence was indirect, European Commissioner Margrethe Vestager indicated that "we certainly shouldn't panic about the way algorithms are affecting the market."[43] Somewhere else she alleges that the collusion between machines without any involvement of human beings is still "science fiction."[44] Nicholas Petit has interpreted this cautious stance as a rejection of faith based antitrust and thus a call for evidence.[45]

---

[41]   Salil K. Mehra, 'Antitrust and the Robo-Seller: Competition in the Time of Algorithms' (Temple University Legal Studies Research Paper Series No. 2015-15, 2015), available at https://papers.ssrn.com/sol3/papers.cfm?abstract_id=2576341 (accessed 30 June 2022). When summarizing the argument, it could be states that "Mehra suggests that the repeated Prisoner Dilemma in a Cournot model will aggregate cooperation with the arrival of robo-sellers or algorithms for the following reasons. Algorithms will enable a firm to detect defection from supra-competitive pricing quicker, reducing the potential profit during the first period of a discounted price. The amount of data algorithms can analyze will also enable them to make more accurate decisions and so prevent errors. Similarly, these algorithms will not be subject to biases that could inspire human salesforce to offer promotions." Van Uytsel (n. 1 above) at 162.

[42]   Maurice E. Stucke and Ariel Ezrachi, 'Two Artificial Neural Networks Meet in an Online Hub and Change the Future (of Competition, Market Dynamics and Society)' (Legal Studies Research Paper Series No. 323, 2017) 8-13, available at https://papers.ssrn.com/sol3/papers.cfm?abstract_id=2949434 (accessed 30 June 2022). The retail gasoline markets in several countries were made more transparent. "Transparency, so was the idea, would facilitate the consumer to identify lower prices and so align their consumption patterns. The reality, however, was different and this could be called a *transparency paradox*. Rather than stimulating competition, the increased transparency actually diminished competition and led to even higher prices." Van Uytsel (n. 41 above) at 162. A recent empirical study by Stephanie Assad et al., unavailable to Stucke and Ezrachi when they were developing their arguments, confirmed that the findings in a traditional business setting also apply when algorithmic pricing is used. See Stephanie Assad, Robert Clark, Daniel Ershov, and Lei Xu, 'Algorithmic Pricing and Competition: Empirical Evidence from the German Retail Gasoline Market' (CESifo Working Paper No. 8521, August 2020), available at https://papers.ssrn.com/sol3/papers.cfm?abstract_id=3682021 (accessed 30 June 2022).

[43]   Margrethe Vestager, 'Algorithms and Competition' (Bundeskartellamt 18th Conference on Competition, 2017), available at https://ec.europa.eu/commission/commissioners/2014-2019/vestager/announcements/bundeskartellamt-18th-conference-competition-berlin-16-march-2017_en (accessed 30 June 2022).

[44]   ibid.

[45]   Nicholas Petit, 'Editorial: Antitrust and Artificial Intelligence: A Research Agenda' (2017) 8(6) *Journal of European Competition Law and Practice* 361, 362. The call for evidence is something with which Cento Veljanovski certainly agree, which is apparent in the following quote: "Although Ezrachi and Stucke wants us to move away from *'slogans'* in this area, they nonetheless contribute their own by describ-

Ashwin Ittoo and Nicolas Petit are among the first scholars to respond to the call for evidence.[46] Ittoo and Petit point out that it is important to use algorithmic learning which is able to adjust itself to reach a specific outcome. In other words, they emphasize the need for a dynamic learning process. Q-learning, a specific model of reinforced learning,[47] offers this function. They further contend that it is important to choose those algorithms that can respond to the behaviour and strategies of other market participants, being multi-agent Q-learning. Among the multi-agent Q-learning technologies, so state Ittoo and Petit, is the Nash Q-learning technology the most likely to render a collusive price setting.[48] Nash Q-learning agents could potentially collude, because the outcome of an algorithm is defined as the best response of one agent to the choice of another agent. Theoretically, the "profit-maximizing Nash Q-learning agents could set their prices in response to each other until a point is reached where no agent has any incentive to deviate from this price level given what it expects others to do."[49]

Following this research, there are several other papers that have argued that a Q-learning algorithm is able to collude as long as it operates in a controlled environment. Often cited in the legal literature are the papers of a group of scholars surrounding Emilios Calvano and of Timo Klein.[50] The group around Calvano let their Q-learning algorithm operate within an oligopoly model "with logit demand and constant marginal costs,"[51] while Klein's Q-learning algorithm competes in an environment of sequential competition.[52] In both models, there is no communication between the algorithms.[53] It should also be noted that, despite arriving at a colluded outcome, not all of these papers are able to explain the reason of the colluded outcome.[54] These studies, by no means, represent the final stage of experimenting with Q-learning. Alterations to the economic environment have been tested in other studies. However, more

---

ing '*algorithm-enhanced conscious parallelism*' as "*Tacit Collusion on Steroids*". To others, this is an exaggerated hypothesis. ... There are reasons to be skeptical about the prospects of widespread machine-based collusion and the difficulties it poses for law enforcement." Veljanovski (n. 8 above) at 55.

[46]   Ittoo and Petit (n. 4 above).

[47]   For more detailed information on the different forms of learning, see Descamps, Klein, and Shier (n. 13 above) at 32–5.

[48]   ibid., 9.

[49]   ibid.

[50]   See respectively, Klein (n. 4 above). Calvano et al. (n. 4 above).

[51]   Calvano et al. (n. 4 above).

[52]   Klein (n. 4 above) at 543–7.

[53]   See respectively, Klein (n. 4 above), at 544. Calvano et al. (n. 4 above) at 3269.

[54]   See Klein (n. 4 above) at 539, stating that "However, exactly how algorithms may lead to autonomous collusion is an open research question."

recently, it has been held that the focus on simple Q-learning may prevent experimenting in complex economic environments. One of the proponents of this view is Matthias Hettich.[55]

Hettich posits that algorithmic collusion may be possible with a more complex type of Q-learning: Deep Q-Network (DQN) algorithm.[56] This kind of algorithm is an enhanced Q-learning algorithm by relying on Deep Neural Networks. His set-up shows that in a duopoly, DQN's systematically set supra-competitive prices. The evolution towards higher prices is much faster than in case of normal Q-learning. It is said that only after 20,000 interactions, the price starts to increase.[57] These supra-competitive prices are not a collusive outcome, but the process towards the higher price setting is similar to achieving collusion. Hettich further mentions that an increase of the number of market participants will slow down the process.[58] If the number of market participants is seven or more firms, the experiment shows that the process towards higher price setting, and eventually collusion, disappears. Higher price setting, and thus also collusion, will also be unlikely if there is heterogeneity among the DQNs. It is made clear that this study is a first step, and thus also still too narrow to draw real world conclusions.[59]

All the above-mentioned models suppose that algorithms will tacitly collude. No communication will occur between the algorithms. Nevertheless, there is also a growing body of research on whether algorithmic communication will ever be possible.[60] This research goes beyond the setting of algorithmic collusion with advanced agreed communication protocols. It is researched on whether algorithms can autonomously learn to develop such a communication protocol. Despite research showing the ability of algorithms to communicate, and even generate cheap talk messages,[61] "further research is required to find out whether algorithms will be able to learn to communicate with the aim of cooperating in a competitive (dilemma-like) environment."[62]

---

[55]   Hettich (n. 4 above).

[56]   ibid., 2.

[57]   ibid., 16.

[58]   ibid., 2 and 16.

[59]   ibid., 16.

[60]   For a summary, see Normann and Stenberg (n. 4 above) at 769–70.

[61]   See, e.g., Kris Cao, Angeliki Lazaridou, Marc Lanctot, Joel Z. Leibo, Karl Tuyls, and Stephen Clark, 'Emergent Communication Through Negotiation' (2018), available at https://arxiv.org/pdf/1804.03980.pdf (accessed 30 June 2022); Jacob W. Crandall, Mayada Oudah, Tennom, Fatimah Ishowo-Oloko, Sherief Abdallah, Jean-François Bonnefon, Manuel Cebrian, Azim Shariff, Michael A. Goodrich, and Iyad Rahwan, 'Cooperating with Machines' (2018) 9(233) *Nature* 1, available at www.nature.com/articles/s41467-017-02597-8.pdf (accessed 30 June 2022).

[62]   Normann and Stenberg (n. 4 above) at 770.

The experimental basis of what has been described above, leads several scholars to the conclusion that autonomous algorithmic collusion is still not a significant problem.[63] Reports supported by enforcement authorities seem to take the same stance.[64] They do not rule out, however, the possibility that, with the advancement of computer science, algorithms will be able to collude without the interference of human beings.[65] Yet, according to Veljanovski, this does not diminish the question of whether it will ever be possible to relinquish any link with human conduct. In the end, human decision will be underlying the order to develop these algorithms and put them into practice. And, taking this kind of stance would eliminate algorithmic collusion as a specific problem within anti-cartel law.[66]

3.2   Algorithmic Homogeneity is Utopia, and so is Algorithmic Tacit Collusion

The literature postulating that the use of algorithms will facilitate tacit collusion assumes "algorithmic homogeneity."[67] Algorithmic homogeneity points to the goal pursued by the algorithm. It is accepted that algorithms will seek profit maximization. This will be characterized by the fact that "all algorithms are programmed to 'monitor price changes and swiftly react to any competitor's price reduction.'"[68] The idea pursued is that each algorithm will move towards the same price in this setting. Though Petit has been the first one to use

---

[63]   Schrepel (n. 6 above). Other limitations on the experimental framework are summarized by John Moore, Etienne Pfister, and Henri Piffaut, 'Some Reflections on Algorithms, Tacit Collusion, and the Regulatory Framework' in David S. Evans, Allen Fels AO, and Catherine Tucker (eds), *The Evolution of Antitrust in the Digital Era: Essays on Competition Policy* (Competition Policy International, 2021), at 90–2.

[64]   See, e.g., JFTC (n. 23 above) at 29–30.

[65]   Timo Klein, '(Mis)understanding Algorithmic Collusion' (2020) *CPI Antitrust Chronicle* 1, 5 and 7 available at https://dev.competitionpolicyinternational.com/wp -content/uploads/2020/07/8-Misunderstanding-Algorithmic-Collusion-Timo-Klein.pdf (accessed 30 June 2022). For the time being, coordination at the level of the algorithm design is required to achieve algorithmic collusion, see Nicolas Eschenbaum, Filip Mellgren, and Philipp Zhan, 'Robust Algorithmic Collusion' (2021), available at https://arxiv.org/pdf/2201.00345.pdf (accessed 30 June 2022).

[66]   Veljanovski (n. 8 above) at 56.

[67]   Petit (n. 45 above) at 361.

[68]   Damien Geradin, 'Algorithmic Tacit Collusion and Individualized Pricing: Are Antitrust Concerns Justified?' (Copenhagen Economics Conference, 2017) 2, available at www.copenhageneconomics.com/dyn/resources/Filelibrary/file/6/66/1498204706/ geradin.pdf (accessed 30 June 2022).

the term algorithmic homogeneity, Dolmans is one of the first to posit that the pricing algorithm could develop different pricing strategies.[69]

The maximization of long-term profits is most likely the message given to the algorithms determining price setting strategies. In the previous section, we have already indicated that competitive pricing strategies may be more optimal in an environment where data is collected on consumer preferences or where this data has led to the customization of the products. Dolmans points out that, with a separate set of information, the algorithm may eventually choose a predatory pricing or any other exclusionary conduct as an optimum strategy to realize the long-term profit. The information may include "rivals' market share, assets, capital reserves, employee count, variable and fixed costs, etc."[70]

Besides the idea that different pricing strategies may be developed by the pricing algorithm, it needs to be investigated whether formulating one goal, i.e. profit maximization, would lead to collusion. Algorithms may need more detailed description to produce a result in one way or another.

3.3   Discussing Algorithmic Tacit Collusion is Fundamentally Unimportant?

The summary above and whatever that follows in the book has also been called fundamentally unimportant.[71] The reason? Scholars argue that, and this is in part a repetition of some of the debates mentioned above, namely that there is a lack of empirical evidence on algorithmic collusion and, if algorithmic collusion occurs, there is nothing new for competition law.

Thibault Schrepel is one of the first to state that

> yet, empirical studies documenting the frequency of the phenomenon in the real-world remain to be produced. One cannot find any qualification of algorithmic collusion in official publications coming from antitrust and competition agencies, in any of the reports given to these agencies, or in the OECD publications. When

---

[69]   Dolmans (n. 5 above) at 8–9.
[70]   ibid., 8.
[71]   Schrepel (n. 6 above). A more fundamental problem for competition law, it is held, is the arrival of blockchain. Blockchain is able to conceal much better than anything else transfers of information, preventing enforcement authorities to observe how competitors monitor rivals' conduct. This could expand the feasibility of collusion beyond oligopolistic markets. See Thibault Schrepel, *Blockchain + Antitrust: The Decentralization Formula* (Edward Elgar 2021) 137–81; Thibault Schrepel, 'Collusion by Blockchain and Smart Contracts' (2019) 33(1) *Harvard Journal of Law & Technology* 117; Stefan Thomas, 'Harmful Signals – Cartel Prohibition and Oligopoly Theory in the Age of Machine Learning' (2019) 15(2–3) *Journal of Competition Law & Economics* 159.

having a look at the litigation brought in the U.S. and in Europe, algorithmic collusion is virtually non-existent.[72]

Klein counterattacks and states that "absence of proof is not the same as proof of absence."[73] With an increasing reference to the use of algorithms in cases and enforcement authorities' reports, Klein insinuates that there may be much more undetected evidence or that the algorithms "may be used to sustain a tacit understanding to keep prices high."[74]

Schrepel also argues that algorithmic collusion does not pose any new problem for the application of competition law. Just like in traditional price-fixing, algorithmic collusion requires the detection and attribution of liability. The former could be addressed by using algorithms to detect collusion, while the latter could be addressed by attributing liability on the management or the developers.[75] As Veljanovski puts it bluntly like this: "Executives are unlikely to be able to hide behind machines."[76] The problem with this view, according to Klein, is that it rejects the idea that algorithms make the act of colluding easier, without necessarily as much communication as in the past, and that a "judicial enforceable remedy for collusive interdependent pricing – irrespective of whether it is tacit or explicit" could be devised.

Veljanovski adds that experimental studies do not show the feasibility of algorithmic collusion in a real-world context. This has led many to argue that "truly autonomous collusion is science fiction."[77] But, so holds Klein, this is the wrong conclusion.[78] The correct conclusion would be that there are no immediate concerns. However, the experiments are gradually progressing and providing answers to shortcomings of earlier experiments. So, as also Veljanovski acknowledges, one should not reject the idea that truly autonomous collusion may eventually be reality.[79]

3.4 Price Discrimination is More Likely than Algorithmic Tacit Collusion

Picking up the thread of a technological perspective on algorithms, Deng's discourse on machine learning seems to imply that not all kind of machine

---

[72] Schrepel (n. 6 above) at 117–18.
[73] Klein (n. 65 above) at 5.
[74] ibid.
[75] Schrepel (n. 6 above) at 118.
[76] Veljanovski (n. 8 above) at 56.
[77] ibid.
[78] Klein (n. 65 above) at 5.
[79] ibid., 7. See also Veljanovski (n. 8 above) at 56.

learning is currently impossible.[80] Deng categorizes three types of machine learning. Above we have already described reinforcement learning, which calls for learning through trial and error.[81] Learning through examples[82] and learning through difference[83] are two other types of machine learning. In the context of the former, Deng explains that algorithms, further qualified as artificial neural networks, could manage to predict the preferences of a consumer based upon his past behaviour.[84] This will enable firms to "offer personalized product options and associated prices."[85]

Behavioural discrimination has also been identified by Ezrachi and Stucke as a possible outcome of the use of algorithms.[86] Damien Geradin explicitly acknowledges the additional claim of Ezrachi and Stucke.[87] Maurice Dolmans, to the contrary, formulates price discrimination as his critique to Ezrachi and Stucke's claim that tacit collusion is the likely outcome of increased price transparency, which in turn is caused by the collection of big data.[88] He further opines that the information gathered may actually allow for price discounts spread through various digital communication channels.[89] Also, Michal S. Gal, in her paper *Algorithms as Illegal Agreements*, describes the possibility that collecting data on consumers may contribute to price differentiation.[90] Data will allow firms to create digital profiles of their consumers and use them to engage in personalized pricing.

The predictions about what this all means for the future differ. Dolmans presumes that firms will move in a direction of product customization.[91] But, products will be differentiated, eventually by combining them with services. Algorithms will have difficulties to "compare 'like for like' prices"[92] and thus also to "achieve collusive equilibria."[93] Though Gal does not dispute that product customization is one way forward, she does not necessarily agree that it neutralizes the algorithms' game towards colluded prices. Algorithms would

---

[80]   Deng (n. 5 above).
[81]   ibid., 85.
[82]   ibid., 82–4.
[83]   ibid., 84.
[84]   ibid.
[85]   ibid.
[86]   Ezrachi and Stucke (n. 2 above) at 83–131.
[87]   Geradin (n. 68 above) at 4.
[88]   Dolmans (n. 5 above) at 9.
[89]   ibid., 4.
[90]   Gal (n. 9 above).
[91]   Dolmans (n. 5 above) at 9.
[92]   ibid.
[93]   ibid.

enable a "quicker and more accurate multifactored analysis"[94] to see which products are seen as alternatives by the consumers.

Gal portrays different views on what may happen if customization is going to be the future. First, collusion may not be on the price anymore.[95] Market segmentation could become a more rational choice to reap supra-competitive profits from the customers. Second, price collusion may only be an option if the data underlying the personalized pricing can either be shared among the competitors or easily be accumulated by the different competitors.[96] For sure, only algorithms will be able to collude on personalized prices. Third, the outcome of algorithms may neither be personalized pricing nor coordinated pricing, but a price that will be nevertheless higher than a competitive price.[97]

Though Gal attributes several paragraphs to price discrimination, and its potential to prevent collusion, she is pessimistic on the likelihood of it to happen.[98] She makes two observations on the reason:

> First, as Amazon learned the hard way, personalized pricing might create a public backlash. Second, and relatedly, in order to avoid personalized pricing, consumers might prefer to browse anonymously. This, in turn, will limit sellers' ability to engage in targeted advertising. The financial loss from the reduced ability to better identify those potential consumers who might buy a product, might well be larger than the loss from not being able to perform personalized pricing. When this is true, personalized pricing will not be practiced.[99]

Despite all the above-mentioned considerations, a recent study of Axel Gautier, Ashwin Ittoo, and Pieter Van Cleynenbreugel (Gautier et al.) points to several technical challenges for reaching price discrimination.[100] The first challenge relates to what Gal has identified as the multi-factored analysis. This analysis, which they call "processing high-dimensional vectors," will require "huge amounts of memory and computational time- an issue referred to as the 'curse of dimensionality'."[101] Reducing the risk of the curse of dimensionality could result in less accurate assessments due to the limited availability of vectors. A second challenge pertains to the model of training the artificial intelligence. Various experiments testing price discrimination use supervised

---

[94] Gal (n. 9 above) at 21.
[95] ibid, 20.
[96] ibid.
[97] ibid.
[98] ibid., 21.
[99] ibid.
[100] Axel Gautier, Ashwin Ittoo, and Pieter Van Cleynenbreugel, 'AI Algorithms, Price Discrimination and Collusion: A Technological, Economic and Legal Perspective' (2020) 50(3) *European Journal of Law and Economics* 405.
[101] ibid., 421.

learning. This would require the manual annotation of data that is "generated by or harvested from common online sources."[102] This is costly and not without mistakes. It is pointed out that solutions exist to this challenge, such as explicitly soliciting consumers on what their willingness to pay is or changing the learning model of the algorithms.[103] A third challenge concerns the scalability of the proposed experimental models. It could be argued that real world datasets are "larger, noisier and contain much many more features"[104] due to which the effectiveness of these models would be negatively affected. Only large firms with "a solid digital backbone and advanced IT infrastructure"[105] would be able to develop appropriate models. Smaller firms may need to rely on these bigger firms' cloud computing services. However, this comes at a cost. The cloud service providers, for which Gautier et al. mention Amazon Web Services, Microsoft Azure, or Google, do not offer the full range of price discrimination tools. Also, many of the cloud computing services are engaged in businesses competing with the customers of the cloud computing services. In short, Gautier et al. consider price discrimination strategies viable for a few players within the digital economy.[106]

3.5   Auditing or Sandbox Testing the Algorithm

Unlike with real-world price fixing schemes, the evidence of algorithmic collusion is something that is readily available at the premises of the firms using it. To prevent that the algorithms would engage in collusive practices, the algorithms could either be audited or taken into a sandbox and tested. Neither of these suggestions seem to be viable for Ezrachi and Stucke.[107] Auditing the algorithm is a feasible option for algorithms that are coded to collude.[108] Software engineers, however, seem to imply that auditing is also possible by reverse-engineering. Not all algorithms, especially not the self-learning ones, will reveal that they, sooner or later, will engage in collusion. Sandbox testing will be an artificial environment in which the algorithm is tested. It is not sure

---

[102] ibid., 422.
[103] ibid., 423.
[104] ibid.
[105] ibid.
[106] ibid.
[107] Ezrachi and Stucke (n. 2 above) at 230–31.
[108] Ibid., at 230. See also Oxera Consulting LLP, 'When Algorithms Set Prices: Winners and Losers' (Discussion Paper, 2017) 30, available at www.regulation.org.uk/library/2017-Oxera-When_algorithms_set_prices-winners_and_losers.pdf (accessed 30 June 2022).

that the algorithm will render a collusive outcome in the sandbox.[109] Equally, the collusive outcome in a sandbox is not necessarily the outcome that will be achieved in a complex real world situation, in which the industry is developing new standards at a rapid pace.[110]

Some of the earliest studies on algorithm auditing have been undertaken by a team of scholars who were at that time linked to Northeastern University. Le Chen, Alan Mislove, and Christo Wilson researched the pricing algorithm(s) of Uber and Amazon Marketplace. Even though these studies were not necessarily directed at understanding whether any of the algorithms could cause a collusive outcome, the empirical approach allows us to make important statements related to collusive outcomes. The Uber audit has shown that it is nearly impossible for competitors to rely on data of competing ride-sharing firms, unless data is made artificially available by one of the firms itself or by reverse-engineering of the competitor. Unless this happens, a collusive outcome or any other pricing strategy impacting competitors will be difficult to achieve. The study also revealed that even within the Uber structure itself the algorithm is not necessarily suggesting the same price to all its drivers. The situation is slightly different in case of Amazon Marketplace. The study has revealed that the use of algorithms tends to drive prices towards the price of the lowest price setter and thus create a form of tacit collusion. Equally, there may be evidence that the low price setting is not kept for a long time. The difference in outcome between these two studies could be attributed to the character of the information used by the algorithm: transparent or opaque. Similar studies have been undertaken by Marcel Wieting and Geza Sapi on an Amazon-like platform in the Netherlands and Belgium and by Assad et al. in relation to the German retail gasoline market. The conclusions of the latter studies are much in line with the findings of Chen, Mislove, and Wilson.

The literature on testing algorithms has been given a new impulse by the article of Joseph Harrington, titled *Developing Competition Law for Collusion by Autonomous Price-Setting Agents*.[111] Harrington surveys the US competition law to state that it requires "a common understanding among firms that they will restrict competition in some manner."[112] To prove the restriction, the enforcement authorities require "express and direct communication that conveys a plan to coordinate behavior." But, the "communication need not to

---

[109] Ezrachi and Stucke (n. 2 above) at 231. There seems to be discussion on the feasibility or desirability to engage in auditing. See Colombo (n. 13 above) at 20.

[110] Ezrachi and Stucke (n. 2 above) at 231.

[111] Harrington (2017) (n. 7 above).

[112] ibid., 22.

be so egregious."[113] As has been mentioned above, plus factors could indicate that parallelism is unnatural and should therefore be punished.[114]

Against this background, Harrington identifies four different views on algorithmic collusion. First, there will be algorithms determining the price based upon "information that would be present under competition, such as past prices, sales, and other market data."[115] It is possible that, based upon the information, the prices will be the same or similar. Absent any form of communication, it is hard to argue that competition law should apply. Even if the evidentiary standard changes, Harrington claims that the firms using the algorithms will not be liable. At the end, managers were acting independently and could not foresee that collusion would be achieved.[116] Second, there will be algorithms reaching a collusive outcome because of their coding. Either by examining the algorithm or by testing through the feeding of data to the algorithm, enforcement authorities will be able to determine whether the employed algorithm is illegal. This kind of algorithms should be *per se* illegal.[117] Third, learning algorithms that seek to enhance efficiency will, in principle, not lead to collusive outcomes. The reason for this claim is that the processing of information[118] for setting the price will fall short of what is necessary to achieve collusion.[119] Fourth, despite the belief in competitive outcomes, there could be cases in which learning algorithms, more in specific estimation-optimization

---

[113] ibid., 26.

[114] See infra Section 4.2 The Need to Create a Rule of Reason.

[115] Harrington (2017) (n. 7 above) at 25.

[116] ibid., 26–7.

[117] ibid., 48–50.

[118] The information that the algorithm will take into consideration is most likely past data of the firm to analyze the relationship between price and profit. This data could be linked to current data on the market conditions. Another source of information could be Big Data, information gathered on from consumers, from sales, or even from rival's firms. ibid., 54–5.

[119] Harrington (2017) (n. 7 above) at 55–6.

algorithms[120] and reinforcement learning algorithms,[121] present colluded outcomes.[122]

To determine whether prohibited algorithms have been used, Harrington suggests two testing approaches: static testing and dynamic testing.[123] The former requires access to the coding,[124] while the latter only permits the tester to observe the input and the output.[125] The problem with static testing is that it will only be applicable to algorithms that are decodable. As suggested by Ulrich Schwalbe, algorithms will likely only achieve coordination if the algorithms can send signals to each other. This requires, with the current state of the art, communication protocols within the algorithms.[126] Static testing will be problematic with deep learning. Inspection of the code will not reveal any information on whether collusion could be achieved. Therefore, the dynamic testing is suggested as alternative. Dynamic testing requires the user to feed the algorithms with information on the market condition and how prices respond to these conditions.[127] There are critiques to this dynamic testing. First, to get an accurate outcome of the dynamic testing, a large set of information may be required. Second, as these algorithms keep on learning, the outcome at the stage of testing may be different than when the algorithm is or was operating in the market.[128]

To overcome the problems identified above, Harrington suggest setting up a research program "for restricting AAs [artificial agents] not to collude, and detecting them when they collude."[129] The research program should be

---

[120] ibid., 57, giving the following definition: "An estimation-optimization algorithm estimates the environment faced by a firm and then determines what conduct performs best for that estimated environment. It can deliver a forecast on performance (e.g., profit or revenue) for any action (e.g., price) or strategy (e.g., pricing algorithm). An estimation-optimization algorithm learns over both the environment and the best action for an environment." ibid., at 58–9.

[121] Harrington (2017) (n. 7 above) at 58–9, giving the following definition: "reinforcement learning fuses these two learning processes by learning directly over actions (or strategies); it figures out what action (or strategy) is best based on how various actions (or strategies) have performed in the past. It does not explicitly estimate the firm's environment (e.g., it does not estimate the firm's demand function) and thus is seen as 'model free' because it is not based on a particular model of the firm's environment." Ibid., 59.

[122] Harrington (2017) (n. 7 above) at 60–62.

[123] ibid., 58.

[124] ibid.

[125] ibid, 59.

[126] Schwalbe (n. 4 above) at 15.

[127] Harrington (2017) (n. 7 above) at 61–2.

[128] ibid., 62. See also Ezrachi and Stucke (n. 2 above) at 230–31.

[129] Harrington (2017) (n. 7 above) at 65.

conducted along three steps: first, a collusion incubator should run tests with algorithms to identify when it produces collusion or competition as outcome; second, identify the properties present when a colluded outcome is achieved and this by comparing with the properties of algorithms leading up to competitive pricing; third, re-test the algorithms that have been instructed not to select certain pricing strategies.[130] Since this kind of research program still has to be undertaken, Harrington is not able to state what kind of properties will be identified as problematic. Yet, he guesses that one of the properties that should be forbidden in an algorithm is that it should not match the rival firm's price. Harrington stresses that his test should not lead to the prohibition of price matching, but to the ban on algorithms that result in price matching.[131] Harrington also indicates that one should investigate to exclude algorithms that are conditioned to act in response to the rival firm's price setting.[132]

The main critique of Harrington's approach is that the auditing will be a "gargantuan task."[133] There will be various algorithms in use. These algorithms will constantly evolve, either by programmers or by self-learning. To avoid continuous examination of algorithms, Schwalbe suggests to counter the problem by coding. At the fundamental level, each pricing algorithm should be coded so that coordination is less likely to happen.[134]

3.6   Algorithmic Consumers to Counterbalance Algorithmic Collusion

Algorithms are not only important on the business side. Michal Gal and Niva Elkin-Koren developed the argument that algorithms will also benefit consumers.[135] Algorithms will be able to "make and execute decisions for the consumers by directly communicating with other systems through the Internet. The algorithm automatically identifies a need, searches for an optimal purchase, and executes the transaction on behalf of the consumer."[136] Algorithms facil-

---

[130]   ibid., 66.

[131]   ibid., 69.

[132]   ibid., 69–70.

[133]   Schwalbe (n. 4 above) at 23. See also Frédéric Marty, 'Algorithmes de Prix, Intelligence Artificielle et Equilibres Collusifs' (Science Po OFCE Working Paper No. 14, 2017) 15, available at www.ofce.sciences-po.fr/pdf/dtravail/WP2017-14.pdf (accessed 30 June 2022).

[134]   Schwalbe (n. 4 above) at 23.

[135]   Michal S. Gal and Niva Elkin-Koren, 'Algorithmic Consumers' (2017) 30(2) *Harvard Journal of Law & Technology* 299.

[136]   Michal S. Gal, 'Algorithmic-Facilitated Coordination - Roundtable on Algorithms and Collusion' (DAF/COMP/WD(2017) 26, 22 June 2017) 4, available at https://one .oecd.org/document/DAF/COMP/WD(2017)26/en/pdf (accessed 30 June 2022).

itating the consumers' transactions have been termed "algorithmic consumers,"[137] "digital butlers,"[138] or "digital assistants."[139] Among the algorithmic consumers could include, for example, Amazon's Alexa, Google Home, or Apple's HomePod.

Gal argues that the algorithmic consumers could function as a counterbalance for the algorithms used by the suppliers. Her argument is centred on three elements: buyer power, the conceptualization of the decisional parameters, and the anonymization of the customer. Algorithmic consumers will represent individual consumers on the market. When the algorithmic consumer groups a large number of users, transactions on the market could become less frequent. The transactions of each individual consumer can now be grouped into one large order by the algorithmic consumer. In such circumstances, suppliers' algorithms may be more inclined to deviate from a coordinated price equilibrium.[140] To circumvent the coordination of the suppliers' algorithms, algorithmic consumers can be coded to "eliminate or at least reduce market failure in the long run."[141] Algorithmic consumers could, for example, be instructed not to buy if coordination is presumed or to apply different purchase strategies. The effectiveness of suppliers' algorithms may depend on their ability to create personalized digital profiles of their customers and "suppliers to increase their profits, by setting the maximum price that each consumer is willing to pay ("personalized pricing")."[142] This kind of price discrimination could be prevented by using an algorithmic consumer as intermediary. An individual consumer's preference will disappear "into one virtual buyer."[143] Gal terms this "anonymization through aggregation."[144]

The biggest critique to the suggestion that algorithmic consumers could constitute a market based solution for the collusion triggered by the suppliers' algorithms is that several of the algorithmic consumers will not be neutral towards individual consumers. The most popular algorithmic consumers are put on the market by large-scale digital platforms. Each of these platforms, as is shown in the case of the European Union against Google, will have their own agenda.[145] Ezrachi has addressed this issue with a reference to the Jim Carey

---

[137] Gal and Elkin-Koren (n. 135 above).
[138] ibid., at 336. See also Stucke and Ezrachi (n. 42 above) at 2.
[139] Stucke and Ezrachi (n. 42 above).
[140] Gal (n. 136 above) at 7.
[141] ibid., 12.
[142] ibid.
[143] Gal and Elkin Koren (n. 135 above) at 331.
[144] ibid.
[145] Ariel Ezrachi and Maurice E. Stucke, 'Algorithmic Collusion: Problems and Counter-Measures - OECD Roundtable on Algorithms and Collusion' (21–23 June 2017) *DAF/COMP/WD(2017)*, available at www.oecd.org/officialdocuments/publi

movie *The Truman Show*, in which "Truman lives an ecosystem in which he was perfectly happy, but it was all a façade. And in the online environment we are not very far from that …"[146] The overreliance on the algorithmic consumer will alienate the individual consumer from the market reality. Individual consumers will not realize that, at the end, they are not getting the best deal imaginable for them.[147]

Neutral counter-algorithms may be required to prevent any of the above-mentioned scenarios. Petit has elaborated significantly on this issue in his presentation *Antitrust and Artificial Intelligence: State of Play.*[148] Enforcement authorities could stimulate the creation of software counteracting virtual coordination. This software could be based on the information the enforcement authorities gather when they are auditing and testing the suppliers' algorithms.[149] Less intrusive market intervention would be if the enforcement authority would specify standards which should be included in the suppliers' algorithms[150] or through pop-ups warning of behavioural discrimination on a website.[151] An alternative would be that the authority just takes a cooperative role and would work with Standard Setting Organizations to formulate the antitrust standards.[152] Active participation in the market, for example through the release of lower prices that could trigger price wars or through instant messages to consumers informing that the platform is not offering the lowest price, is discussed as under the heading of "'digital half' of the competition agency."[153] Petit's list of alternative solutions to the algorithmic consumer is further supplemented by Ezrachi and Stucke. They point

---

cdisplaydocumentpdf/?cote=DAF/COMP/WD%282017%2925&docLanguage=En (accessed 30 June 2022).

[146]   United Nations Conference on Trade and Development (UNCTAD), 'Q&A with Ariel Ezrachi, Professor of Competition Law, Oxford University' (2016), available at http://unctad.org/en/pages/newsdetails.aspx?OriginalVersionID=1362 (accessed 30 June 2022). See also Maria Ioannidou, 'Digital Agoraphobia": An Enforcement Perspective' (Annual ASCOLA Conference, 2018) 9, available at www.law.nyu.edu/sites/default/files/upload_documents/Ioannidou_0.pdf. (accessed 30 June 2022).

[147]   For a detailed analysis of the problem that algorithmic consumers may cause, see Ioannidou (n. 146 above).

[148]   Nicholas Petit, 'Antitrust and Artificial Intelligence: State of Play' (GCLC Lunch Talk: "Algorithms and Markets: Virtual or Virtuous Competition?", 2017), available at www.coleurope.eu/sites/default/files/uploads/event/petit_0.pdf (accessed 30 June 2022).

[149]   ibid., slide 15.

[150]   ibid., slide 16.

[151]   ibid., slide 17.

[152]   ibid., slide 16. The appeal to soft law has also been made by Colombo. See Colombo (n. 13 above) at 21.

[153]   Petit (n. 148 above) at 18.

out that a neutral algorithm could be delivered by a consumer cooperative. If required, the market entrance of this cooperative should be stimulated by the government.[154]

4 CONTAINING TACITLY COLLUDING ALGORITHMS WITH LAW

4.1 The Wide Net of Contemporary Competition Law

Despite the debate on whether algorithms will collude, there is also a literature on how competition law should respond in case algorithms will have a negative effect on the market. When elaborating their taxonomy, Ezrachi and Stucke elaborated how competition law could deal with colluding algorithms. Their argument is that, when no human-made agreements exist, contemporary competition law will face problems. Intent has been proposed for the Predictable Agent model.[155] If the enforcement agency cannot rely on an agreement or intent, which is the case in a Digital Eye model, a new stance towards algorithmic tacit collusion may have to be developed.[156]

The European Union competition law practice may lead to a different conclusion. Jan Blockx, in his paper *Antitrust in Digital Markets in the EU: Policing Price Bots*,[157] argues that intent is not required to establish a competition law infringement. The EU enforcement authority, the Commission, has always emphasized the need to look at " *'expressions'* and *'communications '*"[158] of parties to determine whether there is an infringement of the cartel provision. The intent of the parties has never been taken into consideration, especially not to exempt some companies from their liability. In order for these expressions to be an agreement, Blockx holds, it is sufficient that there has been "an invitation to collude to the other party and that the other party tacitly acquiesces to that invitation."[159] Even in the absence of an invitation, the European Courts have contended that the "communication of commercially sensitive information"[160] from which the other parties have not publicly dis-

---

[154] Ezrachi and Stucke (n. 2 above) at 228–9.
[155] ibid., 56–70.
[156] ibid., 71–81.
[157] Blockx (2017) (n. 8 above).
[158] ibid., 5.
[159] ibid.
[160] ibid.

tanced themselves can be qualified as a competition law infringement. This is commonly known as a concerted practice.[161]

The just-described interpretation the European enforcement authorities have given to its competition law may have important implications for the digital world. Blockx gives an example of this by referring to "multiple competing traders [using] the same supplier for the pricing software and this software improves its performance ('learns') using the data obtained from the traders."[162] Another example is the involvement of "price trackers imbedded in the website of the trader which contractually allow the software to optimize prices of multiple traders."[163] The only gap that may exist in the European competition law exists when the "website is crawled without the consent of its owner and the owner has merely made the pricing information which is crawled public."[164] In terms of the Ezrachi/Stucke taxonomy, Sebastian Felix Janka and Severin Benedict Uhsler argue that this gap is most likely existing in relation to the Predicable Agent and the Digital Eye.[165]

The emphasis on expressions and communications does not take away that intentions are often referred to in European enforcement practice.[166] Assessing conduct in the light of its intention is, however, not done to establish an infringement in the sense of Article 101 of the Treaty of the Functioning of the European Union (TFEU). The intention merely helps establishing the objectives pursued by the conduct. Without any evidence on the intention, the Commission could reach a similar result, be it with a "much more detailed effects analysis."[167] Reverting to intentions is mainly done to facilitate enforcement.

Blockx goes one step further and indicates that EU competition laws imposes on undertakings the obligation to constantly monitor its business relations. This could have important consequences for the debate on algorithms. If an undertaking notices that other undertakings sign vertical agreements with the same algorithm developer, the undertaking should carefully assess

---

[161] On concerted practices and computers, see Andreas Heinemann and Aleksandra Gebicka, 'Can Computers Form Cartels? About the Need for European Institutions to Revise the Concertation Doctrine in the Information Age' 7(7) *Journal of European Competition Law and Practice* 431.

[162] Blockx (2017) (n. 8 above) at 6.

[163] ibid.

[164] ibid.

[165] Janka and Uhsler (n. 14 above) at 120–21.

[166] Blockx (n. 8 above) at 6. See also in the context of Article 102 Treaty on the Functioning of the European Union, Nicolo Zingales, 'Antitrust in the Age of Algorithmic Nudging' (Annual ASCOLA Conference, 2018), available at www.law .nyu.edu/sites/default/files/upload_documents/Zingales.pdf (accessed 30 June 2022).

[167] Blockx (n. 8 above) at 7.

its position. Similarly, there rests an obligation on undertakings to monitor its business to make sure it is compliant to the EU competition law provisions.[168] Therefore, undertakings should only operate algorithms that are designed not to collude. For self-learning price algorithms, this obligation means that the undertaking should take the necessary steps terminate collusion from the moment she is aware of the colluded price setting. Blockx further notices that it is well-established practice in EU jurisprudence that developers of algorithms facilitating collusion may be implicated.[169] Colombo suggests that this will not be the case when developers were complying with instructions from the firm requesting the development of a certain algorithm.[170]

The above-mentioned analysis could be helpful for jurisdictions that have shaped their competition law according to the EU model. EU law seems to be flexible enough "to include information exchange, third-party facilitators, unilateral price signaling, and even being present in the same room as members of the cartel while refusing any involvement and taking no collusive action."[171] It is therefore suggested that the algorithmic collusion is more a US-centred problem and thus of jurisdictions that followed the US model of competition law. In line with this conclusion, both Van Cleynenbreugel and Blockx high-light still other elements within the EU competition law to tackle algorithmic collusion.

Van Cleynenbreugel contends that the notion of "association of under-takings" could function to capture a situation in which undertakings rely on a platform and its algorithmic technologies to sell their products or services. The relationship between the undertakings and this platform could constitute an association of undertakings if there is a governance structure with repre-sentatives of both parties. However, since the MasterCard jurisprudence, this explicit governance structure is not required anymore. It is sufficient that a "commonality of interest" can be deduced from "the processes leading to, and the outcomes obtained in, the decisions adopted by,"[172] in this context, the platform to implement algorithms to achieve a "certain result in terms of pricing and the availability of products."[173] Simplifying the decision-making process, undertakings will seek high profits while distributing their products through the platform.[174] For achieving this high return, the platform will need

---

[168] See also Marty (n. 133 above) at 15.
[169] Blockx (n. 8 above) at 7.
[170] Colombo (n. 13 above) at 17. See also Schwalbe (n. 4 above) at 22.
[171] Veljanovski (n. 8 above) at 57.
[172] Van Cleynenbreugel (n. 8 above) at 435.
[173] ibid., 436.
[174] ibid. A common interest may originate "between the undertakings that use the platform to access customers and the platform's own decision to use algorithms to deliver greater efficiencies within the platform." ibid.

to offer an efficient service. Efficiency can be achieved through implementing, for example, algorithms. So it could be considered that the undertakings "have mandated the platform – at least implicitly – to rely on particular algorithms to deliver such result … A platform may thus have a mandate … to steer the pricing or offering of products in a certain direction."[175] Comparing this with the traditional understanding of association of undertakings, the algorithm thus "replaces the need for physical contact in the framework of a management board within the association of undertakings."[176]

Blockx mentions that the Commission could intervene against algorithms without imposing fines and refers for this purpose to Article 7 of Regulation 1/2003.[177] This Article 7 stipulates that the Commission can bring any infringement to an end, "even in the absence of an intention or negligence."[178] The absence of an intention or negligence warrants, based upon a reasoning to the contrary of Article 23 (2) Regulation 1/2003, the fact that the Commission cannot impose a fine. The following scenarios could, according to Blockx, example an intervention without a fine:

> A pricing bot would be considered to be so ambiguous that it may not have been possible for its designer or user to foresee its anticompetitive character, the Commission can prohibit the practice without a fine … if an anticompetitive practice is identified which causes parallel behavior between a number of undertakings but it would be impossible to identify the undertaking which is to blame for the collusion.[179]

Luca Calzolari, while agreeing with Blockx's suggestion, points to a possible problem. Article 7 of Regulation 1/2003 requires an infringement. As this may be a burden, Calzolari claims that Article 9 of the same regulation may be a better option. This article only requires the Commission to have a competitive concern. Such a competitive concern could be the basis of a commitment decision in which a remedy is formulated to address the concern. Calzolari acknowledges, though, that this option may only be possible due to the practice that has grown in which "the Commission often contacts the undertakings involved and informally notifies them of its interest in receiving commitment proposals."

---

[175] Van Cleynenbreugel (n. 8 above) at 436.
[176] ibid., 438.
[177] Blockx (n. 8 above) at 9–11.
[178] ibid., 10.
[179] ibid., 10–11.

4.2 The Need to Create a Rule of Reason

Gal's journey along the concepts of competition law is slightly braver than Blockx's approach. Whereas Blockx is focusing on whether intent is a necessary element for the concept of agreement and concerted practice under European competition law,[180] Gal expands the research to check whether the use of advanced algorithms can be an element to transform conscious parallelism into an illegal tacit agreement.[181] Starting from the assumption that conscious parallelism is currently outside the scope of competition law, Gal then describes elements that, when performed together with conscious parallelism, would render such a parallelism into a forbidden tacit agreement. These elements, also called "plus factors," are "circumstantial facts or factors ... from which an agreement can be indirectly inferred."[182] One category of plus factors that deserve consideration is the category of facilitating practices. Such practices "are positive, avoidable actions that allow competitors to more easily and effectively achieve coordination by overcoming impediments to coordination, in a way that goes beyond mere interdependence."[183] The question is whether the use of an algorithm could be categorized as a facilitating practice. To use Ezrachi and Stucke's taxonomy, this question should be investigated for the Predictable Agent or Digital Eye model algorithms.[184] There are two further limitations. First, the research can exclude algorithms in which the programmer has consciously incorporated coordinating coding or suppliers have consciously employed such a coded algorithm. The intent of either the programmer or the supplier to engage in the described conduct could constitute the necessary elements for an agreement.[185] Second, the research can neglect algorithms that simply mimic human conscious parallelism. This kind of algorithms would, just like its human equivalent, fall outside the scope of competition law.[186]

To consider whether the use of the remaining algorithms could be qualified as a facilitating practice, and thus as a plus factor, a case-by-case analysis must

---

[180] ibid. See also Blockx (2018) (n. 8 above).

[181] Gal (n. 9 above).

[182] Ibid., 101. See also Dylan I. Ballard and Amar S. Naik, 'Algorithms, Artificial Intelligence, and Joint Conduct' (2017) 1(2) *Competition Policy – International Antitrust Chronicle* 29, 3.

[183] Gal (n. 9 above), at 103. Gal also refers to the current practice of treating facilitating factors as a sub-category of the plus factors. See ibid., 1.

[184] As seen above, the other ones could easily fall within the scope of competition law as all of them are linked to one or another form of an agreement.

[185] Gal (n. 9 above) at 106.

[186] ibid., 107.

be made. When engaging in this analysis, Gal emphasizes four issues.[187] First, Gal indicates that not all algorithms are meant to coordinate prices between competitors. Second, if the facilitating effects originates "from the conditions of the digital world – e.g., increased connectivity,"[188] these effects should not be confused with "facilitating effects of using the algorithm."[189] Third, in case the algorithm is combined with other practices facilitating coordination, the assessment should take both the algorithm and the other practices into consideration. Fourth, the analysis should classify the algorithms into algorithms that facilitate coordination among market players on the one hand and competitors on the other hand. Having these issues in mind, Gal develops a rule of reason to separate acceptable from unacceptable algorithms. This rule of reason analysis constitutes of three questions. Depending on the answer of each question, it is determined whether the use of the algorithm should be prohibited or not. The three questions are as follows:[190]

Does the algorithm facilitate or strengthen in a non-negligible way the ability to reach or maintain a jointly profitable market equilibrium?
   no   →   legal
                yes↓
Is the use of the algorithm justified by neutral or procompetitive considerations?
   no   →   illegal
                yes↓
Do these considerations outweigh the algorithm's coordination-facilitating effects, and are the latter needed in order to enjoy the former?
   yes   →   legal
                no↓
                illegal

Based upon this theoretical description of the rule of reason analysis, Gal provides five examples of potential problematic use of algorithms:

i.   Suppliers consciously use of similar algorithms even when better algorithms are available to them. ...

ii.   Firms make conscious use of similar data on relevant market conditions even when better data sources exist. ...

iii.   Programmers or users of learning algorithms give them similar case studies from which to learn despite those not being the best case studies readily available. ...

iv.   Users take actions that make it easier for their competitors to observe their

---

187   ibid., 110.
188   ibid.
189   ibid.
190   ibid., 112.

v.   algorithms and/or their databases, and their competitors take actions to
         observe them. ...

         The user technologically "locks" the algorithm so that it is difficult to
         change it. ...[191]

Though Gal has limited the rule of reason approach to a specified group of
algorithms, her position should not be understood as relinquishing the need
to question contemporary competition law and theory. At the start of her
argument to establish the need for a rule of reason analysis for the use of
algorithms, Gal engages with the debate of Kaplow and Posner, which centres
on whether classical oligopolistic behaviour can be prosecuted as an unlawful
agreement.[192]

The rule of reason is a US concept. An efficiency defence under European
competition law has to be built on Article 101 (3) TFEU. Colombo claims that
such a defence should be considered for price setting algorithms, presuming
that these algorithms can generate pro-competitive effects for consumers.[193]
Though recognizing that "academic research on the economic impact of
algorithmic pricing is relatively limited,"[194] Colombo refers to likely cost
reductions triggered by the implementation of the algorithms. These reductions may link to lower search costs for the consumer, to more transparency
and so leading to more competition, or to increased production efficiency. The
result, so is argued, would be lower prices for the consumer.[195] Cost reduction
that is passed on to consumers is, however, not the only requirement for the
application of Article 101 (3) TFEU. It is further required that it can be shown
that the restriction created by the algorithm creates an overall improvement in
production or distribution, the restriction is reasonably necessary to attain the
efficiencies and competition should not be totally excluded.

Underlying the above-mentioned approaches is a reconsideration of whether
algorithmic price setting should be considered illegal per se or as object and
whether it is better to adopt an effects based approach towards algorithms
involved in price setting.[196]

---

[191] ibid., 114–15 (detailed explanations excluded).
[192] ibid., 101–10.
[193] Colombo (n. 13 above) at 18–20.
[194] ibid., 19.
[195] ibid.
[196] Thomas (n. 71 above).

4.3   Enhancing Privacy and Reducing Transparency

The collection of data is going to play a vital role in the use of price setting algorithms. The data could be linked to an individual consumer and so constitute her digital profile. Whenever an algorithm recognizes the digital profile, the algorithm could adjust its price setting according to what it can predict about the consumer based upon what it knows. To avoid the algorithm to link us with a specific digital profile, there may be a turn to anonymous browsing.[197]

An alternative to anonymous browsing would be to increase the privacy of the consumers. Ezrachi and Stucke see two viable solutions.[198] On the one hand, these scholars suggest that consumers should be familiarized with the business practices in the digital environment. Increased awareness could be achieved by requesting the websites drawing information from our digital profile for more openness. Several examples of how this could be done are given. Ezrachi and Stucke suggest that pop-up windows could warn the consumer when information is being gathered or used, websites should provide information on claims being made in relation to the price or the availability of products, or a website could reveal that a personalized price is displayed.[199] On the other hand, the scholars opine that a legal interference may be necessary to align the Internet operators with the privacy needed for consumers. Ezrachi and Stucke point out that Europe seems to move in the latter direction with the adoption of the General Data Protection Regulation 2016/679 (GDPR). The GDPR gives the consumers more control over their data.[200]

If there is preparedness to tackle privacy issues, the intervention could focus on reducing price transparency. This intervention focusses on the seller's side rather than on the consumer's side. One possible solution would to encourage firms to allow secretly communicate with buyers. Governments may also intervene to reduce the speed of adjusting prices. To allow for price reductions, the prohibition to swiftly adjust the price could only apply to price increases.[201]

4.4   Compliance

The increased use of algorithms in price setting may require the rethinking of compliance. Several ideas have been proposed.

Starting from the observation that "software developers can be liable for willingly and knowingly designing an algorithm that can implement collu-

---

[197]   Gal (n. 136 above) at 21.
[198]   Ezrachi and Stucke (n. 2 above) at 226–8.
[199]   ibid., 227.
[200]   ibid. See also Dolmans (n. 5 above) at 20.
[201]   Ezrachi and Stucke (n. 2 above) at 229–30.

sion,"[202] Claudia O'Kane and Ioannis Kokkoris stipulate that more attention should be paid towards dealing with software developers, whether belonging to third parties or their own IT department.[203] When a third party is consulted for developing new algorithms, it is suggested that the firm includes a copy of the antitrust compliance scheme in the supply contract.[204] Equally important will be to disseminate this compliance scheme within their own IT department and make sure that the scheme is fully understood.[205] A similar idea has been advocated by Justin Johnson and Daniel Sokol.[206] After speculating on various ideas of how algorithms could contribute to increased trust among competing firms, and thus make collusion likely in a wider range of cases, Johnson and Sokol emphasize that it is necessary that "overseers inquire as to the process that guided both the selection and the development of the algorithm."[207]

When it comes to specific algorithmic collusion scenarios, O'Kane and Kokkoris advocate that, whenever a hub is involved in a price setting strategy, the need for transferring price sensitive information should be examined.[208] Johnson and Sokol warn that none of the "current processes of compliance are well equipped"[209] to deal with scenarios in which the algorithm itself learns to collude. It is not clear whether their suggestion to rely on screens, either improved or enabled by artificial intelligence, is the outcome for filling the gap in compliance. This is unlike their suggestion to adopt screens for a scenario in which the collusion is both on price and online product/service reviews.[210]

---

[202] Claudia O'Kane and Ioannis Kokkoris, 'A Few Reflections on the Recent Caselaw on Algorithmic Collusion' (2020), available at https://papers.ssrn.com/sol3/papers.cfm?abstract_id=3665966 (accessed 30 June 2022).

[203] One of the other suggestion is to make sure that software developers can be caught by competition law. Being the first in line for being liable, Claudia O'Kane and Ioannis Kokkoris hold that they will be more inclined to design algorithms that do not collude. Ibid., at 6. The idea of compliance by design is also mentioned in the paper of Anne-Sophie Thoby, 'Pricing Algorithms & Competition Law: How to think optimally the European competition law framework for pricing algorithms?' (2020) *Competition Forum, Art. n. 0009* 1, 19, available at www.competition-forum.cfom/ (accessed 30 June 2022). The focus on the IT developers could be complemented with a bounty hunter program, offering algorithm developers, programmers or computer technicians an incentive to blow the whistle whenever they are aware collusion prone designs or use of algorithms. See Lamontanaro (n. 13 above) at 1302–08.

[204] O'Kane and Kokkoris (n. 202 above).

[205] ibid., 6–7.

[206] Justin Johnson and D. Daniel Sokol, 'Understanding AI Collusion and Compliance' (2020), available at https://papers.ssrn.com/sol3/papers.cfm?abstract_id=3413882 (accessed 30 June 2022).

[207] ibid., 8.

[208] O'Kane and Kokkoris (n. 202 above) at 6.

[209] Johnson and Sokol (n. 206 above) at 8.

[210] ibid., 10–13.

4.5   Precautionary Antitrust to Tackle Algorithmic Collusion

Algorithms are linked with uncertainty. It is indeterminate whether algorithmic tacit collusion will ever be a problem. Equally, it is often ambiguous whether competition law can apply to the various forms of collusion to which algorithms could contribute. Because of this uncertainty, there has also been debate on whether competition law as such is suitable for legal intervention. This has led to a discussion on the creation of an alternative enforcement tool. This debate has been greatly influenced by Europe and the Commission's work on a New Competition Tool (NCT).[211]

Algorithms have confronted the competition law community with various issues that are still uncertain up until now. It is not clear what the capabilities of algorithms are. Also, it is often not obvious how algorithms operate. These unknowns make it difficult to apply traditional competition law. In order to address, among others, these issues it was argued that a different tool that complements traditional competition law should be created.[212] One of the features of this tool could be the creation of a full-fletched market investigation power. Subsequent to such investigation, structural and behavioural remedies could be part of the sanctioning regime. Structural remedies could relate to the divesture of production capacity, while behavioural remedies could be multiple. Examples are, and some of them were also suggested by Ezrachi and Stucke, "banning generic price announcement,"[213] to "cooperate with testing and

---

[211] See, e.g., Colm Hawkes, 'A Market Investigation Tool to Tackle Algorithmic Tacit Collusion: An Approach for the (Near) Future' (Research Papers in Law 3/2021, 2021), available at www.coleurope.eu/sites/default/files/research-paper/ResearchPaper _3_2021_Colm_Hawkes.pdf (accessed 30 June 2022); John Weche and Thomas Weck, 'Tacit Collusion and the Boundaries of Competition Law: The Parallel Case of Common Ownership and Algorithmic Pricing' (2021) 5(1) *CoRe* 4; Ingrid Vandenborre and Michael J Frese, 'Algorithmic Pricing: Candidate for the New Competition Tool?' (2020), available at https://globalcompetitionreview.com/guide/e-commerce -competition-enforcement-guide/third-edition/article/algorithmic-pricing-candidate -the-new-competition-tool (accessed 30 June 2022); Picht and Loderer (n. 36 above); Thoby (n. 203 above) at 23–4, where the author informs that not only extensive investigative powers is a form of ex ante regulation, but also imposing testing the algorithm in an incubator. For a more extensive discussion of the latter option, see supra Section 3.5 Auditing or Sandbox Testing the Algorithm.

[212] Hawkes (n. 211 above) at 20. See also Picht and Loderer (n. 36 above) at 415, where the authors refer to this as a result-based approach. This approach "entitles authorities to intervene where they detect anticompetitive market outcomes, even if they do not (immediately) manage to prove flaws in algorithmic design or the presence of subjective elements, such as knowledge or intent."

[213] Hawkes (n. 211 above) at 20.

inspection, including ... the algorithmic system,"[214] to "make certain changes to the design and operation of algorithms,"[215] or "reducing the frequency with which companies may adjust prices."[216]

The basis for such an intervention would be risk and not harm. A risk would allow for recognizing "the threats inherent to the ongoing and dynamic changes and abstractions of our pricing systems, it cements the aim of future regulation and it gives regulatory intervention a succinct legal basis."[217] The European Commission has indicated that it was aiming for two different types of risks: a structural risk for competition and a structural lack of competition.[218] While the former refers "to scenarios where certain market characteristics (e.g. network and scale effects, lack of multi-homing and lock-in effects) and the conduct of the companies operating in the markets concerned create a threat for competition,"[219] the latter "refers to a scenario where a market is not working well and not delivering competitive outcomes due to its structure (i.e. a structural market failure)." One of these structural failures could be "oligopolistic market structures with an increased risk for tacit collusion, including markets featuring increased transparency due to algorithm-based technological solutions (which are becoming increasingly prevalent across sectors)."[220]

The shift from harm to risk as the basis for competition law enforcement has been the origin for the concept of "precautionary antitrust."[221] Precautionary

---

[214] ibid.

[215] ibid.

[216] ibid.

[217] Juliane Mendelsohn 'Algorithmic Pricing and Market Coordination – Toward a Notion of "Collusive Risk"' (2020) 78 *THĒMIS-Revista de Derecho* 241, 251.

[218] See Aurelien Portuese, 'The Digital Markets Act: Precaution over Innovation' (2020) *EPiCENTER* 1, 2, available at www.epicenternetwork.eu/wp-content/uploads/2021/06/Digital-Markets-Act-precaution-over-innovation-final.pdf (accessed 30 June 2022).

[219] European Commission, 'Proposal for a Regulation by the Council and the European Parliament Introducing a New Competition Tool' (2020) *Document Ares(2020)2877634* 1, 2, available at https://eur-lex.europa.eu/legal-content/EN/ALL/?uri=PI_COM%3AAres(2020)2877634 (accessed 30 June 2022). See also Portuese (n. 218 above) at 2.

[220] European Commission (n. 219 above). Juliane Mendelsohn, speaking specifically about collusion, uses the term "collusive risk." See Mendelsohn (n. 217 above) at 251.

[221] See, e.g., Aurelien Portuese, 'Precautionary Antitrust: A Precautionary Tale in European Competition Policy' in Klaus Mathis and Avishalom Thor (eds), *Law and Economics of Regulation* (Springer 2021) 203; Aurelien Portuese, 'European Competition Enforcement and the Digital Economy: The Birthplace of Precautionary Antitrust' (The Global Antitrust Institute Report on the Digital Economy 17, 2020), available at https://papers.ssrn.com/sol3/papers.cfm?abstract_id=3733715 (accessed 30 June 2022).

antitrust derives from the precautionary principle, which is a "regulatory principle which prescribes regulatory interventions amid uncertainties, despite absence of harm, for the sake of avoiding a hypothetical risk which may lead to irreversible situations."[222]

Precautionary antitrust did not externalize in the adoption of a broadly conceptualized NCT. The European Commission decided to limit its precautionary antitrust in scope, the gatekeepers to the digital economy, and is for this purpose finalizing the Digital Markets Act.[223] The still-birth of broad NCT has somehow affected further debate on alternative enforcement tools for algorithmic collusion, but not completely killed it.[224]

5　　SITUATING THE BOOK WITHIN THE ABOVE-SUMMARIZED DEBATE

The debate on competition law and algorithmic collusion was mainly driven by the prophecy that algorithms, together with the gathering of Big Data, will – on the one hand – increase the speed with which tacit collusion could be achieved and – on the other hand – enlarge the market scope in which tacit collusion could be realized. This book complements that debate, summarized above, in

---

[222]　Aurelien Portuese, 'The Digital Markets Act: European Precautionary Antitrust' (2021), available at https://itif.org/publications/2021/05/24/digital-markets-act-european -precautionary-antitrust/ (accessed 30 June 2022). The author further states that the "precautionary principle reverses the burden of proof so that it is no longer for the enforcer to demonstrate the need for intervention, but it is for the company to demonstrate the need for enforcers not to intervene. The DMA applies this precautionary logic to digital competition."

[223]　ibid. The Digital Markets Act was finally approved by the European Parliament and the Council of the European Union in July 2022. Regulation (EU) 2022/1925 of the European Parliament and of the Council of 14 September 2022 on contestable and fair markets in the digital sector and amending Directives (EU) 2019/1937 and (EU) 2020/1828 (Digital Markets Act), [2022] OJ L265/1. See also Komninos Assimakis, 'The Digital Markets Act: How Does it Compare with Competition Law?' (2022), available at SSRN: https://ssrn.com/abstract=4136146 (accessed 30 June 2022).

[224]　Vasileios Tsoukalas, 'Should the New Competition Tool be Put Back on the Table to Remedy Algorithmic Tacit Collusion? A Comparative Analysis of the Possibilities under the Current Framework and under the NCT, Drawing on the UK Experience' (2022) 13(3) Journal of European Competition Law & Practice 234. It should be noted that (algorithmic) collusion was extensively discussed during the preparations of the New Competition Tool. Reference to that concept was also made in the consultations with the public. However, neither the Digital Services Act nor the Digital Markets Act have picked up the issue of collusion. See Fabiana Di Porto, Luiss Guido, Tatjana Grote, Gabriele Volpi, and Riccardo Invernizzi, ''I See Something You Don't See'. A Computational Analysis of the Digital Services Act and the Digital Markets Act' (2021) 1 *Stanford Computational Antitrust* 84, 103.

two ways. First, this book offers an insight to what extent the competition laws of the European Union, Australia, India, China, and Japan are suitable to deal with the different forms of algorithmic collusion. Another contribution will claim that competition law as we know it has inherent limitations. Second, this book claims that the technology-focused studies tend to focus on how tacit collusion can be autonomously achieved and so neglect to study what kind of data is fed to the algorithms. For this reason, the book provides an original auditing study focused on e-commerce and a theoretical reflection on existing auditing studies.

Before reflecting on the two issues just described, Chapter 2, written by Thomas Weck, situates the debate algorithmic collusion in the general debate on algorithms and competition law. He thereby draws specific attention to the use of algorithms by platforms.

If the prophecy of algorithms autonomously conspiring on the price were to become reality, enforcement authorities need to analyse whether their respective competition law can effectively deal with the problem or whether their law needs to be amended. The contributions in this book show that the effectiveness of a competition law increases when a broadly defined concept of concerted practices is embedded.

Jan Blockx exemplifies, in Chapter 3, that concerted practices are essential to deal with algorithmic collusion. Based on the practice in the EU, he meticulously argues that such a concept can even deal with collusion by self-learning algorithms.

Two chapters nicely complement this finding. Baskaran Balasingham introduces, in Chapter 4, how Australia has adapted its competition law to better deal with information sharing issues and so incorporated the concept of concerted practice in its respective competition law. In doing so, Balasingham argues that this concept can also be used to deal with algorithmic collusion and examines to what extent this newly introduced concept could be applied to the most egregious forms of such collusion.

Nikita Koradia, Kiran Manokaran, and Zara Saeed inform, in Chapter 5, that also India faces a similar problem to what Australia once had. The absence of the concept of concerted practices in the law prevents India from appropriately dealing with several forms of algorithmic collusion. As the Indian regulator is considering an amendment of its competition law, Koradia, Manokaran, and Saeed analyse whether the suggested concept of concerted practice is sufficient. The situation is slightly different in China and Japan. Both countries have separate provisions to deal with horizontal and vertical agreements, making it difficult to deal with hub and spoke agreements.

Wei Han, Yajie Gao, and Ai Deng detail in Chapter 6, after explaining that price discrimination is a more prevalent issue in China than algorithmic collusion, that China is intending to amend its law to better deal with algorithms, and thus also collusion. However, various other suggestions are made, indicating that the current reform may not reach far enough.

In Chapter 7, Steven Van Uytsel and Yoshiteru Uemura point out that the Japanese competition law has a strict divide in dealing with horizontal and vertical agreements, making it difficult to deal with hub and spoke agreements. However, Van Uytsel and Uemura suggest that it may not be necessary to amend the law to cover algorithmic hub and spoke agreements. In scenarios where the hub, the algorithm, is sufficiently separated from the spokes, they argue that the unfair trade practices provision, applicable to designated vertical and unilateral conduct, could offer.

Yoshiteru Uemura provides an analysis of how the European Commission responded to the use of algorithms in resale price maintenance cases in Chapter 8.

The book also identifies that the technology-driven debate is mainly focusing on whether algorithms could achieve autonomously a collusive outcome. Such research, no matter how valuable, neglects the issue of information availability. Auditing studies may fill this gap.

This book offers, in Chapter 9, a study auditing the online grocery market in Singapore, by Cassey Lee and Gloria Lin, in order to detect whether transparent data enables the algorithms to tacitly collude.

Steven Van Uytsel discusses, in Chapter 10, two auditing studies, one related to Uber and one linked to Amazon, in order to see what the difference is for competition law if data is transparent or not.

2. Algorithms and the limits of antitrust

Thomas Weck[1]

1 INTRODUCTION

This contribution describes the German Monopolies Commission's position on algorithmic collusion and its staff's current line of thinking regarding the role of platforms in this context. The Monopolies Commission is a permanent, independent expert body established by law (§ 44 of the German Competition Act). It has the task to advise the German government and legislature in the areas of competition policy-making, competition law, and regulation. Its reports are accessible on its website, some also in English translation.[2] The Monopolies Commission has repeatedly discussed competition within digital markets in its reports.[3] Its Biennial Report published in summer 2018 includes an analysis on collusion by use of pricing algorithms.[4] A follow-up analysis was published by the German and French competition authorities in November 2019.[5] The Monopolies Commission and the authorities' understanding of digital markets continues to evolve. Over time, the focus has shifted from the

---

[1] The contribution reflects exclusively the personal views of the author. The author used to work as Lead Analyst for the Monopolies Commission, but left the institution after submission of this contribution, which remains unaltered, apart from minor corrections.

[2] See www.monopolkommission.de/en/ (accessed 10 January 2023).

[3] See Monopolkommission, *Hauptgutachten 2000/2001: Netzwettbewerb durch Regulierung* (Nomos 2003) paras 331ff.; Monopolkommission, *Hauptgutachten 2012/2013: Eine Wettbewerbsordnung für die Finanzmärkte* (Nomos 2014) paras 1ff.; Monopolkommission, *Hauptgutachten: Wettbewerb 2016* (Nomos 2016) paras 1174ff.; Monopolkommission, *Hauptgutachten: Wettbewerb 2018* (Nomos 2018) paras 605ff. (all re online markets); Monopolkommission, *Sondergutachten 68: Wettbewerbspolitik: Herausforderung Digitale Märkte* (Nomos 2015) paras 1ff.; Monopolkommission, *Sondergutachten 82: Empfehlungen für einen effektiven und effizienten Digital Markets Act* (Nomos 2021), paras 16ff.

[4] Monopolkommission (2018) (n. 3 above) paras 164ff.

[5] Bundeskartellamt and Autorité de la concurrence, 'Algorithms and Competition' (2019), available at www.autoritedelaconcurrence.fr/sites/default/files/algorithms-and -competition.pdf (accessed 30 June 2022).

economics of platform competition to risks to competition that are associated with the entrenched positions of platform operators and with the use of algorithms by commercial platform users.

The Internet fuels competition both online and offline (to the extent that online services are relevant offline). The key market drivers on the Internet, from a competition perspective, are data, algorithms, and platforms (Section 2). It is an open question whether online algorithms pose new challenges to competition policy, in particular pricing algorithms (Section 3). In the author's view, it may be worthwhile to look more closely at the platforms where such algorithms are used to identify the cases that warrant a closer look (Section 4). In any event, the Monopolies Commission has made several recommendations to elucidate the relevant issues (Section 5).

2   THE DIGITAL ECONOMY
FROM A COMPETITION PERSPECTIVE

The Internet lowers the cost of transactions and information for Internet users.[6] The reduced cost of information means, among other things, that companies may use large amounts of data to render their services or to develop new services (Big Data). Algorithms serve as instruments to analyse and to commercially exploit large amounts of data. Finally, platforms may step between groups of Internet users and act as information and transaction intermediaries.

Data may convey information that is relevant in competition. Thus, data can have a competitive impact, especially where the market is concentrated and where transparency is high. According to the general rules, this competitive impact depends on the market structure (e.g., high market concentration, homogeneous goods etc.), the type and quality of the relevant data and surrounding information (i.e., the value for strategic business decisions), and the quantity of information flows.[7]

Algorithms are tools to analyse and use data to solve a given problem. Online algorithms allow to process large amounts of data quickly. Thus, the market participants can use algorithms to increase market transparency and to react faster to customer requests, or to changes in the market. For instance, ranking algorithms can be used to display search results sorted by relevance,

---

[6]   See Thomas Weck, 'Oushuu – doitsu kyousouhou ni okeru purattofooma, onrain torihiki to deeta' [Platforms, Online Transactions and Data in European and German Competition Law] 836 Kousei Torihiki 80 (Masako Wakui (trans), 2020), regarding this entire section.

[7]   See Commission, Guidelines on the applicability of Article 101 of the Treaty on the Functioning of the European Union to horizontal co-operation agreements (Horizontal Guidelines) [2011] OJ C11/1 paras 75 ff.

making it easier for consumers to choose the products or services that suit them best. Pricing algorithms allow suppliers to adjust their prices quickly to changing market conditions.[8] This chapter focuses mainly on pricing algorithms.

Platforms are a particularly important characteristic of online markets. Platforms allow different groups of Internet users to connect in a fast and easy manner. To that end, online platforms provide a central infrastructure. This has a number of implications. First, online platforms can – and do – influence how the market is organized.[9] Second, by connecting users, platforms facilitate information flows, thereby increasing market transparency. Third, for both the platforms and the users of the platforms, the increased transparency means that they can identify relevant data more easily and use the data in their market reactions. The last point has some relevance for algorithmic collusion in the author's view and will be explored in more detail in Section 4 below.

3 THE ROLE OF (PRICING) ALGORITHMS IN PARTICULAR

As stated before, algorithms are instruments used to analyse and process data on the Internet. In competition policy, there has been a lot of discussion in recent years whether algorithms may contribute to competition problems. The discussion revolves largely around two topics, first, algorithmic collusion and, second, the use of algorithms to price-discriminate.

3.1 Algorithms and Collusion

It is still unclear whether the use of algorithms contributes to collusion in the online world. The reason is that not enough empirical evidence is available, particularly on the use of pricing algorithms. Assuming that collusion were to take place, however, the question is: what are the rules to assess that collusion, and what can the competition authorities do about it?

Before we consider the rules, we need to take into account that collusion is a market outcome from an economic perspective.[10] Collusion exists where prices are higher than under conditions of undistorted competition. From a legal perspective, however, we note that competition law does not prohibit

---

[8]   See, e.g., Monopolkommission (2018) (n. 3 above) paras 164 ff.

[9]   See Jacques Crémer, Yves-Alexandre de Montjoye and Heike Schweitzer, *Competition Policy for the Digital Era: Final Report* (European Commission 2019) 60 ff., also regarding the policy implications currently discussed in the EU.

[10]   Commission, Guidelines on the applicability of Article 101 of the Treaty on the Functioning of the European Union to horizontal co-operation agreements (Horizontal Guidelines) [2011] OJ C11/1 paras 65 ff.

market outcomes. Competition law only prohibits market behaviour to which individual liability can be attached, and which produces the market outcomes.

This is relevant also with regard to algorithmic (and other) collusion. According to EU court jurisprudence, to find liability, we need to look at whether market participants make commercial decisions that allow them to interfere with competition, and to eliminate "the risk usually inherent in any independent change of conduct in one or several markets".[11]

Collusion can take place in either of two ways under EU law. One possibility is that the market participants communicate or engage in market conduct showing their joint intention, for example, to raise prices. This would be cartel behaviour. The collusion in this case would be so-called "explicit collusion". However parallel behaviour not involving an expression of a joint intention would be insufficient to find explicit collusion. Competition law does not hinder companies from individually adapting intelligently to market conditions.[12]

Another possibility of producing a collusive outcome is that market participants jointly exploit a market structure that is itself favourable to collusion. Such a market structure would exist where several companies form a dominant oligopoly.[13] The companies may then decide to ask customers for a price that goes beyond intelligent adaptation to the market because, in a setting of dominance, the market functions do not work properly anymore.[14] That type of joint excessive pricing would amount to so-called "implicit collusion".

In both cases, the market participants make a commercial decision, which they may implement using algorithms. However, it is the commercial decision and not the use of the algorithms that is relevant for establishing liability. That does not change even if the algorithms produce a collusive outcome – for example: excessive prices. Thus, the use of algorithms, as such, is not a problem under EU competition rules.

That being said, the use of algorithms can be a problem when it comes to practically enforcing the rules in a meaningful way. First, we need to consider that collusion is only likely to emerge in markets that have a market structure

---

[11] Case 48-69 *Imperial Chemical Industries v Commission* ECLI:EU:C:1972:70, para 101.

[12] C-609/13 P *Duravit and Others v Commission* ECLI:EU:C:2017:462, para 72.

[13] Joined cases C-395/96 P and C-396/96 P *Compagnie maritime belge transports and Compagnie maritime belge and Dafra-Lines v Commission* ECLI:EU:C:2000:132, para 39. See also Commission, Guidelines for the assessment of horizontal mergers under the Council Regulation on the control of concentrations between undertakings [2004] OJ C31/5 para 39 ff.; Commission, Guidelines for the assessment of non-horizontal mergers under the Council Regulation on the control of concentrations between undertakings [2008] OJ C265/6 paras 79 ff., 119 ff.

[14] Case 27/76 *United Brands v Commission* ECLI:EU:C:1978:22, para 249.

that is, in some way or the other, favourable to collusion. However, where the market conditions are favourable to collusion, companies may coordinate their market behaviour with the help of algorithms even without the need of reaching any sort of agreement or concerted practice. Second, the companies' relevant commercial decisions may take place a long time before any algorithm is used. For example, if companies use self-learning algorithms, we may even have to look at the decision to buy the self-learning algorithm in the competition law assessment. Third, companies are nowadays targeting customers in a more and more context-specific and individualized fashion. This means that product offers and prices are adjusted much more rapidly than in earlier times.

Consequently, even assuming that the likelihood of algorithmic collusion were to increase, proving violations and enforcing the competition rules is likely to become more and more difficult.

3.2   Algorithmic Price Discrimination

The Internet increases price transparency for all market participants. This is generally to the benefit of both merchants and consumers. On the one hand, retailers may use the Internet to compare their prices with those of their competitors, and to adjust their prices if necessary. On the other hand, consumers can search for the best deal for them. In competition, the possibility of price differentiation can help to ensure that consumers receive a better price than if there were only standard prices.

Using pricing algorithms allows merchants to better analyse user data and, thus, to simplify individualized pricing. Of course, consumers may use algorithms as well, for example price-comparison tools. That being said, it is likely that the merchants have advantages over the consumers, at least in the long run. One reason is that the merchants have more funds to invest in their algorithms.[15] Another reason is the above-mentioned tendency of companies to target consumers in a more and more context-specific and individualized fashion. Thus, merchants may find out which groups of consumers are likely to switch less quickly to a more competitive offer than others. However, if customers do not quickly switch to competitors, price differentiation can be used to make customers pay even more than if there were only unit prices.

The problem here is not price differentiation as such, but the structural information asymmetry in online sales. For if merchants are better able to evaluate data than consumers, it may become necessary to consider regulation to compensate for any disadvantages for consumers that may result. Competition law, however, may prove helpful as well. The possibility of price differentiation

---

[15]   Monopolkommission (2018) (n. 3 above) paras 195–6.

militates in favour of a narrower market definition.[16] The ban on the abuse of market power could then possibly be applied more frequently than is currently the case.

4   ALGORITHMIC COLLUSION AND PLATFORMS

It has not been explored so far whether a link exists between the role of online platforms and the potential risk of algorithmic collusion. In the author's view, this is remarkable as several statements above indicate that such a link might indeed exist.[17]

First, it was highlighted before that data exchanges may pose more problems where the market is concentrated, and that also collusion is only likely to emerge in markets where the market structure is favourable to collusion, that is, in concentrated markets with high market transparency. Algorithms would then only be the last element allowing market participants to overcome the obstacles to collusion in a relevant market.

Second, it was said before that platforms – due to their role as information transaction and intermediaries – centralize the market organization to some extent and can act as central rule-setters for their users.

Third, platforms – as intermediaries – typically generate network effects. This may give rise to concentration tendencies, depending also on other factors, such as platform scale, the possibility of parallel use and switching costs, platform differentiation, and user heterogeneity.[18] Concentration is not the same as market power, as long as markets remain contestable. Market power, however, can arise, for example, where the platform has exclusive access to data, or where it is able to extend its gatekeeper function into other areas (build-up of "ecosystems"). This may lead to a situation where markets "tip" permanently in favour of a platform, meaning that the market structure benefitting the platform is perpetuated and the platform is able to attain a monopoly position with its services. It is still unclear under EU law when market tipping may give rise

---

[16]   See U.S. DOJ and FTC, Horizontal Merger Guidelines, version of 19 August 2010, section 3; Monopolkommission (2018) (n. 3 above) para 219, regarding the relevance of price discrimination for the delineation of markets.

[17]   On the following, see also John Weche and Thomas Weck, 'Tacit Collusion and the Boundaries of Competition Law: The Parallel Case of Common Ownership and Algorithmic Pricing' (2021) 5(1) *CoRe* 4, 8.

[18]   See David S. Evans and Richard Schmalensee, 'The Industrial Organization of Markets with Two-Sided Platforms' (2007) 3 *Competition Policy International* 151; David S. Evans and Richard Schmalensee, 'Markets with Two-Sided Platforms' (2008) 1 *Issues in Competition Law and Policy* 667; Monopolkommission (2015) (n. 3 above) paras 36–9, 45 ff.; Monopolkommission (2021) (n. 3 above) para. 6.

to a (structural) abuse of dominance.[19] However, strong indications exist that market concentration and information asymmetries are increasing and have caused market failures to an extent that it is necessary to intervene with permanent regulation of ecosystem operators.[20] The monopolization of platform markets may increase the dependency of commercial and non-commercial users of the platform and, thus, contribute to conditions that allow merchants to collude to the detriment of consumers (especially if only a limited number of merchants is offering the relevant products on the platform).

Fourth, merchants using platforms to sell their products and services typically use pricing algorithms. For them, it is a great benefit of platforms that concentration tendencies generated by the platforms increase market transparency. As was stated before, merchants are in a better position to benefit from improved market transparency than consumers. This is because merchants have more funds to invest in their algorithms and because they have an interest in individualized pricing. However, if merchants are able to price-discriminate more often, that may also indicate that the market is becoming more and more fragmented. In a fragmented market, conditions favourable to collusion may exist more often than in larger and less fragmented markets.

At present, regulators focus mainly on the power of platforms and digital ecosystems and less on collusion among commercial platform users, which may be a result of the monopolization of platform markets.[21] This monopoli-

---

[19] See, however, Case 6-72 *Europemballage Corporation and Continental Can Company v Commission* ECLI:EU:C:1973:22, para 29: "If it can, irrespective of any fault, be regarded as an abuse if an undertaking holds a position so dominant that the objectives of the treaty are circumvented by an alteration to the supply structure which seriously endangers the consumer's freedom of action in the market, such a case necessarily exists, if practically all competition is eliminated."

[20] See Commission, 'Commission Staff Working Document, Impact Assessment Report Accompanying the document Proposal for a Regulation of the European Parliament and the Council on contestable and fair markets in the digital sector (Digital Markets Act)' (15 December 2020) *SWD/2020/363final (Part 1/2)* paras 68 ff.; Jerrold Nadler and David N. Cicilline, 'Investigation of Competition in Digital Markets' (Majority Staff Report, U.S. House of Representatives, 2020), available at https://judiciary.house.gov/uploadedfiles/competition_in_digital_markets.pdf?utm_campaign=4493-519 (accessed 30 June 2022) .

[21] This is indicated, e.g., by the EU Digital Markets Act and the P2B Regulation. See, respectively, Regulation (EU) 2022/1925 of the European Parliament and of the Council of 14 September 2022 on contestable and fair markets in the digital sector and amending Directives (EU) 2019/1937 and (EU) 2020/1828 (Digital Markets Act), [2022] OJ L265/1; Regulation (EU) 2019/1150 of the European Parliament and of the Council of 20 June 2019 on promoting fairness and transparency for business users of online intermediation services, OJ [2019] L 186/57. For the United States, the US bills expected to rein in the power of large platform operators; e.g., the bills for an American

zation issue is important, but it may be necessary to look also beyond. In the author's view, the considerations above, taken together, lead to the question whether platforms in permanently tipped markets may be a market force that contributes to a market structure which increases the potential risk of algorithmic collusion. If that were the case, then the risk of algorithmic collusion might be particularly high for merchants operating on those online platforms with an entrenched market position.

5   MONOPOLIES COMMISSION RECOMMENDATIONS

In the Biennial Report of 2018, the Monopolies Commission called for sector inquiries to obtain empirical evidence. This should allow the determination of whether the use of online algorithms increases the risks to competition. In case the agencies are able to prove that algorithmic collusion is a problem, the Monopolies Commission also made another recommendation. That recommendation goes to the question of who should be held responsible if it remains unclear whether explicit or implicit algorithmic collusion has effectively damaged consumers. In the Monopolies Commission's view, the merchants using the algorithms should prove that they have not harmed consumers (= reversal of the burden of proof).[22]

Regarding platforms, the Monopolies Commission noted that already under the existing rules, platforms may be held responsible for collusion that takes place on the platforms. This is the case if the platforms participated actively and with full knowledge of the facts in the infringement.[23] However, the Monopolies Commission has not developed a position on the structural impact of platforms on algorithmic competition. Thus, it also remained silent on whether the risk of algorithmic collusion is particularly high for merchants operating on online platforms.

The German Federal Cartel Office and the French Autorité de la concurrence on the one hand and the UK Competition and Markets Authority on the

---

Innovation and Choice Online Act (H.R. 3816/S.2992), and an Ending Platform Monopolies Act (H.R. 3825).
[22]   Monopolkommission (2018) (n. 3 above) paras 225 ff., especially paras. 246 ff.
[23]   Monopolkommission (2018) (n. 3 above) paras 252 ff. with reference to Case-194/14 P *AC-Treuhand v Commission* ECLI:EU:C:2015:717, paras 26, 36. Establishing liability under this standard does not pose any particular problems vis-à-vis platforms, but may be difficult vis-à-vis other third parties (e.g., the programmers of algorithms).

other hand published two working papers on algorithms in the meantime.[24] That said, the authorities have not conducted in-depth market studies yet. The two papers acknowledge the potential risks of algorithms, but also highlight that evidence on algorithmic collusion is still scarce. Thus, the Monopolies Commission's calls for obtaining more empirical evidence remain relevant as of now.

6   CONCLUSION

The policy debate on algorithmic collusion developed fast, but it is still unclear to what extent the assumed risks to competition actually exist. In the Monopolies Commission's view, it will be necessary to collect empirical evidence in order to determine the practical relevance and scope of the problem. In the author's own view, it could moreover make sense to investigate whether algorithmic collusion is more likely to occur where merchants use online platforms. In any event, if we were to find out that algorithmic collusion is increasing in online markets, we might run into issues that are known already from the European gasoline markets: a market structure facilitating collusion (i.e., fragmented markets/high concentration, extremely high market transparency), a high risk that this market structure is used to collude (even without the need of explicit agreements), but no real solution to overcome that risk of collusion. In fact, a research paper concerning algorithmic pricing in the German retail gasoline market corroborated the collusion potential of algorithmic pricing in those markets last year.[25] Thus, assuming that the conditions on online platform markets may likewise facilitate collusion, we may have to expect a difficult debate on the measures to be adopted if we find out that algorithmic collusion is indeed a practically relevant issue also in other markets.

---

[24] Bundeskartellamt and Autorité de la concurrence, 'Joint Working Paper – Algorithms and Competition' (2019), available at www.bundeskartellamt.de/ SharedDocs/Publikation/EN/Berichte/Algorithms_and_Competition_Working-Paper .pdf;jsessionid=529D0343BE443999E6FC6FCDB2D74CA8.2_cid362?__blob= publicationFile&v=5 (accessed 10 January 2023); Competition and Markets Authority, 'Algorithms: How they Can Reduce Competition and Harm Consumers' (2021), available at https://assets.publishing.service.gov.uk/government/uploads/system/uploads/ attachment_data/file/954331/Algorithms_++.pdf (accessed 10 January 2023).

[25] Stephanie Assad, Robert Clark, Daniel Ershov, and Lei Xu, 'Algorithmic Pricing and Competition: Empirical Evidence from the German Retail Gasoline Market' (CESifo Working Paper 8521/2020, 2020), available at www.cesifo.org/ en/publikationen/2020/working-paper/algorithmic-pricing-and-competition-empirical -evidence-german (accessed 10 January 2023).

3. Artificially intelligent collusion caught under EU competition law

Jan Blockx[1]

1   INTRODUCTION

Over the last decade or so, our lives have become increasingly digitalized: more and more of it takes place online. This is also true for our shopping habits. If I want to buy a book, say, Isaac Asimov's *I, Robot*, I do not need to go to my local bookstore anymore: if the latter has a website, I may be able to find out online whether it has the book available and at what price, and probably even order it online. At the same time, I can compare my local bookshop's offering with dozens of other bookstores (some of which have brick and mortar shops but others only existing online).

But this transparency is not only available for consumers. All the competing bookstores can also see each other's prices without having to physically visit each other's shops. Already in a 2017 inquiry by the European Commission, about half of the retailers that responded to the Commission's questionnaire tracked online prices of competitors.[2]

The vast amount of data available online invites the use of artificial intelligence (AI) with processing power and speed that far exceed human abilities.

[1]   All comments are welcome at jan.blockx@uantwerpen.be. Beyond the presentation at the conference "Collusion, algorithms and competition law" organized by Kyushu University on 23 November 2019, this Chapter also builds on thoughts presented at the conference on "The Effects of Digitization, Globalization, and Nationalism on Competition Law" organized by ASCOLA and New York University on 21–23 June 2018 and at the Radboud Economic Law Conference organized by Radboud University Nijmegen on 9 June 2017. I am grateful to the participants to these conferences as well as Anne-Marie Van den Bossche, Massimiliano Kadar, Johan van de Gronden, and Michal Gal for comments on earlier drafts. All views expressed and any remaining errors are of course mine.
[2]   European Commission, 'Final Report on the E-commerce Sector Inquiry of 10 May 2017' (SWD (2017) 154 final) para 149, available at http://ec.europa.eu/competition/antitrust/sector_inquiry_swd_en.pdf (accessed 30 June 2022).

Rather than having physical employees track the prices of competitors online, companies can use software, often referred to as "spiders", "scrapers", or "crawlers", that does so. According to the Commission's inquiry referred to above, about two-thirds of retailers tracking online prices of competitors do so using such automatic software programmes.[3]

But why stop there? Rather than only tracking prices online, pricing software can also set prices. Doing so is of course a much more complex task than merely tracking prices, which explains why there are clear examples of this going wrong.[4] But with advances in AI, algorithms become better and better at doing this. They can take into account increasing amounts of demand and supply factors to set pricing and they may even improve their own performance as a result of self-learning from past errors (without human intervention). Algorithms also exhibit several practical advantages compared to humans: they can calculate prices instantly, do not need toilet or coffee breaks, and do not exhibit certain biases that humans have.

Market transparency and price flexibility are conditions for perfect competition and these factors may therefore ensure that price competition is fiercer online, which should in principle benefit consumers. However, other characteristics of online markets may mean that these factors have the opposite effect.[5] Indeed, since the work of Stigler, we know that price transparency and flexibility precisely allow for the detection and punishment of deviations from a collusive outcome.[6] Because of the repeated Prisoner's Dilemmas that the vendors face, this may cause them to increase prices and reduce offerings.[7]

---

[3]   ibid.

[4]   See for example, the incident reported by Michael Eisen, 'Amazon's $23,698,655.93 Book About Flies (2011), available at www.michaeleisen.org/blog/?p= 358 (accessed 30 June 2022), where price algorithms led to a copy of Peter Lawrence's The Making of a Fly being advertised for USD 23,698,655.93.

[5]   See on this already John M. Clark, 'Toward a Concept of Workable Competition' (1940) 30(2) *The American Economic Review* 241.

[6]   See Georg Stigler, 'A Theory of Oligopoly' (1964) 72(1) *Journal of Political Economy* 44.

[7]   OECD, 'Algorithms and Collusion: Background Note by the Secretariat' (2017) 27, available at https://one.oecd.org/document/DAF/COMP(2017)4/en/pdf (accessed 30 June 2022), summarising literature on collusion by algorithms in iterated Prisoner's Dilemmas which shows that the immediate reaction of algorithms favours tit-for-tat strategies. See also Monopolkommission, 'Algorithms and collusion Excerpt from Chapter I of the XXII. Biennial Report of the Monopolies Commission ("Competition 2018") in accordance with Section 44 Paragraph 1 Sentence 1 of the German Act against Restraints of Competition' 6-7, available at www.monopolkommission.de/ images/HG22/Main_Report_XXII_Algorithms_and_Collusion.pdf (accessed 30 June 2022).

Of course, consumers can use algorithms to their benefit as well.[8] Any supra-competitive margins that online retailers make create opportunities for third parties to offer products and services to help consumers get the best deal: this is part of the business model of price comparison websites. But the fear is still that the relatively concentrated number of digital intermediaries and suppliers may gain the upper hand over atomized consumers.[9]

This raises a legal problem since tacit collusions is not, as such, illegal under EU competition law. More than 50 years ago already, the CJEU held that EU antitrust law "does not deprive economic operators of the right to adapt themselves intelligently to the existing and anticipated conduct of their competitors."[10] While the literature has argued that tacit collusion is just as harmful as explicit collusion (cartels),[11] the problem is that it is hard to draw a clear line between intelligent adaptations to competitor behaviour that are pro-competitive and those that are anti-competitive. As a consequence, most scholars (and, as pointed out, the CJEU) consider that tacit collusion in general is lawful.[12] This was not a significant problem in the offline world where the conditions for tacit collusion are not often present. However, the more artificially "intelligent" economic operators become, the better they will be at adapting themselves to the existing and anticipated conduct of their competitors. Tacit collusion may become the norm rather than the exception.

A number of authors have in recent years stated that current antitrust rules may not be able to police supra-competitive price levels (or indeed other undesirable market outcomes) that may result from the use of pricing algo-

---

[8]   For a discussion of the use of algorithms by consumers, see Michal S. Gal and Niva Elkin-Koren, 'Algorithmic Consumers' (2017) 30 *Harvard Journal of Law & Technology* 309.

[9]   ibid, in particular 19 and 29–31; Ariel Ezrachi and Maurice E. Stucke, *Virtual Competition: The Promise and Perils of the Algorithm-Driven Economy* (Harvard University Press 2016) 194–7; Jan-Frederick Göhsl, 'Algorithm Pricing and Article 101 TFEU' (2018) 68 *Wirtschaft und Wettbewerb* 121, 124–5.

[10]   Cases C-40/73 *Suiker Unie and Others v Commission* ECLI:EU:C:1975:174, para 174. See also C-89/85 *Ahlström Osakeyhtiö and Others v Commission* ECLI:EU:C:1993:120, para 71.

[11]   See Richard Posner, *Antitrust Law* (The University of Chicago Press 2001), in particular its chapter 3 "Price fixing and the oligopoly problem", 51–100. Posner also argued that tacit collusion could be covered by section 1 of the Sherman Act (see in particular Richard Posner, 'Oligopoly and the Antitrust Laws: A Suggested Approach' (1968) 21 *Stanford Law Review* 1562) although the vast majority of scholars (and it seems Posner himself today) disagree.

[12]   For a discussion of the situation under EU law, see Nicolas Petit, 'The Oligopoly Problem in EU Competition Law' in Ioannis Liannos and Damien Geradin (eds), *Research Handbook in European Competition Law* (Edward Elgar 2013) 259.

rithms.[13] Most influential have been Ezrachi and Stucke[14] who have argued that "when computer algorithms and machines take over the role of market players, the spectrum of possible infringements may go beyond traditional collusion"[15] and that in some cases this "may result in AI self learning escaping legal scrutiny."[16] Also Ezrachi and Stucke's book *Virtual Competition*, which partially covers AI and collusion, has been the subject of much debate since its publication at the end of 2016.[17] The interest in the topic from enforcers has also become apparent.[18]

This chapter will discuss what tools are available in EU antitrust law to tackle collusion by price bots, based on the existing legislation, the case law of the European courts and the practice of the European Commission. I will argue that, while tacit collusion will continue to present a gap or "crack" in enforcement, there are a number of tools already available to avoid this turning into a chasm.[19] I therefore agree with the European Commission that "[t]o a large extent, pricing algorithms can be analysed by reference to the traditional reasoning and categories used in EU competition law."[20] That does not mean that there are no additional practical issues in detecting collusion but I will touch on these only tangentially.[21]

I will structure this chapter around three legal issues that allegedly raise enforcement challenges in collusion between algorithms: (i) the existence of a (horizontal) agreement, (ii) the relevance of (anti-competitive) intent, and (iii)

---

[13]   Some of the literature is referenced below.

[14]   In fact, many other writings on this topic simply rehash some of the arguments that they have made.

[15]   Ariel Ezrachi and Maurice E. Stucke, 'Artificial Intelligence & Collusion: When Computers Inhibit Competition' (Oxford Legal Studies Research Paper 18/2015, 2015), available at www.law.ox.ac.uk/sites/files/oxlaw/cclpl40.pdf (accessed 30 June 2022).

[16]   ibid, 25.

[17]   Ariel Ezrachi and Maurice E. Stucke, *Virtual Competition: The Promise and Perils of the Algorithm-Driven Economy* (Harvard University Press 2016).

[18]   In addition to other references in this paper, see also Competition & Markets Authority, 'Pricing Algorithms: Economic Working Paper on the Use of Algorithms to Facilitate Collusion and Personalised Pricing' (2018), available at https://assets .publishing.service.gov.uk/government/uploads/system/uploads/attachment_data/file/ 746353/Algorithms_econ_report.pdf (accessed 30 June 2022).

[19]   A fear expressed by Salil K. Mehra, 'Antitrust and the Robo-Seller: Competition in the Time of Algorithms' (2016) 100 *University of Minnesota Law Review* 1323, 1340.

[20]   OECD, 'Algorithms and Collusion – Note from the European Union' (DAF/ COMP/WD(2017)12) 35, available at https://one.oecd.org/document/DAF/COMP/ WD(2017)12/en/pdf (accessed 30 June 2022).

[21]   See on this, for example, Monopolkommission (n. 7 above) 11 and 17–18.

potential liability. The discussion focuses on the "trickiest" scenario discussed by Ezrachi and Stucke, that is, the scenario that would allegedly cause most difficulties for antitrust enforcement, the "Autonomous Machine".

2   EXISTENCE OF A HORIZONTAL AGREEMENT

The first obstacle to antitrust enforcement in an AI environment is said to be the requirement that there is a "concurrence of wills" before parallel behaviour between two undertakings can be considered to fall foul of Article 101 TFEU. In their paper on AI and collusion, Ezrachi and Stucke point out how important this notion of agreement is to the enforcement of horizontal collusion: "While antitrust enforcement predominantly targets corporations, the law considers the nature of illicit conduct through a 'human' prism. Accordingly the focal point for intervention is the presence of an agreement or understanding which reflects a concurrence of wills between the colluding companies' agents."[22]

Article 101 TFEU indeed prohibits "all agreements between undertakings, decisions by associations of undertakings and concerted practices which may affect trade between Member States and which have as their object or effect the prevention, restriction or distortion of competition within the internal market". The European Courts have defined the notion of agreement in the sense of Article 101 TFEU as centring "around the existence of a *concurrence of wills* between at least two parties, the form in which it is manifested being unimportant so long as it constitutes the faithful expression of the parties' *intention*."[23] There is no doubt that the language used to describe the notion of agreement is anthropocentric[24] (or even psychological): it is made by and for humans.

But that does not mean that the law only applies to humans as beings embodied with a psyche. On the contrary, the prohibition of Article 101 TFEU is precisely directed at undertakings, which in most cases are not individuals. Moreover, even when conduct of humans is concerned, it is simply practically impossible to determine their mental "will" or "intention" if this has not been somehow expressed. As a consequence, in practice the European Courts have focused their analysis of the notion of agreement on the "expressions" of the parties, rather than on any presumed or postulated mental states that would

---

[22]   Ezrachi and Stucke (n. 15 above).
[23]   Case T-41/96 *Bayer v Commission* ECLI:EU:T:2000:242, para 69 (emphasis added).
[24]   See in the same context also Ezrachi and Stucke (n. 17 above) at 42 and Mehra (n. 19 above) at 1329. Law in general is of course focused on human conduct: see Yavar Bathaee, 'The Artificial Intelligence Black Box and the Failure of Intent and Causation' (2018) 31(2) *Harvard Journal of Law & Technology* 890, 890–91.

exist behind those expressions.[25] What is more, according to the case law, any thoughts or intentions that a party might privately entertain are not determinative for the existence of an agreement; what matters is what the party expressed to the other party.[26] Rather than "wills" and "intentions", the focus of EU antitrust is therefore on "expressions" and "communications", clearly things that robots and AI are capable of. Robots could just as well enter into an agreement to divide national markets and/or fix the prices and quotas of a product,[27] or express their adherence to a certain pricing policy recommended by a trade association.[28] That it is impossible to observe the "mental state" of the robot while it does so, is irrelevant, just as it is for humans. On this point, in my view, the case law does not present an obstacle to enforcement in an AI environment.

What about the second aspect of the notion of agreement referred to above, that is, the "concurrence" of wills (or of expressions)? The meaning of this "concurrence" goes to the heart of what should be viewed as "collusion" in antitrust law, and this is an area where there traditionally has been a gap in enforcement: purely unilateral conduct is not caught by Article 101 TFEU.[29] Many have argued that the concurrence of wills requires some form of reciprocity[30] but what comes out of the case law is that the requirement of reciprocity is at least very limited. In order for there to be an "agreement" in the sense

---

[25] See already cases C-41/69 *Chemiefarma v Commission* ECLI:EU:C:1970:71, para 112 and T-7/89 *Hercules Chemicals v Commission* ECLI:EU:T:1991:75, para 256, or, in the non-cartel context, case C-209/78 *Van Landewyck v Commission* ECLI:EU:C:1980:248, para 86.

[26] In case C-29/83 *CRAM v Commission* ECLI:EU:C:1984:130, at [1984] ECR 01695 and ECR 01703-4, para 26, the CJEU therefore held that the fact that Schiltz "never intended to observe the agreement" was irrelevant to the question of whether it concluded an agreement or not. In case T-41/96, *Bayer v Commission* ECLI:EU:T:2000:242, para 156, the General Court analysed whether Bayer's dealers "wished to pursue Bayer's objectives or wished to make Bayer believe that they did": if they had done the latter that could have made them party to an agreement, even if they had private reservations about it. Admittedly, the position of the CJEU on appeal was more ambiguous: compare paras 121 and 122 of joined cases C-2/01 P and C-3/01 *BAI v Bayer and Commission* ECLI:EU:C:2004:2.

[27] As humans did in case 41/69 *Chemiefarma v Commission* [1970] ECR 661.

[28] As humans did in case 209/78 *Van Landewyck v Commission* [1980] ECR 3125.

[29] Case C-107/82 *AEG v Commission* ECLI:EU:C:1983:293, para 38; joined cases C-25/84 and C-26/84 *Ford and Ford Europe v Commission* ECLI:EU:C:1985:340, para 21; case T-43/92 *Dunlop Slazenger v Commission* ECLI:EU:T:1994:79, para 56; case T-41/96 *Bayer v Commission* ECLI:EU:T:2000:242, para 66.

[30] See the AG Opinion in case C-74/14 *Eturas and Others* ECLI:EU:C:2015:493, paras 45–47. See also Alison Jones, 'Woodpulp: Concerted Practice and/or Conscious Parallelism?' (1993) *European Competition Law Review* 273, 275–6 and Gerwin Van Gerven and Edurne Navarro Varona, 'The Wood Pulp Case and the Future of Concerted Practices' (1994) 31 *Common Market Law Review* 575, 600 and the refer-

of Article 101 TFEU, it is sufficient that an undertaking tacitly acquiesces to an invitation to collude sent by a competitor.[31] Tacit acquiescence of the recipient of the invitation arises if its business conduct is influenced by that invitation.[32] The CJEU clarified in the *Eturas* judgment that, in order to establish a "concerted practice", it is even sufficient that an undertaking becomes "aware" of commercially sensitive information received from a competitor in order to be regarded as having tacitly assented to a common anticompetitive practice.[33] The recipient can only escape liability by publicly distancing itself from the content of the communication or reporting it to the authorities.[34]

Some authors have argued that the notion of "awareness" of the commercially sensitive communication again provides an anthropocentric hurdle to the application of these principles to AI,[35] but I do not think this is the case. When the CJEU discusses this notion in the *Eturas* case, it points out that there can be a presumption of awareness once communication has been issued. Alleged recipients can rebut such a presumption, according to the CJEU, by "proving that they did not receive that message or that they did not look at the section in question or did not look at it until some time had passed since that dispatch."[36] To transpose this to online price trackers: if my local bookstore changes the prices in its brick and mortar shops but not online, this constitutes a communication that an online price tracker will obviously not be aware of, but if it changes its prices online, an online price tracker can be presumed to be aware of such a change. Indeed, becoming aware of the prices of competitors is the very purpose of an online price tracker.

Finally, what about the "sending" end of the collusion, that is, when is there an invitation to collude or other unlawful communication of commercially sensitive information? When a vendor communicates pricing information to a competitor in a non-public manner such communication will relatively easily be interpreted as an invitation to collude. But what if the communication takes place in a legitimate context, for example, if the data is exchanged

---

ence there to René Joliet, 'La notion de pratique concertée et l'arrêt I.C.I. dans une perspective comparative' (1974) 3(4) *Cahiers de droit européen* 251.

[31]   On the need for an invitation, see joined cases C-2/01 P and C-3/01 *BAI v Bayer and Commission* ECLI:EU:C:2004:2, para 102.

[32]   Cases C-338/00 P *Volkswagen v Commission* ECLI:EU:C:2003:473, para 67 and C-74/04 P *Commission v Volkswagen* ECLI:EU:C:2006:460, para 39.

[33]   Case C-74/14 *Eturas andOthers* ECLI:EU:C:2016:42, para 44.

[34]   Established case law since case T-6/89 *Enichem Anic v Commission* ECLI:EU:T:1991:74, confirmed by case C-49/92 P *Commission v Anic Partecipazioni* ECLI:EU:C:1999:356. Most recently, see case C-74/14 *Eturas and Others* ECLI:EU:C:2016:42, para 28.

[35]   See Göhsl (n. 9 above) at 122.

[36]   Case C-74/14 *Eturas and Others* ECLI:EU:C:2016:42, para 41.

with the supplier of the pricing software to allow this software to improve its performance? Or if the vendor merely makes its pricing information public, ostensibly to allow customers to find that information? Such a communication of pricing information will normally not be problematic under EU competition law. However, evidence of the intentions of the undertakings involved may make a difference here.

3   EVIDENCE OF INTENTIONS[37]

Several authors that have written about artificially intelligent collusion[38] and indeed also in other contexts,[39] mistakenly suggest that an infringement of Article 101 TFEU can only be committed intentionally. This is certainly not the case.

Already Article 23(2) Regulation 1/2003[40] makes it clear that fines may be imposed by the Commission on undertakings that "either intentionally or negligently" infringe Article 101 TFEU. Intention is therefore not necessary even to be fined: negligence suffices. The CJEU has also repeatedly held that an anticompetitive intention is not necessary to establish a restriction to competition in the sense of Article 101 TFEU.[41] There is no "gap" in EU antitrust law when it comes to unintentional infringements.

As a consequence, the fact that pricing information is communicated without anticompetitive intentions does not exclude that such communication gives rise to an unlawful agreement or concerted practice. It is therefore also not excluded that algorithms, self-learning or not, that are written with pro-competitive intentions can still be found to be restrictive of competition.

---

[37] For a more detailed discussion of this topic, see Jan Blockx, *Mens Rea in EU Antitrust Law: When Intentions Matter* (Wolters Kluwer 2020) and Jan Blockx, 'Revaluing the Role of Intent Evidence in EU Antitrust Law' (2019) 3(4) *European Competition and Regulatory Law Review* 354.

[38] Uwe Salaschek and Mariya Serafimova, 'Preissetzungsalgorithmen im Lichte von Art. 101 AEUV' (2018) 68 *Wirtschaft und Wettbewerb* 8, in particular 10–13.

[39] Tobias Lettl, 'Abstimmung im Sinne von Art. 101 Abs. 1 AEUV, § 1 GWB' (2017) 67 *Wirtschaft und Wettbewerb* 422.

[40] Council Regulation (EC) 1/2003 of 16 December 2002 on the implementation of the rules on competition laid down in Articles 81 and 82 of the Treaty, OJ L1/1.

[41] Cases C-551/03 P *General Motors v Commission* ECLI:EU:C:2006:229, para 77; C-8/08 *T-Mobile Netherlands and Others* ECLI:EU:C:2009:343, para 27; C-501/06 P et al. *GlaxoSmithKline Services Unlimited v Commission* ECLI:EU:C:2009:610, para 58; C-32/11 *Allianz Hungaria Biztosito* ECLI:EU:C:2013:160, para 37; C-67/13 P *Cartes Bancaires v Commission* ECLI:EU:C:2014:2204, para 54 and C-286/13 P *Dole Food and Dole Fresh Fruit Europe v Commission* ECLI:EU:C:2015:184, para 118.

However, that does not mean that evidence of the anticompetitive intentions of parties to an alleged agreement or concerted practice is not relevant. The European Courts have systematically held that "there is nothing to prohibit the Commission or the Community courts from taking that intention into account."[42] Indeed, *in practice*, the European Commission and the European Courts have often relied on evidence of intentions and commercial strategies to interpret the conduct of undertakings, in particular if the conduct is ambiguous.

The problem is that the antitrust laws do not exhaustively describe what conduct is prohibited and what conduct is allowed. In those circumstances, it may be useful to look at what the parties drafting the agreement or engaging in the practice themselves believe they are trying to achieve. Obviously, the parties may be wrong: they may think that they are doing something entirely innocuous but in fact restrict competition. But, ordinarily, the parties closest to the agreement or the practice are best placed to assess its objectives.[43] When a team of commercial employees works together or reports to management, they are likely to reveal their intentions in emails and other documents explaining their actions. If a competition authority then gets hold of such internal documents, these may reveal these intentions, and the authority can use this material to interpret the undertaking's conduct.

A good example of how this is relevant in the enforcement of Article 101 TFEU[44] is provided by the recent patent settlement cases, where the Commission, supported in this by the General Court, has used evidence of the intentions of the parties to the settlements to interpret what they were trying to achieve with their agreements and whether these agreements therefore were likely to restrict competition.[45]

---

[42] C-551/03 P, *General Motors v Commission*, ECLI:EU:C:2006:229, paras 77–78 and similar wording in C-8/08, *T-Mobile Netherlands and Others*, ECLI:EU:C:2009:343, para 27; C-501/06 P et al., *GlaxoSmithKline Services Unlimited v Commission*, ECLI:EU:C:2009:610, para 58; C-32/11, *Allianz Hungaria Biztosito*, ECLI:EU:C:2013:160, para 37; C-67/13 P, *Cartes Bancaires v Commission*, ECLI:EU:C:2014:2204, para 54; C-286/13 P, *Dole Food and Dole Fresh Fruit Europe v Commission*, ECLI:EU:C:2015:184, para 118.

[43] See, for a similar argument in the context of unilateral practices: Marina Lao, 'Reclaiming a Role for Intent Evidence in Monopolization Analysis' (2004) 54 *American University Law Review* 151, 157. Contra: Geoffrey A. Manne and E. Marcellus Williamson, 'Hot Docs vs. Cold Economics' (2005) 47 *Arizona Law Review* 609, 620.

[44] Evidence of intentions plays a similar role in abuse of dominance cases under Article 102 TFEU (see, for example, C-549/10 P *Tomra and Others v Commission* ECLI:EU:C:2012:221, paras 19–21) but a discussion of this falls outside of the scope of this book.

[45] See Commission decision of 19 June 2013 in case 39.226 *Lundbeck*, in particular recitals 803–16, 858–66, 950–54, 1000–05, 1075–79 and 1161–66, confirmed by

More to the point here, evidence of intentions has also been considered particularly important to establish the existence of hub-and-spoke collusion. For example, if a retailer shares commercially sensitive information with a supplier it will make a world of difference if the retailer intends such information to be passed on to other retailers.[46] In the world of pricing algorithms, a similar situation may arise when the data provided by a trader is used to improve the performance of pricing software also to the benefit of other traders or when price trackers embedded in the website of the trader contractually allow the software to optimise prices of multiple traders.[47]

In the few price signalling cases that have been published, intentions also play a role but in a different way. Rather than focusing on evidence of subjective intentions, authorities have looked at the possible business purposes (objective intentions) that the communication in question could serve. In *Container Shipping*, for example, the Commission considered that the rate increase announcements had "little value to customers since they may not enable them to plan ahead or compare Prices between Parties":[48] the simple announcement of an intention to increase prices could not be relied on by customers and in any event did not act as a promotion (it only concerned increases, not decreases of prices) and did not allow potential customers to establish the price level. Similarly, in the *Dutch Telecoms* case, the Dutch Competition Authority considered that the price announcements did "not

---

the General Court in case T-472/13 *Lundbeck v Commission* ECLI:EU:T:2016:449, in particular paras 517–33 (judgment subsequently confirmed by the CJEU in case C-591/16 P *Lundbeck v Commission* ECLI:EU:C:2021:243); the Commission decision of 10 December 2013 in case 39.685 *Fentanyl*, in particular recitals 334–59; and the Commission of 9 July 2014 in case 39.612 *Perindopril (Servier)*, largely upheld as regards the infringement of Article 101 TFEU by the General Court in case T-691/14 *Servier and Others v Commission* ECLI:EU:T:2018/922. See also the judgment in case C-307/18 *Generics (UK) and others* ECLI:EU:C:2020:52, in particular paras 56–57.

[46] See in particular, the judgment of the Court of Appeal in England and Wales in case *Argos, Littlewoods and JJB v OFT* [2006] EWCA Civ 1318, paras 91 and 141.

[47] See on this Stefan Schmidt, 'Web-Tracker und Kartellrecht' (2016) 66 *Wirtschaft und Wettbewerb* 572, 574–5. Furthermore, in case traders united by economic links together represent a significant part of the market, they can collectively hold a dominant position (joined cases T-68/89, T-77/89 and T-78/89 *SIV and Others v Commission* ECLI:EU:T:1992:38, para 358) and the use by multiple competing traders of devices strengthening their interdependence (e.g. by using the same pricing software) could be viewed as an abuse of such a collective dominant position. For a critical discussion of this position, see Nicolas Petit, 'The Oligopoly Problem in EU Competition Law' in Ioannis Lianos and Damien Geradin (eds), *Research Handbook in European Competition Law* (Edward Elgar 2013) 259, 335–6, also available at https://papers.ssrn.com/sol3/papers.cfm?abstract_id=1999829 (accessed 30 June 2022).

[48] Commission decision of 7 July 2016 in case 39.850 *Container Shipping*, recital 44.

provide valuable information to consumers or information about future trends in demand that is of general use":[49] the authority had the impression that the price announcements were not meant for consumers (since they were made in a professional journal rather than in consumer-oriented media) and consumers could not rely on them (since it was not clear yet whether the price announcements would actually be carried out).[50] The lack of a lawful business purpose of the communication pointed to an unlawful purpose, namely to signal price increases to competitors.[51]

How does the use of algorithmic pricing affect evidence of intentions? For the assessment of whether the conduct serves a lawful business purpose, not much changes. Such an assessment can be undertaken just as well for conduct authored by robots as by humans. Of course, this assessment is not always easy: conduct may be ambiguous and serve several purposes, some of which may be lawful but others not. But the complete absence of a lawful business purpose should still raise red flags.[52]

For ambiguous conduct, on the other hand, it is probably true that if an algorithm sets prices, there will be much less "chitchat" that can be used for interpretation. The algorithm usually does not work in a team so does not need to explain its conduct. In any event, any explanations that the algorithm would provide are unlikely to be directly intelligible to humans since they will not be phrased in a "human" language.

On the other hand, human beings can also hide their intentions and very often therefore competition authorities cannot use evidence of intentions to interpret their actions. In fact, unless she somehow expresses it, there is no way to determine what goes on in the head of a human person: what objectives she pursued, what factors drove her to a certain action and so on. This

---

[49]   Decision of the Dutch Competition Authority of 7 January 2014 in case 13.0612.53 *T-Mobile, Vodafone, KPN*, recital 44, available at www.acm.nl/sites/default/files/old_publication/publicaties/14326_commitment-decision-regarding-mobile-operators.pdf (accessed 30 June 2022).

[50]   See also the Analysis of agreement containing consent order to aid public comment in *In re Valassis Communications, Inc.*, F.T.C. No. C-4160 (March 14 2006) (consent order), available at www.ftc.gov/enforcement/cases-proceedings/0510008/valassis-communications-inc-matter (accessed 30 June 2022), where DoJ considered that the price announcement in question "would not ordinarily have been disclosed".

[51]   See also Michal S. Gal, 'Algorithms as Illegal Agreements' (2019) 34 *Berkeley Technology Law Journal* 67, 102.

[52]   This analysis could become more complicated, however, if AI systems would develop new business strategies that are difficult for humans to understand (so that do not seem to make sense). However, presumably the businesses that use such sophisticated AI systems will want to have some understanding of what the system is doing and what goals it is pursuing, for example, that it is not pursuing an unprofitable strategy. See also footnote 54 and accompanying text.

is different for algorithms, where at least some of the coding underlying the decision-making can be scrutinized. This is even true for self-learning algorithms: although some of its decision-making may be a black box, certainly not all of it is (contrary to the case of a human person).[53]

In fact, one would expect that the human programmers and users of the algorithms themselves also want to be able to verify that the algorithm is working correctly (pursuing the goals it is meant to pursue) and that they therefore want to have a certain insight into what drives the algorithm in a certain way.[54] Competition authorities can audit the algorithms in a similar manner to see if there is evidence of the "intentions" of the algorithm in its coding – something that, once again, could be helpful, but is not necessary to find an infringement.

The Ethics Guidelines for AI of the High-Level Expert Group of the European Commission also point to the need for trustworthy AI to meet a requirement of transparency, which entails that its decision-making processes should be traceable and explainable.[55] Conversely, any attempt by the developers or users of the algorithm to make its decisional process more non-transparent (e.g. through encryption), could – in the absence of any specific justifications (e.g. cyber security) – warrant additional scrutiny by authorities and more severe punishment.[56]

4   POTENTIAL LIABILITY

A final obstacle to enforcing antitrust rules against algorithms that is often mentioned is the attribution of liability. If pricing bots collude, who should be held responsible for this? Should it be the developers of the algorithm in question, or their users (and beneficiaries)? On what basis could either of them be held liable?[57]

---

[53]   Gal (n. 51 above), 108.

[54]   See, in a more general context, Brent D. Mittelstadt et al., 'The Ethics of Algorithms: Mapping the Debate' (2016) 3(1) *Big Data & Society* 1, 13.

[55]   Independent High-Level Expert Group on Artificial Intelligence set up by the European Commission, 'Ethics Guidelines for Trustworthy AI' (8 April 2019), available at https://ec.europa.eu/newsroom/dae/document.cfm?doc_id=60419 (accessed 30 June 2022).

[56]   The Commission has in some decisions viewed concealment efforts as indicative of an infringement (see, for example, Commission decision of 16 July 2003 in case 38.233 *Wanadoo Interactive*, title G3 and the Commission decision of 8 December 2010 in case 39.309 *LCD*, recital 302), and the Court of First Instance has accepted that steps to conceal collusion can be taken into account as aggravating factor when calculating the fine (see T-338/94 *Finnboard v Commission* ECLI:EU:T:1998:99, para 335).

[57]   I do not deal here with the question of whether the algorithms themselves can be held liable. Point 59 (f) of a resolution of the European Parliament of 16 February

I do not think these questions can be answered in the abstract: it all depends. However, I believe the case law of the CJEU is pretty clear that undertakings cannot take a passive attitude when it comes to antitrust infringements. We have already seen how an undertaking can be liable for participation in a concerted practice if it does not publicly distance itself from commercially sensitive information it receives. Liability for an antitrust infringement can arise not merely as a result of the actions of an undertaking but also from its inactions.

It is well known that in the EU dominant undertakings have a "special responsibility" to ensure that their conduct does not restrict competition.[58] But there is also a "special responsibility" for undertakings to be circumspect in their dealings with competitors and with sensitive information they receive from their competitors. For example, when competitors engage in a lawful joint venture, they must ensure that their lawful cooperation does not have spill-over effects in other markets where their cooperation would not be lawful. To avoid this, undertakings may be under a positive obligation to put in place the necessary safeguards.[59] Similarly, while it is accepted that undertakings envisaging a merger need to exchange certain commercially sensitive information in order to assess whether the transaction is worthwhile, they need to put in place safeguards to ensure that that exchange of information does not result in an infringement of Article 101 TFEU.[60] That undertakings should keep their

---

2017 with recommendations to the Commission on Civil Law Rules on Robotics (P8_ TA(2017)0051) in fact suggested that, in civil law, such liability could be introduced for the most sophisticated autonomous robots. This suggestion has however been criticised.

[58]   First mentioned in case C-322/81 *Nederlandsche Banden Industrie Michelin v Commission* ECLI:EU:C:1983:313, para 57.

[59]   See Commission, 'Guidelines on the applicability of Article 101 of the Treaty on the Functioning of the European Union to horizontal co-operation agreements', OJ C11/1, para 215 which requires parties to a joint purchasing arrangement to ensure that sensitive data collated by the joint venture is not passed on to the parties.

[60]   There are a number of decisions in which the European Commission imposed fines on undertakings for implementing a concentration prior to merger control clearance. In one of the most recent ones (*Altice / PT Portugal* (Case M.7993) Commission Decision [2018]), the Commission also pointed to the unregulated exchange of commercially sensitive information that took place between the merging parties prior to the Commission's merger control review, although it did not make explicit what the limits are that parties should adhere to in this respect. The French Competition Authority was clearer in another decision fining Altice for a case of gun-jumping. It stated that, although "the preparation of a concentration usually gives rise to the exchange of a large amount of information between the acquirer and the seller or target", nevertheless "whatever the reasons for which the companies may need to exchange information, it is their duty to put in place measures that eliminate any communication of strategic information between independent undertakings." ("La préparation d'une opération de concentration donne habituellement lieu à l'échange de nombreuses informations entre l'acquéreur et le vendeur ou la cible" "Quels que soient les motifs pour

business relations under constant review is also attested by the fact that they may infringe Article 101 TFEU by being party to a vertical agreement in case similar vertical agreements are subsequently concluded by other undertakings: in those circumstances, an agreement may become illegal even though it was not illegal when it was originally concluded.[61]

Along the same lines, undertakings that collect commercially sensitive information from their competitors must take the necessary steps to ensure compliance with Article 101 TFEU. If they use pricing bots, they need to ensure that what these bots do is in compliance with the antitrust rules. If the user of a pricing bot fails to take the necessary steps to stop those bots from engaging in collusion, the user can be liable for that collusion, regardless of whether the pricing bot is self-learning or not. Self-learning robots are not so different from sales people who, as not-artificial intelligence, also learn and adapt their commercial strategies. And, just as employers will be liable if their employees commit an antitrust infringement when authorized to act for their employer,[62] undertakings will be liable for the actions of their pricing bots if they use them.[63]

---

lesquels les entreprises pourraient avoir besoin d'échanger des informations, il leur appartient de mettre en place un dispositif qui élimine toute communication entre entreprises indépendantes d'informations stratégiques") (Decision 16-D-24 of the French Competition Authority of 8 November 2016 in case *Altice / SFR*, available at www.aut oritedelaconcurrence.fr/sites/default/files/commitments//16d24.pdf (accessed 30 June 2022).

[61] On the cumulative effect of parallel networks of vertical agreements, see cases C-23/67 *SA Brasserie de Haecht v Consorts Wilkin-Janssen* ECLI:EU:C:1967:54 and C-234/89 *Stergios Delimitis v Henninger Bräu AG* ECLI:EU:C:1991:91. Commission Regulation 2022/720 of 10 May 2022 on the application of Article 101(3) of the Treaty on the Functioning of the European Union to categories of vertical agreements and concerted practices [2022] OJ L134/4 which block exempts vertical agreement if certain thresholds are met, also specifically mentions in its Article 6 that the benefit of the Regulation may be withdrawn in individual cases, including because of "the cumulative effect of parallel networks of similar agreements that restrict buyers of the online intermediation services from offering, selling or reselling goods or services to end users under more favourable conditions on their direct sales channels.".

[62] See joined cases C-100-103/08 *Musique Diffusion française v Commission* ECLI:EU:C:1983:158, para 97, and, more recently, case T-588/08 *Dole Food and Dole Germany v Commission* ECLI:EU:T:2013:130, para 581.

[63] As Acting Chairman of the US Federal Trade Commission Maureen K. Ohlhausen put it in a speech on 23 May 2017: "If it isn't ok for a guy named Bob to do it, then it probably isn't ok for an algorithm to do it either", available at www.ftc.gov/ public-statements/2017/05/should-we-fear-things-go-beep-night-some-initial-thoughts -intersection (accessed 30 June 2022). See, for a similar position in Europe, Niccolò Colombo, 'Virtual Competition: Human Liability vis-à-vis Artificial Intelligence's

Commissioner Vestager has taken this position in a speech in 2017 where she said that "businesses need to know that when they decide to use an automated system, they will be held responsible for what it does."[64] Director-General Laitenberger went even a step further in identifying the positive compliance obligations of companies:

> Imagine that a firm lets a piece of software monitor the prices of rivals and set its own. Let us also imagine that the software works all by itself, taking over the kind of coordination, bargaining and mutual commitment that are necessary to run a cartel. Well, even in this case the firm would still be liable for its actions. To stay on the safe side of the law, it should have programmed the software to prevent collusion in the first place.[65]

Some inspiration may be provided by the requirement of "compliance by design" incorporated in the General Data Protection Regulation (GDPR) which the EU adopted in 2016.[66] Article 25(1) of this regulation provides that the data controller needs to put in place the necessary technical and organizational measures to meet the requirements of the regulation, and this already from the time it sets up its system of data processing. While EU antitrust rules do not foresee such a principle explicitly, one could say that the case law requires compliance by design also in antitrust law.[67] Commissioner Vestager certainly interpreted it this way when she stated that "pricing algorithms need to be built in a way that doesn't allow them to collude."[68]

Anticompetitive Behaviours' (2018) 2 *European Competition and Regulatory Law Review* 11.

[64]   Speech of Commissioner Vestager at the Bundeskartellamt 18th Conference on Competition (Berlin, 16 March 2017), available at https://wayback.archive-it.org/12090/20191129221651/https://ec.europa.eu/commission/commissioners/2014-2019/vestager/announcements/bundeskartellamt-18th-conference-competition-berlin-16-march-2017_en (accessed 30 June 2022).

[65]   Speech of Director-General Laitenberger at the Consumer and Competition Day (Malta, 24 April 2017), available at http://ec.europa.eu/competition/speeches/text/sp2017_06_en.pdf (accessed 30 June 2022).

[66]   Regulation 2016/679 of 27 April 2016 on the protection of natural persons with regard to the processing of personal data and on the free movement of such data, and repealing Directive 95/46/EC, OJ L119/1.

[67]   See on this Frédéric Marty, 'Algorithmes de prix, intelligence artificielle et équilibres collusifs' (2017) 31 *Revue Internationale de Droit Economique* 83, 105.

[68]   Speech of Commissioner Vestager at the Bundeskartellamt 18th Conference on Competition (Berlin, 16 March 2017), available at https://wayback.archive-it.org/12090/20191129221651/https://ec.europa.eu/commission/commissioners/2014-2019/vestager/announcements/bundeskartellamt-18th-conference-competition-berlin-16-march-2017_en (accessed 30 June 2022).

In circumstances where an undertaking does not have sufficient control over the pricing bot for the latter to be considered akin to an employee, liability of the undertaking may not be so immediate. However, even if the pricing algorithm is controlled by an independent service provider, liability of the undertaking using its services can arise, according to the CJEU in the *VM Remonts* judgment, when either (i) the undertaking was aware of the anticompetitive objectives pursued by (the algorithm controlled by) the service provider, or (ii) could reasonably foresee these anticompetitive objectives.[69]

As to the developer of the algorithm (if this is a different economic entity than the user or controller of the algorithm), I believe – contrary to some other authors[70] – that, in the right circumstances, its liability can also be engaged. The case law that a middleman that facilitates collusion by competitors is itself party to that infringement and can be punished for it, is now fairly well established.[71]

In practice, however, ensuring that software is programmed in such a way that it does not breach the antitrust rules, is not obvious. Ideally, one would want to introduce the antitrust rules in the code of algorithms to ensure that they comply with them, but there does not seem to be an easy way to do this. Let us return to Isaac Asimov, the great science fiction writer, whose book I was looking for at the beginning of this Chapter. He developed a series of Laws of Robotics, the first one of which was "A robot may not injure a human being or, through inaction, allow a human being to come to harm." Simple as such a rule seems to be, in many of his books, including *I, Robot*, such rules nevertheless often caused robots to behave in unexpected and undesired ways. There is even more uncertainty in the antitrust rules, as pointed out above. Few antitrust lawyers would agree that a provision as simple as "a pricing algorithm may not harm consumers" or "a pricing algorithm shall not fix prices with other algorithms" would be workable: it is simply too vague and begs the question what counts as "harming consumers" or "price fixing" under the antitrust rules. Like enforcement, compliance is a continuous effort, not something that

---

[69] C-542/14 *VM Remonts* ECLI:EU:C:2016:578, paras 30–31.

[70] See Salaschek and Mariya (n. 38 above) at 15 who fail to take into account the case law in the next footnote in this context.

[71] Cases T-99/04 *AC-Treuhand v Commission* ECLI:EU:T:2008:256; T-27/10 *AC-Treuhand v Commission* ECLI:EU:T:2014:59 and C-194/14 P *AC-Treuhand v Commission* ECLI:EU:C:2015:717; and T-180/15 *Icap and Others v Commission* ECLI:EU:T:2017:795. In addition, if the algorithm becomes a standard in the industry, one can wonder whether the use of that algorithm to facilitate price increases to the detriment of consumers could not be viewed as the abuse of a dominant position as well, available at https://chillingcompetition.com/2016/01/22/ecjs-judgment-in-case-c-7414 -eturas-on-the-scope-of-concerted-practices-and-on-technological-collusion (accessed 30 June 2022)

can be established entirely *a priori*. Compliance will therefore constantly need to be redesigned.

Finally, even if it is unclear who should be responsible for an antitrust infringement, that does not mean that enforcement is entirely impossible. Obviously, the effectiveness of antitrust enforcement is linked to the severity of the sanctions that are imposed for infringements. It is a well-known fact that some cartels have covered the entire world with the exception of the United States because the risk of imprisonment there deterred the cartelists from extending it to American territory.[72] On the other hand, criminalisation of cartels also increases the evidentiary burden of the investigative authorities since the standard of proof in criminal law is generally higher than in civil law.[73] Even in the EU, the punishment of cartels through fines has been viewed as quasi-criminal, which implies that the evidentiary burden is relatively high.[74]

However, as a last resort, EU antitrust law allows for the regulation of practices that are considered to be harmful to competition even if it would not be appropriate to impose a fine. The Commission has in particular proceeded in this way when it found a practice to be anticompetitive that had not been qualified as such in the past.[75] Although the Commission is not prevented from imposing a fine in those circumstances,[76] it can exceptionally not impose a fine on an undertaking even though that undertaking has infringed the EU rules on competition, if there are objective reasons to do so.[77]

In particular, Article 23(2) of Regulation 1/2003 provides that fines may be imposed by the Commission on undertakings that "either intentionally or

---

[72]   See Gregory J. Werden, Scott D. Hammond, and Belinda A. Barnett, 'Recidivism Eliminated: Cartel Enforcement in the United States since 1999' (2011), available at: www.justice.gov/atr/file/518331/download (accessed 30 June 2022):

> On numerous occasions, the Antitrust Division has interviewed members of international cartels who provided first-hand accounts of their participation in cartels that spanned the globe but stopped at the U.S. border because the participants feared going to jail. This eyewitness testimony is compelling evidence that enforcement in the Unites States is deterring cartel activity.

[73]   See the AG Opinion in case T-1/89 *Rhône-Poulenc v Commission* ECLI:EU:T:1991:38, at 1991 ECR II 991.

[74]   Although the CJEU has always avoided the qualification of EU antitrust law as criminal and Article 23(5) of Regulation 1/2003 even explicitly denies that characterisation to fining decisions adopted by the Commission, many have argued that fines in cartel cases should be viewed as quasi-criminal, see, for example, the AG Opinion in case C-681/11 *Schenker & Co. and Others* ECLI:EU:C:2013:126, para 59.

[75]   See, for example, Commission decision of 29 April 2014 in case 39.985 *Motorola – Enforcement of GPRS standard essential patents*, in particular recitals 559–61.

[76]   Case C-457/10 P *AstraZeneca v Commission* ECLI:EU:C:2012:770, para 164.

[77]   Case C-499/11 P *Dow Chemical and Others v Commission* ECLI:EU:C:2013:482, para 47.

negligently" infringe Article 101 TFEU. These two forms of *mens rea* have been interpreted very widely in the case law such that very little culpability seems in fact required in order to impose a fine on an undertaking.[78] In any event, this apparent culpability requirement only concerns the liability for fines and not the existence of an infringement as such. Indeed, even in the absence of an intention or negligence, the Commission may, pursuant to Article 7 of Regulation 1/2003, order an undertaking to bring an infringement to an end and, if necessary, impose structural or behavioural remedies that are necessary to terminate the infringement. Article 24 of Regulation 1/2003 allows the Commission to make compliance with such a decision subject to periodic penalty payments.

So even if, as a theoretical hypothesis, the practice of a pricing bot would be considered to be so ambiguous that it may not have been possible for its designer or user to foresee its anticompetitive character, the Commission can prohibit the practice without a fine. It could also impose an obligation on one or more undertakings to ensure that the practice is stopped (possibly subject to the risk of a periodic penalty payment).

5   CONCLUSION

While the Internet may bring us new products and services and markets which are competitive in ways that seemed unthinkable until very recently, it may also create market inefficiencies. It is therefore worthwhile to look out for any gaps in antitrust enforcement that may arise from the competitive process in virtual markets.

However, it is also important not to underestimate the flexibility allowed by the CJEU's case law in EU antitrust cases. The CJEU has identified unlawful collusion as a consequence of the disclosure of sensitive information from one undertaking to another. Evidence of an anticompetitive intention is not required to establish an infringement, although it is important in practice: whether or not algorithms are more opaque than humans in this respect remains to be seen.

Furthermore, undertakings can be liable for the actions of the (self-learning) algorithms they create or use. Undertakings have a positive obligation to ensure compliance with the EU antitrust rules and cannot plead ignorance of what their employees or price bots are doing. Additionally, even if there would be

---

[78]   Much of the case law on the *mens rea* of Article 23(2) Regulation 1/2003 (and its predecessor Article 15(2)(a) of Regulation 17/62) has, in fact, been about awareness of the antitrust rules (alleged mistakes of law) rather than about intention or negligence. Following the principle that mistakes of law are no excuse, liability then becomes almost strict. For a recent example, see C-681/11 *Schenker & Co. and Others* ECLI:EU:C:2013:404.

circumstances where undertakings could not be found to have been negligent in how they supervise their employees and price bots, the Commission could prohibit practices and ensure compliance through periodic penalty payments.

4. Can the reformed Australian competition law stop algorithmic collusion?

Baskaran Balasingham

1 INTRODUCTION

Algorithms and Big Data are the driving factors behind the rapid growth and success of digital platforms. Pricing algorithms in particular are often used by online retailers and e-commerce platforms like Amazon. The data-driven innovations including price monitoring and efficient price discrimination that stem from pricing algorithms can enhance consumer welfare. On the other hand, pricing algorithms can be deployed as a means to facilitate collusion and can therefore cause consumer harm. When this happens the conduct may not necessarily involve a contract, arrangement or understanding which had to be proven to establish an infringement of the old section 45 of the Australian Competition and Consumer Act 2010 (Cth) (CCA). Under that provision the establishment of an infringement was cumbersome enough when it was solely about the conduct of human beings. How much more difficult would it be now that artificial intelligence and machine learning have entered the picture? In November 2017, and completely unrelated to the technological advancements in relation to potential cartel conduct, the CCA was amended to prohibit concerted practices that have the purpose, effect or likely effect of substantially lessening competition. In the wake of the amendment's entry into force, the Chairman of the Australian Competition and Consumer Commission (ACCC), Rod Sims, expressed confidence that Australia's competition law, particularly with the addition of the new concerted practice prohibition, can deal with algorithms that harm competition.[1]

---

[1]   Rod Sims, 'The ACCC's Approach to Colluding Robots' (Can Robots Collude? Conference, Sydney, 16 November 2017), available at www.accc.gov.au/speech/the -accc's-approach-to-colluding-robots (accessed 30 June 2022).

The aim of this chapter is to analyse the extent to which the new prohibition of concerted practices that were introduced by the Competition and Consumer Amendment (Competition Policy Review) Act 2017 may capture algorithmically facilitated collusion. Given that the new amendment lacks a definition of the term "concerted practices", this chapter argues that the judicial interpretation of this term will be decisive for the scope of the prohibition and the types of algorithmic collusion it may capture. The chapter is structured as follows: the next section sheds light on the link between collusion and facilitating practices. Section 3 explains how the CCA dealt with facilitating practices before the latest amendment. Section 4 sets out the new concerted practice prohibition, and Section 5 subsequently analyses the application of the CCA to algorithmic collusion. Section 6 concludes.

2   COLLUSION AND FACILITATING PRACTICES

Competition inherently involves uncertainty. It is therefore in competing firms' interest to increase their welfare by mitigating this uncertainty. For instance, if they agree not to undercut each other's prices they can more easily charge prices above the competitive level. This form of collusion or coordination is considered anti-competitive as it harms consumer welfare and creates a deadweight loss. Collusion/coordination among firms can take various forms, ranging from tacit collusion in oligopolistic markets to "cooperation agreements". Owing to the characteristics of the market, oligopolies are able to behave in a parallel manner without necessarily entering into an agreement or concerted practice.[2] For economists tacit collusion is as undesirable as explicit collusion. Cooperation agreements, by contrast, are formal and enforceable agreements that can be beneficial to competition as they "can be a means to share risks, save costs, increase investments, pool know-how, enhance product quality and variety, and launch innovation faster".[3] Tacit collusion and cooperation agreements are at opposite ends of a spectrum of inter-firm cooperation, with internalisation ranging from low to high.[4] In between these poles there is conduct that may be anti-competitive. This conduct may take different types of formality. In some countries the prohibition of anti-competitive collusion is not limited to formal contracts but also applies to cooperation achieved

---

[2]   Richard Whish and David Bailey, *Competition Law* (9th edn, Oxford University Press 2019) 570.

[3]   Commission, 'Guidelines on the Applicability of Article 101 of the Treaty on the Functioning of the European Union to Horizontal Co-operation Agreements' (2011) OJ C/11.

[4]   Ioannis Lianos and Valentine Korah, *Competition Law: Analysis, Cases, & Materials* (Oxford University Press 2019) 689.

through informal agreements and concerted practices or concerted action. The concept of "concerted practices" was recently also adopted under the CCA. As known from other jurisdictions it is difficult both to define the type or degree of coordination that may amount to a concerted practice and to apply the prohibition to the facts of any given case.[5] The existence of so-called "facilitating practices" is often crucial to firms' ability to collude. Hay notes that "[t]he term 'facilitating practices' describes various kinds of activities in which firms engage to better enable coordination of their actions and avoid (or at least reduce) competition without the need for a meeting or other forms of explicit communication."[6] Facilitating practices may increase the likelihood of collusion, but may turn out to be neutral or even be beneficial for the competitive nature of the market.[7] Much of the difficulty with concerted practices stems from determining to what extent they diminish uncertainty in the market. The examples of information sharing and the use of algorithms illustrate this difficulty.

2.1   Information Sharing

It is not unusual or entirely illegal for firms to share information with each other. Full market transparency is one of the hallmarks of a perfectly competitive market.[8] The communication of information between market participants can solve the problem of information asymmetries and thus lead to more efficient markets. Sharing of information may for example help firms to improve their internal efficiency through benchmarking against each other's best practices and save costs by reducing their inventories or dealing with unstable demand.[9] The main benefits of enhanced market transparency for consumers are lower search costs and enhanced choice.[10] However, information sharing can under certain circumstances facilitate tacit collusion between firms. According to the economic literature the competitive effects of information sharing generally depend on (1) the underlying market structure; (2) the

---

[5]   Whish and Bailey (n. 2 above) at 115.

[6]   George A. Hay, 'Facilitating Practices' in Wayne D. Collins, Joseph Angland and American Bar Association (eds), *Issues in Competition Law and Policy* (Vol 1, American Bar Association 2008) 1189.

[7]   OECD, 'Policy Roundtables: Facilitating Practices in Oligopolies 2007' *DAF/COMP (2008)24* (2008), 128, available at www.oecd.org/daf/competition/41472165.pdf (accessed 30 June 2022).

[8]   OECD, 'Policy Roundtables: Information Exchanges between Competitors under Competition Law' *DAF/COMP(2010)37* (2010), available at www.oecd.org/competition/cartels/48379006.pdf (accessed 30 June 2022).

[9]   Commission (n. 3 above) at para 57.

[10]   ibid.

impact of the communication on the level of transparency within the market; and (3) the characteristics of the information shared and the manner of its communication.[11]

With regard to the market structure, information sharing (and facilitating practices in general) are more likely to cause competitive concerns in an oligopolistic market.[12] The potential for collusion is even greater where such a market is characterised by a higher degree of concentration, with a small group of players who interact regularly; high barriers to entry; a low degree of product differentiation; stable demand conditions; and symmetric costs.[13] Where the supply side of a market is already prone to coordination due to those pre-existing structural factors, increased transparency may potentially facilitate collusive outcomes.[14] Moreover, apart from whether the communication of information is "private", or is made to the public at large, the characteristics of the information shared are likely to affect its collusive potential, most importantly whether the information relates to past, current or future matters; whether it is aggregated (i.e. industry-wide) or disaggregated (i.e. firm-specific); the degree of commitment inherent in the communication and the degree of verifiability of the information; the degree of sensitivity of the subject matter; and the frequency and timing of the exchange of information.[15] It is clear from the above that the collusive potential of information sharing needs to be assessed on a case-by-case basis.

2.2   Algorithmic Collusion

Apart from digital platforms and Big Data, artificial intelligence and machine learning are significant drivers of change in markets and market structures.[16] Algorithms as one of the most well-known applications of artificial intelligence and machine learning are becoming ubiquitous in today's economy.[17]

---

[11]   Kathryn Tomasic, 'Price Signalling' Amendments to the Competition and Consumer Act 2010 (Cth): A Principled Response to the Problem of Tacit Collusion?' (2012) 19 *Competition & Consumer Law Journal* 176, 179.

[12]   OECD (n. 7 above) at 9; Hay (n. 6 above) at 1189.

[13]   Tomasic (n. 11 above) at 180.

[14]   ibid., at 181.

[15]   ibid., at 186–7.

[16]   See Ariel Ezrachi and Maurice E. Stucke, *Virtual Competition: The Promise and Perils of the Algorithm-driven Economy* (Harvard University Press 2016) 15; Thorsten Käseberg and Jonas von Kalben, 'Herausforderungen der Künstlichen Intelligenz für die Wettbewerbspolitik' (2018) 68 *Wirtschaft und Wettbewerb* 2, 2.

[17]   Ai Deng, 'What Do We Know About Algorithmic Tacit Collusion' (2018) 33 *Antitrust* 88, 93. The EU's E-Commerce Sector Enquiry revealed that two-thirds of online retailers that monitor rivals' prices already use an automated price monitor-

Algorithms collect, cluster and analyse large sets of data faster and more accurately than humanly possible. Fed with these pieces of information, algorithms are capable of analysing entire markets as well as the behaviour of each individual consumer.[18] This allows algorithms to determine and adapt product prices individually and to tailor them to specific consumers, based on their buying habits and reservation prices at a certain time.[19] Apart from yielding positive effects for an individual firm, the use of algorithms can also raise overall market efficiency.[20] As with information sharing, the use of algorithms can increase transparency in the market.[21]

On the other hand, algorithms may facilitate tacit collusion in a number of ways. First, an enhanced capacity to process large amounts of data helps competing firms to understand each other's production functions and business strategies.[22] Second, the use of algorithms lowers the risk of unintentional destabilisation of a cartel caused by defection from the supra-competitive equilibrium which is more likely to arise when corporate actors make mistakes when they try to meet this equilibrium by adapting their transaction conditions.[23] Third, algorithms are not prone to human biases such as the tendency to favour short-term and/or personal gains from breaching the collusive equilibrium over long-term and/or company gains from upholding a cartel.[24] Finally, algorithms tend to increase the frequency and reduce the latency of transactions between colluding firms, thus making price undercutting less likely to go unnoticed long enough to yield attractive deviation gains.[25]

In their seminal work Ariel Ezrachi and Maurice M. Stucke identify four potential scenarios in which the use of algorithms may raise antitrust concerns.[26] The level of sophistication of algorithms and their use in the market,

---

ing software (European Commission, Staff Working Document, 'Final Report on the E-Commerce Sector Inquiry' *SWD(2017) 154 final* (2017), para 603).

[18] Sebastian Janka and Severin Uhsler, 'Antitrust 4.0 – the Rise of Artificial Intelligence and Emerging Challenges to Antitrust Law' (2018) 39 *European Competition Law Review* 112.

[19] ibid., at 112; Käseberg and von Kalben (n. 16) at 3.

[20] OECD, 'Algorithms and Collusion – Background Note by the Secretariat' *DAF/COMP(2017)4* (2017), 12–16.

[21] See Ezrachi and Stucke (n. 16 above).

[22] Peter Picht and Benedikt Freund, 'Competition (Law) in the Era of Algorithms' (2018) 39 *European Competition Law Review* 403, 405

[23] ibid.

[24] Salil K. Mehra, 'Antitrust and the Robo-Seller: Competition in the Time of Algorithms' (2016) 100 *Minnesota Law Review* 1323, 1328; see also Ariel Ezrachi and Maurice E. Stucke, 'Artificial Intelligence & Collusion: When Computers Inhibit Competition' (2017) 2017(5) *University of Illinois Law Review* 1792.

[25] Picht and Freund (n. 22 above) at 405.

[26] See Ezrachi and Stucke (n. 16 above) at 36–7 and 39–81.

as well as the challenge for competition law enforcement between these four scenarios differs greatly. In the first two scenarios algorithms are used to facilitate humanly agreed upon collusion, whereas in the last two scenarios the algorithms are more advanced and their use can result in tacit collusion. In the first scenario, the "Messenger" scenario, humans collude and use algorithms to execute their will.[27] In the second scenario, the "Hub and Spoke", the parties to the collusive conduct exchange sensitive information using a single pricing algorithm to determine their market prices.[28] In the third scenario, the "Predictable Agent", each firm unilaterally programs its algorithm to monitor price changes, swiftly reacts to any competitors' price reductions and follows price increases as long as they are sustainable. The algorithms are likely to engage in predictive analytics to build forecasts by studying real-time, historical and third-party data.[29] Finally, in the fourth scenario, the "Digital Eye", the algorithms are self-learning and able to optimise their performance by reflecting on past decisions in order to maximise profits.[30] As the scope of this chapter is limited to algorithmically facilitated collusion, Section 5 below will analyse whether Australian competition law is applicable to the first two scenarios.

3   THE TREATMENT OF FACILITATING PRACTICES BEFORE THE HARPER REFORM

3.1   Outline of the Pre-Amendment Prohibitions under the CCA

Australia's first effective competition statute was the Trade Practices Act 1974. In 2010, the Act was re-named the Competition and Consumer Act 2010, but the provisions remained mostly unchanged until the entry into force of the Competition and Consumer Amendment (Competition Policy Review) Act 2017. Part IV of the Act proscribes certain forms of conduct that distort competition. A few provisions are prohibited without regard to whether or not the conduct is in fact harmful to competition in individual cases (so-called "per se prohibitions"). Most other provisions by now are only prohibited if the conduct has certain economic consequences – these provisions are subject to a "substantial lessening of competition" (SLC) test. In 2009, new cartel laws including criminal penalties were introduced. Collusive conduct may since then be caught either by the cartel laws[31] or by section 45. The cartel laws set

---

[27]   ibid., at 36.
[28]   ibid.
[29]   ibid., at 61.
[30]   ibid.
[31]   CCA, Division 1 of Part IV, Sections 45AA–45AU.

out per se prohibitions (and include criminal and civil prohibitions that operate concurrently) for provisions that contain a "cartel provision" as defined in section 45AD. If a provision does not meet this definition, it may still be caught by section 45 if it has the purpose, effect or likely effect of substantially lessening competition. Given the narrow scope of the cartel laws, facilitating practices were, and still are, more likely to be caught under section 45 which can be thought of as a catch-all provision for anti-competitive arrangements.[32]

3.1.1 Contract, arrangement or understanding

Irrespective of whether the cartel laws or section 45(1) applied to facilitating practices under the pre-2017 Act, the first element that needed to be proved was the existence of a contract, arrangement or understanding (CAU). In *ACCC v. Leahy*, Justice Gray explained that the terms "contract, arrangement and understanding" encompass a "spectrum of consensual dealings".[33] These concepts are considered to be related, overlapping and along a scale of formality – with "contract" at the higher end and "understanding" at the lower end, and "arrangement" somewhere in between.[34] At least this appears to be the contemporary view,[35] stemming from Justice Peter Gray's opinion in *ACCC v. Leahy* where he interpreted each term. A "contract" is understood by its ordinary common law meaning, that is, it involves offer and acceptance between the parties, resulting in a meeting of minds and being supported by good consideration, and being accompanied with sufficient certainty and intention.[36] Justice Gray therefore described it as a consensual dealing with a high degree of formality.[37] The term "arrangement" is less clearly understood and prone to

---

[32] Arlen Duke, *Corones' Competition Law in Australia* (7th edn, Thompson Reuters 2019) 402.

[33] *ACCC v. Leahy Petroleum Pty Ltd* [2007] FCA 794, para 24.

[34] Caron Beaton-Wells and Brent Fisse, *Australian Cartel Regulation: Law, Policy and Practice in an International Context* (Cambridge University Press 2011) 39.

[35] Ibid; ACCC, *Petrol Prices and Australian Consumers: Report of the ACCC Inquiry into the Price of Unleaded Petrol* (ACCC 2007) 228.

[36] *ACCC v. Leahy*, para 25. Justice Gray stated:
The term 'contract' is well understood by lawyers. A contract is the result of the acceptance by one party of an offer made by another, resulting in the minds of the two parties being at one as to the agreement they have made. It must be supported by good consideration, have sufficient certainty of terms that it be possible to determine what has been agreed, and be accompanied by an intention on the part of the parties that a legally binding relationship should be established by it. (ibid). See also *Hughes v. Western Australian Cricket Association* [1986] 19 FCR 10, 32.

[37] *ACCC v. Leahy*, para 25.

a more elastic meaning.[38] An arrangement lacks some of the essential elements of a contract, and if not express negotiation, it must at the very least involve express communication between the parties.[39] Justice Gray noted that the word "understanding" is "intended to connote a less precise dealing than either a contract or arrangement".[40] Unlike an arrangement, an understanding can be tacit so long as there is a meeting of minds.[41]

While arrangements and understandings are intended to catch dealings which are less formal and may not give rise to a legally binding contract, courts have concluded that both concepts require three elements: communication, consensus and commitment.[42] Communication giving rise to an arrangement may be implicit in some act rather than express words, and can be as informal as a wink or nod.[43] There must be consensus as to what is to be done by at least one party. A mere hope or expectation as to what will happen will not be sufficient.[44] Mutuality between the parties is not required, although in prac-

---

[38]   ibid., para 26. Justice Gray argued:
The word 'arrangement' is less clearly understood, and more susceptible of elasticity as to its meaning. In general, it appears to connote a consensual dealing lacking some of the essential elements that would otherwise make it a contract. For instance, a dealing that would otherwise be a contract may be described as an 'arrangement' if the parties to it intended not to create a legally binding relationship, but only to give expression to their intentions as to the obligations that each felt morally bound to adhere to in relation to what was to pass between them, or to be carried out by them. Of course, an arrangement might be a broader concept than this, because it is a term the boundaries of which have not been fixed in the traditional understanding of lawyers.
(ibid).

[39]   ibid.

[40]   ibid., para 27. Justice Gray stated: "The word 'understanding' is obviously intended to connote a less precise dealing than either a contract or arrangement. This is so because of the meaning of the word 'understanding' itself, and because, in the terms of s 45(2)(a), the parties to it may 'arrive at' it instead of making it." (ibid).

[41]   ibid., para 28. Justice Gray used the word 'tacit' to refer to understandings 'arrived at by each party, either by words or acts, signifying an intention to act in a particular way in relation to a matter of concern to another party' (ibid.).

[42]   *ACCC v. Construction, Forestry, Mining and Energy Union* [2008] FCA 678, para 10. Apart from communication, consensus and commitment it is also necessary to prove consent. The parties must have consented to a course of action which will often be implicit and rarely controversial where other elements are established. However, it will exclude e.g. agreements that are reached through duress (Philip Clarke et al., *Competition Law and Policy: Cases and Materials* (3rd edn, Oxford University Press 2011) 241.

[43]   *ACCC v. Leahy*, para 26.

[44]   ibid., para 28; *TPC v. Email Ltd* [1980] FLR 383, 385; *Stationers Supply Pty Ltd v. Victorian Authorised Newsagents Association Ltd* [1993] 44 FCR 35, 61; *News Ltd v. Australian Rugby Football League Ltd* [1996] 64 FCR 410, 571–2.

tice there is usually reciprocity of obligations.[45] The most controversial and problematic requirement for establishing an arrangement or understanding is to show that at least one party made a commitment to act in a particular way.[46] It is sufficient if the commitment involves a "moral obligation, or obligation binding in honour"[47] only, but independently held hopes or beliefs will not be sufficient. The High Court has never directly stipulated this requirement. However, it denied the ACCC special leave to appeal the judgment of the Full Federal Court in *Apco v. ACCC*,[48] where the latter endorsed this requirement, as the High Court did not consider that the Full Federal Court's decision raised any serious issues of interpretation.[49]

The ACCC argued that the interpretation has made it difficult to prove the existence of a CAU.[50] Notably the ACCC had little success in bringing information-sharing cases as it often failed to establish the commitment requirement, and *ACCC v. Leahy* is probably the low water-mark case.[51] In that case, the ACCC alleged that a number of petrol station proprietors entered into eight separate arrangements or understandings to fix the retail price of petrol. To prove its case, the ACCC presented circumstantial evidence, and admissions made in compulsory examinations. It also relied on direct evidence, however, which the court deemed to be unhelpful as it was evidence of general patterns and practices rather than events on any specific date.[52] The Federal Court held that, although there could be no doubt that petrol station proprietors passed information from one to another about the levels of retail petrol prices on a number of occasions, that did not necessarily indicate that they had come to an arrangement or understanding.[53] Justice Gray noted that

> [i]n a competitive market involving a number of competitors, information about the prices of others is certainly one of the most useful factors in the setting of a dealer's own prices. In such a market, there is a tendency for prices of homogeneous commodities to move towards uniformity across the market. Petrol is such a commodity.

---

[45] *ACCC v. Amcor Printing Papers Group Ltd* [2000] 169 ALR 344, 359–60.

[46] Rhonda Smith and Arlen Duke, 'Agreements and Competition Law in Australia' (2014) 22 *Competition & Consumer Law Journal* 54, 73; Michael Gvozdenovic, 'Concerted Practices and Statutory Interpretation: An Affirmation of the Jurisprudence on "Contracts, Arrangements and Understandings"' (2019) 26 *Competition & Consumer Law Journal* 213, 223; Clarke et al. (n. 42 above) at 246.

[47] *ACCC v. Leahy*, para 940.

[48] *Apco Service Stations Pty Ltd v. ACCC* [2005] 159 FCR 452.

[49] *ACCC v. Apco Service Stations Pty Ltd* [2006] HCA Trans 272.

[50] ACCC (n. 35 above) at 228.

[51] Russell V. Miller, *Miller's Australian Competition Law and Policy* (3rd edn, Thomson Reuters 2018) 167.

[52] *ACCC v. Leahy*, para 922.

[53] ibid., para 922.

The public display of board prices by all or most competitors would ensure a high degree of uniformity in the market in any event. Telephone calls and face-to-face conversations were other ways in which information about prices was conveyed.[54]

The court held that no commitment had been established. It explained that

advanced notice of the proposed implementation of a decision already made to increase prices would provide a competitor with the advantage of more time, but cannot itself be indicative of the existence of an arrangement or understanding containing a provision to fix prices. There are additional elements that need to be established.[55]

The decision and reasoning in *Leahy* highlights two problems in relation to the former section 45: first, the high threshold for catching price information exchange under this provision, and second, the difficulties associated with both direct and circumstantial evidence in those cases.[56] *ACCC v. Leahy* has been consistently followed, as a result of which, without more, the exchange of pricing information was not caught prior to the last amendment.[57] The more recent *Australian Egg Cartel* case once more underlined the ACCC's struggle to establish, on the balance of probabilities, the existence of a CAU.[58]

---

[54]   ibid., paras 922–3.

[55]   ibid., para 925.

[56]   Lindsay Foster and Hanna Kaci, 'Concerted Practices: A Contravention Without a Definition' (2018) 26 *Competition and Consumer Law Journal* 1, 6.

[57]   ibid.

[58]   See *ACCC v. Australian Egg Corporation Ltd* [2017] FCAFC 152, paras 95–8 and 107. The conduct in question in this case related to a meeting by the Australian Egg Corporation Limited (AECL), an industry body that monitors egg production and the demand for eggs in Australia. In 2012, the AECL requested a meeting of the 25 largest egg producers to address the oversupply of eggs. The crisis summit was attended by 19 of those producers. The ACCC alleged that the AECL and other participants contravened the CCA's cartel laws by attempting to induce egg producers to make an agreement or arrive at an understanding to limit egg supply. The primary judge distinguished between a circumstance where industry participants are brought to an appreciation that it is in their interest to act in a particular way, independently of what others are doing, and a circumstance where industry participants are invited to agree to act in a certain way with the expectation of reciprocal conduct by others. The latter is in breach of the cartel laws, whereas the former is not (*ACCC v. Australian Egg Corporation Ltd* [2016] FCA 69, para 381). The primary judge held that even though at least two respondents intended for participants to limit egg supply, there was no intention for that to occur by inducing partiucpants to enter into an arrangement or understanding to take collective action and that due to the lack of mutuality or reciprocity of obligations the conduct did not breach the cartel laws (ibid., at para 383). On appeal the Full Federal Court affirmed the primary judge's distinction . The Court held

3.1.2   Purpose, effect, likely effect of substantial lessening competition

Subsequent to establishing a CAU, the prohibition in old section 45(1) required establishing that the agreement had the purpose, effect or likely effect of substantially lessening competition in a market. The proscribed anti-competitive purpose, effect or likely effect are alternative rather than cumulative conditions. The courts have interpreted the "purpose" of a provision to involve an enquiry into the subjective purpose of the parties to the CAU.[59] This subjective purpose needs to be ascertained from the evidence of the mental state of the parties responsible for inserting the provision in the CAU, although inferences may also be inferred from the party's conduct.[60] From section 4F of the Act it also follows that the prescribed purpose of the provision does not need to be the sole purpose, so long as it is a "substantial" purpose.[61] Where the purpose of a provision cannot be established it will suffice to show that it has the effect of substantially lessening competition. Where a provision does not produce actual effects, it is possible that it many contravene section 45(1) on the basis of its likely effects. There has been some debate as to the precise meaning of the word "likely". In *News Ltd v. Australian Rugby Football League Ltd*, the Full Federal Court found that the term should be interpreted more broadly to mean a "real or not remote chance" rather than "probable".[62] The determination of whether a provision has the likely effect of substantially lessening competition requires applying a counterfactual test which compares the likely state of competition in the future with the impugned conduct and the likely state of competition in the future without the impugned conduct.[63]

While there is no legislative definition of the SLC concept, it is in essence where a practice interferes with the competitive process in a meaningful way.[64] Even though the concept is composite it requires that meaning is given

---

that an industry body may perform an educative or information providing role towards its members without contravening cartel and associated provisions. As a general proposition, it may be said that an industry body may, in the interests of its members and of the industry, provide information to its members and suggest that they examine their present practices and consider changing them (*ACCC v. Australian Egg Corporation Ltd* [2017] FCAFC 152, para 98).

[59]   *News Ltd v. South Sydney District Rugby League Football Club Ltd* [2003] HCA 45, paras 18, 46, 65, and 216.

[60]   Duke (n. 32 above) at 412.

[61]   CCA, Section 4F(1)(b)(ii).

[62]   *News Ltd v. Australian Rugby League Football Ltd,* (n. 44) para 343.

[63]   *Outbound Marine Australia Pty Ltd v. Hecar Investments (No 6) Pty Ltd* [1982] 66 FLR 120, paras 123–4.

[64]   ACCC, 'Guidelines on Concerted Practices' (August 2018), para 4.19.

to each individual term.[65] In other words, it is necessary to understand what "competition" means in a particular context, whether that competition has been "lessened", and whether the lessening is "substantial".[66] First of all, "competition" within the meaning of section 45 denotes competition in any market in which a corporation is a party, or any related body corporate to such corporation, supplies or acquires or is likely to supply or acquire, goods or services, or would but for the provision supply or acquire, or be likely to supply or acquire, goods or services.[67] "Lessening competition" includes "preventing or hindering competition".[68] Finally the word "substantial" according to the High Court means that the loss of competition must be "meaningful or relevant to the competitive process".[69]

3.2   The Price Signalling Laws

Price signalling laws were introduced by the controversial Competition and Consumer Amendment Act (No 1) 2011. The new legislation comprised a per se prohibition on the private disclosure of pricing information to competitors, as well as a prohibition on the public price disclosure that were made to substantially lessen competition. These prohibitions were introduced to cover the limitations in the cartel laws and section 45 which were blatantly laid open in *Leahy*.[70] The concern was that a party might "signal" a price (or other) change to a competitor but such conduct would not be caught by the cartel law or section 45. The ACCC's 2007 Petrol Report emphasised that, in light of the court's restrictive construction of the word "understanding", the anti-competitive exchange of retail petrol prices between competitors would not amount to a "price-fixing understanding" for the purposes of section 45 and therefore is outside the scope of the CCA.[71]

The price signalling legislation was only applied to banking services and included a number of exceptions. Apart from this rather limited scope, the effectiveness of this legislation was further constrained by the complex draft-

---

[65]   Peter Armitage, 'The Evolution of the "Substantial Lessening of Competition" Test – A Review of Case Law' (2016) 44 *Australian Business Law Review* 74, 84.

[66]   Caitlin Davies and Luke Wainscoat, 'Not Quite a Cartel: Applying the New Concerted Practices Prohibition' (2017) 25 *Competition & Consumer Law Journal* 173, 193; see *Stirling Harbour Services Pty Ltd v. Bunbury Port Authority* [2000] FCA 38, para 113.

[67]   CCA, section 45(3)(a).

[68]   ibid., section 4G.

[69]   *Rural Press Ltd v. ACCC* [2003] HCA 75, para 41.

[70]   See Rod Sims, 'ACCC Priorities in Enforcing Competition Law' (12th Competition Law Conference, Sydney, 5 May 2012).

[71]   ACCC (n. 35 above), at 228.

ing of the provisions, which were highly prescriptive, in an attempt to exclude pro-competitive or benign price disclosure from the ambit of the prohibitions.[72] These aspects eventually led to the failure of the price signalling regime which was demonstrated by the fact that no proceedings were ever instituted by the ACCC under these laws. The Harper Committee concluded that the price signalling provisions were not fit for purpose and should be repealed. In particular, it expressed the view that competition laws should apply generally across the economy, not to particular sectors and that there is no policy rationale for price signalling laws to apply only to the banking sector.[73]

4   THE NEW PROHIBITION OF CONCERTED PRACTICES

Due to the limited scope of the price signalling laws, the gap identified by the ACCC in the 2007 Petrol Report effectively remained: the CCA did not apply where two or more competitors engaged in a facilitating practice that is likely to substantially lessen competition, unless the parties had reached at least an understanding.[74] In the ACCC's view the requirement to establish mutual commitment for there to be an understanding set a high threshold.[75] This requirement appears not only formalistic but also inconsistent with the potential anti-competitive effect of facilitating practices which may be adopted with or without an explicit understanding.[76] As noted by Walker "[t]he 'success' of both explicit agreements and other types of facilitating practices in sustaining supra-competitive prices has nothing to do with whether the conduct involves any sort of moral or other 'commitment' by the parties".[77]

When the Harper Committee launched a root and branch reform of the CCA in 2013, it recommended repealing the price signalling laws and expanding section 45 to apply to contracts, arrangements, understandings *and* concerted practices.[78] The government accepted those recommendations in the

---

[72]   Foster and Kaci (n. 56 above) at 2–3.

[73]   Commonwealth of Australia, 'Competition Policy Review: Final Report' (March 2015), 372 (Harper Review).

[74]   ibid., 370–1.

[75]   ACCC, 'Submission to the Competition Policy Review – Response to the Draft Report' (26 November 2014) 43–4.

[76]   See George A. Hay, 'Facilitating Practices: The Ethyl Case' in John E. Kwoka and Lawrence J. White (eds.), *The Antitrust Revolution: Economics, Competition, and Policy* (3rd edn, Oxford University Press 1999) 189.

[77]   Jill Walker, 'Agreements, Communication and Facilitating Practices: Where is the Harm?' (Paper presented at the Law Council Trade Practices Workshop, Gold Coast, 21 August 2010) 3.

[78]   Harper Review (n. 73 above) at 370–1.

Competition and Consumer Amendment (Competition Policy Review) Bill 2017.[79] Section 45(1)(c) of the CCA now provides that "a corporation must not ... engage with one or more persons in a concerted practice that has the purpose, or has or is likely to have the effect, of substantially lessening competition". The amended CCA does not define the term "concerted practices". In the *Guidelines on concerted practices* the ACCC sets out how it currently proposes to interpret section 45(1)(c) but it also lacks a definition. The interpretation of the term is ultimately the responsibility of the Australian courts.[80] This section sets out the guidance on the concept of concerted practices provided in Australian legislative material and discusses the usefulness of the European concept for Australia.

4.1   Guidance in Australian Legislative Material

The Explanatory Memorandum to the 2017 Bill refers to the Harper Committee's position that it is unnecessary to introduce a legislative definition of "concerted practices", as the word "concerted" has a "clear and practical meaning".[81] The Explanatory Memorandum explains that a legislative definition was contemplated, but ultimately not adopted.[82] It reasoned that although a legislative definition would potentially increase certainty as to what does and does not constitute a concerted practice, this would require a focus on determining whether conduct fits within detailed technical provisions, rather than making a principled assessment of the conduct as a whole.[83] The Committee was concerned that this approach might inadvertently exclude conduct which should be deemed to be a "concerted practice".[84] Instead, it decided to provide additional guidance as to the typical features of a concerted practice whilst also leaving scope within section 45 to apply the concept to new forms of

---

[79]   The Competition and Consumer (Competition Policy Review) Bill 2017 (2017 Bill) passed both House of Parliament and received Royal Assent on 27 October 2017. It entered into force on 6 November 2017.

[80]   ACCC (n. 64 above) at 2.

[81]   Explanatory Memorandum, *Competition and Consumer Amendment (Competition Policy Review) Bill 2017*, para 3.17, available at https://parlinfo.aph.gov.au/parlInfo/download/legislation/ems/r5851_ems_0b6ffc49-7398-409a-8e46-4873853a475f/upload_pdf/625422.pdf;fileType=application%2Fpdf (accessed 30 June 2022). In its Final Report the Harper Committee states that the "word 'concerted' means jointly arranged or carried out or co-ordinated. Hence, a concerted practice between market participants is a practice that is jointly arranged or carried out or co-ordinated between the participants." (Harper Review (n. 73 above) at 371).

[82]   Explanatory Memorandum (n. 81 above), at para 15.44.

[83]   ibid.

[84]   ibid.

anti-competitive conduct as they arise.[85] According to the Committee this option increases certainty and at the same time lowers the risk of inappropriately limiting the scope,[86] thus retaining a "flexible and principled application of the concept".[87] While this approach leaves businesses with uncertainty until the courts come up with an interpretation, it provides the ACCC with flexibility as the how to approach the concerted practices prohibition.[88]

The Explanatory Memorandum describes a "concerted practice" as "any form of cooperation between two or more firms (or people) or conduct that would be likely to establish such cooperation, where this conduct substitutes, or would be likely to substitute, cooperation in place of the uncertainty of competition."[89]

Lindsay Foster and Hanna Kaci criticise this characterisation, which stems from the definition of concerted practices under EU competition law as discussed below, since "it merely shifts the question of construction from the proper construction of 'concertation' to the interpretation of equally ambiguous terms such as 'cooperation' and 'co-ordination'".[90] The definition by the Court of Justice of the European Union (CJEU) is not sound as the concept of cooperation itself is vague.[91]

Possibly more useful for the interpretation of a "concerted practice" is the distinction between this concept and the other concepts of section 45(1). The Explanatory Memorandum sets out that a concerted practice is intended to capture conduct that falls short of a CAU as the courts have interpreted each of those terms in section 45.[92] Highlighting the distinction between a concerted practice and an understanding, the Explanatory Memorandum notes that the former does not require any commitment. It states that "a concerted practice may exist even if none of the parties is obliged, either legally or morally, to act in any particular way".[93] The *Guidelines on concerted practices* confirm this point.[94]

---

[85]   ibid., at para 15.45.

[86]   ibid.

[87]   ibid., at para 3.18.

[88]   Rob Nicholls and Deniz Kayis, 'Concerted Practices Contested: Evidentiary Thresholds' (2017) 25 *Competition & Consumer Law Journal* 125, 128.

[89]   Explanatory Memorandum (n. 81 above), at para 3.19.

[90]   Foster and Kaci (n. 56 above) at 7.

[91]   Oliver Black, *Conceptual Foundations of Antitrust* (Cambridge University Press 2005) 141–2.

[92]   Explanatory Memorandum (n. 81 above), at para 3.21.

[93]   ibid., at para 3.22.

[94]   ACCC (n. 64 above), at para 3.3.

In order to fathom the scope of the concerted practice prohibition, it may also be practical to think of the type of behaviour that would not be captured.[95] The Explanatory Memorandum clarifies that the concept is not intended to catch mere innocent parallel behaviour, for example, where two firms who are determining their prices independently happen to charge similar prices for the same product.[96] Similarly, the concept is not intended to catch conduct such as the public disclosure of pricing information which facilitates price comparison by consumers, as this conduct is beneficial to competition.[97] Finally, the Explanatory Memorandum and the *Guidelines on concerted practices* also set out some examples that illustrate a concerted practice.

4.2   The European Concept of Concerted Practice

The Exposure Draft's Explanatory Materials expressly state that the interpretation of the concept should be "informed by international approaches to the same concept, where appropriate".[98] In giving evidence to Parliament in 2016, the ACCC Chairman supported the Harper Committee's recommendation to "copy" European and US law on concerted practices. Yet, the *Guidelines on concerted practices* mainly refer to the concept in the EU and UK, and do not mention the US at all.[99]

In Europe the concept of "concerted practice" has been described as "nebulous".[100] On the one hand, the Court sought to institute effective competition law enforcement that takes into account different forms of collusion and the available evidence. On the other hand, the Court tried to ensure that the concept is not unduly wide so as to render the scope of Article 101 TFEU practically unlimited.[101] However, the jurisprudence of the EU Courts suggests they favoured the former. In light of many different forms that concerted practices can take and the highly fact-specific nature of cases dealing with those practices, the EU and UK courts have deliberately refrained from construing the expression "concerted practice" in a formalistic or narrow manner

---

[95]   Duke (n. 32 above) at 424.
[96]   Explanatory Memorandum (n. 81 above), at para 3.25.
[97]   ibid., para 3.26.
[98]   Commonwealth of Australia, Explanatory Materials, Exposure Draft – Competition and Consumer Amendment (Competition Policy Review) Bill 2016, para 3.18.
[99]   ACCC (n. 64 above), at para 1.4. The 2017 amendment of the CCA was arguably more influenced by EU competition law than US antitrust law.
[100]   Lianos and Korah (n. 4 above) at 388. See also Black (n. 91 above) at 141.
[101]   ibid., 388–9.

in order not to define or limit what may amount to a concerted practice.[102] Commentators attribute the concept's success in regulating informal agreements to its wide definition.[103] As intended by the Court, the concept has enabled the Commission to bring proceedings under Article 101 of the TFEU against collusive conduct that would have remained uncovered if one was able to only employ the concept of "agreement".[104] In *Dyestuffs*, the Court held that the object of bringing concerted practices within Article 101 was to prohibit "a form of coordination between undertakings which, short of the conclusion of an agreement properly so-called, knowingly substitutes practical cooperation between the undertakings for the risks of competition."[105] In *Suiker Unie*, the Court emphasised the importance of each market participant to determine its conduct and strategy on the market independently from its competitors.[106] Yet, it also noted that the requirement of independence does not proscribe firms to adapt themselves intelligently to their competitors, it strictly precludes conduct that could that could influence conduct on the market or disclose one's future conduct on the market.[107] Even though a concerted practice does not require an actual plan[108] it is suggested that it involves reciprocal cooperation or a joint intention of firms to conduct themselves in a specific way, disclosed through direct or indirect contact, with the purpose of influencing the actions of an actual or potential rival or to reveal to them the course of conduct that will or may be adopted on the market.[109] This is satisfied where one firm discloses its intentions or conduct on the market to another when the other requests it, or at the very least accepts it.[110] A concerted practice thus involves some subjective element (i.e. some form of "mental consensus whereby practical cooperation is knowingly substituted for competition"), a material element (i.e. conduct on

---

[102] *Argos Ltd v. OFT* [2006] EWCA Civ 1318, para 22. See also *Tesco Stores Ltd v. OFT* [2012] CAT 31, para 56; Whish and Bailey (n. 2 above) at 118.

[103] Joanna Goyder, Albertina Albors-Llorens, *Goyder's EC Competition Law* (5th edn, Oxford University Press 2009) 88. See Federico Ghezzi and Mariateresa Maggiolino, 'Bridging EU Concerted Practices with US Concerted Actions' (2014) 10 *Journal of Competition Law and Economics* 647; Foster and Kaci (n. 56 above) at 21.

[104] Lianos and Korah (n. 4 above) at 389.

[105] Case 48/69 *Imperial Chemical Industries v. Commission* ECLI:EU:C:1972:70, para 64.

[106] Joined Cases 40/73 etc. *Coöperatieve Vereniging "Suiker Unie" UA and Others v. Commission* ECLI:EU:C:1975:174, para 173.

[107] ibid., para 174.

[108] ibid., paras 173–4.

[109] ibid., paras 173–4. See also Alison Jones and Brenda Sufrin, *EU Competition Law: Text, Cases, and Materials* (6th edn, Oxford University Press 2016) 153.

[110] Cases T-25/95 etc. *Cimenteries CBR SA v. Commission* ECLI:EU:T:2000:77, para 1849; Whish and Bailey (n. 2) at 119.

the market pursuant to collusion), and a causal relation between the subjective and the material elements [111]

4.3   How Relevant is the European Concept for Australia?

Some commentators have cautioned against readily emulating the definition and scope of the European concerted practice concept under the Australian competition law.[112] Others think that Australian courts are unlikely to adopt the wide scope of the European concept.[113] Apart from the general caution against adopting principles relevant to the laws of other countries "uncritically and without regard to the context on which they were developed",[114] the case law of the EU Courts is considered of limited value.[115] As noted by Justice Kevin Lindgren it is not only the text of the foreign legislation that is relevant, its underlying concepts and assumptions must also be taken into account.[116]

An important underlying assumption in relation to the European concerted practice concept, as confirmed in *Eturas*,[117] is the evidential presumption concerning the subjective element. The CJEU established a rebuttable presumption that concertation has been followed where firms take part, even passively, in discussions with competitors and remain active on the market thereafter.[118] This presumption forms an integral part of EU law.[119] It is often decisive in EU cases and clearly distinguishes EU law from Australian law.[120] According to Sara Brooks, with the existence of this presumption under Australian law, the outcome in the petrol cases would have been different.[121] Commentators

---

[111] Case C-199/92 P *Hüls AG v. Commission* ECLI:EU:C:1999:358, para. 161. See also Case C-8/08 *T-Mobile Netherlands and Others v. Raad van bestuur van de Nederlandse Mededingingsautoriteit* ECLI:EU:C:2009:343, paras 38–9. See also Lianos and Korah (n. 4 above) at 391.

[112] See Davies and Wainscoat (n. 66 above) at 190–3; Gvozdenovic (n. 46 above) at 229–32.

[113] Foster and Kaci (n. 56 above) at 21.

[114] *Boral Besser Masonry Ltd v. ACCC* (2003) 215 CLR 374, para 126.

[115] Gvozdenovic (n. 46 above) at 230–2.

[116] Kevin Lindgren, 'The Courts' Role in Statutory Interpretation: The Relevance of Overseas Case Law to Australia's GST' (FCA) [2009] *Federal Justice Scholarship* 13.

[117] Case C-74/14 *"Eturas" UAB and Others v. Lietuvos Respublikos konkurencijos taryba* ECLI:EU:C:2016:42. See Section 5 below.

[118] *Hüls AG*, paras 158–66. See also Commission (n. 3 above) at para 62.

[119] *T-Mobile*, para 52.

[120] Sara Brooks, 'Regulation of Anticompetitive "Understandings" and Price Signalling in Australia – A European Perspective' (2011) 39 *Australian Business Law Review* 309, 320.

[121] ibid., 320–1.

argue that Australian courts are unlikely to adopt such a presumption.[122] The Federal Court more recently found that attending and not objecting to conduct proposed at a meeting of competitors is insufficient to constitute a "commitment".[123] It is questionable whether Australian law will embrace the presumption in the absence of a specific legislative direction to that effect.[124] In any event, this presumption would be inappropriate as the new concerted practices prohibition requires a purpose, effect, or likely effect of substantially lessening competition,[125] whereas under EU law a concerted practice is caught even in the absence of anti-competitive effects on the market.[126]

Another difference between the Australian and the European concepts may be the requirement of reciprocity. Under EU law the subjective element appears to require reciprocal cooperation or a joint intention to conduct themselves in a specific way, whereas under Australian law this does not seem to be the case. In *Morphett Arms Hotel v. TPC*, the Full Federal Court found that an understanding does not require reciprocity.[127] Courts have followed this approach numerous times,[128] but there are equally as many cases where the courts have deemed it unnecessary to authoritatively determine the issue.[129] Although a unilateral obligation is sufficient, the courts have acknowledged

---

[122] See Caron Beaton-Wells and Brent Fisse, 'Competition Policy Review: Supplementary Submission' (12 November 2014), available at https://brentfisse.com/wp-content/uploads/2020/07/Beaton-Wells__Fisse_Supplementary_Submission_CPR_121114.pdf (accessed 30 June 2022).

[123] *ACCC v. Olex Australia Pty Ltd* [2017] FCA 222, at para 560. In this case the ACCC alleged that Olex and Prysmian, the two largest Australian manufacturers of electrical cable, wholesalers, various executives and the Electrical Wholesalers Association of Australia engaged in price fixing and market sharing. The ACCC argued that the proposed conduct had a substantial purpose of creating a disincentive for contractors and end-users to purchase cable directly from the manufacturers (or Olex alone). However, the Federal Court held that Olex did not have a purpose of preventing or limiting supply to those customers or to allocated them to the wholesalers. Supplying those customers directly was an important part of Olex's business which it wanted to grow. While the two cases are difficult to compare, a distinguishing factor between *Olex* and *Eturas* is that the alleged conduct in the former case was not in the defendant's commercial interest.

[124] Beaton-Wells and Fisse (n. 34 above) at 10.

[125] ibid., 10.

[126] *Hüls v. Commission*, at para 163.

[127] *Morphett Arms Hotel Pty Ltd v. TPC* (1980) 30 ALR 88, para 91.

[128] See e.g. *ACCC v. Amcor Printing Papers Group Ltd* (2000) 169 ALR 344, para 75; *ACCC v. Rural Press* (2002) 118 FCR 236, para 79.

[129] *Morphett Arms Hotel*, para 89; *TPC v. Service Station Association Ltd* (1993) 44 FCR 206; *ACCC v. Leahy*, para 41; *ACCC v. TF Woollam and Son Pty Ltd* (2011) 196 FCR 212, para 55; *ACCC v. Australian Egg Corporation Ltd* [2017] FCAFC 152, para 96.

that such cases would be rare and difficult to envisage.[130] Since the threshold for satisfying the subjective element to establish a concerted practice is lower than for an understanding, it can be argued that the concerted practice prohibition under Australian law should not require reciprocity. This seems to be confirmed by the Explanatory Memorandum.[131] In light of the above the European concerted practice concept is not readily applicable under Australian law.

5 ALGORITHMIC-FACILITATED COLLUSION UNDER THE CCA

As mentioned above, in two of the four scenarios of algorithmic collusion identified by Ezrachi and Stucke, firms use algorithms to facilitate their cartel.[132] This section analyses to what extent the reformed CCA is applicable to these two scenarios.

5.1 The Messenger Scenario

In the Messenger scenario algorithms are used to execute the wills of the colluding firms' corporate actors.[133] This scenario is the least cumbersome from an antitrust enforcement perspective as the concept of "agreement" in the broad sense can undoubtedly be applied.[134] The meeting of minds is between human beings and they merely use algorithms to facilitate tasks which they would otherwise do themselves including the implementation, monitoring and policing of the cartel.[135] Algorithms can most likely execute those tasks more efficiently since human errors and emotions can be ruled out. There have been a number of cases around the world in which competition authorities

---

[130] Nicholas Wendon, 'Division 1A of the Competition and Consumer Act 2010 (Cth): A Critique' (2013) 21 *Australian Journal of Competition and Consumer Law* 181, 183 (citing *TPC v. Email Ltd* (1980) 43 FLR 383; *ACCC v. Leahy*; *TPC v. Service Station Association Ltd* (1993) 44 FCR 206; *TPC v. Parkfield Operations Pty Ltd* (1985) 7 FCR 534). Since no case to date has established an understanding without reciprocity between the parties, an argument against this requirement "is no longer credible" (Warren Pengilley, 'What Is Required to Prove a "Contract, Arrangement or Understanding"?' (2006) 13 *Competition and Consumer Law Journal* 241. It has therefore been suggested that an understanding cannot be unilateral and must involve mutual obligations (Gvozdenovic (n. 46 above) at 224). See also *ACCC v. Air New Zealand Ltd* (2014) 319 ALR 388).

[131] Explanatory Memorandum, at para 3.22.

[132] Ezrachi and Stucke (n. 16 above) at 36–7.

[133] ibid., 36.

[134] ibid., 39.

[135] ibid., 36.

and courts were confronted with the *Messenger* scenario. One of the earliest cases was *United States v. David Topkins*[136] where the members of the cartel used algorithms to coordinate changes to their respective prices for the sale of posters.

Rob Nicholls and Brent Fisse argue that competitors could make use of algorithms for weaker forms of communication that do not involve a CAU as the element of commitment is lacking. In this case, there may nonetheless be an infringement under the new section 45.[137] As mentioned above, the Australian legislator's rationale for introducing the concerted practice prohibition was to bring within the ambit of section 45 price signalling or information exchange cases where there is no requisite commitment. However, a more significant obstacle might be satisfying the SLC test. A specific issue when applying the SLC test in a case involving algorithmic collusion is whether evidence could be presented that directly demonstrates that there is a substantial lessening of competition with the algorithm and no substantial lessening of competition in the absence of the algorithm or with an alternative (less anti-competitive) algorithm.[138] Hence, despite the wider scope of the new section 45, bringing a successful case against firms that engage in a Messenger-type algorithmic collusion might still be difficult for the ACCC.

5.2   The Hub and Spoke Scenario

In the Hub and Spoke scenario, cartel participants use a single pricing algorithm to determine their market prices.[139] The concept of a "hub and spoke" agreement has long been recognised in competition law enforcement. Hub and spoke agreements were the subject of a number of US antitrust landmark judgments,[140] as well as high-profile investigations in the UK[141] and EU. A hub and spoke agreement typically involves the use of vertical restraints as facilitating practices in the operation of a horizontal agreement. For instance, if retailers want to fix prices they can each enter a vertical agreement with an upstream firm which acts as a common agent in order to facilitate collusion amongst

---

[136]   *United States v. David Topkins*, Case3:15-cr-00201-WHO.

[137]   Rob Nicholls and Brent Fisse, 'Concerted Practices and Algorithmic Coordination: Does the New Australian Law Compute?' (2018) 26 *Competition & Consumer Law Journal* 82, 88.

[138]   ibid., 96.

[139]   Ezrachi and Stucke (n. 16 above) at 36.

[140]   See e.g. *Interstate Circuit, Inc v. United States*, 306 U.S. 208; *Toys "R" Us, Inc v. FTC*, 221 F.3d 928 (7th Cir. 2000).

[141]   OFT, *Agreements between Hasbro UK Ltd and distributors fixing the price of Hasbro toys and games*, CA98/18/2002, 28 November 2002; OFT, *Price-fixing of Replica Football Kit*, CA98/06/2003, 1 August 2003.

them.[142] While the conclusion of those multiple vertical restraints makes the collusion possible in the first place, the enforcement of those restraints facilitates the monitoring of prices, and even punishment for breaching the collusive agreement.[143] The upstream firm is the "hub" and the vertical agreements between the upstream firm and each retailer form the "spokes". Similarly, multiple manufacturers can collude by using a common downstream firm as distributor, as happened in the *Apple e-books* case that was investigated by the DOJ and the European Commission.[144] Under Australian law, the case law appears to suggest that a horizontal arrangement or understanding between the spokes can be established indirectly by demonstrating the vertical contact between the spokes and the hub.[145] In Europe the position seems to be similar.[146] By contrast, under US law it is the presence of a horizontal agreement among the spokes, that is, the "rim" of the wheel, that renders these vertical agreements anti-competitive.[147] A hub and spoke constellation without a rim is merely a set of vertical agreements that result in parallel conduct and is therefore not illegal.[148]

In the context of automated systems, the algorithm functions as the hub to facilitate collusion amongst its common users. Unlike in the Messenger scenario, the algorithm does not merely execute the orders of humans. Instead the use of the same pricing algorithm stabilises prices and softens competition.[149] The recent *Eturas* case in the EU illustrates how algorithms could potentially be applied in the Hub and Spoke scenario. In this case several Lithuanian travel agencies had entered into a licensing contract with Eturas to use its online travel booking system. The licensing contract did not contain a provision that would allow Eturas to alter the travel agencies' prices. Following a survey on discount rates amongst the travel agencies, Eturas' internal messaging system

---

[142]   Matthew Bennett et al., 'Resale Price Maintenance: Explaining the Controversy, and Small Steps Towards a More Nuanced Policy' (2010) 33 *Fordham International Law Journal* 1278, 1291.

[143]   ibid.

[144]   *United States v. Apple, Inc*, 791 F.3d 290 (2d Cir. 2015); Commission Decision of 25 July 2013, Case COMP/AT.39847 – E-books, available at https://ec.europa .eu/competition/antitrust/cases/dec_docs/39847/39847_27536_4.pdf (accessed 30 June 2022).

[145]   See *News Ltd v. Australian Rugby Football League Ltd* (n. 44).

[146]   Janka and Uhsler (n. 18 above) at 118.

[147]   Joseph E. Harrington, 'How Do Hub-and-Spoke Cartels Operate? Lessons from Nine Case Studies' (24 August 2018) 54, available at papers.ssrn.com/sol3/papers.cfm ?abstract_id=3238244 (accessed 30 June 2022).

[148]   ibid; Barak Orbach, 'Hub-and-Spoke Conspiracies' (2016) 15(3) *Antitrust Source* 1, 3.

[149]   Ezrachi and Stucke (n. 16 above) at 48.

informed the latter that it had set a maximum discount rate of 3 per cent on travel packages. Although it was still possible for each travel agency to grant a higher discount this required to take additional technical steps in order to do so.[150] The setup was clearly a hub and spoke agreement with Eturas as the hub and the travel agencies at the rim of the wheel with vertical communication alongside the spokes.[151] The question that the CJEU had to answer was whether the mere passive reception of a notice on the restriction of discounts could amount to a concerted practice.[152] The Court held that the passive reception of the notice justifies the presumption that the recipient was aware of the notice's content. This awareness might amount to a concerted practice under Article 101(1) of the TFEU.[153] Yet, according to the Court, the recipients must have the opportunity to rebut the presumed infringement of Article 101(1) of the TFEU, for example, by publicly distancing themselves from the alleged concerted practice or by giving informing competition authorities.[154]

Australian courts were concerned with alleged hub and spoke agreements in two more recent cases. The most recent one was the *Australian Egg Cartel* case where the ACCC failed to prove the existence of an arrangement or understanding between an association of egg producers, its managing director and some egg producers. The court drew a distinction between two situations: in the first situation industry participants are being brought to an appreciation of what is in their interests, independently of what others are doing, to act in a particular manner. This situation did not involve a contravention of the CCA, at least before the amendment. In the second situation industry participants are being invited to agree to act in a certain way in the expectation of reciprocal conduct by others. Such conduct was and still is a breach of the CCA.[155] Regarding the latter, the court held that there was insufficient evidence for finding a form of collective action involving reciprocal obligations or understanding by the egg producers.[156]

If the scope of the new concerted practice prohibition in section 45(1)(c) is interpreted as broadly as the European concept, then the Hub and Spoke scenario could finally be caught by the CCA more easily. However, there are two major obstacles for bringing a successful case. First, as mentioned above in contrast to EU law, Australian law lacks an evidential presumption. It is

---

[150] *Eturas*, at paras 5–11.
[151] Janka and Uhsler (n. 18 above) at 116; *Eturas*, para 27.
[152] *Eturas*, at para 25.
[153] ibid., at para 50.
[154] ibid., at para 28; Case C-194/14 P *AC-Treuhand v. Commission* ECLI:EU:C:2015:717, para 31.
[155] See *ACCC v. Australian Egg Corporation Ltd*, (n. 155) para 75.
[156] ibid., at para 83.

unclear under Australian law whether awareness of the common algorithm would be required for a finding of a concerted practice or whether it suffices that the parties should have been aware of the common algorithm (as suggested by the CJEU in *Eturas*).[157] The second obstacle, as above with regard to the Messenger scenario and also as illustrated in *ACCC v. Air New Zealand*,[158] is the SLC test. The ACCC alleged that Air New Zealand exchanged information about future surcharge pricing intentions with other airlines through surveys and meetings conducted by an industry association. The trail court noted that the exchange of future pricing intentions would not always substantially lessen competition.[159] Overall, due to the absence of an evidential presumption and the possible high threshold set by the SLC test, the ACCC might struggle to bring successful cases against hub and spoke cartels that are facilitated by algorithms.

6   CONCLUDING REMARKS

In Australia, the Competition and Consumer Amendment (Competition Policy Review) Act 2017 recently introduced a concerted practice prohibition. The pre-Amendment CCA only prohibited contracts, arrangements or understandings that had the purpose, effect or likely effect of substantially lessening competition. Even when seeking to establish an understanding, which is the least formal type of consensual dealing, the ACCC had to show that at least one party had made a commitment to act in a particular way. In the past, the ACCC was often unsuccessful in cases that involved facilitating practices such as information sharing and price signalling as it failed to establish the commitment element. Moreover, the price signalling laws that were introduced in 2011 to fill the gap in the CCA were highly ineffective due to their very limited scope and complex drafting. In the meantime, with the advancement of technology cartelisation has become more sophisticated. Algorithms may not only be used to enhance a firm's efficiency in the market but may also be misused to engage in price-fixing. Algorithmically facilitated collusion poses challenges in terms of competition law enforcement. Nonetheless, days after the amendment entered into force, the ACCC Chairman was confident that Australian competition law, particularly with the addition of the new concerted practice prohibition can capture algorithmic collusion. While the Australian concept of concerted practice, which lacks a definition in the Act, was heavily influenced by the European concept in Article 101 of the TFEU, the latter

---

[157] Nicholls and Fisse (n. 137 above) at 97.
[158] *ACCC v. Air New Zealand Ltd* [2014] FCA 1157.
[159] ibid., at para 1107.

is not readily applicable under Australian law. The evidential presumption under EU law that concertation has been followed where firms take part, even passively, in discussions with rivals and remain active on the market thereafter does not exist under Australian law. This presumption would be inappropriate as the new concerted practices prohibition requires a purpose, effect or likely effect of substantially lessening competition, whereas in EU law a concerted practice is caught even in the absence of anti-competitive effects on the market. However, such presumption, as suggested in the CJEU's *Eturas* case, could prove to be decisive in catching algorithm-facilitated hub and spoke agreements. Besides facilitating those kind of agreements algorithms could be used for the implementation, monitoring and policing of cartel agreements that were negotiated by humans. Where the use of algorithms does not involve a CAU because the element of commitment cannot be established, the new concerted practice prohibition could capture such conduct. Yet, again the SLC test needs to be met in order to establish an infringement of section 45. Overall the new concerted practice prohibition in section 45(1)(c) will be useful in cases where algorithms facilitate collusion but bringing successful cases may nevertheless be difficult.

5. Tackling algorithmic collusion: the scope of the Indian Competition Act

Nikita Koradia, Kiran Manokaran and Zara Saeed[1]

1   INTRODUCTION

The existence of algorithms is not new to economies worldwide. They have been in existence for thousands of years. However, it is very recently that with digitalization, economies have started becoming mindful to it from competition law perspective. Digitalization has not only changed the perspective of consumers towards businesses, but it has also impacted the ideology of businesses on how to conduct business. The change in the ideology of business can be seen from the change in importance attached to the data which has become the new currency. Digitalization has brought the issues faced due to algorithms on the forefront.

Algorithms have become an inevitable part of the modern economy. Their importance in today's world cannot be understated. Some scholars consider algorithms to have a windfall effect on economies for the advantages that they offer in terms of automation, predictive analysis, increased efficiency and better quality. Alternatively, some scholars contend the impact automation of human-decision making might have on competition in the market. This narrative was evidenced when two competitors selling second-hand copies of the book *The Making of a Fly* entered into a price war by way of algorithms shooting the price of the book to $23,698,655.96.[2] The situation gave a sneak-peak

---

[1]   This chapter is a shortened version of an earlier publication, Nikita Koradia, Kiran Manokaran, and Zara Saeed, 'Algorithmic Collusion and Indian Competition Act: Suggestions to Tackle Inadequacies and Naivety' in Steven Van Uytsel (ed.), *The Digital Economy and Competition Law in Asia* (Springer 2021). The authors have a license from Springer to re-publish the content.
[2]   Manon van Roozendaal, 'Algorithms: Teenage Troublemakers of EU Competition Law – A Closer Look at Algorithms as the New Price-Fixing Tool in EU Competition Law' (European Law Institute Young Lawyers Award, 2018), available at

into what can happen when algorithms are left alone or unsupervised. This issue has not been left unaddressed and various reports and interdisciplinary research have been conducted on the effect/dangers of algorithms on competition in the market more so where they can be used actively by companies to distort competition in the market.

One of the biggest concerns that was raised was of algorithms as facilitators of collusion. The concerns highlighted how algorithms could be used to collude in innovative and unusual ways which do not fit within the contours of the definition of agreement as we understand it in a traditional antitrust sense. The digital markets have made it conducive to collude through algorithms as there is more transparency in the market, the frequency of communication is higher and the price fluctuations are so frequent that it is highly improbable to detect anti-competitive activity in the market. Research has pointed out how algorithms can lead to collusion through hub-and-spoke or tacitly. The other scenario that has been debated about is the collusion reached by deep learning algorithms without any human intervention.

The Chapter shall highlight how algorithms can be used to collude in novel ways in the competition landscape of India. Section 2 deals with the definition of agreement under the Indian Competition Act 2002 (Competition Act)[3] and whether the definition needs to be revisited to address algorithmic collusion. This Section deals with how tacit collusion can be an inevitable consequence of price setting through algorithms and can get aggravated with differing market structures and how a perfectly competitive market can imitate an oligopoly market. The third Section deals with the developing jurisprudence of hub-and-spoke in India with special emphasis on the case against Uber for price fixing. It also emphasizes the recent amendments proposed under the Competition Act with respect to hub-and-spoke and how the Competition Commission of India (CCI) can deal with hub-and-spoke through algorithms differently. The third Section also deals with the digital eye scenario and questions whether such circumstances can raise competition concerns in the near future. Section 5 concludes.

---

www.europeanlawinstitute.eu/fileadmin/user_upload/p_eli/YLA_Award/Submission _ELI_Young_Lawyers_Award_Manon_van_Roozendaal_2018.pdf (accessed 30 June 2022).

    3   Competition Act, 2002, available at www.cci.gov.in/sites/default/files/cci_pdf/ competitionact2012.pdf (accessed 30 June 2022) (Competition Act).

2 ANTI-COMPETITIVE AGREEMENTS UNDER THE INDIAN COMPETITION LAW

In India, the regulation of competition was formerly governed by the Monopolies and Restrictive Trade Practices Act, 1969 (MRTP Act)[4] which was rather narrow in its ambit. Even the definition of "agreements" in the erstwhile MRTP Act simply defined the term to include any arrangement or understanding, whether or not intended to be enforced by legal proceedings.[5] However, pursuant to the wave of liberalization in the country since the early 1990s[6] and the ever-changing market conditions as a consequence of rapid economic development, it was felt that the MRTP Act was becoming obsolete.[7] Consequently, the High Level Committee on Competition Policy and Law (also known as the Raghavan Committee) was constituted to examine and suggest reforms to the existing Competition Law regime in light of the growing liberalization and globalization.[8] Pursuant to the Raghavan Committee's recommendations, the Competition Act was legislated with a much greater scope so as to tackle emerging issues in the Competition Law and it provides for one of the widest definitions for "agreements" when compared with the antitrust laws of other jurisdictions.

2.1 The Definition and Scope of Anti-Competitive Agreements

The Competition Act defines an "agreement" to include any arrangement, understanding or action in concert, whether or not, such arrangement, understanding or action in concert is formal or in writing or is intended to be

---

[4] The Monopolies and Restrictive Trade Practices Act, 1969, available at www.mca.gov.in/Ministry/actsbills/pdf/The_Monopolies_and_Restrictive_Trade_Practices_Act_1969.pdf (accessed 30 June 2022) (MRTP Act).

[5] MRTP Act, Section 2 (a): "agreement includes any arrangement or understanding, whether or not it is intended that such agreement shall be enforceable (apart from any provision of this Act) by legal proceedings."

[6] Rashmi Banga and Abhijit Das (eds.), *Twenty Years of India's Liberalization: Experiences and Lessons* (United Nations Conference on Trade and Development, 2012).

[7] The Finance Minister on 27 February 1999 declared in the budget speech that MRTP Act has become obsolete in light of international economic developments relating to Competition Law.

[8] Raghavan Committee, 'Report of High-Level Committee on Competition Policy Law' (2013), available at https://theindiancompetitionlaw.files.wordpress.com/2013/02/report_of_high_level_committee_on_competition_policy_law_svs_raghavan_committee.pdf (accessed 30 June 2022).

enforceable by legal proceedings.[9] In comparison with the erstwhile definition of agreement in the MRTP Act, it can be seen that Section 2(b) of the Competition Act provides for a wider scope by including in its ambit "action in concert" which is akin to the concept of "concerted practice" in the EU and "collusion" in the US.

It further clarifies that there is no requirement as to the form of agreement.[10] As the CCI observed in *Re: Alleged Anti-Competitive Conduct by Maruti Suzuki India Limited* that agreements restraining competition are generally made in smoke-filled rooms and therefore it is difficult to find formal/written agreements.[11] Thus, the definition is a wide one as it is inclusive and non-exhaustive. The understanding required by the definition may even be tacit and the definition covers situations where the parties act on the basis of a nod or a wink. The Competition Act further widens the scope while addressing "anti-competitive" agreements. It prohibits enterprises and persons (including association of enterprises and persons) from entering into any agreement with respect to the production, supply, distribution, storage, acquisition or control of goods or provision of services which causes or is likely to cause an appreciable adverse effect on competition within India.[12] Any agreement entered in contravention of the same is void.[13] In addition to the same, the act specifically addresses agreements between enterprises engaged in identical or similar trade of goods or provision of services (horizontal agreements)[14] and agreements between enterprises at different stages of the production chain in different markets (vertical agreements).[15]

Section 3 (3) of the Competition Act, in particular, has been given a large sweep by the language used in the same. The Section reads as:

> Any agreement entered into between enterprises or associations of enterprises or persons or associations of persons or between any person and enterprise or practice carried on, or decision taken by, any association of enterprises or association of persons, including cartels, engaged in identical or similar trade of goods or provision of services ...

---

[9] Competition Act, Section 2 (b): "agreement includes any arrangement or understanding or action in concert: (i) whether or not, such arrangement, understanding or action is formal or in writing; or (ii) whether or not such arrangement, understanding or action is intended to be enforceable by legal proceedings."

[10] *Technip S.A. vs. S. M. S. Holding Pvt. Ltd.* (2005) 5 SCC 465.

[11] Competition Commission of India (CCI), Suo Motu Case No. 01 of 2019, in Re: Alleged Anti-Competitive Conduct by Maruti Suzuki India Limited (MSIL) in implementing discount control policy vis-à-vis dealers.

[12] Competition Act, Section 3 (1).

[13] ibid., at Section 3 (2).

[14] ibid., at Section 3 (3).

[15] ibid., at Section 3 (4).

This Section also expressly provides an illustrative and non-exhaustive list of such agreements.

As can be seen from the language used in the provision, in addition to including "agreements" as defined under Section 2 (b) of the Competition Act which includes any arrangement, understanding and action in concert, the provision also includes practices carried on or decisions taken by any association of enterprises or persons, and cartels. The Competition Act defines a "practice" to include any practice relating to the carrying on of any trade by a person or enterprise.[16] Trade has been defined to mean any trade, business, industry, profession or occupation relating to the production, supply distribution, storage or control of goods and includes the provision of any services.[17] The term "decision" has not been defined and thus it follows the ordinary English meaning. In the Kerala Cine Exhibitors Association,[18] the joint decision taken by the opposite parties to boycott the films which were displayed in the theatres of the members of the informant was held to have resulted in restricting the distribution of film in the market.

Although the terms "practice carried on" and "decision taken" exists in addition to the term "agreements" in Section 3(3) of the Competition Act, which could provide for a wider interpretation so as to include practices and decisions independent of an agreement, the CCI has rather restrictively interpreted the provision by holding that mere existence of a practice or decision among enterprises without an underlying agreement or understanding would not be covered in the provision's sweep. A practice to be covered under Section 3 (3) of the Competition Act should be the result of an agreement, express or implied.[19] It would be noteworthy to extract the observations of Mr. R. Prasad, Member of CCI in his dissenting order in *M/s. Metalrod Ltd vs. M/s. Religare Finvest Ltd*, in this regard:

> ... there is a feeling of some different inference on the term "agreement". There is a view that Section 3(3) Indian Competition Act 2002 is wider in scope than Section 3(1) Indian Competition Act 2002 as Section 3(1) Indian Competition Act 2002 deals only with any agreement whereas Section 3(3) Indian Competition Act 2002, in addition to any agreement, also covers practises carried on or decision taken by which results in [appreciable adverse effect on competition (AAEC)]. The fact that the Indian Competition Act 2002 uses, these three terms also indicates that "agreement", "practises carried on" and "decision taken" are envisaged as distinct

---

16   ibid., at Section 2 (m).
17   ibid., at Section 2 (x).
18   CCI, Case No. 45 of 2012, *Kerala Cine Exhibitors Association vs. Kerala Film Exhibitors Association*.
19   CCI, Case No. 5 of 2009, *Neeraj Malhotra vs. Deustche Post Bank Home Finance*.

and distinguishable. A "follow the leader" syndrome may lead to anti-competitive "practises carried on" and "decision taken" without being an "agreement". But these would still be actionable under Section 3(3) if they result in acts covered under sub-clauses (a) to (d). The inference drawn cannot be subscribed to. Section 3(1) Indian Competition Act 2002 is the covering Section of the entire Chapter on "Prohibition of agreements" and it is the broader provisions which covers both Section 3(3) and Section 3(4) Indian Competition Act 2002. In fact, in Section 3(1) Indian Competition Act 2002 two situations i.e. 3(3) and 3(4) have been envisaged. It means that any contravention of Sections 3(3) and 3(4) Indian Competition Act 2002, the contravention of Section 3(1) Indian Competition Act 2002 has to be there. Section 3(1) Indian Competition Act 2002 is inherent and implicit in Section 3(3) and 3(4) Indian Competition Act 2002. It also cannot be concluded that "practises carried on" or "decision taken by" as provided in Section 3(3) Indian Competition Act 2002can be without any "agreement". Agreement is a necessary element in all the Sections provided under Section 3. It is the crux of the Chapter "Prohibition of agreements". Unless there is an agreement, there can't be prohibition of agreements. Thus, a contravention of Section 3(3) Indian Competition Act 2002 without having an agreement cannot be visualized. This presumption is further strengthened by the fact that in Section 19(3) Indian Competition Act 2002 it is clearly mentioned that "the Commission shall, while determining whether an agreement has an AAEC under Section 3, have due regard to all or any of the following factors, namely (a) to (f)."[20]

Thus, for the application of Section 3(3) of the Competition Act, it is necessary to establish the existence of an agreement in any form between the enterprises. The use of different phraseology merely reflects the legislature's intention to provide a very wide definition of the term agreement in contrast to how agreements are understood under civil law.[21] Even if one were to take a view that the specific use of the words "practice" and "decision" in addition to a predefined term "agreement" is to be construed as independent categories, the provision uses those terms only in relation to "association of enterprises or persons" and not enterprises and persons individually. Thus, independent business conduct would not be covered under Section 3(3) in any event.

A crucial feature of Section 3(3) of the Competition Act is that it, upon establishing the existence of a horizontal agreement, the provision presumes the agreement to have an appreciable adverse effect on competition (AAEC), thereby shifting the burden of proof on the accused enterprises to prove that their agreement is not anti-competitive in terms of the factors listed in Section

---

[20] CCI, Case No. 28 of 2010, *M/S Metalrod Ltd vs. M/S. Religare Finvest Ltd –* Dissenting Order of Mr. R. Prasad, Member.
[21] CCI, Case 59 of 2011, **Shri Jyoti Swaroop Arora vs. M/S Tulip Infratech Ltd. &** *Ors*.

19(3) of the Competition Act.[22] The presumption as to the AAEC is a rebuttable one and the accused enterprises must be given the opportunity to rebut the same.[23] The Indian jurisprudence on the law of presumption is well settled such that the terms "shall presume" as found in Section 3(3) of the Competition Act would only raise a rebuttable presumption.[24] The Supreme Court of India has held that "a presumption not in itself evidence but only makes a prima facie case for the party in whose favour it exists. It indicates the person on whom burden of proof lies."[25] Thus, upon establishing the existence of a horizontal agreement, the onus is on the accused enterprise to demonstrate that the pro-competitive effects of the agreement outweigh the anti-competitive effects. The position in India is, thus, different from the US's per se rule where further enquiry as to the anti-competitive effects ceases upon establishing the presence of a horizontal agreement.[26]

2.2   Tacit Collusion and Action in Concert within Section 3 of the Competition Act

As seen from the definition, the presence of an agreement can also be through its more elusive form of "action in concert". The Raghavan Committee consciously included "action in concert" to cover situations of tacit and informal arrangements between enterprises. The Committee observes the following in its report:

> In principle, any kind of agreement (including oral and informal agreements and arrangements) could be illegal, if it violates the law. In the case of written or formal

---

[22]   Section 19 (3) of the Competition Act:
       The Commission shall, while determining whether an agreement has an appreciable adverse effect on competition under Section 3, have due regard to all or any of the following factors, namely: –
       (a)   creation of barriers to new entrants in the market;
       (b)   driving existing competitors out of the market;
       (c)   foreclosure of competition by hindering entry into the market;
       (d)   accrual of benefits to consumers;
       (e)   improvements in production or distribution of goods or provision of services; or
       (f)   promotion of technical, scientific and economic development by means of production or distribution of goods or provision of service.
[23]   CCI, Case No. 20/201, *M/s Santuka Associates Pvt. Ltd. vs. All India Organization of Chemists and Druggist &3 ors*, para 28.3.
[24]   *Sodhi Transport Co. & another vs. State of UP and another*, 1986 AIR 1099.
[25]   ibid., at para 3. Also see *AR Antuley vs. RS Nayak*, 1984 SCR (2) 495; *Noor Aga vs. Union of India*, CA No. 1034 of 2008.
[26]   *United States vs. Socony-Vacuum Oil Co., Inc.*, 310 U.S. 150 (1940).

agreements, there can be no legal controversy. On the other hand, in the case of oral or informal agreements, it is necessary to prove the existence of an agreement. Proof will generally be based on circumstantial evidence, and parallelism of action between firms can indicate this. It follows that any prohibitions should also apply to what in the UK law are known as "concerted practises". Although the distinction between these and agreements are often imprecise, a concerted practice exists when there is informal cooperation without a formal agreement.[27]

Thus, even an informal co-operation can be construed as an agreement for the purpose of Section 3 of the Competition Act through the devise of "action in concert". The exact scope and ambit of "action in concert" has been the subject of scrutiny and deliberation in several cases. It is well known that parallel behaviour in markets, particularly in oligopolistic markets,[28] can occur as a natural reaction to market factors even in the absence of any agreement to not compete. Therefore, discourse as to the full reach of the notion of "action in concert" has always run its course bearing caution to not trample on independent prudent behaviour of businesses that reflects parallelism. The CCI has time and again held that mere parallel behaviour would not fall within the scope of "action in concert" and emphasized the need for circumstantial evidence (in the form of plus factors) establishing that there is meeting of minds.[29] Thus, the CCI relies on the existence of certain "plus factors" to infer "meeting of minds" and establish collusion.[30] Plus factors, as defined by the commission, "are economic actions and outcomes, above and beyond parallel conduct by oligopolistic firms, that are largely inconsistent with unilateral conduct but largely consistent with coordinated action."[31] The CCI has also held that particular actions of competitors can be construed as evidence of concerted practice where there is no plausible alternative.[32]

The emphasis on "meeting of minds" again takes the test under Section 2 (b) and Section 3 of the Competition Act to whether there was some kind of understanding or arrangement between the enterprises that appear to be acting in co-ordination. Thus, an attempt to prove an "agreement" through the device of "action in concert" would boil down to establishing a "meeting of minds" between the enterprises exhibiting parallelism.

---

[27] Raghavan Committee (n. 8 above).

[28] Richard A. Posner, 'Oligopoly and the Antitrust Laws: A Suggested Approach' (1968) 21 *Stan. L. Rev.* 1562.

[29] CCI, Case 7 of 2013, *Re: Chief, Materials Manager – I.*

[30] CCI, MRTP Case: RTPE No. 20 of 2008, *All India Tires Dealers Federation vs. Tire Manufacturers.*

[31] ibid., at para 123.

[32] ibid.

While CCI has been conscious in avoiding overreach under "action in concert" it has also been vigilant in scrutinizing those that seek to escape the clutches of Section 3 of the Competition Act through the guise of "conscious parallelism". In *Re M/s Sheth & Co*,[33] while adjudicating allegations of collusive bidding, the commission noted that price parallelism coupled with peculiar market conditions like few enterprises with same owners, stringently standardized product, predictable demand, and other such plus factors point towards collusive tactics adopted by accused enterprises and held their actions to be in violation of Section 3(1) read with Section 3(3) (a) and Section 3(3) (d) of the Competition Act.[34] Therefore, in ensuring that the protective mantle of "conscious parallelism" does not clothe culpable enterprises with immunity,[35] the CCI has examined carefully any joint behaviour with the varying facts and circumstances of each case which could potentially contribute as a plus factor in determining the existence of "meeting of minds".

However, the approach to determining the adequacy of plus factors in holding parallel behaviours as collusive and not conscious has somewhat been inconsistent. The frequently cited examples to demonstrate the inconsistence are the *Cement Manufacturers* case[36] and the *Tire Manufacturers* case.[37] In the *Cement Manufacturers* case, the CCI decided that a group of cement manufacturers were involved in forming a cartel which attributed in a significant increase in cement prices. It further held that the cement manufacturers had transgressed the limits in sharing of sensitive information pertaining to price, production and supply, through the platform created by their trade association which had facilitated in price and production parallelism in a concerted manner.[38] Although it recognized that the relevant market had an oligopolistic setup, it rejected the defence of consequential interdependence and decided against the cement manufacturers by relying on the minutes of their trade association meeting to support a finding of collusion.[39]

Curiously, the *Tire Manufacturers* case, which was decided in the same year,[40] had near similar fact and yet witnessed a different verdict from the

---

[33]   CCI, Suo Motu Case No. 04 of 2013, *In Re: M/s Sheth and Co, and Others* (Suo Motu Case No. 04 of 2013).

[34]   ibid., at para 38.

[35]   *Theatre Enterprises Inc. vs. Paramount Film Distributing Corp*, 346 U.S. 537 (1954).

[36]   CCI, Case No. 29 of 2010, *Builders Association of India vs. Cement Manufacturers' Association*.

[37]   *All India Tires Dealers Federation vs. Tire Manufacturers*.

[38]   ibid., at para 284.

[39]   ibid., at para 285.

[40]   The Cement Manufacturer Case was decided on 20 June 2012 whereas the Tire Manufacturer Case was decided on 30.10.2012.

CCI. Even in this case, the CCI categorized the tire market to be an oligopolistic market in nature, as in the *Cement Manufacturers* case. However, the Commission was of the opinion, that by taking the conduct of the tire companies into consideration, there wasn't enough proof that the tire companies acted together in limiting the production and increasing the price of tires in the market.

While it is pertinent to note, that the Commission had applied the same principles to determine the merits of both the cases, in the *Tire Manufacturers* case, the CCI took a view that there was "no specific pattern" to conclude a formation of an agreement between the parties.[41] Despite the visible parallelism among the tire manufacturers in terms of pricing and production, and the recorded exchange of information[42] among the manufacturers through the platform created by their trade association, the CCI, while conceding that the actions of the tire manufacturers does display some characteristics of a cartel, held that the evidences were inadequate to establish the existence of a cartel.[43] This is in stark contrast to the approach adopted by the CCI in the *Cement Manufacturers* case.

In a more recent case of *Rajasthan Cylinders and Containers Limited vs. Union of India and another*,[44] the CCI had ruled that suppliers of Liquefied Petroleum Gas (LPG) Cylinders to the Indian Oil Corporation Ltd had been involved in cartelization, thereby influencing and rigging the prices, and subsequently, violating the provisions of Section 3(3)(d) of the Competition Act. However, the Supreme Court of India (Supreme Court) set aside the CCI's findings and the Competition Appellate Tribunal's (COMPAT) decision which upheld the CCI's order. The Supreme Court was of the view that, the CCI's conclusions were based on the plus factors including but not limited to market conditions, presence of the number of players, and submission of identical bids (with varying costs) that it had taken into account[45] and that these factors were "only one side of the coin"[46] and had to be evaluated by keeping the ground realities in place. Both the COMPAT and, subsequently,

---

[41] Priya Urs and Rishi Shroff, 'The Cement and Tyre Cartels: What India Can Learn from the US and EU' (2007) 6(2) *Indian Law Journal*, available at www.indialawjournal.org/archives/volume6/issue-2/article4.html (accessed 30 June 2022).

[42] The CCI, like in the Cement Case, referred to the minutes of the meeting of the Tire Manufacturers Trade Association (ATMA).

[43] CCI, Case No. 29 of 2010, *Builders Association of India vs. Cement Manufacturers' Association*, para 365.

[44] *Rajasthan Cylinders and Containers Limited vs. Union of India and another*, Civil Appeal No. 3546 of 2014.

[45] ibid.

[46] ibid., at para 88.

the Supreme Court accepted the theory of oligopolistic interdependence[47] and held the parallel conduct to be a consequence of the structure of the market.

Therefore, despite the broad language of Sections 2 and 3 (3) of the Competition Act which is capable of capturing a wide range of anti-competitive conduct within its ambit, the inconsistency with respect to the acceptability of evidence in order to establish plus factors, and the zealous differences to the oligopolistic defence somewhat muddles the true practicable scope of the provision.

2.3   Standard of Proof

The CCI has also been mindful of the difficulties in proving the existence of such agreements and has held that the standard of proof is "preponderance of probability" while observing that "[i]n most cases, the existence of an anti-competitive practice or agreement must be inferred from a number of coincidences and indicia which, taken together, may, in the absence of another plausible explanation, constitute evidence of the existence of an agreement."[48] Preponderance of probability is the standard of proof required mostly in civil and administrative proceedings.[49] It simply refers to the greater weight of evidence required to decide in favour of one side.[50] If the holistic appreciation of all the evidence makes the existence of a fact more probable than the other possible versions of fact, then the standard has been said to have been met with respect to the existence of that probable fact.[51] It is often contrasted with the more stringent standard of "beyond reasonable doubt" followed in criminal proceedings which requires a fact to be established beyond any reasonable doubt and if there are two possible versions of the fact that can be inferred from the evidence, the courts would accept the version favouring the innocence of the accused.

---

[47]   Richard Whish and David Bailey, *Competition Law* (9th edn, Oxford University Press 2018).

[48]   CCI, Case of 1 of 2012, Director General (Supplies & Disposals) vs. M/s Puja Enterprises Basti and Ors. The standard has also been affirmed by the Supreme Court in *Rajasthan Cylinders and Containers*.

[49]   *Union of India and Others vs. Hindustan Development Corporation and Others*, (1993) 3 SCC 499.

[50]   Black's Law Dictionary, 11th Edition.

[51]   Some have defined the standard as requiring at least 51 per cent probability as to the existence of a fact. Available at: www.legalmatch.com/law-library/article/preponderance-of-the-evidence-vs-beyond-a-reasonable-doubt.html (accessed 30 June 2022).

An attempt was made to challenge this standard in *Re: Western Coalfields Limited*.[52] It was contended that since the proceedings under the Act have penal consequences, the standard of proof under Section 3 ought to be beyond reasonable doubt and not the preponderance of probability.[53] The Commission rejected the argument by relying on the decision of COMPAT in *International Cylinder (P) Ltd vs. Competition Commission of India* which justified adopting the more liberal standard of preponderance of probability in light of the difficulty in establishing the existence of such agreements in reality. COMPAT observed as follows:

> The burden in this behalf cannot be equated with the burden in the criminal cases where the prosecution has to prove the allegation beyond the reasonable doubt. A strong probability would be enough to come to the conclusion about the breach of the provisions of the Competition Act. Some of the learned counsel argued that their participation or the preconcerted agreement would have to be proved beyond doubt. We do not think so. It is obvious that an agreement cannot be easily proved because it may be a wink or a nod or even a telephone call. What is required to be proved is a strong probability in favour of a pre-concerted agreement and the factors which we have highlighted go a long way in that direction and as plus factors ...

Thus, the CCI has struck a balance in terms of adopting a lesser threshold of proof considering the practical difficulties in proving agreements. In fact, the Indian Courts have been more inclined to endorse the test laid down by the European Court of Justice in *Imperial Chemical Industries Ltd vs. Commission of the European Communities*[54] in tackling the issue of concerted practice.[55] The Supreme Court, reflecting on the observations made by the European Court of Justice in *Dyestuffs*,[56] rejected the oligopolistic defence of the appel-

---

[52] CCI, Case No. 34 of 2015, *Re: Western Coalfields Limited*.

[53] ibid., at para 13.5.

[54] Case 48-69, [1972] ECR 619.

[55] See also, CCI, Case 1 of 2014, *In Re: Alleged Cartelization in Supply of LPG Cylinders*.

[56] See case in n. 54, para 65:

> By its very nature, then, the concerted practice does not have all the elements of a contract but may inter alia arise out of coordination which becomes apparent from the behaviour of the participants. Although parallel behaviour may not itself if identified with a concerted practice, it may however amount to strong evidence of such a practice if it leads to conditions of competition which do not respond to the normal conditions of the market, having regard to the nature of the products, the size and number of the undertakings, and the volume of the said market. Such is the case especially where the parallel behaviour is such as to permit the parties to seek price equilibrium at a different level from that which would have resulted from competition, and to crystallise the status quo to the detriment of effective

lants in a bid-rigging setup and further emphasized the need to consider the plus factors as a whole and not in isolation.[57]

3   INVOLVING ALGORITHMS IN ANTI-COMPETITIVE AGREEMENTS

Ariel Ezrachi and Maurice E. Stucke have raised four major concerns from a competition law perspective that can arise due to algorithms.[58] They distinguish between four scenarios: messenger, hub-and-spoke, tacit collusion and digital eye. Among these scenarios, there are those that use the algorithms to implement or give effect to an explicit agreement which shall fall within the definition of agreement in contravention of Section 3(3) of Competition Act. There are equally scenarios in which there is a unilateral use of pricing algorithms which could result in coordinated outcomes not explicitly barred by the Competition Act.[59] For the purpose of this chapter, hub-and-spoke, tacit collusion and digital eye will be discussed. In the end, the messenger scenario, in which algorithms are used to give effect to an explicit agreement, can be easily dealt with under the Competition Act.

3.1   Algorithms in a Hub-and-Spoke Scenario

In most jurisdictions, direct communication between market players with an intention to behave in an anti-competitive manner and consequently disrupting welfare of the consumers can be categorized as collusion. However, in most circumstances, these market players do not directly exchange information but rather adopt sophisticated forms of collusion. One such form of collusion is known as hub-and-spoke arrangement where an entity at a different level of supply chain (hub) coordinates a horizontal conspiracy amongst competitors (spoke) (together hub-and-spoke) at a different level of supply chain by way of a series of vertical agreements.[60] From a competition law perspective, such

---

freedom of movement of the products in the [internal] market and free choice by consumers of their suppliers.

[57]   *Excel Corp Care Ltd. vs. CCI*, (2017) 8 SCC 47.

[58]   Ariel Ezrachi and Maurice E. Stucke, 'Artificial Intelligence & Collusion: When Computers Inhibit Competition' (2017) *U. Ill. L. Rev.* 1775.

[59]   Competition & Markets Authority, 'Pricing Algorithms- Economic Working Paper on the Use of Algorithms to Facilitate Collusion and Personalised Pricing' (2018), available at https://assets.publishing.service.gov.uk/government/uploads/system/uploads/attachment_data/file/746353/Algorithms_econ_report.pdf   (accessed 30 June 2022).

[60]   Craig G. Falls and Celeste C. Saravia, 'Analyzing Incentives and Liability in "Hub-and-Spoke" Conspiracies' (2015), available at www.cornerstone.com/

arrangement can raise concerns due to indirect information exchange amongst the competitors without any direct communication which can lead to collusive outcome.[61]

While analysing the hub-and-spoke scenario, Ezrachi and Stucke raise a legitimate challenge in detecting algorithm collusion where the collusion may be facilitated amongst the competitors by way of a hub or a third-party facilitator.[62] While the hub-and-spoke scenario is in itself anti-competitive in nature, the presence of pricing algorithms[63] and repricing software,[64] supporting the hub-and-spoke arrangement may likely cause the anti-competitive output in a technologically governed market, to exacerbate.

Even though the existence of hub-and-spoke is inherently counterintuitive,[65] it still exists and poses a challenge specifically in less mature jurisdictions where detection could be difficult owing to the sophistication required by the authorities to deal with such arrangements. It becomes a serious concern, specifically in India, owing to the absence of jurisprudence and cases that have addressed the issue of hub-and-spoke except for the case of *Samir Agrawal vs. ANI technologies* (Uber case).[66] The reluctance by the authorities in recognizing the hybrid model of vertical and horizontal agreements is attributable to the negligible amount of cases present on the subject matter in India.

Publications/Articles/Analyzing-Incentives-and-Liability-in-Hub-and-Spo.pdf (accessed 30 June 2022).

[61] OECD, 'Roundtable on Hub-and-Spoke Arrangements – Background Note' (2019), available at https://one.oecd.org/document/DAF/COMP(2019)14/en/pdf (accessed 30 June 2022).

[62] Ezrachi and Stucke (n. 58 above).

[63] An algorithm that uses price as an input, and/or uses a computational procedure to determine price as an output.

[64] Price adjustments implemented by an algorithm in response to changes in demand, inventory, or competitors' prices.

[65] Falls and Saravia (n. 60 above) (the reason is no party at a different level of the distribution chain would want to give a higher bargaining power by increasing the market power of either upstream players or downstream players in the market. It follows the same analogy to why vertical agreements might not raise anti-competitive concerns usually owing to the parties having counter incentives in a negotiation unlike a horizontal agreement where the incentives are aligned. This is specifically true where the hub or the third-party facilitators does not have any interest in the functioning of the upstream or downstream suppliers. E.g., where a person merely provides the same pricing algorithms to the competitors. Hence, the algorithm provider's interest is independent to the functioning or the working of the companies situated at different level of production/distribution chain).

[66] Competition Appeal (AT) No.11 OF 2019

This reluctance stands testified from the recent proposed amendment to the Competition Act, the Competition Bill 2020, [67] wherein they have acknowledged that such conduct exists in the market. Most of the developed jurisdictions such as the US[68] and the EU[69] do not have detailed guidelines on whether and under what circumstance hub-and-spoke conspiracy should come under a per se or a rule of reason approach. India, after United Kingdom,[70] remains one of the only jurisdictions that has explicitly proposed a combination of horizontal and vertical agreements, thus hub-and-spoke, to have a presumed appreciable adverse effect in the market through the Competition Bill 2020. In terms of certainty of legal test on how hub-and-spoke must be treated (whether it should have presumed AAEC under Section 3(3) of the Competition Act or judged under rule of reason under Section 3(4) of the Competition Act), the Competition Bill 2020 has laid a very clear stance. Despite these new suggestions, this Section shall recognize the limited jurisprudence developed in India pertaining to hub-and-spoke and investigate how far the Competition Act is equipped to deal with hub-and-spoke arising in digital markets by way of algorithms.

The difference between hub-and-spoke in a traditional sense and a new kind of hub-and-spoke in the algorithm driven world has gained much relevance in the debate of how far algorithms can ease collusion.[71] The traditional understanding of hub-and-spoke needs to be slightly more expansive when dealing with algorithms. The hub-and-spoke scenario in cases involving algorithms does not necessarily deal with a hub who is either at the upstream or downstream supply chain but rather a common intermediary or an algorithm

---

[67]   The Bill proposes to add a proviso to Section 3 (3) of the Competition Act providing that any Enterprise or Association, though not engaged in identical or similar trade will be presumed to be a part of the Horizontal Agreement/Cartel if it actively participates in the furtherance of such an agreement.

[68]   The only Section dealing with horizontal collusion is Section 1 of the Sherman act. The courts through decisional practices have widened the scope by including hub-and-spoke as a per se offence where horizontal coordination could be proved. However, there isn't any guidelines on what shall constitute.

[69]   Article 101 TFEU does not mention about hub-and-spoke instead there is a mention of this in the guidelines for information exchange under Guidelines on the applicability of Article 101 of the Treaty on the Functioning of the European Union to horizontal co-operation agreements, available at: https://eur-lex.europa.eu/legal -content/EN/TXT/HTML/?uri=OJ:C:2011:011:FULL&from=EN (accessed 30 June 2022).

[70]   Okeoghene Odudu, 'Indirect Information Exchange: The Constituent Elements of Hub and Spoke Collusion' (2011) 7(2) *Eur. Comp. J.* 205.

[71]   In a traditional hub-and-spoke cartel, the hub is usually at the upstream or downstream level of the supply chain and coordinates the agreement amongst the spokes at a different level of the same supply chain.

developer (third-party facilitator) who is entirely unrelated to the colluding parties.[72] It is important to differentiate between the two elusive and intertwined concepts of hub-and-spoke as it determines the liability to be foisted on the third-party and/or hub. This Section will presume that there is a difference between a hub and a third-party facilitator.

3.1.1 Potential scenarios under hub-and-spoke

There are broadly two main umbrella functions that an algorithm performs: first is to collect information and second is to analyse the information (data). All the other functions flow from these two main functions. The function of an algorithm is like any human brain where after they analyse the information they make pricing decisions keeping in mind that the product is priced above the marginal cost but below a competitor cost.[73] This leads to a dynamic competitive market where algorithms determine prices for commodities after collecting the information from the market and then analysing it in their favour independently. However, where they do not follow the norms mentioned above it can lead to unsolicited outcomes for the market as well as for themselves. The making of a fly case was one such unwanted outcome that was a result of a poorly documented algorithm.[74]

The unsolicited outcomes to the market can also be a result of information sharing amongst these algorithms which limits their capability of determining prices independently. The other issue that can arise from a competition policy perspective is where businesses who do not have the resources or do not wish to make their own algorithms outsource it from a third party.

The above issue can raise four kinds of scenarios from a competition law perspective:

1. First, where the competing businesses outsource the algorithm to the same third party which might provide the same pricing algorithms to all the competing companies.[75] This will lead to the algorithms reacting in

---

[72] OECD (n. 61 above).

[73] The optimal pricing decisions by a company must be a price above its own marginal cost but below the competitors cost. Hence, the competitors cost must be above their marginal cost.

[74] Both the parties had set an algorithm to match the competitors price which led to an upward spiral in prices. The result was a result of a poorly documented algorithm wherein in order to match the prices of its competitor the algorithm started calling the shots and led to upward spiral of prices, the book being priced at $23,698,655.93. Dionysios S. Demetis and Allen S. Lee, 'When Humans Using the IT Artifact Becomes IT Using the Human Artefact' (2018) 19(10) *J. Assoc. Inf. Syst* 929.

[75] OECD, 'Algorithms and Collusion: Competition Policy in the Digital Age' (2017), available at www.oecd.org/daf/competition/Algorithms-and-colllusion -competition-policy-in-the-digital-age.pdf (accessed 30 June 2022).

the similar manner to any change in the market conditions and therefore determining the pricing decisions in parallel, which can inevitably result in price parallelism assuming the products are homogenous and the input feed is similar across the competitors.[76] This scenario presumes that the competing businesses were not aware of each other's decisions but the third party was aware of it. The first sub-issue is how far a third party can be made liable for providing the same algorithm to competing parties where it is a prudent commercial and cost-saving decision though it has resulted in a perverse outcome in the market.[77] The second sub-issue is how far the competing business ought to have been aware that the algorithms so outsourced could have possibly resulted in anti-competitive outcomes. The answer to the first sub-issue is quite straightforward. The third party is under no obligation to not provide the same algorithm to the competing companies. Even if they are not allowed, it shall not be within the purview of the Competition Act and raises a bigger question of corporate governance and contracts. The second sub-issue could point towards the fact that where there is no strategic communication or exchange of information that reduces uncertainty in the market between the parties, it shall not come within the definition of concerted practices under Section 3(3) of Competition Act.[78] The second sub-issue could also point to the solution that antitrust by compliance could be imposed on the companies

---

[76]   ibid.

[77]   This is a commercial decision making as they will not have to build different algorithms for each of the party.

[78]   Any agreement entered into between enterprises or associations of enterprises or persons or associations of persons or between any person and enterprise or practice carried on, or decision taken by, any association of enterprises or association of persons, including cartels, engaged in identical or similar trade of goods or provision of services, which –
   (a)   directly or indirectly determines purchase or sale prices;
   (b)   limits or controls production, supply, markets, technical development, investment or provision of services;
   (c)   shares the market or source of production or provision of services by way of allocation of geographical area of market, or type of goods or services, or number of customers in the market or any other similar way;
   (d)   directly or indirectly results in bid rigging or collusive bidding, shall be presumed to have an appreciable adverse effect on competition: Provided that nothing contained in this sub-Section shall apply to any agreement entered into by way of joint ventures if such agreement increases efficiency in production, supply, distribution, storage, acquisition or control of goods or provision of services. Explanation. – For the purposes of this sub-Section, "bid rigging" means any agreement, between enterprises or persons referred to in sub-Section (3) engaged in identical or similar production or trading of goods or provision of services, which has the effect

and the algorithm providers.[79] It shall be discussed in the latter part of the chapter.

2. The second scenario that can arise is where the third-party platform fixes prices between the competing parties who can be imputed to be aware or unaware of the collusion. This argument can draw parallels with the concept of unified price setting model for all service providers by the platform. [80] The first sub-issue is the incentive behind the third party in setting the prices in a totally unrelated market or at a different level of the supply chain which will essentially benefit the downstream or the upstream parties. While the second sub-issue that can arise is how far the act of the third party can be considered an imputed knowledge to the competing companies to be indicted under concerted practises in violation of the Competition Act or can it be considered imputed knowledge inevitably on them signing up for the services of the third party. This scenario can be illustrated by way of the Uber business model wherein Uber as a platform fixes the prices using algorithms that can be charged by the drivers (service providers) without the drivers having an agreement with each other.[81] This can be specifically seen in the surge pricing phenomenon.[82] The incentive behind Uber doing this is straightforward. Uber charges a certain percentage of fixed commission[83] from the drivers on each trip.[84] The higher the price charged by the drivers to the consumers the higher the commission that will be received by Uber. From the competition law perspective, one argument could be that this unilateral act by the third party shall not come within the definition of collusion to be indicted under Section 3(3) of Competition Act at present even though the outcome is

---

of eliminating or reducing competition for bids or adversely affecting or manipulating the process for bidding.

[79]   OECD (n. 75 above).

[80]   Julian Nowag, 'When Sharing Platforms Fix Sellers' Prices' (Lund University Legal Research Paper Series, LundLawCompWP 1/2018, 2018), available at https://ssrn.com/abstract=3217193 (accessed 30 June 2022).

[81]   Competition Appeal (AT) No.11 OF 2019.

[82]   Under this phenomena prices adjust in response to demand and supply in real time. Juan-Camilo Castillo, 'Who Benefits from Surge Pricing' (2022), available at https://papers.ssrn.com/sol3/papers.cfm?abstract_id=3245533.

[83]   Lee Chen, Alan Mislove and Christo Wilson, 'Peeking beneath the Hood of Uber' (2015), available at www.ftc.gov/system/files/documents/public_comments/2015/09/00011-97592.pdf (accessed 30 June 2022).

[84]   Ariel Ezrachi and Maurice E. Stucke, 'Two Artificial Neural Networks Meet in an Online Hub and Change the Future (of Competition, Market Dynamics and Society)' (2017), available at https://papers.ssrn.com/sol3/papers.cfm?abstract_id=2949434 (accessed 30 June 2022).

undesirable to consumer welfare.[85] This situation can draw parallels to the fourth scenario mentioned below. However, the answer could vary where the third-party is a platform and the service providers sign up with cognizance of such a unified price setting model. In this situation, the defence of a unilateral act by the platform might not hold good. The second sub-issue on whether the drivers shall be considered to have imputed knowledge shall be answered in the latter part while dealing with *Samir Agrawal vs. ANI Technologies* case.[86] The third sub-issue that can arise in this context is what if the platform is unable to provide differential pricing due to the oligopolistic nature of the market where the best price is the common price set by the platform. Can a pricing scheme which is more consumer-welfare enhancing even though it is achieved through a hard-core restraint be considered to rebut the presumption of AAEC under Section 3(3) of Competition Act.

3.   The third scenario that can arise from a competition law perspective is where the competing parties collude with each other on prices by way of a facilitator (algorithm provider).[87] In this particular setting, the competing parties by way of vertical agreements with the third-party/hub exchange information through hub with each other to facilitate collusion between them. This is the traditional form of hub-and-spoke conspiracy.[88] The question in this is where there are a series of vertical agreements facilitating a horizontal agreement amongst the competitors, how shall the competition law in India deal with it. The second sub-issue that can arise is what is the incentive in this case for the third-party to coordinate the agreement amongst the competitors in an unrelated market.

An extension to the third scenario is a situation where, though the competing parties are not explicitly colluding with each other,[89] they are aware or may be aware that all of them are using a similar algorithms from the same third

---

[85]   In this scenario, the author presumes that the parties who are signing up are unaware of collusion amongst themselves, and the knowledge through signing up for a unified price setting mechanism shall not be imputed on them. In that situation, if Uber fixes prices on behalf of them without their knowledge it becomes a unilateral act.

[86]   Competition Appeal (AT) No.11 OF 2019.

[87]   OECD (n. 75 above).

[88]   Rodrigo Londono van Rutten and Caroline Buts, 'Hub and Spoke Cartels: Incentives, Mechanisms and Stability' (2019) 1 *CoRe3* 4.

[89]   It differs from the first situation as in the first situation the competing parties were not aware of all of them using the similar algorithms from the third party.

party.[90] This is also called the predictable agent scenario.[91] This will help them to predict the competitors pricing decisions and adjust their pricing strategically. This scenario shall have the effect of information exchange with reduced uncertainty and more transparency which might give rise to a tacit collusion outcome.[92] The question that can arise is how far the algorithm provider can be called a hub. The second sub-issue this scenario advances is, if there is a difference between a hub who plays a more intervening role in the hub-and-spoke conspiracy and a third party provider who is merely providing an algorithm without playing an interventionist role in the entire collusive strategy. This particular issue is raised even in the first concern where the third party is the only one who is aware of all competing businesses using the similar algorithms and nothing more. Using similar algorithms might inevitably result in parallel prices in the market but without any interventionist role in bringing out the collusive equilibria by the third party. The question once again is can a third-party provider who falls short of being a hub be liable for being a party to the anti-competitive agreement which is seminal in tying the liability to a hub or a third-party facilitator in prompting collusion amongst competitors. It is important to address the difference between the hub and third party facilitator as, if it is considered a hub with an interventionist role the antitrust liability encircling it, would be graver vis-à-vis a third-party facilitator where he might not be considered a party to the anti-competitive agreement. The predictable agent scenario will be dealt with under the heading of tacit collusion.[93] The difference between a hub and a third-party facilitator shall be dealt in later part of this chapter.[94]

4.   The fourth scenario could be where the third-party acts as an invisible hand and determines the prices amongst the competing parties without them knowing. There hasn't been a case on this scenario, but it is likely possible that such a situation can arise and can produce unwarranted outcomes in the market.[95] The incentive behind the third-party acting invisibly to determine prices could be to make its services more profitable by allocating more profits to the software users. This can happen in a situation for instance in the *Eturas* case where the operator of booking system

---

[90]   Competition & Markets Authority (n. 59 above).
[91]   Ariel Ezrachi and Maurice E. Stucke, 'Sustainable and Unchallenged Algorithmic Tacit Collusion' (2018), available at https://papers.ssrn.com/sol3/papers.cfm?abstract_id=3282235 (accessed 30 June 2022).
[92]   Competition & Markets Authority (n. 59 above).
[93]   See Section 3.2, "Predictable Agent."
[94]   See Section 3.1.3, "Legislative Gap under Section 3(3) of Competition Act."
[95]   Liability for outsourced algorithmic collusion – A practical approximation.

got in place a discount control mechanism wherein the operators could not give discount beyond 3 per cent.[96] In this case Eturas informed all the operators to adhere to the maximum discount, however if in a situation, he would have not informed them regarding the maximum discount but would have set the algorithm to not provide a discount beyond 3 per cent he would have been able to fix prices as an invisible hand without knowledge of the affecting firms. Such unilateral conduct of the invisible hand shall not fit within the contours of Section 3(3) of Competition Act for the lack of agreement/concert amongst the competing parties.

3.1.2   Hub-and-spoke scenarios and the Competition Act

The concept of hub-and-spoke is novel to the jurisprudence under the Indian Competition Law 2002. There are only three Indian cases that mention hub-and-spoke. Out of the three cases it was only in the case of *Samir Agrawal v. ANI Technologies*[97] that the hub-and-spoke arrangement allegation actually went to trial. The other two cases, revolving on a hub-and-spoke arrangement which was effectuated by way of RPM, were never pursued by the CCI and hence never investigated. Even though there is limited jurisprudence developed in India with regards to hub-and-spoke, CCI recently came up with the Competition Bill 2020 which mentioned hub-and-spoke agreements being covered under the anti-competitive agreements under Section 3 of the Competition Act.

The chapter shall first discuss the various cases that raised the allegation of hub-and-spoke under the Indian Competition Law 2002. The case of *Fx Enterprise Solutions Pvt. Ltd and Anr. vs. Hyundai Motor India Pvt. Ltd* and the case of Uber in India, shall illustrate the position of India on hub-and-spoke arrangements. After, the chapter shall elaborate on how far the amendment, the Competition Bill 2020, shall equip the commission to deal with complex hub-and-spoke scenarios.

a.   *Fx Enterprise Solutions Pvt. Ltd and Anr. vs. Hyundai Motor India Pvt. Ltd*

The CCI, in *Fx Enterprise Solutions Pvt. Ltd and Anr*,[98] passed a judgment against Hyundai holding them liable for RPM, which was overturned by NCLAT,[99] on the premise of lack of evidences to substantiate the claim.

---

[96]   Case C-74/14 *"Eturas" UAB and Others v. Lietuvos Respublikos konkurencijos taryba* ECLI:EU:C:2016:4.

[97]   Competition Appeal (AT) No.11 of 2019.

[98]   CCI, Case no. 36 and 82 of 2014, *Fx Enterprise Solutions Pvt. Ltd. and Another vs. Hyundai Motor India Pvt. Ltd.*

[99]   Competition Appeal (AT) No. 06 of 2017.

The NCLAT, while reversing the judgment, reasoned that the CCI failed to undertake an independent investigation into the claims and relied solely on the Director General's (DG) investigation report. Despite the reversal of the CCI's decision, it is pertinent to discuss the CCI's stand in the *Hyundai* case in order to throw light on the Commission's approach in tackling an allegation of hub-and-spoke. In this case the claimants instituted proceedings before the CCI against Hyundai Motor India Limited (Hyundai) for fixing the maximum resale price and the maximum discount that could be charged by the dealers of Hyundai to its customers.

Maximum resale price maintenance, coupled with the maximum discount fixed by Hyundai effectively acted as a minimum price floor "including the dealer's margin" which stripped away any price competition amongst the dealers. Hyundai admitted that they had mechanisms in place through which they could keep a check on dealers trying to undercut the prescribed prices or who had a discount scheme. If caught, they were to be penalized and it could also result in the termination of their Hyundai dealership. Hyundai's argument in support of appointing mystery shopping agencies to keep a check on dealers deviating from the mandated price was to penalize those dealers who were secretly jeopardizing the financial health of others. The data was collected on discounts being given by all the dealers and shared with each of them in an email thread. The violating dealer's information was shared with other dealers. The penalty ranged from Indian Rupees Two Hundred Thousand (INR 200,000) per violation up to Indian Rupees Eight Million (INR 8,000,000). This acted as a deterrent for all dealers to not deviate from the price mandate given by Hyundai.[100]

From the facts, the CCI inferred that the dealers would have essentially competed on discounts, if not for the discount control mechanism in place. The email thread which communicated to all the dealers the discounts offered by other dealers was a commercially sensitive information exchange wherein the dealers exactly knew what their competing dealers were charging implying that the dealers were conscious of the prices being charged by their competing businesses. The penalties collected from dealers who did not adhere to the discount mandate were distributed amongst the non-violating dealers. It was also evidenced that Hyundai used to meet with its dealers on a monthly basis to discuss prices charged and discounts offered by the dealer which categorically indicates that all the dealers exchanged commercially sensitive information,

---

[100] A higher penalty in itself is not conclusive proof of collusion. *United States vs. Parke, Davis & Co*, 362 US 29 (1960).

were aware of the mandate and agreed to carry on such activity in concert.[101] However, the CCI did not pursue the case of horizontal agreement amongst the retailers.

The case can draw parallels with the facts of *United States v. Parke, Davis & Co*,[102] wherein the retailers were given the suggested resale prices in advance by way of a retail catalogue that was circulated amongst all of them. The company went ahead to impress upon all the retailers that the prices were being adhered to by all of them and if anyone deviated from the prices or advertised the discounts, he shall be "put in line". Each retailor was personally visited to make them cognizant of resale prices. The retailors agreed to adhere to the prices based on a common understanding that everyone else was also adhering to it. The exchange of commercially sensitive information coupled with a commitment by the parties to act on it with a common understanding was sufficient to constitute undue restraint of trade.[103]

INFORMATION EXCHANGE UNDER INDIAN COMPETITION LAW

The Competition Act has, under Section 2(b),[104] one of the widest definitions of agreement vis-à-vis any other jurisdiction and includes arrangement, understanding and concerted practices.[105] The provision dealing with horizontal collusion under Section 3(3) of the Competition Act is wide enough to include an "agreement, practices carried on or decision taken" in which practice as defined under Section 2(m) of the Competition Act[106] includes any practice relating to the carrying on of any trade by a person or an enterprise; and is of

---

[101] The SIA 'VM Remonts' (formerly SIA 'DIV un KO') and *Others vs. Konkurences padome* (2016) highlighted conditions to prove a concerted action: (1) The undertaking knew about the anti-competitive intention and intended to contribute; (2) The undertaking could have reasonable foreseen and was prepared to accept the risk.

[102] *United States vs. Parke, Davis & Co.*

[103] ibid.

[104] "(b) 'agreement' includes any arrangement or understanding or action in concert (i) whether or not, such arrangement, understanding or action is formal or in writing; or (ii) whether or not such arrangement, understanding or action is intended to be enforceable by legal proceedings."

[105] The concept of concerted practice comprises an informal cooperation between undertakings, without the conclusion of an agreement, substituting the risks of competition. [S]uch a practice is a form of coordination between undertakings by which, without it having been taken to the stage where an agreement properly so-called has been concluded, practical cooperation between them is knowingly substituted for the risks of competition.
Case C-8/08 – *T-Mobile Netherlands v. Raad van Bestuur van de Nederlandse Mededingings Autoriteit* [2009], para 26.

[106] Competition Act, Section 2 (m), stating that "practice" includes any practice relating to the carrying on of any trade by a person or an enterprise.

wide amplitude to include the practice of exchanging commercially sensitive information which can have AAEC in the market. Information exchange under competition law has not been defined nor has the commission issued any guidelines. However, it has been found to be anti-competitive through various judicial decisions under Section 3(3) of the Competition Act.

In a recent judgment,[107] the CCI held that the exchange of commercially sensitive information in itself shall not amount to anti-competitive activity but it may be considered as a plus factor and the Commission must establish the test of commitment[108] amongst the colluding parties to prove collusion. The test of commitment as laid down in EU jurisdiction states that it must be proved by the commission that the colluding parties not only received that information but also acted upon it.[109] However, this test has been diluted post the *Eturas* case[110] wherein the regulator held that the dispatch of information to all travel agents through a platform shall be anti-competitive and that parties must show they have done some overt act to distance themselves from such message. In this case where the burden was shifted onto the parties to prove that they did not read the email or they tried in all capacities to distance themselves from the conduct which is very different from all the other cases involving hub-and-spoke where the burden still remains on the plaintiff to prove agreement amongst the spokes. It was held in this case that "the presumption of innocence in primary law does not preclude a domestic court from presuming awareness of a message from the date of its dispatch in light of further objective."[111]

The National Company Law Appellate Tribunal (NCLAT) in an appeal in the *Cement Manufacturers* case[112] held that exchange of commercially sensitive information shall amount to evidence of collusion if it reduces the

---

[107] CCI, Suo Motu Case No. 01 of 2017 *In Re: Alleged Cartelization in Flashlights Market in India.*

[108] In that regard, the Court of Justice has held that, subject to proof to the contrary, which the economic operators concerned must adduce, it must be presumed that the undertakings taking part in the concerted action and remaining active on the market take account of the information exchanged with their competitors in determining their conduct on that market. In particular, the Court of Justice has concluded that such a concerted practice is caught by Article 101(1) TFEU, even in the absence of anticompetitive effects on that market. C 8/08, *T-Mobile Netherlands and Others*, EU:C:2009:343, para 51, 2015, C 286/13 P, *Dole Food and Dole Fresh Fruit Europe v. Commission*, EU:C:2015:184, para 127.

[109] *"Eturas" UAB and Others.*

[110] ibid.

[111] ibid.

[112] *Ambuja Cements Limited & Ors vs. CCI*, TA(AT) (Compt) No. 22 of 2017, order dated 25 July 2018, sub judiced in Supreme Court.

strategic uncertainty amongst the alleged collusive parties.[113] What information constitutes "reduced strategic uncertainty" has not been elaborated under Indian Competition law.[114] The fact that the dealers of Hyundai adhered to the discount control mechanism and to the resale prices since the deterrent penalty was really high and the dealers did act on RPM and discount mandate qualified the test of commitment. However nowhere in the judgment is it unequivocally mentioned that the dealers and the manufacturer exchanged price sensitive information which was anti-competitive in nature. But the same could be inferred from the nature of the market,[115] information exchange,[116] the monitoring policy, frequency of information exchange, deterrent penalty which was ignored by the commission absolutely.

As was illustrated in *United States vs. Parke, Davis & Co*,[117] it was made clear by Hyundai that all the dealers were impressed upon the same expectation and hence such negotiations were a part of the concerted action to minimize price competition amongst the dealers. The dealers were all informed of each other's prices and any deviations by the violating dealer. It was an attempt to carry on a common understanding that each of them observe the directed prices.[118] It is

---

[113] In so far as concerns, in particular, the exchange of information between competitors, it should be recalled that the criteria of coordination and cooperation necessary for determining the existence of a concerted practice are to be understood in the light of the notion inherent in the Treaty provisions on competition, according to which each economic operator must determine independently the policy which he intends to adopt on the common market.
(*T-Mobile Netherlands and Others*, para 32 and *Dole Food and Dole Fresh Fruit Europe vs. Commission*, para 119).

[114] In particular, an exchange of information which is capable of removing uncertainty between participants as regards the timing, extent and details of the modifications to be adopted by the undertakings concerned in their conduct on the market must be regarded as pursuing an anticompetitive object (see *Dole Food and Dole Fresh Fruit Europe vs. Commission*, para 122; see also, to that effect, judgment *T-Mobile Netherlands and Others*, para 41).

[115] The automobile market is an oligopoly market in India and hence information exchange on prices and discounts to be offered by the dealers reduces strategic certainty in the market making it more conducive to concertation.

[116] The nature of information that was exchanged reduced any incentive between the dealers to compete since they could either compete on prices which was fixed through RPM or on discounts that they could offer which was also curtailed. Hence there was no parameter on which the dealers could have possibly competed. The nature of information exchanged was also not taken into consideration. The mere exchange of commercially sensitive information does not amount to conclusive proof of collusion but can used as a plus factor.

[117] *United States vs. Parke, Davis & Co*; Comments: The Parke, Davis case: Refusal to deal and the Sherman Act (1961) *Duke L.J.* 127.

[118] *United States vs. Parke, Davis & Co*.

interesting to note that NCLAT while deciding the appeal completely ignored the admission by Hyundai of impressing upon each dealer the resale price as well the discount control mechanism. Rather than going into the merits of the appeal, the NCLAT chose to reverse the case on the grounds of inability of the CCI to conduct an independent inquiry from the DG's investigation.

It was also contended that the discount control mechanism was Implemented on behalf of the dealers, however the contention stopped at that and the commission failed to dwell into the veracity of the claim. The CCI held Hyundai liable for vertical restraint under Section 3 (4I) together with Section 3 (1) of the Competition Act for RPM which was over-ruled by NCLAT. The contention of a hub-and-spoke arrangement between Hyundai and its dealers was not brought to investigation by the CCI under Section 26 (1) of the Competition Act, even though it was brought up by the complainant.[119] The Director-General (DG) merely made an investigation on the vertical agreement between the dealers and Hyundai. The question that still remains is whether the DG could have *suo motu* made a case under the horizontal prohibition while investigating vertical anti-competitive agreement. As was held under the *Grasim Industries* case,[120] the DG does not have the power to go beyond the claim referred to it by the CCI under Section 26 (1) of the Competition Act.[121] However, in the *Hyundai vs. CCI* case,[122] the Madras High Court has relied on Section 26 (1) of the Competition Act[123] to state that, if the subject matter of information is already known to the CCI, the new information on that same subject matter can be added to the previous information and no *prima facie* case need to be made by the CCI.[124] However, whether the new information could fall under the proviso to Section 26 (1), which includes an inquiry into a horizontal agreement while investigating a vertical agreement, remains debatable. According to the author the heading under which both horizontal and vertical agreement fall, is anti-competitive agreements under Section 3 of

---

[119] Procedure for inquiry on complaints under Section 19 of the Competition Act.

[120] CCI, Case No 62/2016, *CCI vs. M/s Grasim Industries*.

[121] Section 26 of the Competition Act lays down the procedure for those under inquiry.

[122] WP Nos. 31808 and 31809 of 2012; Hyundai Motor India Limited vs. CCI.

[123] On receipt of a reference from the Central Government or a State Government or a statutory authority or on its own knowledge or information received under Section 19, if the Commission is of the opinion that there exists a prima facie case, it shall direct the Director General to cause an investigation to be made into the matter: Provided that if the subject matter of an information received is, in the opinion of the Commission, substantially the same as or has been covered by any previous information received.

[124] *Hyundai Motor India Ltd vs. CCI*, Competition Appeal (AT) No. 6 of 2017, decided on 19 September 2018.

the Competition Act. Therefore, if the DG finds the presence of a horizontal agreement supported by vertical agreements, the author does not think that the CCI needs to form a separate *prima facie* opinion on that issue and it can be accommodated under the proviso to Section 26 (1) of the Competition Act. If so, the DG on various occasions in its report pointed out towards the existence of a horizontal coordination amongst the dealers but did not observe the same to be a case of hub-and-spoke.

The approach by the CCI would have been better suited if the allegation pertained to both the RPM and a claim under Section 3(3) of the Competition Act. The author suggests this as, assuming Hyundai would have been able to give pro-competitive justification for implementing RPM, in case of allegation under Section 3(3) of the Competition Act the reversal in burden of proof would have shifted the onus on Hyundai to prove that its act did not have AAEC in the market. The author does not suggest over-regulation by the CCI. However, where it was *prima facie* evident that a horizontal conspiracy existed, the CCI should have brought the claim under Section3(3) of the Competition Act.

If either the CCI or the NCLAT had positively determined the arrangement between Hyundai and its dealers to be a case of hub-and-spoke, it would have been a classic example of Type II hub-and-spoke under the three-pronged taxonomy[125] proposed by Falls and Saravia in their article titled 'Analysing Incentives and Liability in "Hub-and-spoke" Conspiracies'.[126] The Type II hub-and-spoke consist of reduced competition at the level of horizontal participants which could be either at the upstream or downstream level which is given effect by vertical agreements with the third party at the different level of supply chain. This is usually effected by way of RPM wherein the manufacturer's downstream dealers conspire amongst themselves to remove intra-brand competition by asking the manufacturer to impose RPM.[127]

There was clear evidence, produced during investigation, that all dealers were aware of each other's conduct and consciously continued to adhere to the RPM policy, therefore it met the requirement of the definition of agreement under Section 2(b) and of horizontal conduct under Section 3(3) of the Competition Act raising the presumption of AAEC in the market. However, the CCI chose not to pursue the case under Section 3(3) and the NCLAT did not even go into the merits of Hyundai's admission of adherence to such policy

---

[125]   Rob Nicholls, 'Algorithm-Driven Business Conduct: Competition and Collusion. Centre for Law Markets and Regulations' (2018), available at http://unsworks.unsw.edu.au/fapi/datastream/unsworks:52475/bin7174fba5-902f-4331-801c-8f59532b77fb?view=true (accessed 30 June 2022).

[126]   Falls and Saravia (n. 60).

[127]   Craig Callery, 'Should the European Union Embrace or Exercise Leegin's "Rule of Reason"?' (2011) 32 *European Competition Law Review* 42.

by all the dealers, which shows the sluggishness and inability of the commission to evolve and acknowledge the existence of hub-and-spoke. The OECD report mentions:

> Opting for an RPM case instead of a full-blown hub-and-spoke investigation could serve as a shortcut, at least under legal frameworks where RPM is considered an infringement by object, like in the EU.[128] Since RPM is the commonly used tool to implement hub-and-spoke arrangements, a competition agency that puts an end to the RPM will also disrupt the underlying hub-and-spoke arrangement. It cannot function without. The legal requirements for an RPM case are certainly lower. An agency needs to prove that a price related communication between a supplier and a retailer amounted to RPM, but no more than that. This would constitute an object violation of Art. 101 (1) TFEU and its national equivalents, without the need for further analysis of effects or efficiencies or of complicated tri- or multilateral relationships.[129]

It could be seen that the CCI had an opportunity to establish the precedent for hub-and-spoke but chose not to do so either due to its inability to deal with such complex arrangements or due to the lack of investigative tools to decipher horizontal collusion or merely because it wanted to opt for a short-cut.

b.   *The Uber case in India*

India was one of the only jurisdictions, after the US,[130] to institute a suit against Uber for price fixing and facilitating a cartel between the drivers by acting as a hub/third-party provider.

The private ride hailing services essentially function on the machine learning model wherein it seeks to match the demands of the passengers to the drivers by taking real time, real demand, distance of the passenger to the driver, the length of the journey etc. into account while deciding the fares to

---

[128] "RPM is currently listed as one of the hard-core violations that make any vertical agreement ineligible for an exemption from Art. 101 (1) within the framework of the Vertical Block Exemption Regulation, Art. 4 (a) VBER – Commission Regulation No 330/2010. The European Commission has started the process of the review of the VBER, and the debate about the correct placement of RPM as a hard-core, object infringement can be expected to be one of the main discussion topics for the years to come", available at: http://ec.europa.eu/competition/consultations/2018_vber/index_en .html (accessed 30 June 2022).

[129] OECD, 'Corporate Governance Factbook 2019' (2019), available at www.oecd .org/corporate/Corporate-Governance-Factbook.pdf (accessed 30 June 2022).

[130] *Meyer vs. Uber Technologies, Inc.*, No. 16-2750 (2d Cir. 2017).

be charged.[131] It operates in real time and changes the price charged at each moment depending on the demand and other factors.[132]

The allegation against Uber pertained to it acting as a platform in the form of a third-party intermediary to exchange commercially sensitive information amongst the drivers who have been held to be independent contractors.[133] The claim was that Uber fixed prices on behalf of the drivers and hence constituted a hub-and-spoke conspiracy where the drivers acted as spokes. However, for the claim of hub-and-spoke to succeed it has to be proved that there was a horizontal agreement amongst the Uber drivers. The fact that the drivers signed up to Uber knowing that other drivers would also follow the price determined by the common platform, hence an element of understanding for constituting agreement under Section 2(b) of the Competition Act can be inferred. The question then remains whether the commission and the NCLAT belittled the anti-competitive business model or once again showed its incompetence to deal with such an arrangement. It is ironic that Indian competition law is one of the most expansive and flexible laws compared to other jurisdictions and yet decisional practice nullifies the scope of the law.

The argument by the CCI as well as NCLAT while dismissing the case against Uber rested on lack of evidence of conspiracy between the drivers.[134] The commission expounded that the application of hub-and-spoke mandatorily requires collusion amongst the parties at the horizontal level. The mere accession of drivers to a common unified price setting mechanism is not a proof of agreement amongst the drivers inter-se. The mere allocation of pricing power to a common third party does not prove agreement between the drivers and hence there is no substance to the allegation of price fixing by Uber through hub-and-spoke.[135] The conservative approach of the CCI and NCLAT in deciding this case could also be due to the inability to interpret Section 3(3) of the Competition Act to include enterprise or association of enterprises who might not be in a similar/identical trade and hence could not be presumed to be a part of the agreement.

The Uber case in India missed the whole essence of hub-and-spoke. The Uber case in India points out to the second scenario mentioned above wherein

---

[131] Hai Wang and Hai Yang, 'Ridesourcing Systems: A Framework and Review' (2019), available at https://papers.ssrn.com/sol3/papers.cfm?abstract_id=3375259 (accessed 30 June 2022).

[132] Kenji Lee, 'Algorithm Collusion and its Implications for Competition Law and Policy' (2018), available at https://papers.ssrn.com/sol3/papers.cfm?abstract_id=3213296 (accessed 30 June 2022).

[133] Competition Appeal (AT) No. 11 of 2019.

[134] Competition Act, Section 2(b).

[135] ibid., at Section 2(b).

the third party provides the purpose and also the method to reach to that purpose. However, one set of arguments could be that the knowledge among the competitors to settle on the same algorithm could not be inferred to mean existence of agreement amongst them. The drivers are so widespread that it is impossible for them to agree with each other for there to be a horizontal conspiracy, rather they have no say in the business model adopted by Uber. The problem if one exists is with the business model of Uber and not the fact that knowledge can be wrongfully attributed to the drivers for using Uber in parallel. The case was merely based on assumptions and, unlike the US case against Uber for price fixing,[136] where in order to get the petition admitted the plaintiff did give proofs of meetings held between the drivers and the representatives of Uber, such evidences were never raised in the case against Uber in India.[137] Moreover, for the hub-and-spoke concept to be applied the competition authorities have to strictly prove an agreement between the competitors as per the United States position.[138] This position however seems to have got a little diluted in the European Union after the *Eturas* case[139] where the knowledge amongst the competitors was presumed and they had to discard the burden that they did an overt act to distance themselves from such agreement. India has yet not settled on its approach to dealing with algorithm price setting.

The other set of arguments could be where the service providers are competitors and not agents or do not form one single economic entity with the platform, theoretically the platform fixing prices on their behalf through algorithms could very well come within the prohibition under Section 3(3)(a) of Competition Act by way of hub-and-spoke.[140]

If the second set of arguments hold true which the author thinks they should as the service providers and the platform does not form a part of one single economic entity since the service providers and the platform nor the service providers amongst themselves shared the cost nor pursued a common economic goal.[141] In the Indian context, there is no sufficient control that Uber exercise over the service providers and a lack of central decision-making power,

---

[136] *Meyer vs. Uber Technologies, Inc.*

[137] Competition Appeal (AT) No. 11 of 2019.

[138] The evidence must prove defendants had the intent to adhere to an agreement that was designed to achieve an unlawful objective; specific intent to restrain trade is not required; *Meyer vs. Uber Technologies*, Inc., No. 16-2750 (2d Cir. 2017).

[139] *"Eturas" UAB and Others*.

[140] OECD (n. 61 above).

[141] Mark Anderson and Max Huffman, 'The Sharing Economy Meets the Sherman Act: Is UBER a Firm, a Cartel or Something in Between?' (2017) 3 *Columbia Business Law Review* 859.

which takes them out of the purview of single economic entity defence.[142] In the *Honda* case,[143] it was held that "the exemption of single economic entity stems from the inseparability of the economic interests[144] of the parties to the agreement."[145] The closest model Uber could come to is the structure of a membership organization.[146] One argument could be that if Uber resembles a membership organization, in the USA context, Uber could be treated under rule of reason if they offer a new product or in the absence of such uniform price fixing they would not have been able to offer this product at all.[147] This could be a convincing defence that could be used by Uber to justify its business model, however it is unlikely that this argument would succeed as Uber does not necessarily fit the contours of a membership organization. This is so as sellers do not come together to make Uber nor do sellers have any autonomy or say in the price fixed by the platform which is usually the case in membership organizations. Also, there are instances where the interests of Uber and sellers may not be aligned[148] and hence nullifying the argument of Uber being a membership organization.[149] Uber's Business model might not even fit the joint venture defence since there needs to be a sharing of risk and pooling of assets amongst the parties which in this present case is absent.[150] Uber's relationship with the sellers cannot categorically be put under the vertical agreements as we understand under Section 3(4) of the Competition Act since there is no product that is being sold by Uber to its sellers which could be resold by the seller to the consumers. Section 3(4) of the Competition Act covers agreement amongst enterprises at different stages of the production chain in different markets in relation to the trade of goods or provision of services. Firstly, Section 3(4) of the Competition Act talks about presence at different stages of the production

---

[142] CCI, Case No. 52 of 2012, *Exclusive Motors Pvt. Limited Informant vs. Automobili Lamborghini S.P.A. Opposite Party.*

[143] CCI, Case No. 03/2011.

[144] Footnote added. The economic interests pursued by Uber and their drivers are substantially different; Uber acts as a marketplace where buyers meet the seller.

[145] Piyush Gupta, 'Single Economic Entity and Corporate Separatedness Doctrine: A Juxtaposition' (2019), available at www.mondaq.com/india/antitrust-eu-competition/788042/single-economic-entity-and-corporate-separatedness-doctrine-a-juxtaposition (accessed 30 June 2022).

[146] Julian Nowag, 'When Sharing Platforms Fix Sellers' Prices' (2018) 6(3) *J. Antitrust Enf.* 382.

[147] *Broadcast Music, Inc. vs. Columbia Broadcasting System*, 441 US 1 (1979).

[148] Nowag (n. 146 above). "If there is an increase in the overall number of transactions, the platform might accept a reduction in the prices. On the other hand, sellers pay negligible attention to the number of transactions, and pay heed to the number and price of transactions conducted by them."

[149] Nowag (n. 146 above).

[150] *Texaco Inc. vs. Dagher*, 547 U.S. 1 (2006).

chain to mean that the goods produced by one enterprise acts as an input for the other enterprise. In this particular scenario, there are no goods or services that are being sold by Uber to the sellers for it to act as an input. Instead they are acting like a marketplace where consumers come and buy the goods or services from the sellers who are present on the marketplace.

The closest model through which Uber could be indicted is by categorizing it as a hub-and-spoke through agency. In hub-and-spoke, through brokerage/agency,[151] a hub acts as broker/agent who can fix prices on behalf of their client to receive higher commission or reward payments or fees. For instance, in *Re Insurance Brokerage Antitrust Litigation* the dual role of insurance brokers who acted as consultants to the customers taking insurance and producers for the insurers.[152] The Uber model could be slightly differentiated from the above case wherein Uber the agent fixes prices on behalf of the principal (the sellers) and bears no risk of transaction between the principal and the final consumer.[153] This is different from the traditional agency relationship wherein the agency also bears the risk of acting on behalf of the principal. The traditional agency agreements are outside the scope of competition law.[154] However, a hub-and-spoke through agency represents in essence a typical hub-and-spoke conspiracy, wherein the hub does not bear the risk of performance of the principal to the consumers. Rather it merely acts as a platform for the sellers and the buyers to interact. The problem commences where the agent who fixes the price for one principal starts doing it for multiple principals eventually leading to a cartel behaviour amongst the principals situated at the same level of the supply chain. The incentive for the platform to do so is very straightforward.[155] The higher the aggregate transactions of all the principals with their consumers the higher the fees of the platform.[156] The platform does not care about individual principal's transaction rather it is more concerned the aggregate transaction of all the principals just like in a typical hub-and-spoke cartel where the facilitator benefits when the entire cartel becomes profitable.[157]

---

[151] Agency as we understand traditionally must be distinguished from what we understand under antitrust since agency would be a defence for antitrust as agent acts on behalf of the principal and therefore they cannot be considered two separate entities for the purpose of agreement.

[152] William J. Kolasky and Kathryn McNeece, 'Contingent Commissions and the Antitrust Laws: What Can We Learn from The In re Insurance Brokerage Antitrust Litigation?' (2015) 108 (2619) *Antitrust & Trade Regulation Report* 1.

[153] Commission Guidelines on Vertical Restraints, [2010] OJ C130/01, para 6.

[154] Nowag (n. 146 above).

[155] ibid.

[156] ibid.

[157] ibid.

The conscious and simultaneous signing up of drivers to unified price setting by the platforms should be considered an imputed knowledge. Hence, the business model of Uber must be presumed to have AAEC in the market. The act of Uber where drivers knowingly sign up for an invisible hand determining the prices for all of them commonly is presumed to have appreciable adverse effect on the market and thus, under Section 3(3) of Competition Act, reversing the burden of proof to Uber. Uber should prove that its price-setting strategy did not have AAEC in the market. It was not for the CCI or the NCLAT to determine the AAEC in the market, rather, the business model, if elaborated extensively or understood extensively, it could have per se acted as a proof of collusion and the burden of proof should have been reversed. It was for Uber to prove that it was consumer welfare enhancing and rebut the presumption under Section 3(3) of the Competition Act.

A similar case was instituted by the Luxemburg Competition Commission against Webtaxi,[158] which worked with the same business model as Uber.[159] The Luxembourg Competition Authority presumed that the agreement restricted competition by object and is void under Article 101(2) TFEU. However, it was rebutted on account of efficiency justification mentioned under Article 101(3) TFEU.[160] This result was reached by seeking answers to the following questions. First, in the absence of an Uber-like business model, would consumers be charged more or less, i.e. would the model increase consumer welfare? Second, could such a business model exist without prices being coordinated centrally? Third, what impact will the business model have on competition in the market? Fourth, could an alternative business model offer the same services but be less restrictive?[161] A similar approach by CCI could have brought more clarity in deciphering the competitive constraints posed by such business models.

---

[158] Conseil de la Concurrence, (Luxembourg Competition Authority), Decision of 7 June 2018 no. 2018-FO-01, Webtaxi Sarl.

[159] Available at: http://webtaxi.mobi/business-model (accessed 30 June 2022). The Webtaxi Model resembles the Uber Model in its functioning as a platform where sellers and buyers meet and hence an analogy can be drawn on the case being decided on same principle.

[160] The commission said that the service will be of no use to the consumers without the unified price setting and hence it met all the requirements under efficiency justification.

[161] OECD (n. 61 above).

COULD THE UBER CASE HAVE MISSED THE EXISTENCE OF SECTION 3(1) OF COMPETITION ACT?

The Competition Act has given the widest amplitude to anti-competitive agreements under Section 3, by bifurcating it into three segments: Section 3(3)[162] deals with horizontal agreements, Section 3(4)[163] deals with vertical agreements and, as per the interpretation of CCI in the case of *Ramakant Kini*,[164] Section 3(1) deals with commercial agreements between enterprises which cannot be categorized either under horizontal or vertical agreements as defined under Section 3(3) or 3(4) respectively, but have AAEC in the market nonetheless.

This interpretation came in the background of an agreement between a stem cell bank and a hospital wherein anyone who wanted to enrol for stem cell banking procedure could only do it with the Cryobank with which the hospital had an agreement to the exclusion of any other stem cell banking services.[165] The CCI held that this type of agreement shall not fall within the wording of Section 3(4) of the Competition Act since the stem cell bank and the hospital were not operating at different levels of the same production chain which is a pre-requisite for vertical agreements to fall under Section 3(4) of the Competition Act. However, since it did have appreciable adverse effect it could be brought within Section 3(1) of the Competition Act. The CCI stated that "Section 3(3) of the Indian Competition Act 2002 and Section 3(4) are expansion of Section 3(1) but are not exhaustive of the scope of Section 3(1) of the Indian Competition Act 2002."[166] Though the case was appealed and the penalty was reversed by the COMPAT,[167] the standalone applicability of Section 3(1) of Competition Act by the CCI as recognized in this case could bring any agreement between enterprises irrespective of their horizontal or vertical relations, if the agreement has AAEC in the market, within Section 3 infringement.

The Uber case brought in front of the CCI and NCLAT a different type of agreement that necessarily did not fit within the contours of Section 3(3) the Competition Act as they were not present at the same level of supply chain and 3(4) the Competition Act as Uber and the service providers were not present

---

[162] Competition Act, Section 3 (3).
[163] ibid., at Section 3 (4).
[164] CCI, Case no. 39 of 2012, *Hiranandani and Ramakant Kini vs. CCI*.
[165] ibid.
[166] ibid., at 135.
[167] Competition Appellate Tribunal New Delhi appeal no. 19 of 2014 Under Section 53-B of the Competition Act, 2002 against the order dated 5 February 2014 passed by the CCI in Case No. 39/2012.

at different levels of the same production chain as well.[168] However, it is unde-
batable that the business model in itself did not allow the service providers to
offer its services for a price lesser than what was fixed by the platform, that is,
Uber, even if they wanted. Hence, the business model did not allow the service
providers to compete with each other on prices which is essentially the goal of
competition law. Hence it was a commercial agreement that should have been
brought under Section 3(1) of the Competition Act to assess the appreciable
adverse effect it had on competition by basing itself on its own jurisprudence.
The argument that it could be consumer welfare enhancing could be assessed
while determining appreciable adverse effect factors mentioned under Section
19(3) of the Competition Act. However, the commission failed to take cognizance of the jurisprudence of Section 3(1) of the Competition Act to bring
Uber under the purview of competition law. Also, its wavering mind-set to
rely on standalone applicability of Section 3(1) the Competition Act post the
Ramakant Kini case[169] shows its reluctance in applying such an expansive
interpretation of the Section.[170]

3.1.3 Legislative gap under Section 3(3) of Competition Act

Under the India's legislative framework, the prohibition of anti-competitive
agreements is dealt under Section 3 Competition Act. It is modelled upon
Article 101 TFEU.[171] However, the regulation of an agreement presumed to

---

[168] As was held in a dissenting judgement by Gita Gouri, member of commission,
in the case *Hiranandani and Ramakant Kini vs. CCI.* She held the hospital as a platform which puts the doctors, stem cell banks and other services provided in the hospital
etc. in contact with the patients who are provided these services through the hospital as
a platform, hence it is a two sided market.

[169] *Hiranandani and Ramakant Kini vs. CCI.*

[170] ibid., at 189.

[171] The following shall be prohibited as incompatible with the internal market: all
agreements between undertakings, decisions by associations of undertakings and
concerted practices which may affect trade between Member States and which
have as their object or effect the prevention, restriction or distortion of competition within the internal market, and in particular those which:

(a) directly or indirectly fix purchase or selling prices or any other trading
conditions;

(b) limit or control production, markets, technical development, or
investment;

(c) share markets or sources of supply;

(d) apply dissimilar conditions to equivalent transactions with other trading
parties, thereby placing them at a competitive disadvantage;

(e) make the conclusion of contracts subject to acceptance by the other
parties of supplementary obligations which, by their nature or according to commercial usage, have no connection with the subject of such
contracts.

have AAEC under Indian competition law is stricter than in the European Union.

Article 101(2) TFEU states that any decision taken by or agreement shall be void. The legislators have not mentioned the concerted practices being presumed void.[172] However, under Indian law "any agreement, decision or practices carried on" shall be presumed to have affected the market adversely. Section 2 (b) of the Competition Act defines agreement which include any arrangement, understanding or action in concert. Section 3(3) of the Competition Act states

> [a]ny agreement entered into between enterprises or associations of enterprises or persons or associations of persons or between any person and enterprise or practice carried on, or decision taken by, any association of enterprises or association of persons, including cartels, engaged in identical or similar trade of goods or provision of services which shall limit prices or control output shall be presumed to have AAEC in the market.

Section 2 (b) read with Section 3(3) raises a presumption, against concerted practices automatically and considers them void.

Further, the scope of Section 3(3) of the Competition Act is extremely wide and does not only prohibit agreements which have been concluded through express communication but also communication that facilitates coordination or cooperation amongst the competing parties in any manner including exchange of commercially sensitive information. However, Section 3(3) of the Competition Act restricts itself to agreements, including exchange of information, amongst enterprises engaged in identical or similar trade of business. A traditional hub-and-spoke where the parties in the upstream level acting as

---

Any agreements or decisions prohibited pursuant to this Article shall be automatically void.
The provisions of paragraph 1 may, however, be declared inapplicable in the case of:
- any agreement or category of agreements between undertakings,
- any decision or category of decisions by associations of undertakings,
- any concerted practice or category of concerted practices, which contributes to improving the production or distribution of goods or to promoting technical or economic progress, while allowing consumers a fair share of the resulting benefit, and which does not:
  (a)   impose on the undertakings concerned restrictions which are not indispensable to the attainment of these objectives;
  (b)   afford such undertakings the possibility of eliminating competition in respect of a substantial part of the products in question.

[172] Jose Rivas, 'Why does Article 101(2) TFEU not List Concerted Practises?' (2013) *Kluwer Competition Law Blog*, available at http://competitionlawblog.kluwercomp etitionlaw.com/2013/04/23/ (accessed 30 June 2022).

hub are either manufacturer/supplier/dealer and are facilitating a collusion in the downstream level amongst their retailers (spokes) shall be considered to be a part of such agreement and covered under Section 3(3) of the Competition Act. The definite mention of identical or similar trade of goods might not cover within its ambit a third-party provider who is neither in the similar or identical trade of business but is a party absolutely unrelated to the trade.

The problem might arise where the hub is absolutely in an unrelated business to that of spokes or is merely acting as a platform where sellers and buyers meet. This category of hub-and-spoke have become more prevalent wherein competing companies at the same level of supply chain adopt similar algorithms from the same third-party or use the third-party to facilitate collusion amongst them or acts as a platform and fixes prices on behalf of the competitors causing price parallelism and hence needs address.

3.1.4   The future of hub-and-spoke in India, the Competition Bill 2020

The CCI recently proposed, in the Competition Bill 2020, to amend the existing Competition Act. The Competition Bill 2020 recommends to amend Section 3(3) of the Competition Act to include the following proviso:

> Provided further that an enterprise or association of enterprises or person or association of persons though not engaged in identical or similar trade shall be presumed to be part of the agreement under this sub-Section if it actively participates in the furtherance of such an agreement.[173]

The new proviso has expressly brought within its sweep hub-and-spoke conspiracies and has categorically stated that such conspiracies shall be presumed to have appreciable adverse effect in the market. This new proviso would bring a lot of clarity to how hub-and-spoke must be treated under Indian law. The proviso has further clarified the irrelevance of the hub's existence in similar or identical trade and has qualified any party who plays an intervening role in facilitating collusion to be a part of such agreement even if in unrelated business, hence having presumed appreciable adverse effect in the market. India remains one of the only jurisdictions to have mentioned such prohibition emphatically in its legislative mandate and thereby placing hub-and-spoke arrangement under "restriction by object doctrine".[174]

---

[173] Provided further that enterprise or association of enterprises or persons or association of persons though not engaged in identical or similar trade shall be presumed to be part of the agreement under this sub-Section if it actively participates in furtherance of such an agreement.

[174] It has been brought under Section 3(3) read with Section 3(1) which deals with agreements presumed to have appreciable adverse effect in the market and have the

The proviso has also drawn a difference between an active hub and a third party who is a mere facilitator. The above discussion is raised in the initial part of the chapter where the author has tried to differentiate between a hub and a third-party facilitator. The proviso states "if it actively participates in the furtherance of such an agreement" thereby expressly limiting the application of the future Section 3(3) to those third parties who take an active interest in furthering the goal of restricting competition in the market.[175] However, what still remains debatable is when do we say that a third party has become a hub and/or falls short of becoming a hub.

The proposed amendment to Section 3 of the Competition Act[176] explicitly mentions the need for active participation in the furtherance of an anti-competitive agreement. This could be interpreted to mean that the law recognizes the difference between the active role of a hub and the passive role of a third party. As per the proviso only the hub, which plays an active role could be considered a party to the agreement, would be indicted under Section 3 of the Competition Act.

Most of the hub-and-spoke cases in various jurisdictions have had a hub who is either active or has more than a passive role in facilitating collusion. The hub has taken up various roles. It was determined the hubs' responsibilities in a collusion has been more than a mere bystander.

The hubs have either acted as retailors/manufacturers/distributors who have actively fixed prices at the downstream level/upstream level. For instance in the *Interstate Circuit* case[177] or *Toys 'R' Us* case,[178] both Interstate Circuit and Toys 'R' US, respectively at the downstream and upstream level of the supply chain, fixed prices at a different level to facilitate collusion. In some cases, hub acts as a broker who can fix prices on behalf of their client to receive higher commission or reward payments. For instance, in *Re: Insurance Brokerage Antitrust Litigation*, insurance brokers acted in a dual role. They were both consultants to the customers taking insurance and producers for the insurers.[179]

---

effect of restricting competition by the very purpose of their existence and hence are void.

[175] A hub may be considered an active party when it partakes any commercial or economic interest in the activities of the spokes.

[176] Provided further that enterprise or association of enterprises or persons or association of persons though not engaged in identical or similar trade shall be presumed to be part of the agreement under this sub-Section if it actively participates in furtherance of such an agreement.

[177] *Interstate Circuit, Inc. vs. United States*, 306 U.S. 208 (1939).

[178] *Toys 'R' Us, Inc. vs. Federal Trade Commission*, Seventh Circuit No. 98-4107 (1999).

[179] William Kolasky and Kathryn McNeece, 'Contingent Commissions and the Antitrust Laws: What Can We learn from the In: Re Insurance Brokerage Antitrust Litigation?' (2015) 108 (2619) *Antitrust & Trade Regulation Report* 6.

They helped the insurers in bid rigging, allocating customers and exchanged commercially sensitive information to receive higher commission. The third type of role that a hub can assume is that of an interested third-party facilitator who though not related to the business in the affected market has some interest in inducing anti-competitive activity in that market. For instance, in the *Apple E-Book* case, Apple (hub) wanted to launch an iBook store and facilitated collusion by fixing prices amongst book publishers through MFN clauses and exchanged information between the publishers in order to compete with Amazon who had already established Kindle.

In all the above roles assumed by the hub, the hub has always had an incentive to facilitate collusion in a different market. What constitutes an active role of a hub in collusion could be deciphered from the assumption of an incentive theory. The author suggests that what constitutes an active role shall be determined on a case to case basis keeping in mind the incentive for the third-party to involve itself in such an anti-competitive activity and the kind of role it has played in encouraging collusion.[180] Transposing this theory to the situation where the third-party is a mere algorithm provider and no more, if it actively participates in facilitating collusion for receiving kickback payments or some part of the increased joint profit, then the third-party can be assumed to have an interventionist role in the collusion and must be treated similar to horizontal parties. If the algorithm provider does no more than providing algorithm to the competing parties, it is unlikely that the act of the third party shall be considered a part of hub-and-spoke conspiracy. The other standard that could be used to determine the liability of a hub could be inferred from the standard laid down in the *AC Treuhand* case, which states:

> to contribute to the common objectives pursued, and that the undertaking in question was aware of the substantive conduct planned or implemented by other undertakings or that it could reasonably have foreseen that conduct and that it was ready to accept the attendant risk.[181]

Unlike in the European Union, where guidelines determine that the type, nature and length of infringement should be taken into consideration on an individual basis while imposing fines on the parties,[182] the Competition Act has

---

[180] This shall take into account exchange of commercially sensitive information, through the hub, setting the algorithms by collecting all data from competing companies and using the same input feed, being told to monitor the deviating parties and inform other parties of the deviation if any, sanctioning the deviating parties, imposing discount control mechanisms, consciously facilitating price fixing etc.

[181] Case C-194/14 P, *AC-Treuhand AG v. European Commission*.

[182] Guidelines on the method of setting fines imposed pursuant to Article 23(2)(a) of Regulation No 1/2003 (2006/C 210/02).

no such provision in law. However, this way of calculating the fine has been established through jurisprudence. In the case of *Dry-Cell Batteries*,[183] the CCI levied penalties on individual enterprises keeping in mind their market share and how far they could dictate the terms of the anti-competitive conduct. The same standard can also be followed wherein the fine imposed on the third party shall be determined on a case to case basis as per the role of the hub in aiding and easing collusion.

Should India adopt the public distancing approach as in the Eturas case to deal with indirect information exchange?
India's stance on information exchange is the proof of exchange of commercially sensitive information and the "commitment standard" for it to come within the purview of alleged horizontal agreement.[184] The EU's stance before the *Eturas* case was also similar. However, the *Eturas* case changed the subtleties for cases involving pricing algorithms. The approach adopted by the commission reiterated the ANIC presumption with more objectivity.[185] The court in the case mentioned various ways in which public distancing can be effected: first, oppose such a concerted move to all the alleged concerting parties; second, inform the administrator and the users of the site; third, inform the competition authorities of such an act; fourth, apply the discount above the cap repeatedly.[186] The effectiveness of the first option is doubtful particularly in platform collusion where the parties might not know the other concerting parties. However, the second and the third option shall help meet the goal of public distancing. The fourth option could be feasible but it might also strictly mean that the party is trying to cheat on the cartel.[187] The second impediment to giving discounts above the mandated cap would also mean additional technical

---

[183] CCI, Suo Motu Case No. 03 of 2017, In Re: Anticompetitive conduct in the Dry-Cell Batteries Market in India.

[184] Comments (n. 117 above).

[185] Available at: https://eur-lex.europa.eu/legal-content/EN/TXT/HTML/?uri= CELEX:61992CJ0049&from=EN (accessed 30 June 2022). As is clear from the very terms of Article 85(1) of the Treaty (now Article 81(1) EC), a concerted practice implies, besides undertakings' concerting together, conduct on the market pursuant to those collusive practices, and a relationship of cause and effect between the two. Subject to proof to the contrary, which it is for the economic operators concerned to adduce, there must be a presumption that the undertakings participating in concerting arrangements and remaining active on the market take account of the information exchanged with their competitors when determining their conduct on that market, particularly when they concert together on a regular basis over a long period.

[186] *"Eturas" UAB and Others*. Katri Havu and Neža Zupančič, 'Case Comment: Collusion and Online Platforms in Eturas' (2016) 11(2) *Comp. Law Rev.* 255.

[187] van Roozendaal (n. 2 above).

changes to be done by the party which in all circumstances a party might not be willing to undertake.

For public distancing, the burden of proof is often reversed and imposed on the companies present at the meetings. The reversal of burden of proof does not conflict with the presumption of innocence where the parties had reasonable opportunity to rebut the presumption without taking extraordinary steps or was not too difficult.[188] For instance, in *Boel vs. Commission*,[189] the companies who attended the meetings where commercially sensitive information was exchanged,[190] the onus was on the parties to prove that they had taken sufficient steps to publicly distance themselves from what was discussed in the meetings or they informed authorities of the nature of the meetings.[191] The Competition Act could also apply the reversal of burden of proof standard in order to deal with scenarios arising from hub-and-spoke arrangement.

3.2 The Predictable Agent Scenario

The predictable agent scenario refers to a situation where enterprises employ algorithms in such a way that produces a predictable outcome and reacts in a given way to changing market conditions, in the absence of adequate evidence to establish any kind of an agreement between the enterprises.[192] Therefore, the characteristic features of a predictable agent set up would be the presence of a unilateral development or deployment of an algorithm by an enterprise, to accomplish an intended result with the knowledge that there might be other similarly developed algorithms in the market used by its competitors, without any joint understanding to collude. For the purpose of the following analysis, the author assumes the base conditions of algorithmic tacit collusion as posited by Ezrachi and Stucke.[193]

One of the conundrums brought about by the advent of algorithm driven pricing is that it expands the characteristics of the "oligopoly problem" to any type of digital market. As noted by various scholars, there can be "conscious parallelism" or "oligopolistic interdependence" in certain circumstances where

---

[188] *"Eturas" UAB and Others. Sodhi Transport Co. & another vs. State of UP and another*, 1986 AIR 1099.

[189] Case T-142/89, *Usines Gustave Boël SA vs. Commission of the European Communities* ECLI:EU:T:1995:63.

[190] (i) The nature of the information being exchanged; (ii) the structure of the market in which the counterparts participate; and (iii) whether the information exchange is likely to improve transparency within this market.

[191] Nicholls (n. 125 above).

[192] ibid.

[193] Ariel Ezrachi and Maurice E. Strucke, 'Sustainable and Unchallenged Algorithmic Tacit Collusion' (2020) 17(2) *Nw. J. Tech. & Intel. Prop.* 217.

enterprises might be able to coordinate their price without colluding in the conventional sense.[194] Due to the high interdependence, it has been theorized that players in an oligopolistic market would invariably attempt to match each other's price.[195] With the algorithms, competitors can constantly monitor each other's price and immediately retaliate without any time lag,[196] if one of the competitors attempt to undercut the price. Further, the ease at which information exchange can be facilitated in the digital market makes regulation of the same next to impossible. Thus, any attempt at reduction of price by once competitor would invariably force other players to imitate the same thus placing all the competitors at a disadvantage with none having any real benefit. This extreme price transparency neutralizes any incentive to compete and would rather push the players to maintain a supra competitive pricing sustained by a tacit collusion.[197]

The issue with enforcement, however, lies in bringing such a tacit collusion within the sweep of Section 3 of the Competition Act. Like most jurisdictions, not all forms of parallel behaviour are prohibited by the Competition Act. Parallelism caused as a product of independent and unilateral actions by the competitors remains to be outside the scope of the Competition Act. As provided in the analysis above for "action in concert", parallelism can be prohibited as tacit collusion only when it is possible to establish "meeting of minds" through plus factors. So far, CCI has been relying on factors such as parallelism in distribution and production, correlation between price change and meeting/communication among the competitors and other similar factors to establish a meeting of minds.[198] However, in terms of the change in market dynamics brought about by algorithms, these factors may no longer be indicative of an active conspiracy.[199] Thus, the requirement of establishing meeting of minds poses practical difficulties in effectively tackling algorithmic tacit

---

[194] Richard A. Posner, *Antitrust Law* (2nd edn, University of Chicago Press, 2001) at 52–3. Also see JA Rahl, 'Conspiracy and the Anti-Trust Laws' (1950) 44 *U. Ill. L. Rev.* 743.

[195] Edward J. Green, Robert C. Marshall, and Leslie M. Marx, 'Tacit Collusion in Oligopoly' in Roger D. Blair and Daniel D. Sokol (eds.), *Oxford Handbook of International Antitrust Economics* (Vol 2., Oxford University Press 2014) at 464.

[196] Richard A. Posner argued in his 1968 article 'Oligopoly and the Antitrust Laws: A Suggested Approach', that the presence of time lag between the price leader and rest of the oligopolistic players would still afford the former an advantage. Posner (n. 28 above).

[197] Ezrachi and Stucke (n. 91 above).

[198] *All India Tires Dealers Federation vs. Tire Manufacturers*; *Builders Association of India vs. Cement Manufacturers' Association.*

[199] As such, CCI has been inconsistent in its approach towards plus factors. See supra notes 42 and 116.

collusion although the language of Section 3 of the Competition Act is wide enough to cover the same.

In the predictable agent setup, there is conscious parallelism at the human level, where the enterprises deploy their corresponding pricing algorithm being fully aware that their competitors are likely to do the same.[200] The enterprises are able to program (unilaterally) the logic behind the pricing algorithm such that it yields increased profit. In so programming the algorithm, each enterprise knows that a favourable strategy would be to follow the price increase of others and they are also aware that other competitors could opt for a similar program.[201] It could also be the case where all the enterprises use the same algorithm purchased from a third party thereby making the outcome more predictable.[202] Thus, a supra competitive pricing can be sustained through unilateral actions of the enterprises which may only fall under the conventional understanding of conscious parallelism, and if so would fall outside the scope of Section 3 of the Competition Act for failure to establish meeting of minds.

However, a peculiar feature of this setup is the "knowledge" or "awareness" component. When the enterprises program the algorithms to match the prices of their competitors, with the knowledge that there is a high likelihood their competitors would do the same and should there be a reciprocal action from its competitors, shouldn't such reciprocal mindset be construed as a meeting of minds. The assumption of awareness or knowledge of the competitors is arguably not misplaced since it is a very predictable behaviour in a highly transparent digital market. The commonality of awareness among the competitors coupled with the likelihood of reciprocation that is commensurate with an algorithm driven digital market places an expectation in the minds of the enterprises that their competitors would likely act in the same way. This mutual expectation can be read as a "meeting of minds". The wide definition of agreement under the Competition Act would, in the opinion of the author, allow room for such an interpretation. This notion has also been characterized as a "unilateral contract" which would be construed more as an agreement than as individual behaviour.[203]

Thus, in an algorithmic driven digital market as described above, owing to the peculiar market conditions and awareness of the enterprises which are commonplace in such a market, India can seriously consider an amendment to introduce a reversal of burden of proof where,[204] instead of presuming the

---

[200] Ezrachi and Stucke (n. 91 above).
[201] ibid.
[202] ibid.
[203] Posner (n. 28 above) at 1576.
[204] Such reversal of burden of has already been proposed by various authors in the context of presuming the adverse effects of a collusive act. See Ezrachi and Stucke

AAEC of such parallel actions, it presumes the existence of meeting of minds. Thus, this proposal stipulates that in the face of a parallel behaviour among competitors in a digital market, the DG only needs to establish the AAEC of such parallel behaviour, upon which the CCI would presume the existence of the meeting of minds among the competitors. Needless to say, this presumption would be a rebuttable one in accordance with the existing jurisprudence on presumptions[205] and the accused enterprises must be allowed a reasonable opportunity to justify their conduct to be a unilateral business decision motivated by market forces and not just a mindless mirroring of the competitors' pricing to achieve supra-competitive profits.

To further augment the justifications as to the presumption of "meeting of minds" and the corresponding reversal of burden of proof, it must be pointed out that, unlike the digital eye scenario, the enterprises consciously design the algorithm in such a way that collusion is a very likely and predictable outcome. This aspect on part of the enterprises calls for a more stringent approach in enquiry against algorithmic collusions.

This proposal can be problematic at a first glance. Due to the frequency with which such parallel behaviour may occur, some have even observed that a presumption as to underlying communication between the enterprises may not be readily accepted and industrial awareness may not be adequate to substitute meeting of minds.[206] However, the rules of the game that governed the brick and mortar world have significantly changed in the context of digital markets ruled by algorithms, thus necessitating a more radical approach in tackling algorithmic tacit collusion. The proposal must certainly be scrutinized so as to not dampen innovation in the market, which can only be achieved through more deliberation on presuming "meeting of minds" and ameliorating any adverse side effects of the same. However, such an approach should not be discarded without giving its due place in the discourse of regulating digital markets.

3.3   The Digital Eye or Self-Learning Scenario

The fourth category of algorithmic collusion identified by Ezrachi and Stucke[207] is their digital eye scenario, here referred to as a self-learning scenario. In this scenario, enterprises use self-learning algorithms to maximize their profits or accomplish similar targets. A self-learning algorithm is one

---

(n. 193 above) at 258. But such a presumption of AAEC already exists in India. See Section 3 (3) of the Competition Act.

[205]   *Sodhi Transport Co. & another vs. State of UP and another*, 1986 AIR 1099.

[206]   Ezrachi and Strucke (n. 193 above).

[207]   Ezrachi and Stucke (n 58 above) at 1782.

where, in addition to the initial inputs entered into it, the algorithm learns from its own experiences. Further, the scenario contemplates that the enterprises, though are aware that tacit collusion could be one of the possible outcomes, do not necessarily intended it.[208] The enterprise using a self-learning algorithm is often only able to set the targets to be accomplished (such as profit maximization) by the algorithm with having little to no control over how the targets are achieved by it. The algorithms, having the ability to learn and improve from its experiences, has the potential to observe the patterns of other pricing algorithm used by the competitors and deem it optimal to coordinate a supra competitive price in a sustainable way. This situation poses unique problems since the self-learning algorithms are able to produce collusive outputs through coordination at an AI level. As OEDC observed in its 2017 report, "[i]t is still not clear how machine learning algorithms may actually reach a collusive outcome."[209] Due to the nature of these self-learning algorithms, the collusive outcome can be achieved with very little inputs from the enterprises, which may be regarded as too indirect or remote to attribute any liability on the enterprises for the collusive act of the algorithm. Thus, an anti-competitive collusion can be achieved in the absence of any kind of agreement or common intent among the competing enterprises.[210]

Unlike the predictable agent set up, where the enterprises knowingly employ an algorithm with complete awareness as to a predictable possibility of a collusive outcome being reached, thereby providing a basis to infer an intent to collude, the digital eye scenario operates in the absence of any such intent, thus rendering any consequential tacit collusion as an unintended by-product. This being the case, it has been viewed that such anti-competitive collusions of self-learning algorithms may escape legal scrutiny.[211]

3.3.1   Are algorithms colluding in the sense of Section 3(3) of the Competition Act?

The unique automated nature of self-learning algorithms creates a situation that could potentially be unregulated by the Competition Act in its present existence. When two or more enterprises employ a self-learning algorithm that is programmed to optimize profit, it is possible that these algorithms while considering the various factors to fix prices, may commonly discover conscious parallelism as a sustainable strategy to maintain supra-competitive prices. As noted in the predictable agent set up, it is also possible that the enter-

---

[208] ibid, at 1795.
[209] OECD (n. 75 above).
[210] Ezrachi and Stucke (n. 58 above) at 1783.
[211] ibid., at 1796.

prises procured the self-learning algorithm from the same algorithm developer, thereby increasing the likelihood of tacit collusion amongst the algorithms since there would be a lot of similarity in its programming. Further, due to the algorithm's ability to constantly monitor the other algorithms' prices and retaliate in the event of an undercut by one of the competitors, enforcing the parallelism is significantly easier. For the same reasons, the other self-learning algorithms would eventually learn that undercutting the prices is never profitable and would begin to reasonably expect reciprocation in the event of a price increase. Thus, the algorithms, conscious that parallelism would yield supra-competitive profit and reasonably certain that reciprocity is exercised by the other algorithm, would be indulging in an anti-competitive agreement in terms of Section 3 (3) of the Competition Act. There is one single requirement not covered: an algorithm is neither an enterprise nor a person.

In India, the requirement of agreement, despite its broad definition, requires that it be entered into by enterprises or persons, both of which have been defined under the Competition Act.[212] Thus, an agreement purely between

---

[212] Section 2 (h)of the Competition Act states that "enterprise" means a person or a department of the Government, who or which is, or has been, engaged in any activity, relating to the production, storage, supply, distribution, acquisition or control of articles or goods, or the provision of services, of any kind, or in investment, or in the business of acquiring, holding, underwriting or dealing with shares, debentures or other securities of any other body corporate, either directly or through one or more of its units or divisions or subsidiaries, whether such unit or division or subsidiary is located at the same place where the enterprise is located or at a different place or at different places, but does not include any activity of the Government relatable to the sovereign functions of the Government; Section (L) of the Indian Competition At 2002 states that "person" includes –

(i)	an individual;
(ii)	a Hindu undivided family;
(iii)	a company;
(iv)	a firm;
(v)	an association of persons or a body of individuals, whether incorporated or not, in India or outside India;
(vi)	any corporation established by or under any Central, State or Provincial Act or a Government company as defined in Section 617 of the Companies Act, 1956 (1 of 1956);
(vii)	anybody corporate incorporated by or under the laws of a country outside India;
(viii)	a co-operative society registered under any law relating to co-operative societies;
(ix)	a local authority;
(x)	every artificial juridical person, not falling within any of the preceding sub-clauses;

algorithms without it being attributable to the enterprises would not trigger Section 3 of the Competition Act.

Therefore, an amendment in the Competition Act is needed to cover situations of anti-competitive collusions orchestrated by deep learning algorithms. Bearing in mind the peculiarities of the digital market and the ease with which collusion can be affected by use of algorithms, it would be naïve on part of India to hold on to a provision prohibiting anti-competitive agreements that was designed for the brick and mortar markets. An easy approach would be to enforce a complete prohibition on the use of deep learning algorithms since it is near impossible to regulate and control the way they operate. Further, the law in its present form may be inadequate to place any liability on the enterprise that uses such an algorithm. However, such a move would be a step backward for businesses considering that there is a general shift of marketplaces from the brick and mortar world to the digital platforms across all industries. Hence there is a necessity to explore innovative solutions for harmonizing dependency on deep learning algorithms and a need for maintaining pro-competitive equilibrium in the market.

3.3.2   Can the liability be shifted to the enterprise?

The problem posed by the self-learning algorithms to competition regimes all over the world is novel, unique and evolving. This being the case, any solution devised to allay the challenges posed by the digital eye scenario should also be innovative and adaptable to the dynamic nature of the digital market. An angle worth considering to make the enterprise accountable for the actions of its algorithm would be the principles of agency under contract law. Accordingly, if the algorithm can be said to be an autonomous agent of the enterprise, the enterprise can be made liable for the actions of the agent. However, the biggest hurdle to make this theory practicable is the grant of personhood to the algorithms so that they may qualify as agents of the enterprise.

The essence of the principle of agency is encapsulated by the Latin maxim *qui facit per alium facit per se*, which means "he who acts through another does the act himself". Under the Indian Contract Act of 1872 (Contract Act), the law governing agency is covered under Chapter 10.[213] As per the provisions of the Chapter 10, an agent is a person employed to do an act for another or to represent another in dealings with third persons.[214] The Contract Act further

---

(xi)   "practice" includes all activities carried on by the departments of the Central Government dealing with atomic energy, currency, defence and space.

[213] Chapter 10 of the Indian Contract Act comprises Sections 182 to 238.

[214] Section 182 of the Contract Act 1857 states that "agent" and "principal" defined: "An agent is a person employed to do any act for another, or to represent another in

describes who may be an agent under Section 184, which imposes additional requirements as to the age and mental soundness of the agent. The term "person" is not defined under the Contract Act,[215] but the Competition Act provides for a wide definition of "person".[216] However, as per the definition an algorithm would not fit in any of the categories mentioned therein, except for the final category of "artificial juristic person" provided that India considers favourably passing an amendment recognizing self-learning algorithms as an artificial juristic person and as an agent of the enterprise employing it.

The grant of personhood for artificial intelligence (AI) is a debate in itself. With the increase in use of automation in several industries coupled with advancements in AI, jurisdiction across the globe ought to seriously think about its stance on granting personhood to AI to navigate across an array of legal issues concerning the same including determining the liability of their actions and several experts have already theorized the pros and cons for the same.[217] If AI and self-learning algorithms are considered persons, they could be regarded as an agent of the enterprise that employed it and thus make the latter liable for its actions, including violations under competition law.

Section 188 of the Contract Act does raise a concern since it provides that the extent of authority of an agent is "to do every lawful thing which is necessary in order" to do the act entrusted to it. Therefore, one could argue that the autonomous agent (self-learning algorithm) choosing to unlawfully collude in fixing prices would be outside the scope of the law and thus fail to transfer the liability onto the principal (enterprise). However, the provision was drafted keeping in mind a person capable of knowing what is lawful and unlawful on his/her own, and acting with reasonable care so as to not breach any law. In case of an algorithm, it can only be programmed to abide by the laws. Therefore, care must be taken by the enterprise or the developer to program the algorithms in such a way that it does not violate the provisions of competition act. Failure to program the algorithms accordingly must result in liability. This approach might be regarded as farfetched without more analysis as to the

---

dealings with third persons. The person for whom such act is done, or who is so represented, is called the principal."

[215] When a term is not defined in a particular legislation the practice is to adopt the definition provided for the term in the General Clauses Act of 1977. The said act defines a person (in Section 2 (30) of the General Clauses Act) to include any company or association or body of individuals, whether incorporated or not. However, the author relies on the definition of 'person' in the competition act for the purpose of the present analysis.

[216] Competition Act, Section 2 (L).

[217] Samir Chopra and Laurence White, "Artificial Agents' Personhood in Law and Philosophy' (2004) (Proceedings of the 16th European Conference on Artificial Intelligence, Valencia, 22–27 August 2014) at 635.

exact way in which such pricing algorithms are designed and the ramifications of granting personhood to such algorithms or deeming them to be agents of enterprises as a legal fiction. However, while treading on unchartered territories of legal conundrums such as the self-learning algorithms, it is necessary that all avenues of solutions are explored. There are other suggestions such as implementing "algorithm by design" and establishing specialized agencies to monitor and investigate algorithmic collusion in detail. They are discussed in greater detail in the recommendation Section.

4   CONCLUSION

For any legal system to withstand the test of time it must be able to adapt to the changing contours of science and society. This is particularly true for Competition Law given the dynamic nature of the markets and its rapid expansion into the digital platforms. The digitization of trade and businesses have without a doubt contributed to the betterment of commerce and consumer welfare. But the advent of these innovations brings along with it a new set of problems that were not envisaged while the antitrust framework was formulated in India, thereby creating a dire need for timely reforms in its approach to algorithms.

India's response to the emerging problems for algorithmic collusion is still nascent and short-sighted. In terms of the legislation, the Competition Act, 2002 requires significant amendments so as to bring algorithmic collusions within the sweep of Section 3 and to vest the statutory agencies with the necessary powers to effectively investigate collusion on digital platforms. While the Competition Amendment Act, 2020 is certainly a step forward, it has limited itself only to the issue of hub-and-spoke, thereby leaving much to be desired in addressing issues of tacit algorithmic collusions and regulation of self-learning algorithms. Considering the practical impediments in proving the element of "agreement" in an algorithmic set up, it is also necessary to seriously consider a presumption as to the existence of "meeting of minds", when parallel conduct has an AAEC in the digital markets. Further, the commission should match the technological influx in the market with its own dedicated digital wing, screening algorithms and periodic market studies to pro-actively detect collusive patterns in the digital markets.

Given the enigmatic nature of the algorithm problem, there may yet be new dimensions to the adverse impact it may have on competition. Therefore, it is imperative that the CCI and NCLAT be mindful of the same and consider a more liberal approach in interpreting the provisions of the Competition Act such that the issues arising out of algorithmic collusions are adequately dealt with. Thus, a coordinated effort by all three organs of the government – the legislature, the executive and the judiciary, is necessary to ensure that the benefits accrued from a strong competitive digital market reach the consumers.

6. Challenges brought by and in response to algorithms: the perspective of China's Anti-Monopoly Law

Wei Han, Yajie Gao and Ai Deng[1]

1   INTRODUCTION

It has only been around 15 years since the Anti-Monopoly Law of the PRC (AML) came into effect in 2008.[2] During the same period, China's digital economy has seen strong growth. A large percentage of companies in this nascent industry are data- or algorithm-driven. One such example is Toutiao, a Chinese content platform and its popular 'personalized recommendation' product. However, innovative products also come with their risks. In early 2018, the so-called 'Shashu' phenomenon was one of the most hotly debated topics in China. 'Shashu' refers to algorithmic price discrimination by online platforms where longer-term consumers are charged less favourable prices,[3]

---

[1]   This chapter draws heavily from a previous article 'Algorithmic Price Discrimination on Online Platforms and Antitrust Enforcement in China's Digital Economy' published by the Antitrust Source (Wei Han, Yajie Gao and Ai Deng, August 2018) and the presentation titled 'Challenges Brought by and Response to Algorithmic Collusion: China's Perspective' (Wei Han, Yajie Gao) for the 'Collusion, Algorithms and Competition Law' conference held in Kyushu University on 23 November 2019.

[2]   The 2008 Anti-Monopoly Law of the PRC was amended by the Standing Committee of the National People's Congress in June 2022. For comments on the amended law, please find: Han Wei, Li Liang, *The New Anti-Monopoly Law of the People's Republic of China: Changes and Remaining Issues*, CPI Columns, Asia, August 2022

[3]   Based on 120 times of hailing a taxi through Meituan, an experiment shows that, on average, longer-term consumers pay 3.1 per cent more than newly registered consumers. 'Big Data Shashu? Experiment Shows Didi Charges 70 per cent Higher Than Expected and Meituan Charges Longer-Term Users 3 per cert More Expensive' *view.inews.qq.com* (9 June 2021), available at https://view.inews.qq.com/wxn2/20210609V0919H00 (in Chinese) (accessed 30 June 2022). With support of algorithms and big data on consumers' online activities, online platforms could easily obtain consumers' profiles, thus providing personalized products and/or services, such as charg-

a practice suspected of constituting abuse of dominance.[4] In addition to price discrimination, algorithms might also facilitate collusion,[5] although discrimination through algorithms has attracted more public attention in China.

The Chinese authorities have taken a cautious regulatory position in the digital economy. Abuse of dominance or anti-competitive agreement directly involving algorithms has yet been investigated nor sanctioned by the Chinese competition authority. The Government Working Reports delivered during the 'Two Sessions'[6] in three consecutive years (2017, 2018 and 2019) made it clear that the Chinese government intends to encourage innovation and promote the healthy development of nascent industries by formulating regulatory rules that are 'tolerant and prudent'.[7] Indeed, in the past few years,

---

ing higher prices to longer-term consumers because of longer usage history, stronger reliance on the platform accordingly and less reluctance to turn to rivals. Please be noted that 'Shashu' is not a legal phrase and the definition provided in the main text is only a literal interpretation of '杀熟'. In China, 'Shashu' covers more general discrimination, such as criminatory prices based on different smart phone configurations. For example: Beijing Consumer Association, 'Beijing Consumer Association Releases the Survey Results of Internet Consumption Big Data "Shashu" Problem' (1 March 2022), available at www.bj315.org/xfdc/202203/t20220301_32335.shtml (in Chinese) (accessed 30 June 2022)

[4]   Anti-Monopoly Law of the People's Republic of China, adopted at the 29th Meeting of the Standing Committee of the National People's Congress (30 August 2007) (AML), Article 17 (1), 'Undertakings holding dominant market positions are prohibited from doing the following by abusing their dominant market positions: ... (6) without justifiable reasons, applying differential prices and other transaction terms among their trading counterparts who are on an equal footing ...'

[5]   Terrell McSweeny and Brian O'Dea, 'The Implications of Algorithmic Pricing for Coordinated Effects Analysis and Price Discrimination Markets in Antitrust Enforcement' (2017) 32 *Antitrust* 75, 79.

[6]   'Two Sessions' is the abbreviation of the 'National People's Congress of the People's Republic of China' and the 'Chinese People's Political Consultative Conference', which is the most important political event in China held every March since 1959. Representatives of the 'Two Sessions' gather, summarize and transmit information and requests from the Chinese people to the Communist Party of China.

[7]   Chinese Central Government, 'Government Working Report - Delivered by LI Keqiang, Premier of the State Council' (5th Session of the 12th National People's Congress on 16 March 2017), available at www.gov.cn/guowuyuan/2017-03/16/content_5177940.htm (in Chinese) (accessed 30 June 2022), holding that 'We will formulate regulatory rules for nascent industries in keeping with the principle of encouraging innovation and conducting regulation in a tolerant and prudent way, and guide and promote the healthy development of emerging industries ...'; Chinese Central Government, 'Government Working Report - Delivered by LI Keqiang, Premier of the State Council' (1st Session of the 13th National People's Congress on 5 March 2018), available at www.gov.cn/zhuanti/2018lh/2018zfgzbg/zfgzbg.htm (in Chinese) (accessed 30 June 2022); Chinese Central Government, 'Government Working Report - Delivered by LI Keqiang, Premier of the State Council' (2nd Session of the 13th

the Chinese authorities have closely followed the principle of 'tolerance and prudence' in regulating the digital economy.

Against the backdrop of the 'tolerance and prudence' regulatory principle, algorithmic pricing has nevertheless garnered significant public interest and has recently caught the attention of regulators. In May 2018, Mao Zhang, the head of the State Administration for Market Regulation (SAMR) by then, published an article, in which 'Shashu' was listed as one of the regulatory challenges.[8] The public, on the other hand, has called for timely anti-monopoly enforcement. For example, in 2017, a Chinese lawyer brought a complaint against Apple, alleging abuse of dominance by Apple in running its App Store.[9] Some have also paid attention to the potential 'price collusion' through algorithm by online car-hailing platforms.[10] Indeed, 'algorithmic collusion' is among the buzz phrases in academic discussions in recent years.

The rest of the chapter is organized as follows. In Section 2, we introduce China's anti-monopoly legislation in relation to anti-competitive agreement and abuse of market dominance. Section 3 discusses both *status quo* and relevant challenges with respect to the enforcement in the two areas above. We discuss remedies in Section 4 and our proposals in Section 5. Section 6 concludes.

2   LEGISLATION

2.1   Algorithmic Price Discrimination

The legal basis for regulating price discrimination in the AML is the prohibition of abuse of dominance, not price discrimination *per se*. Article 22 AML lists a series of prohibited conduct, including 'without justifiable reasons, undertakings holding dominant market position are prohibited from applying differential prices and other transaction terms among their trading counter-

---

National People's Congress on 5 March 2019), available at www.gov.cn/premier/2019 -03/16/content_5374314.htm (in Chinese) (accessed 30 June 2022).

[8]   Mao Zhang, 'Push Forward the Reform and Innovation of Market Supervision' (2 May 2018), available at www.gov.cn/xinwen/2018-05/02/content_5287445.htm (in Chinese) (accessed 30 June 2022).

[9]   Jing Wan, 'Chinese Lawyer Complains About Apple's Suspected Monopoly – Comments Made by Experts on Side Effects Brought by Suspected Abuse of Dominant Market Position' *Legal Daily* (10 August 2017), available at www.legaldaily.com .cn/index_article/content/2017-08/10/content_7277805.htm?node=5955 (in Chinese) (accessed 30 June 2022).

[10]   For example, Jiayi Wang, 'Price Monopoly Issues in Relation to the Application of Computing Algorithms' (in Chinese) (Master Thesis, Shanghai International Studies University 2018).

parts who are on an equal footing'. Article 19 of the Interim Provisions on Prohibiting Abuse of Dominant Market Position[11] enacted by the SAMR in July 2019 provides more detailed guidance by explicitly listing discriminatory conduct and justifiable reasons. It also defines the term 'equal footing'.[12]

Discrimination is often associated with unfairness. Indeed, some in China criticize algorithmic discrimination, such as 'Shashu' through big data, precisely from the perspective of fairness.[13] But how should the question of fairness be addressed in competition enforcement? The Roundtable on Price Discrimination held by the Organisation for Economic Co-operation and Development (OECD) in 2016 identified three different effects of price discrimination, '(1) it can exclude rivals and thereby lead to the exploitation of consumers; (2) it can exploit consumers directly; and (3) in upstream markets, it can exploit intermediate customers and create distortionary effects that harm consumers in downstream markets'. The Roundtable emphasized that '[i]n each case, it is the effect on consumers, and not the fairness of the discrimination, that determines the acceptability of the discrimination'.[14] In other words, competition law may not be the right tool to address the fairness standard. Therefore, what role, if any, should fairness play in competition enforcement is a question that the Chinese antitrust agency should consider.

Article 1 of the AML makes clear that the policy goals of China's competition law are multifaceted, '[t]his Law is enacted for the purpose of preventing and restraining monopolistic conduct, protecting fair market competition, encouraging innovation, enhancing economic efficiency, safeguarding the interests of consumers and the interests of the society as a whole, and promot-

---

[11] Interim Provisions on Prohibiting Abuse of Dominant Market Position, promulgated by the State Administration for Market Regulation (SAMR) on 25 July 2019 and effective as of 1 September 2019.

[12] Interim Provisions on Prohibiting Abuse of Dominant Market Position, 'Equal Footing refers to the situation under which there is no difference among all the counterparties which could substantially affect the transaction in terms of transaction security, transaction cost, scope and ability, credit record, transaction link, transaction duration and others.'

[13] For example, Junhai Liu, a professor from the Renmin University of China, argues that big data 'shashu' infringes consumers right to know, right to choose and right to fair trade. Fei Sun and Peng Yin, 'Local Laws and Regulations Are Enacted to Constrain Big Data "Shashu"' *XINHUANET* (7 June 2021), available at www .xinhuanet.com/fortune/2021-06/07/c_1127539823.htm (in Chinese) (accessed 30 June 2022).

[14] OECD, 'Executive Summary of the Roundtable on Price Discrimination: Annex to the Summary Record of the 126th meeting of the Competition Committee 29–30 November 2016' *DAF/COMP/M(2016)2/ANN5* (9 February 2018) 2, available at www .oecd.org/officialdocuments/publicdisplaydocumentpdf/?cote=DAF/COMP/M(2016)2/ ANN5&docLanguage=En (accessed 30 June 2022).

ing the healthy development of socialist market economy'. Note that the AML protects 'fair market competition', but not explicitly '*free market competition*'. The academic community in China, however, has recognized that 'the main goal of anti-monopoly law is to protect free competition'.[15] So exactly how the Chinese antitrust agency interprets Article 1 of the AML when approaching issues such as algorithmic discrimination that can be easily associated with the fairness standard is a key question.

Among all the abuses explicitly prohibited by Article 22 of the AML, we could find only one reference to 'fairness'.[16] In our opinion, when analysing discrimination cases, the Chinese antitrust agency should avoid interpreting Article 1 of the AML mechanically to regard fairness as a key standard. More specifically, we believe that the antitrust agency should combine Article 7 of the AML (general provision of abuse)[17] with Article 22 of the AML (special provision of abuse) to assess whether algorithmic price discrimination has eliminated or restricted competition. We would caution against arbitrarily expanding the interpretation of Article 1 of the AML to include fairness as a legislative goal. In other words, the emphasis should be on the freedom of competition.

2.2 Algorithmic Collusion

Algorithmic collusion can result from an anti-competitive illegal agreement. According to Article 16 of the AML, 'Anti-competitive agreement refers to agreement, decision or other concerted practice which eliminates or restricts competition.' This definition of anti-competitive agreement is similar to Article 101 of the Treaty on the Functioning of the European Union (TFEU). But there are also differences. In addition to the lack of requirement for such an agreement to 'affect trade between Member States' due to institutional differences between the two jurisdictions, Article 16 of the AML, unlike the Article 101 of the TFEU, does not explicitly mention the 'object or effect' element.[18] China does not introduce the dichotomy of 'object or effect' to the 2022 AML.

---

[15] Xiaoye Wang, *The Anti-Monopoly Law* (in Chinese) (Law Press China 2011) 35.

[16] AML, Article 17(1), holding that 'Undertakings holding dominant market positions are prohibited from (1) selling commodities at unfairly high prices or buying commodities at unfairly low prices …'

[17] ibid., Article 6, which says that 'Undertakings holding a dominant position on the market may not abuse such position to eliminate or restrict competition.'

[18] Treaty on the Functioning of the European Union [2012] OJ C/326, Article 101, stipulating that

1. The following shall be prohibited as incompatible with the internal market: all agreements between undertakings, decisions by associations of undertakings and concerted practices which may affect trade between Member States and which

In theory, 'anti-competitive agreement' can be interpreted broadly, especially if one takes into account all 'other concerted practice'. Since the consolidation of the anti-monopoly departments affiliated with the National Development and Reform Commission (NDRC), the Ministry of Commerce (MOFCOM), and the State Administration for Industry and Commerce (SAIC) under the Anti-Monopoly Bureau of the SAMR in 2018, the SAMR has amended the AML with a series of supporting regulations. For example, Article 6 of the Interim Provisions on Prohibiting Anti-Competitive Agreement lists elements which shall be considered when identifying 'other concerted practice'.[19] What's clear from Article 6 is that 'communication of intention or exchange of information' is one of the pre-conditions. What's not clear, however, is whether tacit 'meeting of minds' through algorithm qualifies as one as well.

No matter whether it is 'concurrence of wills' and some form of manifestation in the EU,[20] the 'unity of purpose or a common design and understanding, or a meeting of minds' and 'a conscious commitment to a common scheme' in the US,[21] instant and complicated interactions between competitors facilitated by algorithms have brought challenges to the traditional definition of 'agreement'.[22] From the technical perspective, can algorithms learn to collude without human intervention and without any communication? If so, is there anything competition authorities could do, to the extent that such algorithmic tacit collusion leads to supra-competitive prices for consumers? Do the competition authorities have the legal tools to address such concerns? The related technical and legal uncertainty can not only make it difficult for the competition authority to carry out enforcement actions but can also make it difficult for

---

have as their object or effect the prevention, restriction or distortion of competition within the internal market, and in particular those which ...

[19] Interim Provisions on Prohibiting Anti-Competitive Agreement, Article 6, which states that

When identifying other concerted practice, the following elements shall be considered: 1. whether there is any consistency among conducts of relevant undertakings; 2. whether relevant undertakings have communicated intention or exchanged information; 3. whether relevant undertakings could provide reasonable explanation to the consistency; and 4. structure, competition status, changes and others of relevant market.

[20] Case T-41/96 *Bayer AG vs Commission* ECLI:EU:T:2000:242, para 173.

[21] *Interstate Circuit Inc. vs United States*, 306 US 208, 810 (1939); *Am. Tobacco Co. vs United States*, 328 U.S. 781, 809–10 (1946), 810. *Monsanto Co. vs Spray- Rite Serv. Corp.*, 465 U.S. 752, 768 (1984); *In re Flat Glass*, 385 F.3d, 357.

[22] OECD, 'Algorithms and Collusion: Competition Policy in the Digital Age' (2017) 36–9, available at www.oecd.org/competition/algorithms-collusion-competition-policy-in-the-digital-age.htm (accessed 30 June 2022).

undertakings to understand what types of conduct are prohibited or not when it comes to the use of algorithms.[23]

Exploring whether the traditional definition of 'anti-competitive agreement' is still valid is one of the focuses in the on-going revision of the AML. Mr. Jianzhong Shi, a professor from the China University of Political Science and Law, organized a research group to draft the amendment to the AML. The research group mainly consists of Chinese anti-monopoly scholars. The draft amendment prohibits explicit algorithmic collusion, including algorithm-facilitated 'hub-and-spoke' cartels.[24] Definition of 'anti-competitive agreement' remains the same, in accordance with Article 16 of 2022 AML.

3   ENFORCEMENT

3.1   Algorithmic Price Discrimination

On the issue of 'Shashu' through big data, there has been no known investigation by the Chinese anti-monopoly agencies, despite the public call for

---

[23]   It is worth noting that both legal and economic scholars have started exploring these issues more carefully. For some recent literature, see Joseph E. Harrington, 'Developing Competition Law for Collusion by Autonomous Artificial Agents' (2019) 14 *Journal of Competition Law & Economics* 638 and Ai Deng, 'What Do We Know About Algorithmic Tacit Collusion?' (2018) 33(1) *Antitrust* 88.

[24]   Competition Law.CN, 'Amendment to the AML Proposed by Experts – Comparison to the AML', available at www.competitionlaw.cn/info/1138/26864.htm (in Chinese) (accessed 30 June 2022). The new Article 15 of the AML would provide 'Undertakings are prohibited from entering into anti-competitive agreement through algorithms or any other technical methods forbidden by this Chapter. Online platform operator is prohibited from organizing or coordinating registered merchants to reach anti-competitive agreement forbidden by this Chapter.' Business operators could make use of algorithms to enter into and implement hub-and-spoke cartels, thus constituting a type of algorithmic collusion. Anti-Monopoly Guidelines of the Anti-Monopoly Commission of the State Council for the Sector of Platform Economy, effective as of 7 February 2021 and China's first systematic anti-monopoly guidance specifically applicable to the digital economy, prescribes that (Article 8),

> The intra-platform business operators with competitive relationship may enter in to hub-and-spoke agreement that has the effect of a horizontal monopoly agreement by making use of the vertical relationship with the platform operator or through organization or coordination by the platform operator. In analyzing whether the agreement falls within the monopoly agreements regulated by Article 13 and Article 14 of the Anti-monopoly Law of the PRC, whether the intra-platform operators with competitive relationship enter into and implement the monopoly agreement through methods such as technical means, platform rules, data and algorithm to exclude or restrict the completion in the relevant markets may be taken into consideration.

intervention. Nevertheless, in the past decade, some abuse of dominance cases investigated by the agencies did involve certain discriminatory conduct, although none directly concerned price discrimination. The investigation of the Pizhou Branch of Xuzhou Tobacco Company by the Jiangsu Branch of the SAIC in 2014[25] and the investigation of Inner Mongolia Chifeng Salt Company by the Inner Mongolia Branch of the SAIC in 2016[26] are two typical abuse of dominance cases that involve discriminatory conduct. The investigated companies in both cases are state-owned enterprises.

In addition, in 2018, the Hubei Branch of the SAIC investigated and disciplined a private enterprise, Hubei Yinxingtuo Gangbu Ltd., whose business includes vehicle roll-on-roll-off services; cargo (excluding explosive and dangerous goods) loading, transportation and storage; port support services; and transportation insurance.[27] The competition agency found that, as the only provider of Yiyu Line roll-on-roll-off shipping services in the Sichuan River upstream route, the company gave preferential treatment to Yichang H Transportation Ltd. (H-company), a company with which it had a business relationship, over other transportation companies. Specifically, Hubei Yinxingtuo Gangbu Ltd. not only prioritized the loading of H-Company's ships over others, but also assigned '*more valuable*' vehicles for the H-Company to ship, violating Article 22 of the AML.

3.2 Algorithmic Element in the Substantive Analysis of Abuse of Dominance Cases

In April 2021, the SAMR declared to penalize Alibaba for abusing its dominant position in China's online retail platform service market. The following are among the elements that contribute to Alibaba's dominance: Alibaba determines the listings and presentation of intra-platform business operators and products through formulating intra-platform rules and setting algorithms; Alibaba has deep pockets and advanced technologies, such as those supported

---

[25] Administrative Punitive Decision of Jiangsu Branch of the SAIC, Su Gong Shang An Zi [2014] No. 00578, 29 September 2014, available at www.samr.gov.cn/fldj/tzgg/xzcf/201703/t20170309_301549.html (in Chinese) (accessed 30 June 2022).

[26] Administrative Punitive Decision of Inner Mongolia Branch of the SAIC, Nei Gong Shang Chu Fa Zi [2016] No. 4, 16 August 2016, available at www.samr.gov.cn/fldj/tzgg/xzcf/201703/t20170309_301547.html (in Chinese) (accessed 30 June 2022).

[27] Administrative Punitive Decision of Hubei Branch of the SAIC, E Gong Shang Chu Zi [2018] No. 201, 9 January 2018, available at www.samr.gov.cn/fldj/tzgg/xzcf/201802/t20180208_301597.html (in Chinese) (accessed 30 June 2022).

by algorithms. Besides, algorithm is also an essential to facilitate Alibaba's imposition of 'either-or', or exclusive, provisions.[28]

Similarly, in October 2021, the SAMR punished Meituan for abusing the dominant position in China's online catering takeaway platform service market through imposing 'either-or', or exclusive, provisions. The SAMR opined that online catering takeaway platform services and offline catering services did not constitute the same relevant product market. From the perspective of business-operator-side demand substitutability, online catering takeaway platform services could reach a much wider scale of consumers, with the help of online marketing, big data analysis, algorithms and other internet technologies, while offline catering services could only reach limited consumers due to restrictions on information dissemination, geographic locations and so on. Online catering takeaway platform services work much more efficiently than offline catering services because of big data, algorithms and other internet technologies. Establishment of algorithmic systems is among the reasons why foreign online catering takeaway platforms could not enter China in a timely and effective manner, thus leading to a relevant geographic market of China.[29] The following are some of the reasons why the SAMR considered Meituan had a dominant position in China's online catering takeaway platform service market: Meituan controls the listings and presentation of intra-platform catering business operators and products through formulating intra-platform rules, setting algorithms, artificial intervention and so on, thus controlling the traffic intra-platform business operators could obtain and imposing decisive influence over their business decisions; Meituan has deep pockets and advanced technologies, such as accurate consumer profiles generated by algorithmic systems to provide personalized and targeted services and supervise whether intra-platform catering business operators are also active on competing platforms.[30]

3.3   Algorithmic Collusion

It is undeniable that algorithms have increased market transparency, sped up decision-making, and improved undertakings' ability to respond to the competitors' strategy. But, as discussed above, algorithmic collusion, especially

---

[28]   Administrative Punitive Decision of the SAMR, Guo Shi Jian Chu [2021] No. 28, 10 April 2021, available at www.samr.gov.cn/fldj/tzgg/xzcf/202104/t20210409 _327698.html (in Chinese) (accessed 30 June 2022).

[29]   Administrative Punitive Decision of the SAMR, Guo Shi Jian Chu Fa [2021] No. 74, 8 October 2021, available at www.samr.gov.cn/xw/zj/202110/t20211008_335364 .html (in Chinese) (accessed 30 June 2022)

[30]   ibid.

algorithmic tacit collusion, presents several challenges to antitrust enforcement.[31] In this regard, competition authorities need to first better understand how such algorithmic 'tacit collusion' might work. We will return to this topic below. Here we note that the Chinese competition authority has experience in investigating and sanctioning 'concerted practice'. That experience could be of great help in the enforcement against potential 'algorithmic collusion' in the future.

Since the Chinese competition authority has not investigated any 'algorithmic collusion', in the following, we discuss a case involving a 'concerted practice' that has been found to violate the AML. In the Estrozolam case, the NDRC believed that Changzhou Siyao had reached and implemented an anti-competitive agreement with others, even though it did not explicitly accept Huazhong Pharmacy's offer to cease external supply and increase prices. There was also no evidence that Changzhou Siyao had communicated with the other two companies about price increases after the meeting. The NDRC rejected Changzhou Siyao's argument that the price increase was its own independent decision. The NDRC put forward three reasons for its decision: (1) Changzhou Siyao sent representative(s) to the meeting, during which the price increase was discussed; (2) there was no evidence showing that Changzhou Siyao explicitly objected to the competitors' proposal to increase price; and (3) Changzhou Siyao did not proactively report the meeting to the NDRC, even though it was aware that sensitive commercial information (i.e., price) was discussed during the meeting.[32]

4   REMEDIES

4.1   Legislation in Relation to Algorithmic Price Discrimination and Algorithmic Collusion in China

Even if algorithmic price discrimination or algorithmic collusion[33] by online platforms were determined to be anti-competitive, whether the AML could

---

[31]   OECD (n. 22 above) 11–18 and 24–32.

[32]   Administrative Punitive Decision of the National Development and Reform Commission, Fa Gai Ban Jia Jian Chu Fa [2016] No. 7, July 2016, available at www .samr.gov.cn/fldj/tzgg/xzcf/202003/t20200326_313481.html (in Chinese) (accessed 30 June 2022).

[33]   The academia has discussed the intersection between price discrimination and algorithmic collusion, for example: Salil K. Mehra, 'Price Discrimination-Driven Algorithmic Collusion: Platforms for Durable Cartels' (Temple University Legal Studies Research Paper No. 2020-35, 2020), available at https://papers.ssrn.com/sol3/ papers.cfm?abstract_id=3699032 (accessed 30 June 2022).

provide sufficient and effective remedies is still an open question. Chinese anti-monopoly law provides a legal basis for structural and behavioural remedies only for review of concentrations,[34] but not for anti-competitive agreements or abuse of market dominance. Relevant remedies could only be imposed in accordance with Articles 56 and 57 of the AML,[35] explicitly consisting of: (1) discontinuance of the violation; (2) confiscation of unlawful gains; and (3) imposition of administrative fines.

It is worth noting that, in the review of abuse of dominance cases, competition agencies from the US and the EU have imposed behavioural remedies on high-tech companies, requiring these companies to abide by certain behavioural obligations for a certain period of time. For example, as recently as 2017, the European Commission imposed a series of behavioural obligations on Google.[36] In the Microsoft operating system case, the US District Court for the District of Columbia required Microsoft to disclose protocols used in server/client communications so as to promote and improve the interoperability between Windows desktop PCs and non-Windows servers and other products.[37]

Until now, the AML has only explicitly required companies found having abused their dominant market position or entered into and/or implemented anti-competitive agreement to '*discontinue (the) violation*'. In some respects, this is a 'non-action' obligation. This means that the Chinese antitrust agency might face certain obstacles when imposing proactive behavioural remedies. If we go back to one of the three remedies in the AML, '*discontinuance of violation*' only requires the companies to cease the illegal conduct under investigation, but not to proactively engage in other actions. As an example, in the Tetra Pak case that was investigated by the SAIC, Tetra Pak was required not to: (1) tie in packing materials when supplying equipment and technical services without justifiable reasons; (2) restrict the supply of kraft back papers from packing paper suppliers to third parties without justifiable reasons; or (3) design and implement loyalty discounts that would eliminate or restrict competition in the packing material market. We note that Article 53 of the AML stipulates that an antitrust investigation may be suspended if the firm under investigation 'commits itself to adopting specific measures to eliminate the

---

[34]   The Ministry of Commerce, 'Provisions of the Ministry of Commerce on Imposing Restrictive Conditions on the Concentration of Business Operators (for Trial Implementation)' promulgated on 12 April 2014 and effective as of 1 May 2015.

[35]   AML, Articles 46 and 47.

[36]   Commission Decision of 27 June 2017, *Case AT.39740 – Google Search (Shopping)*, available at https://ec.europa.eu/competition/antitrust/cases/dec_docs/39740/39740_14996_3.pdf (accessed 30 June 2022).

[37]   *United States v. Microsoft Corp.*, 253 F.3d 34 (D.C. Cir. 2001).

consequences of their conduct within a certain period of time'. Therefore, in some ways, Article 53 may be interpreted as the potential legal basis for proactive remedies. Of course, it remains to be seen if Article 53 will be interpreted in this way for cartel and abuse of dominance conduct in practice.

Again, to the extent algorithmic price discrimination or algorithmic collusion by online platforms were deemed illegal, whether and how aggressively the Chinese antitrust agency would pursue proactive behavioural remedies under the AML still remains unclear. This is largely due to the lack of precedents as well as the associated challenges, some of which are discussed in this chapter.

In terms of designing such remedies, increasing algorithmic transparency has also been proposed as an option. In fact, the banking regulation in China has already incorporated a similar requirement.[38] Nevertheless, whether it is proper for the anti-monopoly agency to directly tackle transparency problem is also a question. Even if one ignores the legislative obstacles mentioned above, how to design and supervise behavioural remedies to increase algorithm transparency is another challenge.

4.2   Enforcement Against Algorithmic Price Discrimination in China

To the extent that algorithmic price discrimination by online platforms falls under the scope of the AML, one logical way to interpret the remedy of 'discontinuance of violation' is to simply discontinue price discrimination. As a result, the antitrust agency may impose non-discrimination obligations or even broader fair, reasonable and non-discriminatory (FRAND) obligations on the online platforms. Although non-discrimination or FRAND obligations have not been imposed in cartel or abuse of dominance cases, the MOFCOM has imposed non-discrimination obligations, including FRAND obligations, in a number of conditionally cleared merger cases during the last ten years. For example, in the case of Bayer's acquisition of Monsanto, which was conditionally cleared in March 2018, the MOFCOM found that the resultant concentration could potentially eliminate or restrict competition in the global digital agriculture market and imposed a behavioural remedy on the merged

---

[38]   People's Bank of China, China Banking and Insurance Regulatory Commission, China Securities Regulatory Commission & State Administration of Foreign Exchange, 'Guiding Opinions on Regulating the Asset Management Businesses of Financial Institutions' (April 2018), Article 23,

> The financial institutions shall report the main parameters of AI models and the main logic of assets allocation to the relevant financial regulatory authorities for record-filing, set up separate smart management accounts for investors, fully remind investors of the inherent defects and application risks of AI algorithms …

entity to allow all Chinese digital agricultural software applications to connect to its digital agricultural platforms 'in accordance with fair, reasonable and non-discriminatory provisions', and to allow all Chinese users to access its digital agricultural products or applications for a pre-specified number of years.[39]

With the institutional reform in early 2018 and the establishment of the SAMR, merger review and investigation of cartels and abuse of dominance have been consolidated within a single agency, as are the staff from the three agencies. With the consolidation, it is possible that MOFCOM's experience in the past decade with non-discrimination or FRAND remedies may influence the design and implementation of remedies in abuse of dominance cases, including those that involve algorithmic discrimination.

Although the non-discrimination or FRAND remedies might seem like an obvious choice for addressing algorithmic discrimination, if it is determined to be anti-competitive, we want to emphasize that in practice their application may not be straightforward.[40] Specifically, what can be deemed as non-discriminatory in algorithmic design may not be so clear. In the standard essential patent (SEP) context, FRAND obligations refer to non-discrimination among 'similarly situated' licensees, not all licensees. Whether a condition such as 'similarly situated' should apply if FRAND-like obligations were imposed on algorithmic discrimination, and what types of users would be deemed as 'similarly situated', remain to be answered. Aside from this challenge, the mechanisms for implementing and monitoring such remedies also need to be carefully designed.

---

[39] The MOFCOM Announcement No. 31 of 2018 on Anti-Monopoly Review Decision Concerning the Conditional Approval of Concentration of Undertakings in the Case of Acquisition of Equity Interests of Monsanto Company by Bayer Aktiengesellschaft Kwa Investment Co. (13 March 2018), available at http://fldj .mofcom.gov.cn/article/ztxx/201803/20180302719123.shtml (in Chinese) (accessed 30 June 2022).

[40] With the emergence of big data and the advancements of machine learning and artificial intelligence, algorithmic fairness has attracted a great deal of interest in the public and academic domains. In fact, multiple definitions of algorithmic fairness have been put forward by scholars and researchers. For an economic perspective, see, Jon Kleinberg, Jens Ludwig, Sendhil Mullainathan and Ashesh Rambachan, 'Algorithmic Fairness' (2018) 108 *AEA Papers and Proceedings* 22.

4.3   Require Algorithms to be More Transparent as a Way to Address Both Algorithmic Price Discrimination and Algorithmic Collusion?

On the various issues resulting from the use of algorithms, including algorithmic discrimination and algorithmic collusion, the global community has begun to consider promoting algorithmic transparency as a safeguard. In 2017, the Association for Computing Machinery US Public Policy Council issued a statement on algorithmic transparency and accountability, listing several principles to support the benefits of algorithmic decision-making while addressing concerns with the potential for harmful bias and discrimination.[41] Margrethe Vestager, the European Commissioner for Competition, also advocated that companies are obligated to design algorithms in accordance with data protection and antitrust laws and regulations.[42] The former German Chancellor, Angela Merkel, has expressed similar opinions, calling on Internet giants, such as Meta[43] and Google, to disclose their algorithms, saying that: 'The algorithms must be made public ... These algorithms, when they are not transparent, can lead to a distortion of our perception. They narrow our breath of information.'[44]

Of course, promoting algorithmic transparency is not without its own limitations and challenges. As noted by the OECD,

> [E]nforcing algorithmic transparency and accountability might turn out to be a challenging task in practice, especially when facing black box algorithms ... Merely publishing (or disclosing to a regulator) the source code of the algorithm may not be a sufficient transparency measure. Complete transparency would require that someone could explain why any particular outcome was produced, but that might

---

[41] Association for Computing Machinery US Public Policy Council, 'Statement on Algorithmic Transparency and Accountability' (2017), available at www.acm.org/binaries/content/assets/public-policy/2017_usacm_statement_algorithms.pdf (accessed 30 June 2022).

[42] Margrethe Vestager, 'Algorithms and Competition' (Speech at the Bundeskartellamt 18th Conference on Competition, 16 March 2017), available at https://ec.europa.eu/commission/commissioners/2014-2019/vestager/announcements/bundeskartellamt-18th-conference-competition-berlin-16-march-2017_en (accessed on 30 June 2022).

[43] Facebook renamed itself Meta in October 2021.

[44] Harriet Agerholm, 'Angela Merkel Says Internet Search Engines Are "Distorting Perception" and Algorithms Should Be Revealed' *Independent* (27 October 2016), available at www.independent.co.uk/news/angela-merkel-says-internet-search-engines-endangering-debate-algorithms-should-be-revealed-a7383811.html (accessed 30 June 2022).

be an impossible task when machine learning systems have made autonomous decisions that have not been instructed by anyone.[45]

In China, with respect to algorithmic discrimination such as 'Shashu' through big data, some hold that such conduct has infringed consumers' rights to information about firms' pricing practices.[46] Therefore, in the context of using antitrust enforcement to address algorithmic discrimination, the public may also demand increased algorithmic transparency in the future. However, whether it is appropriate to use the AML to require or dictate algorithmic transparency remains uncertain. Furthermore, even if one ignores the legal obstacles to imposing behavioural remedies mentioned above, how to implement and supervise behavioural obligations to increase algorithmic transparency, while at the same time avoiding the potentially chilling effect on market innovation, will be a challenge.

5   OUR PROPOSALS

5.1   Understand the Development and Evolution of the Theories of Harm in the Digital Economy

China's digital economy is developing rapidly. Mobile payment, bike-sharing, online shopping are being adopted at a rate that is among the fastest in the

---

[45] OECD (n. 22 above). It is worth noting that these comments also reflect the fact that antitrust authorities typically lack the requisite technical expertise. In the academic community, Ezrachi and Stucke, and Harrington, have proposed ways to better understand the impact of algorithms on competitive outcomes. See Ariel Ezrachi and Maurice E. Stucke, *Virtual Competition: The Promise and Perils of the Algorithm-Driven Economy* (Harvard University Press 2016); Harrington (n. 23); Ai Deng, one of the authors of this chapter, gives reasons why algorithmic transparency is not always necessary to detect anti-competitive algorithms. See Ai Deng, '4 Reasons Why We May Not See Colluding Robots Anytime Soon' (2017) *Law360*, available at https://papers.ssrn .com/sol3/papers.cfm?abstract_id=3271904 (accessed 30 June 2022). In a later section, we argue that having a robust expert support system will substantially enhance the capabilities of Chinese antitrust agencies in the digital economy. We also note that the research field of explainable AI (XAI) precisely aims to make machine learning algorithms understandable to humans. For an exploration of XAI's role in antitrust compliance, see Ai Deng, 'From the Dark Side to the Bright Side: Exploring Algorithmic Antitrust Compliance' (2019), available at https://papers.ssrn.com/sol3/papers.cfm ?abstract_id=3334164 (accessed 30 June 2022).

[46] Jing Chen, 'Didi, CTrip and Other Companies Exposed to Apply Shashu, Suspected of Infringing Right to Information of Consumers' *China Economic Net* (30 March 2018), available at www.ce.cn/xwzx/gnsz/gdxw/201803/30/t20180330 _28662738.shtml (in Chinese) (accessed 30 June 2022).

world. With the increasing adoption of digital services also comes public scepticism that the new modes of competition actually work for consumers. In fact, as noted above, there have been controversies around the use of big data and algorithms in China in recent years. New modes of competition enabled by the digital economy have also challenged the effectiveness of the traditional anti-monopoly legal system. Are the traditional theories and tools of analysing potential harm to competition still applicable in the digital economy?[47] Are the issues related to data and algorithms really 'new' competition issues? We note that the vagueness of the purpose of the AML – there are additional rights and interests protected by the AML beyond consumer welfare, as reflected in Article 1 – as well as the vagueness of other provisions leave room for new theories of harm to be developed. For example, should privacy protection be considered as one type of right protected by the AML? This is a topic being heatedly debated all over the world right at this moment.

In reality, the legal environment in China is more complex. With the promulgation of a series of new laws like the Cybersecurity Law of the PRC, the Data Security Law of the PRC and the Personal Information Protection Law of the PRC in recent years, it is no easy task for the Chinese anti-monopoly agency to balance the promotion of openness to data and transparency in algorithms to enhance competition on the one hand, and the protection of personal information on the other.[48]

In December 2021, together the Cyberspace Administration of China, the Ministry of Industry and Information Technology, the Ministry of Public Security and the State Administration for Market Regulation released the Provisions on Administration of Algorithmic Recommendation in the Internet Information Service, effective as of 1 March 2022. The Provisions were enacted to meet the need to further promote the comprehensive governance of Internet information service algorithms and the need to actively promote

---

[47] For a discussion of this question, see CEPS, 'Competition Policy in the Digital Economy: Towards a New Theory of Harm?' (Seminar Organized by the CEPS Digital Forum, 1 June 2016), available at www.ceps.eu/ceps-events/competition-policy-in-the -digital-economy-towards-a-new-theory-of-harm/ (accessed 30 June 2022).

[48] Wei Han and Yajie Gao, 'Promote Openness or Strengthen Protection? Application of Law to Data Competition in China' (2018) *CPI Antitrust Chronicle*, available at www.competitionpolicyinternational.com/wp-content/uploads/2018/05/ CPI-Han-Gao.pdf (accessed 30 June 2022). In addition, mergers and acquisitions in the digital arena are rather common in China. In early 2018, the acquisition of Eleme by Alibaba and the acquisition of Mobike by Meituan attracted much attention in Chinese society. Issues raised by these transactions, such as pre-emptive acquisition of disruptive innovators, input foreclosure, and even the applicability of the theory of conglomerate leverage, are also well worth the Chinese anti-monopoly agency's attention.

the healthy development of algorithm recommendation services, providing regulatory basis for governing big data 'Shashu'.[49]

As the digital economy continues to develop, the Chinese authorities should proactively think about how the AML could be applied to technical innovations in the future. We should ask, among other questions, how one should analyse new issues and problems under the traditional antitrust framework. We believe that the antitrust agency should approach innovations from the perspective of antitrust based on harm to competition. Ultimately, the agency should try to understand innovative business models and market competition from comprehensive technical, business, economic and legal perspectives.

5.2   Promoting the Use of Technologies in the Anti-Monopoly Enforcement

From the aspect of enforcement, China has emphasized, and we believe, will continue to emphasize the importance of applying Internet technologies to supervision and regulation. In China's judicial system, the Internet courts[50] established in recent years have heard cases online and accepted electronic evidence gathered through blockchain.[51] There is huge potential for the compe-

---

[49]   State Council of the People's Republic of China, 'Official Interpretation of the Provisions on Administration of Algorithmic Recommendation in the Internet Information Service' (4 January 2022), available at www.gov.cn/zhengce/2022-01/04/content_5666428.htm (in Chinese) (accessed 30 June 2022).

[50]   Provisions of the Supreme People's Court on Several Issues Concerning Trial of Cases by the Internet Courts (FA SHI [2018] No. 16), promulgated on 3 September 2018 and effective as of 7 September 2018, Article 1, 'The Internet courts shall try cases online and the litigation segments including case acceptance, service, mediation, evidence exchange, pre-trial preparation, court hearing and judgment announcement shall generally be completed online …'. ibid., Article 2, 'The Internet courts in Beijing, Guangzhou and Hangzhou shall have jurisdiction on centralized basis over the following first-instance cases within the jurisdiction of the city where they are respectively located that shall be accepted by the basic people's courts …'

[51]   ibid., Article 11,
         Where the authenticity of the electronic data provided by the parties concerned can be proved through electronic signature, trusted time stamp, hash check, block chain or any other technical means of collection, fixation and tamper-proofing of evidence or be authenticated through the platform for electronic collection and storage of evidence, the Internet courts shall confirm the authenticity of such electronic data …'.
Man Liu, 'Demystify the Beijing Internet Court: Entrance Through Scanning Face While Judgment of Simplified Case Written Automatically' (Southern Metropolis Daily, 10 September 2018), available at www.sohu.com/a/252923313_161795 (in Chinese) (accessed 30 June 2022).

tition authority to apply digital technologies to enforcement.[52] It could not only facilitate detection of 'algorithmic collusion' but would also help alleviate the serious shortage of manpower in China's anti-monopoly agency. Russia, for example, has developed a system, the 'BIG DIGITAL CAT'[53] to detect collusion. Several other international agencies such as UK's CMA have also developed cartel-detection technologies.

5.3 Encourage and Promote Independent Digital Assistants

The emergence of digital assistants, digital butlers,[54] algorithmic assistants or algorithmic consumers has revolutionized how we purchase and consume products and services. Maurice E. Stucke and Ariel Ezrachi defined the digital assistant as 'a tool which caters to users' needs, excels at anticipating their wants, and delivers a personalized online environment'.[55] Internet conglomerates all over the world have introduced their digital assistants, such as Amazon's Alexa, Apple's Siri, Google's Assistant, Microsoft's Cortana, Facebook's Marvin, Baidu's Duer, Alibaba's Xiaomi and Tencent's Dingdang. Digital assistants could bring huge benefits to ultimate consumers, through increasing buyer power, restraining seller power, lowering transaction costs, mitigating side effects of algorithmic discrimination and disrupting algorithmic collusion. Nevertheless, digital assistant is not a panacea. Only when the digital assistant is provided by undertakings independent from the Internet conglomerates could it effectively play a counterbalancing role against these same market players. Of course, we should also keep in mind the relevant privacy and democracy concerns and other risks brought by these digital assistant technologies.

5.4 Protect the Right of Defence

According to Article 22 of the AML, discriminatory conduct by online platforms with dominant market positions may be illegal only if they do not have

---

[52] For an exploration of how technologies could be leveraged, see, for example, Deng (n. 45); Ai Deng, 'Cartel Detection and Monitoring: A Look Forward' (2017) 5 *Journal of Antitrust Enforcement* 488.

[53] Federal Antimonopoly Service of the Russian Federation, 'FAS Creates a New Web-Service: "Big Digital Cat"' (22 October 2018), available at http://en.fas.gov.ru/press-center/news/detail.html?id=53478 (accessed 30 June 2022).

[54] Michal Gal and Niva Elkin-Koren, 'Algorithmic Consumers' (2017) 30 *Harvard Journal of Law and Technology* 309.

[55] Maurice E. Stucke and Ariel Ezrachi, 'How Digital Assistants Can Harm Our Economy, Privacy and Democracy' (2018) 32 *Berkeley Technology Law Journal* 1239.

'justifiable reasons' for doing so. This offers companies a way to defend themselves by identifying justifiable reasons.[56] Article 19 of the Interim Provisions on Prohibiting Abuse of Dominant Market Position promulgated by the SAMR in September 2019 offers some guidance on what may qualify as such justifiable reasons. Specifically, the following elements will be taken into account: (1) whether the act in question meets the actual needs of the counterparty and is in line with legitimate trading convention and industry practices; (2) whether the act in question is related to promotions provided to new customers on the first transaction within a reasonable period; and (3) whether there are other reasons to justify the discriminatory act.

China's advocacy for 'tolerant and prudent' regulation for nascent industries is mainly aimed at avoiding excessive intervention that inhibits incentives for innovation. From the perspective of antitrust enforcement, full protection of the rights of enterprises to defend themselves, an open attitude towards a dynamic efficiency defence, as well as procedural justice, are important safeguards for the 'tolerant and prudent' regulation.

5.5   Promote Research Efforts and Establish an Expert Support System

Research into antitrust issues with respect to algorithms is still at early stage.[57] The limited experience also calls for a prudent antitrust enforcement approach to algorithmic discrimination by online platforms. Excessive law enforcement can easily lead to chilling effects on innovation, which could in turn undermine consumer welfare.

The broad antitrust community still lacks sufficient understanding of how algorithms work, and the full extent of the impact artificial intelligence may have on business models and market competition. Considering the limited knowledge that we possess at this early stage; an important step is to conduct market research and industry surveys. For new problems such as algorithmic discrimination, China's antitrust law enforcement agency should conduct

---

[56]   In the three abuse of dominance cases discussed above, the companies under investigation all tried to defend their conduct, although none of the defences was accepted in the end.

[57]   Some recent research includes Deng (n. 23); Ai Deng, 'When Machines Learn to Collude: Lessons from a Recent Research Study on Artificial Intelligence' (2017), available at https://ssrn.com/abstract=3029662 (accessed 30 June 2022); Ai Deng, 'An Antitrust Lawyer's Guide to Machine Learning' (2018) 32 *Antitrust* 82; Harrington (n. 23); Emilio Calvano, Giacomo Calzolari, Vincenzo Denicolò, and Sergio Pastorello, 'Artificial Intelligence, Algorithmic Pricing and Collusion' (2019) 110 *American Economic Review* 3267.

market research as soon as possible to understand the applications of big data and algorithms in China's digital market and identify major potential issues to lay a good foundation for potential antitrust law enforcement in the future.

As a start, it would be helpful for the antitrust agency to have some basic knowledge of the relevant technologies used in algorithmic discrimination to fully understand the conduct. In addition to inviting technical experts to assist in actual investigations, a longer-term solution for the newly established SAMR is to consider setting up an independent technical support department. In fact, the 'technical investigators' instituted within the Chinese court system is a good example of such a mechanism, and a similar model could be adopted by the antitrust agency. Since 2015, these 'technical investigators' have helped with complicated technical issues in the intellectual property courts in Beijing, Shanghai, Guangzhou and other cities.[58] In early 2018, as part of the government restructuring, the State Intellectual Property Office, which has a large number of experienced technical experts, was consolidated into the SAMR. Accordingly, the SAMR could consider taking advantage of in-house technical expertise to better deal with issues such as algorithmic discrimination in today's digital economy.

5.6   Leverage the Public in the Anti-Monopoly Enforcement

In order to increase efficiency and to address the shortage in manpower, the SAMR is advised to strengthen the deterrent effects of the law and turn to the public for leads. The 'Provisional Measures to Reward Complaint against Serious Illegal Conducts in Market Supervision (Draft for Comments)' (Provisional Measures to Reward Complaint) released jointly by the SAMR and the Ministry of Finance on 19 November 2019 is a good start.[59] These measures set out to encourage public report of any suspected anti-competitive agreement by offering a reward as high as two million CNY, as a way to maintain an economic environment with fair competition and to crack down on illegal conduct.[60] Article 4, in particular, introduces the scope of the

---

[58]   Hong Hao, 'Technical Investigator Has Been Introduced to the Chinese People's Court' (18 May 2018) *People's Daily*, available at http://hb.people.com.cn/n2/2018/0518/c192237-31594437.html (in Chinese) (accessed 30 June 2022).

[59]   SAMR, 'Provisional Measures to Reward Complaint against Serious Illegal Conducts in Market Supervision (Draft for Comments)' (19 November 2019), available at www.samr.gov.cn/hd/zjdc/201911/t20191119_308625.html (in Chinese) (accessed 30 June 2022).

[60]   ibid., Article 13,
    The upper limit for rewarding the complaint could be no more than one million CNY. As for complaint against systematic and regional risks which have or would cause serious social damages, relevant reward could be more than one

measures and the types of illegal conduct in breach of the competition law.[61] Note that while the Chinese competition legal system mainly consists of the 'Anti-Monopoly Law' and the 'Anti-Unfair Competition Law', the Provisional Measures apply to breaches of either of these laws.

5.7   Special Suggestions for Cracking Down on (Algorithmic) Collusion

We believe that the leniency programme will play an increasingly important role in combating collusion including explicit algorithmic collusion in China.[62] Among all the anti-competitive agreements or concerted practices already investigated and sanctioned in China, a large percentage of the investigations benefited from the leniency programme. An important observation here is that the idea of a leniency programme is in stark contrast to the notion of 'harmony', an essence of the Chinese culture. Chinese companies are confronted with this cultural obstacle whenever they consider applying for leniency. Accordingly, provisions pertaining to leniency shall be presented more clearly to help the Chinese undertakings better understand and anticipate potential legal results, such as the promulgation of the Guidelines for the Application of the Leniency Program to Horizontal Anti-Competitive Agreement in October 2020.[63]

Finally, unlike the UK[64] and other jurisdictions, only bid rigging could potentially trigger criminal liability in China.[65] In practice, enforcement

---

million CNY but no more than two million CNY. The exact number shall be determined by the financial department at central or provincial level together with the SAMR.

[61]   ibid., Article 4, 'This Provisional Provisions apply to complaints against the following serious illegal conducts: … (2) gross violation of competition law, and other laws and regulations in relation to intellectual property, cracking down pyramid sale …'.

[62]   Tacit algorithm collusion where algorithms learn to collude without human intervention is a subtler issue and we refer the readers to more recent research for more discussion. Deng (n. 23); Deng (n. 52); Deng (n. 57); Harrington (n. 23 above).

[63]   Guidelines for the Application of the Leniency Program to Horizontal Anti-Competitive Agreement, promulgated by the Anti-Monopoly Commission of the State Council on and effective as of 18 September 2020.

[64]   Enterprise Act 2002, Part 6, Cartel Offence.

[65]   The National People's Congress, Criminal Law of the P.R.C., promulgated in and effective as of 1997, Article 223,

Bidders who act in collusion with each other in offering bidding prices and thus jeopardize the interests of bid-inviters or of other bidders, if the circumstances are serious, shall be sentenced to fixed-term imprisonment of not more than three years or criminal detention and shall also, or shall only, be fined. If a bidder and bid-inviter act in collusion with each other in bidding and thus jeopardize the

of the Criminal Law of the PRC (Criminal Law) also tends to impose less severe penalties. Because it is much more difficult to incorporate new criminal conduct into Criminal Law, the Chinese academic circle has started discussing whether criminal liability shall be imposed on undertakings that are part of anti-competitive agreements, especially horizontal anti-competitive agreements.

6   CONCLUSION

This chapter explores the challenges the Chinese competition authority faces in dealing with competition issues raised by algorithms and big data. Indeed, given that no administrative antitrust decision has been issued against algorithmic price discrimination or algorithmic collusion so far, there remains a great deal of uncertainty as to how the SAMR would enforce anti-monopoly law in this area. It is important to recognize that price discrimination can be pro-competitive and can increase consumer welfare under certain circumstances.[66] We believe a cautious approach to antitrust enforcement regarding online platforms' algorithmic discrimination is warranted.

To better address the potential regulatory challenges, we have recommended in this article several pre-emptive measures that the SAMR could take. In order to more comprehensively understand both the *status quo* and the prospects of anti-monopoly enforcement in China's digital economy, a good knowledge of anti-monopoly law itself is not enough. It is also necessary to understand the broader regulatory environment in China, including China's opening its market to the outside world, it's providing a level playing field to market players both home and abroad,[67] its continued emphasis on the 'tolerant

---

lawful interests of the State, the collective or citizens, they shall be punished according to the provisions of the preceding paragraph.

[66]   For an exposition of the economics of price discrimination, see James C. Cooper, Luke Froeb, Daniel P. O'Brien and Steven Tschantz, 'Does Price Discrimination Intensify Competition? Implications for Antitrust' (2005) 72 *Antitrust Law Journal* 327.

[67]   For example, the State Council, 'Guiding Opinions on Promoting the Legal and Sound Development of the Online Economies' (August 2019). The State Council, 'Regulations on Improving Business Environment' (October 2019). The Communist Party of China, 'Decision of the Central Committee of the Communist Party of China on Adhering to and Perfecting the Socialist System with Chinese Characteristics and Promoting the Modernization of the National Governance System and Governance Capabilities', GOV.CN, 5 November 2019, 6. 'Uphold and improve the basic socialist economic system and promote high-quality economic development' – (3) *'Speed up the improvement of the socialist market economy system. Establish a high-standard market system, improve a fair competition system ... Strengthen the basic status of competition policy, implement a fair competition review system, and strengthen and improve*

and prudent' principle, and the fair competition review system introduced in 2016.[68]

anti-monopoly and anti-unfair competition law enforcement...'; (5) '*Construct a new level of open economy ... protect the legitimate rights and interests of foreign invest- ment, promote fair competition between domestic and foreign enterprises...*', availa- ble at www.gov.cn/xinwen/2019-11/05/content_5449034.htm (in Chinese) (accessed 30 June 2022).

[68]   The State Council, 'Opinion of the State Council on Establishing a Fair Competition Review System in the Construction of the Market System' (June 2016), available   at   www.gov.cn/zhengce/content/2016-06/14/content_5082066.htm   (in Chinese) (accessed 30 June 2022). The National Development and Reform Commission, the Ministry of Finance, the Ministry of Commerce, the State Administration for Industry and Commerce and the Legal Office of the State Council, 'Rules for the Implementation of the Fair Competition Review System (Interim)' (October 2017), available at www.gov.cn/xinwen/201710/5234731.htm (in Chinese) (accessed 30 June 2022).

7. Algorithmic collusion and the Japanese antimonopoly law

Steven Van Uytsel and Yoshiteru Uemura

1 INTRODUCTION

The Japan Fair Trade Commission (JFTC) sponsored the Study Group on Competition Policy in Digital Markets (Study Group)[1] to issue its Algorithms or the AI and Competition Policy Report (Algorithm Report or Report).[2] This report was prepared following eight meetings involving the Study Group members between July 2020 and March 2021 and discusses the intersection between algorithms (artificial intelligence) and competition law.[3] The Study Group held that the Japanese Act on Prohibition of Private Monopolization and Maintenance of Fair Trade (Antimonopoly Act or AMA)[4] is relatively well-equipped to deal with collusion brought about by algorithms.[5]

This chapter partially agrees with the Study Group's findings. As long as the dehumanized price setting by algorithms can be linked to the conduct of human actors within competing firms, the JFTC has no enforcement issues besides having to find sufficient evidence to substantiate the existence of human conduct.[6] However, not all algorithmic price settings allow for the establishment of a link between the conduct of human actors within competing

---

[1] JFTC, 'The Study Group on Competition Policy in Digital Markets Released the Report on Algorithms/AI and Competition Policy' (21 March 2021), available at www .jftc.go.jp/en/pressreleases/yearly-2021/March/210331.html (accessed 30 June 2022).

[2] JFTC, 'Report on the Study Group on Competition Policy in Digital Markets "Algorithms/AI and Competition Policy"' (21 March 2021), available at www.jftc.go .jp/en/pressreleases/yearly-2021/March/210331004.pdf (accessed 30 June 2022).

[3] ibid. (the preliminary part to the report titled *The Study Group on Competition Policy in Digital Markets, Chronology of Discussions*).

[4] Law No. 54 of 1974, Shiteki Dokusen no Kinshi oyobi Kousei Torihiki Kakuho ni kan suru Houritsu (Dokusen Kinshi Hou), Law Concerning the Prohibition of Private Monopolies and the Assurance of Fair Trade (hereinafter AMA).

[5] JFTC (n. 2 above) at 31.

[6] ibid., 23–31.

firms, and the Algorithm Report does not fully address such scenarios. One example of an unaddressed scenario is when an algorithm takes the role of a third-party collusion facilitator; such facilitators have troubled the JFTC.[7] The conceptualization of the AMA is such that third-party cartel facilitators are difficult to bring within the existing cartel provision of the AMA. We argue that it may be necessary to reconsider the factual situation of what is currently considered an algorithmic third-party cartel facilitator. In doing so, other provisions within the AMA, such as unfair trade practices, may offer a solution to further deal with algorithmic price setting.

The first part of the Algorithm Report is devoted to algorithmic collusion. The Algorithm Report links back to the taxonomy of algorithmic collusion; its taxonomy was developed in the academic literature to facilitate a shared understanding of the concept. This study highlights the main points included in the definitional section (Section 2). In its elaboration of the different scenarios, the Algorithm Report informs that the AMA has few problems in terms of its applicability to algorithmic collusion. We hold that this view is based on a human-centred approach to algorithmic collusion scenarios (Section 3). The problem with this human-centred approach is that not all algorithmic collusion scenarios are covered, especially when an algorithm acts as a third-party cartel facilitator. This chapter explains why such a scenario is problematic for the AMA (Section 4). While explaining the algorithm as a third-party cartel facilitator scenario, we demonstrate that the classic example for this scenario, that is, the algorithm used by Uber Technologies, Inc. (Uber), is controversial. Elucidating this controversy, we introduce an alternative AMA application to the factual situation of the Uber algorithm, and this through unfair trade practices (Section 5). We conclude by stating that the AMA can tackle algorithmic collusion, especially when collusion can be reduced to human conduct. For such problematic scenarios, it is worthwhile to investigate whether other provisions of the AMA, such as unfair trade practices, could apply to the factual situation (Section 6).

2   THE ALGORITHM REPORT AND THE ALGORITHMIC COLLUSION TAXONOMY

Ariel Ezrachi and Maurice E. Stucke wrote in their book, *Virtual Competition, The Promise and Perils of the Algorithmic-Driven Economy*, that "the upsurge of algorithms, Big Data, and super platforms will hasten the end of compe-

---

    [7]   Steven Van Uytsel, 'Algorithmic Hub-and-Spoke Cartels: A Japanese Perspective' in Steven Van Uytsel (ed.), *The Digital Economy and Competition Law in Asia* (Springer 2021) 193.

tition law as we know it."[8] In an earlier paper, "Artificial Intelligence and Collusion: When Computers Inhibit Competition," these scholars had justified this statement by alluding that "when computer algorithms and machines take over the role of market players, the spectrum of possible infringements may go beyond traditional collusion."[9] The traditional collusion, so contend Ezrachi and Stucke, "reflects a concurrence of wills between the colluding companies' agents. Illegality is triggered when companies, through their directors, officers, employees, agents, or controlling shareholders, operate in concert to limit or distort competition."[10] This human-centred cause of illegality may be on the verge of ending; pricing algorithms could take over any of the roles traditionally played by the companies' agents.

To better understand this, Ezrachi and Stucke divided the role pricing algorithms can play concerning collusion into four scenarios: messenger, hub-and-spoke, predicable agent, and digital eye.[11] This taxonomy has been the basis for discussing algorithmic collusion, even in terms of alternative names having been developed for these scenarios.[12] For example, the Secretariat of the Organisation for Economic Co-operation and Development (OECD) distinguishes between monitoring algorithms, parallel algorithms, signalling

---

[8] Ariel Ezrachi and Maurice E. Stucke, *Virtual Competition: The Promise and Perils of the Algorithm-Driven Economy* (Harvard University Press 2016) 233.

[9] Ariel Ezrachi and Maurice E. Stucke, 'Artificial Intelligence & Collusion: When Computers Inhibit Competition' (The University of Oxford Centre for Competition Law and Policy, Working Paper CCLP (L) 40, 2017) 7, available at www.law.ox.ac.uk/sites/files/oxlaw/cclpl40.pdf (accessed 30 June 2022).

[10] Ariel Ezrachi and Maurice E. Stucke, 'Artificial Intelligence & Collusion: When Computers Inhibit Competition' (2017) 5(1) *University of Illinois Law Review* 1775, 1782. For a summary and examples, see Ulrich Schwalbe, 'Algorithms, Machine Learning, and Collusion' (2018), available at https://papers.ssrn.com/sol3/papers.cfm?abstract_id=3232631 (accessed 30 June 2022).

[11] Ezrachi and Stucke (n. 8 above) at 35–71.

[12] See, e.g., Gintarė Surblytė-Namavičienė, *Competition and Regulation in the Data Economy: Does Artificial Intelligence Demand a New Balance?* (Edward Elgar 2020) at 155–78; Aurelien Portuese, 'Prologue: Algorithmic Antitrust – A Primer' in Aurelien Portuese (ed.), *Algorithmic Antitrust* (Springer 2022); Lorenz Marx, Christian Ritz, and Jonas Weller, 'Liability for Outsourced Algorithmic Collusion – A Practical Approximation' (2019) 2 *Concurrences* 1, available at www.concurrences.com/IMG/pdf/_08.concurrences_2-2019_legal_practices_marx_et_al.pdf?50150/0f71319df3abe8b18a7387586dc4488bc3713519 (accessed 30 June 2022); Nicolo Colombo, 'Virtual Competition: Human Liability Vis-à-Vis Artificial Intelligence's Anticompetitive Behaviours' (2018) 2(1) *European Competition and Regulatory Law Review* 11; Sebastian Felix Janka and Severin Benedict Uhsler, 'Antitrust 4.0 – The Rise of Artificial Intelligence and Emerging Challenges to Antitrust Law' 39(3) *E.C.L.R.* 112.

algorithms, and self-learning algorithms.[13] Despite the different terminology, the understanding of the different scenarios is the same. Since the Algorithm Report refers to the OECD,[14] this taxonomy is used throughout this chapter.

The scenario of a monitoring algorithm describes how an algorithm takes the role of implementing, monitoring, and policing collusion that humans have discussed and approved in advance.[15] A parallel algorithm is a scenario wherein a single algorithm determines the price of firms competing in the same market.[16] A signalling algorithm exemplifies a scenario wherein different algorithms of independent firms predict a similar price outcome based on the observable market conditions.[17] A self-learning algorithm autonomously determines the price in the function of a predetermined goal, such as profit maximization.[18]

The Algorithm Report summarizes the main characteristics of all four scenarios, but two have received special attention: the parallel algorithm and the signalling algorithm.

The Algorithm Report holds that the parallel algorithm can be achieved in two ways. First, competing firms may agree on the price and use the same algorithm to configure the prices according to the agreement. For example, the Study Group puts forward "an algorithm that automatically adjusts prices according to market changes";[19] thus, it is no longer necessary to renegotiate the original agreement based upon the changed circumstances.[20] The algorithm is thus used to facilitate the implementation of an earlier made agreement.[21] Second, a third party may initiate the parallel use of the same algorithm.[22] This could be because competing firms ask for the development of a specific algo-

---

[13]   OECD, 'Algorithms and Collusion – Background Note by the Secretariat' (DAF/Comp(2017)4, 2018) 24–32, available at https://one.oecd.org/document/DAF/COMP(2017)4/en/pdf (accessed 30 June 2022). Niccolò Colombo terms the four categories as follows: classical digital cartel, inadvertent hub-and-spoke, tacit algorithmic collusion, and dystopian virtual reality. See Nicholas Colombo, 'Virtual Competition: Human Liability Vis-à-Vis Artificial Intelligence's Anticompetitive Behaviours' (2018) 2(1) *European Competition and Regulatory Law Review* 11, 12–14.

[14]   JFTC (n. 2 above) at 17.

[15]   Ezrachi and Stucke (n. 8 above) at 39

[16]   ibid., 46–50.

[17]   ibid., 61.

[18]   ibid., 71.

[19]   JFTC (n. 2 above), at 19.

[20]   ibid.

[21]   ibid. The Algorithm Report does not explain the extent to which this scenario differs from a monitoring algorithm. We could presume that the specificity in this scenario is that the same algorithm is used among competitors, while that is not necessarily the case with a monitoring algorithm.

[22]   ibid.

rithm.[23] Although each firm independently implements the algorithm, there is a shared knowledge that the industry relies on the same algorithm. Another possibility is that a third party, that is, a vendor of algorithms, provides the industry with a similar algorithm without the users' knowledge of the users.[24] The third party acts as a hub in price coordination in both cases. Therefore, the above-described scenarios can be perceived as components of a hub-and-spoke cartel,[25] which differs from the classical hub-and-spoke. The Algorithm Report states that algorithmic hub-and-spoke cartel does not require exchanging information directly among the spokes or awareness that the price is coordinated.[26]

The signalling algorithm argues the Algorithm Report is a scenario wherein a designated firm provides information, called signals, to the market and monitors how competing firms react to these signals.[27] A price-fixing agreement is attained when each competing firm indicates that the same price is implemented. Because this type of scenario is digitized, the exchange of signals is swift and invisible to customers. The fastness and obscurity create worries when using the signalling algorithm because these features increase the attractiveness of acting as a signalling firm.[28] Unlike in the offline world, where the signalling firm is likely to lose customers due to its early price increase, signalling firms in an online world can keep their customers.[29]

3   THE ALGORITHM REPORT'S FOCUS ON HUMAN INTERACTION AMONG COMPETING FIRMS

3.1   In Search for Communication between Humans

After detailing how algorithms may contribute to collusion, the Algorithm Report investigates whether the AMA can be applied. Central in this investigation is whether the implementation of the algorithm can be linked to the human conduct of representatives of competing firms. This approach allowed the Study Group to analyze the AMA's application to algorithmic collusion based upon communication.[30]

---

[23]   ibid.,
[24]   ibid., 20.
[25]   ibid.
[26]   ibid., 21.
[27]   ibid.
[28]   ibid.
[29]   ibid.
[30]   ibid., 23.

The core provision of the AMA concerning collusion is Article 3, which prohibits unreasonable restraints of trade. The Study Group reports that unreasonable trade restraints include firms "mutually communicating with other firms to thereby arrange in concert with such other firms, the price, sales volume, production quantity, etc. of any product, which each firm should intrinsically determine by itself (cartel)."[31] It is further indicated that "in concert with other firms" is the most crucial prong, requiring communication between the firms regarding price or quantity.[32]

Communication falls into two categories: firms can explicitly communicate the price or quantity, or the communication can be tacit. If the enforcement agency can find documents on this explicit communication, such as emails, meeting reports, etc., unreasonable restraint of trade can be easily established.[33] However, the Study Group correctly specifies that, due to the illegal characteristics of the communication, firms tend to avoid direct communication, making it tricky for the enforcement agency to establish an infringement. When a firm adjusts its prices to match competitors after observing their price settings, judging that it would bring more economic benefit, it could be a case of tacit communication.[34] This kind of parallel behaviour is outside the scope of the AMA.

Considering the analysis of communication, the Study Group makes four observations.

First, a monitoring algorithm should be no problem under the AMA. A monitoring algorithm always operates based upon a prior human-made agreement. Thus, there must have been some form of communication. The algorithm either monitors the implementation or sets the prices according to that agreement. The AMA would be applied to human-made agreements, and the presence of the algorithm is, as such, does not contribute to establishing an infringement.[35] If the human-made agreement involves an algorithm sending out signals, we could add that there would be no problem applying the AMA. Of course, in all of these cases, the JFTC needs to find sufficient evidence of the communication.

Second, parallel algorithms could be within the AMA scope if users mutually recognize that the commonly used algorithm leads to coordinated price setting. The mutual recognition of the purpose of the algorithm, which is ultimately exemplified with price-setting not influenced by the firms inde-

---

[31] ibid.
[32] ibid., 23–4.
[33] ibid., 24.
[34] ibid.
[35] ibid, 26.

pendently, could be considered communication of intent.[36] There is no explicit recognition in the Algorithm Report that the Uber algorithm can be categorized within this parallel algorithm scenario. The Study Group recognizes that if firms are unaware that they are employing parallel algorithms, the unreasonable restraint of trade provision may not apply. There is no communication of intention.[37]

Third, simply publishing a price, thus signalling the future price setting, would not automatically be an infringement under the AMA. Such an infringement occurs if the price increase can only be explained as interdependent action between the competitors.[38] Japan's lack of case law made the Study Group examine the United States and Europe. The elements that could indicate that the price increase is not the result of an independent business decision include information transmission that is not valuable for consumers, strange symbols as signals, or postponing already published prices. The Study Group further indicates that if such a price transmission is complemented with a similar price increase among the competitors, the enforcement agency could conclude on the communication of intention.[39] The Algorithm Report does not mention how much this is possible for an algorithm to do without an underlying human-made agreement and thus communication.

Fourth, the Study Group sees it as unlikely for firms to adopt self-learning algorithms anytime soon. Experiments with reinforced machine learning algorithms have shown that a concerted outcome can be achieved; however, this outcome is dictated by a stable testing environment. It is not certain that the outcome would be the same in an actual market situation.[40] Even within the stable testing environment, the situation was not bright for firms implementing the algorithm. Before achieving the concerted outcome, a firm would have to sustain substantial losses in the testing environment.[41] To be complete, though, the Study Group added that, even if this kind of algorithm hit the market, the AMA would not apply. The Study Group implied that the algorithms could make no communication of intent; such communication is only possible for firms implementing self-learning algorithms. If these firms use such algorithms "with a mutual recognition that the use of their algorithms leads to price coordination,"[42] then an unreasonable restraint of trade could probably

---

[36] ibid., 26–7.
[37] ibid., 27.
[38] ibid., 28.
[39] ibid., 28–9.
[40] ibid., 29.
[41] ibid.
[42] ibid., 30 n. 51.

be found. However, this would be an example of looking for a human actor to address the concerted action of algorithms.

3.2   The Competing Firm Trap in the Algorithm Report

It is one thing to try to humanize the dehumanized price setting and so require finding some form of communication between representatives. It is another thing to limit the focus on the need for these representatives to work for competing firms. This automatically elaborates the algorithmic scenarios wherein the third-party cartel facilitator is not sufficiently highlighted.

The emphasis on competing firms is mainly present in the parallel algorithm. The Algorithm Report indicates that the management of competing firms may turn to the same algorithm to implement future changes of a human-made cartel agreement.[43] The algorithm updates the constellation of the cartel agreement based upon the changing market circumstances. This could be a variation of the example developed by the OECD, of whom the Secretariat held that use of a pricing algorithm can be inspired to follow a market leader, "who in turn would be responsible for programming the dynamic pricing algorithm that fixes prices above the competitive level."[44] Another example, also inspired by the OECD, is the case whereby competing firms agree to order an algorithm with a third party to implement it among the competing firms.[45] In both cases, the human interaction is horizontal because the cartel's communication is among competing firms. Also, the algorithm in both examples is operating among the competing firms.

However, there may have been no communication between representatives from competing firms; the Algorithm Report underscores this possibility as well. When discussing the application of the AMA to algorithmic collusion, the Algorithm Report states that a third-party algorithm developer may sell the same algorithm to competing firms without them knowing it.[46] The implementation of this algorithm is still at the level of horizontally competing firms. Yet, the third-party algorithm developer does not necessarily have to leave the implementation of the algorithm to competing firms. It is even conceivable that the developer's actual algorithm implementation is done based on the

---

[43]   ibid., 19

[44]   OECD (n. 13 above) at 27. See also Antonio Capobianco and Pedro Gonzaga, 'Algorithms and Competition: Friends or Foes' (2017) 1(2) *Competition Policy International – Antitrust Chronicle* 1, 4, available at www.competitionpolicyint ernational.com/wp-content/uploads/2017/08/CPI-Capobianco-Gonzaga.pdf. (accessed 30 June 2022).

[45]   OECD (n. 13 above) at 27.

[46]   JFTC (n. 2 above) at 27.

information provided by the algorithm users (this scenario is not developed in the Algorithm Report).[47] Some of these users would be service providers, while others would be service takers. The service providers would potentially be competitors.

Less futuristic than the example above, but therefore not less important, is the situation wherein the collusion is facilitated by a firm in a vertical business relationship or a third party outside the business relationship. While the former can be a supplier or manufacturer, the latter could be a trade association or an accountancy firm.[48] The Algorithm Report has also not taken a position toward applying the AMA to these cartel facilitators.

The observations mentioned above tell us two things. As long as the implementation of an algorithm can be linked to the communication of human representatives of competing firms, there should be no problem with applying the AMA. From the moment that this kind of communication is absent, the application of the AMA is no longer certain. The latter may be explained by the AMA's difficulty in dealing with cartel facilitators, being actors external to cartel participants' competitive ring.

4   THE AMA'S AMBIVALENT RELATIONSHIP WITH CARTEL FACILITATORS

4.1   The Conceptualization of the AMA and the Cartel Facilitator's Conundrum

The Algorithm Report found few problems for the AMA in dealing with algorithmic collusion. This stance may be explained because the Algorithm Report did not consider all scenarios wherein an algorithm could contribute to collusion. We have pointed out that implementing an algorithm by a cartel facilitator is not sufficiently addressed. Also, the situation where the developer operates the algorithm may require more attention. Extra attention is warranted in these situations because the AMA created a conservative JFTC approach regarding cartel facilitators.

When the AMA was conceptualized, cartel agreements were categorized as infringements under Article 4 of the AMA.[49] However, this Article was abolished in 1953, when Japan regained its sovereignty and power to amend

---

[47] Cf. ibid., 17–32.
[48] Van Uytsel (n. 7 above) at 207–13.
[49] Alex Y. Seita and Jiro Tamura, 'Historical Background of Japan's Antimonopoly Law' (1994) 1 *University of Illinois Law Review* 115, 170.

its laws.[50] The question arose about how the remaining Article 3 of the AMA should be applied to cartel agreements. The explanatory provision of the unreasonable restraint of trade prong of Article 3 of the AMA, Article 2 (6) of the AMA,[51] determined that a cartel agreement is only illegal when it mutually restricts the business activities among competitors.[52] The term "mutually restrict" is one of the more peculiar characteristics of the AMA's Article 3 and Article 2(6), which created a conundrum of dealing with facilitators of a cartel under the AMA. Two Tokyo High Court decisions, still frequently cited in the literature, offered a solution to the conundrum.

The earliest decision on dealing with cartel facilitators was the Tokyo High Court decision in the Asahi Newspaper Co. case of 9 March 1953.[53] The Asahi Newspaper Co. case was about territorial division, whereby the newspaper publishers' distributors each became responsible for a specific territory. The JFTC was only able to prove agreements between the publishers and the distributors. There was no evidence for concluding that the vertical agreements implemented a horizontal agreement between the publishers. The Tokyo High Court held that the former Article 4 of the AMA could not be applied because the publishers and the distributors were not "independent enterprises in a competitive relationship."[54] The court also stressed that the agreement had to have "common restrictions on business activity by mutual agreement."[55] This should be interpreted that all anti-competitive agreement participants should be aware of and enjoy the agreement's effects.[56] It was presumed that this interpretation of former Article 4 of the AMA would extend to the unreasonable restraint of trade prong of Article 3 of the AMA.[57]

---

[50]   Masako Wakui, *Antimonopoly Law: Competition Law and Policy in Japan* (Independently Published 2018), 250. The content of the abolished Article 4 of the AMA is included in the book.

[51]   This Article 2(6) of the AMA specifies that:
   The term "unreasonable restraint of trade" as used in this Act means such business activities, by which any enterprise, by contract, agreement or any other means irrespective of its name, in concert with other enterprises, mutually restrict or conduct their business activities in such a manner as to fix, maintain or increase prices, or to limit production, technology, products, facilities or counterparties, thereby causing, contrary to the public interest, a substantial restraint of competition in any particular field of trade.

[52]   Wakui (n. 50 above) at 75–80.

[53]   Tokyo High Court (Newspaper Distribution Case), 9 March 1953, 3 Shinketsushu 4.

[54]   Wakui (n. 50 above) at 76–7.

[55]   ibid., 77.

[56]   ibid.

[57]   ibid.

The Asahi Newspaper Co. case had far-fetching consequences. One of the most often cited consequences is that the AMA's unreasonable restraint prong of Article 3 only applies to horizontal agreements. Vertical agreements, no matter how severe the anti-competitive harm they cause, are outside the scope of application.[58] A less-cited consequence is the inability to apply Article 3 to non-competing enterprises playing a role in setting up an unreasonable restraint of trade or to enterprises that do not cause the same restraint of trade.[59] More concretely formulated, the JFTC did not punish cartel facilitators[60] or enterprises that remained passive within the cartel.[61] This view has been upheld for 40 years.[62]

A Tokyo High Court decision of 1993 has changed the JFTC's position. In the Social Insurance Agency Seal case, the Tokyo High Court had to decide whether a non-qualified bidder in a bid-rigging scheme, Hitachi Information Systems (Hitachi), could be included in an action based on Article 3.[63] In the end, as a non-qualified bidder, Hitachi held that it was not in a competitive relationship with the three bidding firms and should therefore not be held liable under Article 3. Furthermore, Hitachi argued that it was not operating its business in the same particular field of trade as the bidding firm.

The Tokyo High Court contended that none of these arguments should be considered valid. First, the 1953 Asahi Newspaper Co. case was based on former Article 4 of the AMA. When deciding the Social Insurance Agency Seal case, Article 4's function was taken over by Article 3 in combination with

---

[58] ibid., 77–8; Shingo Seryo, 'Cartel and Bid Rigging' (2007), available at www .jftc.go.jp/eacpf/05/jicatext/aug31.pdf (accessed 30 June 2022).

[59] Wakui (n. 50 above) at 78.

[60] For the absence of a discussion on this issue Wakui (n. 50 above) at 76–8; Etsuko Kameoka, *Competition Law and Policy in Japan and the EU* (Edward Elgar 2014) at 37–56; Akira Inoue, *Antitrust Enforcement in Japan: History, Rhetoric and Law of the Antimonopoly Act* (Dai-Ichi Hoki 2012), at 59–64; Seryo (n. 58 above) at 11–12.

[61] Kameoka (n. 60 above) at 50–1 (giving the example of a cartel member remaining passive). Another example of a different restriction would be if one enterprise would deal in territory A and the other in territory B, despite this being one type of a restriction, i.e. a territorial division.

[62] Wakui (n. 50 above) at 78. Other cases have confirmed this view. See Japan Fair Trade Commission (Hokkaido Butter Co. Case), 18 September 1950, 2 FTC Decision Reports 108; Tokyo High Court (Toho-Shintoho Case), 7 December 1953, Gyosei Jiken Saiban Reishu 4(12) 3215. The latter case is explicit: "unreasonable restraint of trade is formed where independent enterprises in mutual competition jointly impose certain restrictions upon each other and thereby restrain their free business activities. ... if mutuality is lacking in the restriction, an unreasonable restraint of trade does not occur."

[63] Tokyo High Court (Social Insurance Agency Seal Case), 14 December 1993, 46-III Koto Saibansho Keiji Hanreishu 322.

Article 2(6). The latter's conceptualization is slightly different from former Article 4 of the AMA. Article 3, in combination with Article 2(6), explicitly requires finding a restraint of competition. Hence, it would be more consistent with the article's tone to consider the firms contributing to the restraint rather than their mutual relationships. Once this position was taken, the Court could develop a new view on cartel facilitators.[64] For the application of Article 2(6) of the AMA, the Court could now decide that: (1) the firms could be active in different fields of trade; (2) the firms could be in the same or similar competitive relationship; (3) a mutual restraint does not require restraint in the same manner. Applied to the Social Insurance Agency Seal case, the Court held that it should be sufficient that a firm's free business activities are compromised by taking part in the anti-competitive conduct – collusive bidding in this case. This is the case when the facilitating firm is effectively[65] or in essence[66] "in a competitive relationship with the other participants."[67]

The Tokyo High Court's stance in the Social Insurance Agency Seal case was followed by the JFTC in two bid-rigging cases: The Video Machine case and the Okinawa Aluminum Sash case.[68] Moreover, the *Guideline Under the Antimonopoly Act Concerning Distribution and Trade Practices* adopted language indicating that it is somehow sufficient that each firm's business activities are limited (not necessarily in the same way), and anti-competitive conduct should be directed to the achievement of a common purpose.[69]

The Tokyo High Court's shift mentioned above responds to critiques from several scholars concerning the 1953 Asahi Newspaper Co. case and the subsequent interpretation of Article 2(6) of the AMA. Conversely, Wakui states that the 1993 Social Insurance Agency Seal case has not been extended to agreements whereby horizontal and vertical elements are intertwined in a collusive agreement. She mentions that there are, therefore, still a few arguments that the scope of the AMA's Article 2(6) "should be expanded to include non-horizontal restrictions, which may be necessary to regulate *hub-and-spoke cartel*, wherein a non-competitor acts either as a ringleader or as a facilitator."[70]

---

[64]   Seryo (n. 58 above) at 12.
[65]   Wakui (n. 50 above) at 79.
[66]   Kameoka (n. 60 above) at 45.
[67]   Wakui (n. 50 above) at 79.
[68]   Seryo (n. 58 above) at 12; Kameoka (n. 60 above) at 45.
[69]   This is especially reflected in note 2 of the Guideline Under the Antimonopoly Act Concerning Distribution and Trade Practices. Available at: www.jftc.go.jp/en/legislation_gls/imonopoly_guidelines_files/DistributionSystemsAndBusinessPractices.pdf (accessed 30 June 2022).
[70]   Wakui (n. 50 above) at 80. Such an explicit request may be understood against the background of the Social Insurance Agency Seal case, which requires a competitive relationship (Kameoka (n. 60 above), at 45) or, as Wakui notes, "the defendant [needs

The demand for an explicit statement on the AMA's Article 2(6) position toward hub-and-spoke cartels could also be justified because two categories of facilitators are regulated either by another AMA article or by a law outside AMA. These two facilitators are trade associations and bureaucrats.[71] The former is regulated by the AMA's Article 8, while the latter was "remedied by the enactment of the Act on the Elimination and Prevention of Involvement in Bid Rigging, etc., and the Punishments for Acts by Employees that Harm Fairness of Bidding."[72]

4.2   Algorithmic Cartel Facilitators and the AMA

The Study Group could respond to the ambivalent position of the JFTC toward cartel facilitators in a hub-and-spoke setting. Particular attention should have been paid to algorithms implemented by third-party cartel facilitators, specifically, those that are not competing price leaders, trade associations, or bureaucrats. Provided the cartel facilitator is one of these, there is no problem applying the AMA. The algorithm applied by the price leader can be caught by Article 3 of the AMA,[73] while the ones used by a trade association and a bureaucrat fall under the special regulatory regimes.[74] The AMA application is problematic if the third-party cartel facilitators are, for example, accountancy firms or algorithm developers.

An accountancy firm can fulfil the role of a hub through an algorithm, gathering digital information necessary for operating an algorithm to set the price for competing firms. The exchange of information between the competing firms is thus indirect, and the price is not set through any competing firms. It is done centrally by the algorithm activated by the accountancy firm. It is hard to argue that the accountancy firm is in a competitive relationship with the horizontally competing firms. Without an explicit JFTC statement in this regard, it may be difficult to firmly state that the algorithm's action could be caught by Article 3 of the AMA and lead to a sanction.[75] At best, the JFTC can prove that there has been communication between the horizontally competing

---

to be] somehow engaged in business relating to the relevant product." (Wakui (n. 50 above) at 80).

[71]   Van Uytsel (n. 7 above) at 207–12.

[72]   Masako Wakui, 'Bid Rigging Initiated by Government Officials: The Conjuncture of Collusion and Corruption in Japan' in Thomas Cheng, Sandra Marco Colino, and Burton Ong (eds.), *Cartels in Asia: Law & Practice* (Wolters Kluwer (HK) 2015) 45.

[73]   JFTC (n. 2 above) at 19.

[74]   Van Uytsel (n. 7 above) at 207–12.

[75]   ibid., 212–13.

firms and establish a traditional form of collusion; the accountancy firm will escape the AMA application.

Another example is when an algorithm developer operates the algorithm it has developed; a third party implements an algorithm and thus acts as a hub between competing firms. A popular example in this context is, probably due to the special mention by Ezrachi and Stucke, the algorithm operated by Uber.[76] Elaborating on this example, both authors have stated that:

> [i]f the drivers independently agreed among themselves to charge the same base rate (or surge rate), they would be guilty of price fixing. Yet in the case of Uber a vertical agreement is present between the hub (the algorithm developer) and the spokes (the Uber drivers) ... the first few drivers who joined Uber's platform – while agreeing to use the algorithm – did not necessarily agree to fix the prices for taxi services. But what about the later drivers, who sign up after Uber dominate the ... local market? If these drivers understood that, by joining Uber, they all would receive the same rate and the same percentage of any monopoly profits, have they essentially become a hub-and-spoke conspiracy?[77]

Ezrachi and Stucke are cautious about answering their question positively,[78] indicating that the effects may resemble horizontal collusion but acknowledging that the conditions for a traditional hub-and-spoke cartel are likely not fulfilled.[79] For this, one may need to look at the kind of information exchanged.[80] Drivers communicate to the Uber algorithm when opening their shop, that is, they become available as a driver at the car's location within the city. Riders transfers the information they need to travel from point A to B, thus indicating their position. With the positions known, the algorithm calculates the time before a driver can pick up the rider. Drivers could be scarce, causing the algorithm to increase the price, incentivizing other drivers to come online, or encouraging the riders to seek other transportation. The question is whether the exchange of information by drivers can be said to be price-sensitive. One driver does not indicate their price for other drivers to follow through the communication of the algorithm, raising the question, despite claims to the opposite,[81] whether a developer-deployed Uber-like algorithm exemplifies

---

[76]   Ezrachi and Stucke (n. 8 above) at 50–2.
[77]   ibid., 53.
[78]   ibid., 54.
[79]   ibid.
[80]   Van Uytsel (n. 7 above) at 215.
[81]   Anne-Sophie Thoby, 'Pricing Algorithms & Competition Law: How to Think Optimally the European Competition Law Framework for Pricing Algorithms?' (Competition Forum, Art. N. 0009, 2020), available at https://competition-forum.com/wp-content/uploads/2020/12/art.-n%C2%B00009.pdf (accessed 30 June 2022).

a hub-and-spoke agreement. This has led to an extensive debate on qualifying the Uber-like algorithm,[82] which we address in the next section.[83]

If the current Uber algorithm does not nicely fit the hub-and-spoke constellation, would it still be possible to conceive an environment in which it would? If we examine Uber's business model, we know that the central algorithm currently sets the price for a ride; drivers do not have an option to deviate from this price except to lower it.[84] Imagine that Uber adjusts its app and gives its drivers power over a substantial part of the price. Equally, riders would be allowed to choose which car they prefer based upon the different prices and the estimated waiting time for the respective drivers to arrive. This kind of environment encourages intra-brand competition. In other words, the Uber drivers become internal competitors; however, the drivers' power to set a substantial part of the price enables them to share price-sensitive information with each other. The Uber algorithm could collect the price choice of the lowest price setter and, for example, show this information to other nearby drivers, allowing them to conspire on the price indirectly. While this may initially be the lowest price, repetitive interaction with the system may lead to a higher price.

The alternative business model may bring the developer-deployed algorithm within a hub-and-spoke agreement. The following elements, many related to information sharing, may need to be addressed to formulate a definite view. Does the information communicated among the drivers constitute sensitive

---

[82]   See, e.g., Jorn Kloostra, 'Algorithmic Pricing: A Concern for Platform Workers?' (2021) *ELLJ* 1; Pinar Akman, 'Online Platforms, Agency, and Competition Law: Mind the Gap' (2019) 43 (2) *Fordham International Law Journal* 209; Julian Nowag, 'When Sharing Platforms Fix Sellers' Prices' (LundLawCompWP 1/2018, 2018), available at https://papers.ssrn.com/sol3/papers.cfm?abstract_id=3217193 (accessed 30 June 2022); Mark Anderson and Max Huffman, 'Sharing Economy Meets the Sherman Act: Is Uber a Firm, a Cartel, or Something in Between?' (2017) *Colum. Bus. L. Rev.* 859; Julian Nowag, 'The UBER-Cartel? UBER between Labour and Competition Law' (LundLawCompWP 1/2016, 2016), available at https://papers.ssrn.com/sol3/papers .cfm?abstract_id=2826652 (accessed 30 June 2022).

[83]   See Section 5.1 "Qualifying an Uber-like Algorithm."

[84]   Le Chen, Alan Mislove, and Christo Wilson, 'Peeking Beneath the Hood of Uber' (Internet Measurement Conference, Tokyo, 28–30 October 2015) 2, available at www .ccs.neu.edu/home/amislove/publications/Uber-IMC.pdf (accessed 30 June 2022). See also Ezrachi and Stucke (n. 8) at 50–54; But see Pinar Akman, 'Online Platforms, Agency, and Competition Law: Mind the Gap' (2019) 43 (2) *Fordham International Law Journal* 209, 265 and 285 n. 314, where she indicates that Pinar Akman reported in her extensive study on online platforms that the control over the price may vary depending on the geographical area. She states that "[t]he figure provided by Uber is a 'recommended fare' and the driver can agree a lesser (but not greater) sum with the passenger" and "Uber drivers can also request different fares than that recommended by Uber's algorithm in that they can accept a lower sum from the rider."

information and reduce "strategic uncertainty and increase ... the risk of limiting competition."[85] Is there a legitimate reason why information is shared with competing drivers? To what extent are competing drivers relying on such information to set their prices? Answers to these questions may conclude that a cartel is established among the competing drivers. Articles 3 and 2(6) of the AMA may apply to drivers, but what about the algorithm and its developer? It is necessary to prove the presence of communication between parties that are, in essence, in a competitive relationship with each other to apply Articles 3 and 2(6) of the AMA to this scenario. Will the Uber platform and its algorithm in the alternative Uber business model be, in essence, in a competitive relationship with the drivers as long as it only offers a service to private car drivers to valorize their rides?

5   REVIEWING AN UBER-LIKE ALGORITHM IN THE AMA CONTEXT

5.1   Qualifying an Uber-like Algorithm

The Algorithm Report considers two scenarios wherein a parallel algorithm could be used. One scenario involves the competing firms being aware of the parallel use of the same algorithm; in the other scenario, the competing firms are unaware. According to the Algorithm Report, the Study Group only considers the first scenario within the scope of collusion and the ambit of the AMA's Article 3. The second scenario is outside the scope of Article 3, or at least the unreasonable restraint of trade prong;[86] however, this does not mean that the AMA cannot be applied to the second scenario. The Algorithm Report indicates that the scenario resembles more a situation of unilateral conduct than collusion; unilateral conduct is where a firm with market power deprives other firms of freely deciding their own business activities.[87] This form of control can be caught by the private monopolization prong of Article 3, which applies to unilateral conduct and is further explained in Article 2(7) of the AMA.[88]

Would that mean that the Algorithm Report considers the Uber-like algorithm an example of a forbidden parallel algorithm? The drivers are indeed aware that they are using the same algorithm for setting the price. There is nothing in the Algorithm Report that confirms or denies this interpretation.

---

[85]   Lucas de Carvalho Silveira Bueno, 'Hub and Spoke Cartels vs. RPM: Differences, Interactions and the Concurrence of Wills' Theory of Harm' (2020), available at https://papers.ssrn.com/sol3/papers.cfm?abstract_id=3732767 (accessed 30 June 2022).

[86]   JFTC (n. 2 above) at 27.

[87]   ibid.

[88]   ibid.

The Algorithm Report does not seek any connection with the debate on qualifying the relationship between Uber and its drivers.

Building on the understanding that the relationship should not necessarily be considered within the field of labour law,[89] a rich debate emerged within the competition law literature on qualifying the relationship between Uber and its drivers. Both horizontal and vertical agreements were considered. The debate has highlighted the qualification as a membership agreement and a joint venture agreement among the horizontal agreements. A resale price maintenance (RPM) agreement, a subcontracting agreement, and an agency agreement are the vertical agreements comparing Uber's relationship with its drivers.

The comparison with a membership agreement is made because Uber and its drivers may look like a membership organization formed to offer a new service with a coordinated price. However, substantial differences force a different conclusion. A membership organization usually grows up from the bottom, from the members, who keep some form of control over the decision-making process to keep the organization's interest aligned with that of its members.[90] Uber is not established through an agreement of drivers and does not provide the drivers any power over the decision-making process. Moreover, Uber's interests are not necessarily aligned with the drivers, especially when Uber sets the fees received from the drivers.[91]

The relationship between Uber and the drivers could be considered a joint venture because there is revenue sharing between the platform and the drivers.[92] However, a joint venture commonly requires pooling resources to offer services and share risks and profits. Neither of these is the case. Moreover, as

---

[89] Koolstra (n. 82 above) at 9. It may be argued that if a court finds that the platform workers are "false self-employees," the platform company is likely to change its business model. Another indicator that the platform worker can be considered as self-employed is the Yodel case of the European Court of Justice. See Case C-692/19, *B v. Yodel Delivery Network Ltd*, ECLI:EU:C:2020:288. For a more detailed discussion of the case, see, e.g., Antonio Aloisi, '"Time Is Running Out": The Yodel Order and Its Implications for Platform Work in the EU' (2020) 13(2) *Italian Labour Law e-Journal* 67.

[90] See Nowag (2018) (n. 82 above) at 12; Anderson and Huffman (n. 82 above) at 904–5.

[91] See Nowag (2018) (n. 82 above) at 12–13; Anderson and Huffman (n. 82 above) at 905.

[92] See Nowag (2018) (n. 82 above) at 13; Anderson and Huffman (n. 82 above) at 905–6.

indicated above, the drivers do not have any input regarding the platform's decision-making processes.[93]

The Uber business model may qualify as an RPM agreement because Uber sets the drivers' price; however, for an RPM agreement to cover the relationship between Uber and its drivers, the drivers should be reselling a product that Uber has put on the market. In other words, there must be a transfer of a product from one production level or distribution chain to the other. Without such a transfer, the Uber drivers deliver a service, and it is impossible to approach the relationship between Uber and its drivers with an RPM agreement.[94]

Equalling the relationship between Uber and its drivers with a subcontracting agreement would require Uber (the contractor) to provide the technology and goods necessary to implement the drivers' (the subcontractor) task. This implies that the drivers perform "the service on behalf of the contractor (platform), and the platform, therefore, is the one who ultimately provides the service."[95] Such a setting would require the Uber platform to be the ultimate receiver of the ride price, and the driver would be remunerated for performed work. Also, Uber would have complete control over its drivers for the performance of the contract. Since this is not Uber's business model, it has been held that a subcontracting agreement cannot qualify the relationship between Uber and its drivers.[96]

Qualifying the relationship between Uber and its drivers as an agency agreement would mean that one of the parties (the agent) has the power to negotiate contracts on behalf of the other (the principal). Two views have been developed. On the one hand, the seller could be regarded as the platform's agent for whose behalf she performs services.[97] On the other hand, the seller could be viewed as the principal for whom the platform (the agent) acts as a "mediator in the conclusion of agreements between workers and the customers."[98] Whatever position is taken, agency agreements fall outside the application scope of most competition laws because the principal and the agent are consid-

---

[93]   See Nowag (2018) (n. 82 above) at 13; Anderson and Huffman (n. 83 above) at 906.

[94]   See Nowag (2018) (n. 82 above) at 14–15; Anderson and Huffman (n. 83 above) at 903–4.

[95]   Koolstra (n. 82 above) at 10. See also Nowag (2018) (n. 82 above) at 17 n. 105.

[96]   ibid., at 10. This author has pointed out that this parallel would not be much different from considering the platform worker as an employee in terms of competition law. Competition law would not apply.

[97]   Koolstra (n. 83 above) at 9. See also Nowag (2018) (n. 82 above) at 17, where he argues that a distinction should be made beween a genuine agency agreement and one that resembles a hub-and-spoke agreement.

[98]   Koolstra (n. 82 above) at 9. See also, Akman (n. 82 above).

ered part of a single economic unity.[99] The danger of creating a gap in applying competition law, which Pinar Akman called the platform gap, leads to two different suggestions.[100] If the platform is only offering a service to facilitate the service offering of firms, competition law should not apply. When the platform competes with the service providers on the platform, competition law should apply.[101] The immediate ramification for a platform like Uber would be that the platform is brought under competition law's ambit, but that the law does not apply because Uber behaves itself as competitive neutral towards the actors on its platform.[102]

The ease with which the Algorithm Reports accepts the AMA's application toward an Uber-like algorithm is thus in stark contrast to the conclusions in the international debate, where there is a divide between applying competition law and not.

5.2   Offering an Alternative View for the Application of the AMA to Uber: Unfair Trade Practice

If one sides with the Nowag analysis, which concludes that "it is difficult to consider the platforms and the sellers as one economic unit for the purposes of competition law,"[103] the application of competition law to Uber and its drivers could be discussed. This discussion's appearance depends on qualifying the relationship between Uber and its drivers and conceptualizing the competition law. Japan may offer a unique perspective because the AMA has a peculiar feature: unfair trade practices.[104]

Unfair trade practices – declared illegal in Article 19 of the AMA and further explained in the JFTC's General Designation of Unfair Trade Practices[105] –

---

[99]   Akman (n. 82 above) at 242–56. See also Nowag (2018) (n. 82 above) at 17.
[100]   Akman (n. 82 above) at 295–315.
[101]   ibid., 298.
[102]   ibid., 303–4.
[103]   Nowag (2018) (n. 82 above) at 17–18. The reason for this conclusion is "the seller on the platforms do not pool their resources and share their risk, and not do the sellers with the platforms."
[104]   Wakui notes that the unfair trade practices do not apply in case of agency agreements. She denotes that "[w]hen a party acts as an agent of another party who are engaged in the act of price restriction, there is no violation." However, she adds that this only applies in cases of actual agency. It is necessary to look at whether the principal bears the risk concerning the transaction and whether the transaction is on the principal's own account or not to assess whether there is an actual agency agreement. Masako Wakui, *Antimonopoly Law: Competition Law and Policy in Japan* (Arima Publishing 2008) 156.
[105]   The JFTC issued the General Designation of Unfair Trade Practices in 1953. The 1953 Designation included 12 broadly worded items, including, among others, "refus-

comprise a list of 15 designations: concerted refusal to trade, other refusal to trade, discriminatory consideration, discriminatory treatment on trade terms, discriminatory treatment in a trade association, unjust low price sales, unjust high price purchasing, deceptive customer inducement, customer inducement by unjust benefits, tie-in sales, trading on exclusive terms, trading on restrictive terms, unjust interference with appointment of officer in one's transacting party, and interference with a competitor's transactions.[106] In short, unfair trade practices cover mainly vertical agreements or unilateral conduct.

Uber's business model must be analyzed to see whether one of the above designations could apply. Two services have been highlighted in the literature.[107] First, Uber offers brokerage between drivers and riders. The platform allows drivers to show their availability while permitting riders to request a ride from one point to another. Second, Uber also offers a price-setting service, which drivers cannot refuse. The price-setting service is always to be included in the driver's subscription package. It offers advantages to both drivers and riders; drivers are certain about the payment, while riders are guaranteed a fair price. A driver cannot charge more than the Uber algorithm's calculation; however, the opposite might be possible.[108] In other words, the algorithm fixes the maximum price for a ride.

Uber creates a vertical price restriction by setting the maximum price level; however, as described above, a product must be resold to apply the legal reasoning of an RPM.[109] Since the Uber business model lacks this transaction, another type of infringement must be found within the AMA. Among the different practices that the JFTC designates as unfair trade is Paragraph 12 of the

---

als to deal, price discrimination, predatory or unfair pricing practices, customer and supplies restrictions, tying arrangements, and abuses of dominant bargaining position." The 1953 General Designation was revised in 1982 (1982 General Designation) to include a total of 16 designations that could be captured by the following broad categories: refusal to deal, discriminatory pricing or treatment, unfair pricing, unfair inducement, and coercion (including tying), exclusive dealing, resale price maintenance, exclusive or restrictive dealing, resale price maintenance, abuse of dominant bargaining position and interference with a competitor's transaction. A last revision of the 1982 General Designation, together with Article 2(9) AMA, occurred in 2009. This revision reduced the designations to 15. John O. Haley, *Antitrust in Germany and Japan: The First Fifty Years, 1947–1998* (University of Washington Press 2001) 53.

[106]   ibid.

[107]   Nowag (2018) (n. 82 above) at 17.

[108]   Akman (n. 84 above) at 265 and 285 n. 314.

[109]   In general, Nowag (2018) (n. 82 above) at 14–15; Anderson and Huffman (n. 82 above) at 903–4. On the fact that resale price maintenance requires the sale of a good in Japan, Wakui (n. 6 above) at 190.

General Designation of 2009 (2009 General Designation),[110] which describes trading on restrictive terms. Trading on restrictive terms is a form of conditional dealing whereby an unjust trade restriction is imposed on an enterprise, and this unjust restriction does not amount to an RPM, Article 2(9) of the AMA, or exclusive dealing (Paragraph 11 of the 2009 General Designation).

One example of trading on restrictive terms is when a supplier sets the price for a service downstream; this is a situation in which no product is being offered for resale.[111] More recently, the JFTC sought to apply this provision to parity clauses, thus for situations when a platform demands its sellers do not lower the price on other platforms to guarantee similar prices across platforms.[112] The JFTC has yet to explain the precise operation of Paragraph 12 of the 2009 General Designation regarding the sharing economy.[113] This has to do with the operational setting of the unfair trade practices where trading on restrictive terms belongs. Any explanation of the scope of Paragraph 12 of the 2009 General Designation must be done in a cease-and-desist order.[114] However, such an order only follows when the enterprise under investigation receives a notification. Many enterprises respond to this notification.[115] Consequently, the JFTC has had little chance to elaborate on the application modalities of this provision. For example, in recent history, the JFTC had the opportunity to provide its view on the parity clause because Amazon decided to voluntarily delete the parity clause from the Marketplace. Since Amazon changed its behaviour before the notification, the JFTC closed the investigation without explaining Paragraph 12 of the 2009 General Designation.[116]

---

[110] JFTC, 'Designation of Unfair Trade Practices' (Fair Trade Commission Public Notice No. 15 of June 18' 1982 as revised in 2009), available at: www.jftc.go.jp/en/legislation_gls/unfairtradepractices.html (accessed 30 June 2022).

[111] Wakui (n. 50 above) at 191. Other examples are selective distribution and territorial restrictions and bans on parallel imports, sales methods, wholesale, and dealing with competitors.

[112] ibid.

[113] For an overview of JFTC actions against digital platforms, see Steven Van Uytsel and Yoshiteru Uemura, 'Regulating Competition Law between Digital Platforms: The Japan Fair Trade Commission's Preference for Unfair Trade Practice' in Steven Van Uytsel (ed.), *The Digital Economy and Competition Law in Asia* (Springer 2021) 45–73; Kazuhiko Fuchikawa, 'Regulations of Digital Platform Markets Under the Japanese Antimonopoly Act: Does the Regulation of Unfair Trade Practices Solve the Gordian Knot of Digital Markets?' (2020) 65(1) *The Antitrust Bulletin* 102–19.

[114] Wakui (n. 50 above) at 140. It is also stipulated that only the unfair trade practices qualified in the AML can be subject to a surcharge. For a short description of the problem see, Van Uytsel and Uemura (n. 113 above) at 45.

[115] Van Uytsel and Uemura (n. 113 above) at 45. The process of notification has recently been changed to a commitment procedure.

[116] ibid.

The limited information drawn from applying trading on restrictive terms to the new economy can be somewhat complemented with information from a few older cases. Among these older cases, especially concerning price setting, the Twentieth Century Fox Japan and Kobayashi Kosé cases are the most often cited.[117] The former case concerns a film distributor restricting the freedom of movie theatres to offer discounts on admission fees. The latter involves a case in which a perm solution manufacturer, Kobayashi Kosé (now Kosé Corporation), determined the price of perming services in beauty parlours.[118] Both pricing practices were considered trading on restrictive terms because the freedom of competition restriction was done by setting the price without a product resold. The JFTC did not consider justifying the unjust lessening of competition in either case, despite the possibility being available. In fact, to date, there is no case in which the JFTC has considered any justification for price restrictions. It is probably against any applicable case law background that Wakui hinted at the analytical framework for RPMs to deal with price restrictions qualified as conditional dealing unfair trade practices.[119]

Like trading on restrictive terms, RPMs are a form of conditional dealing, reducing free competition. The basic approach is that such free competition lessening is presumed because the RPM eliminates intra-brand price competition among retailers. It is up to the defendant to rebut such a presumption by proving there is no reduction of free competition or that pro-competitive effects outbalance the restriction. One such pro-competitive effect could be the existence of substantial inter-brand competition, whereas another effect could be avoiding a double marginalization.[120]

To assess these pro-competitive effects, the defendant must put forward a market definition, requiring the naming of competitors and the calculation of each respective market share. Depending on the outcome, it can be argued that sufficient alternatives are challenging Uber, or, if there are no alternatives, Uber's market power must be tempered by preventing the drivers from adding another monopoly mark-up to the platform algorithm's determined price.

Whether the above reasoning could be applied to Uber in Japan remains to be seen. Uber did not originally succeed in transplanting its business model to Japan. Strict regulation prevented the roll-out of ride-sharing with

---

[117]   Wakui (n. 50 above) at 191.

[118]   ibid., 191–2.

[119]   ibid, 191.

[120]   Free riding may not be relevant in the context of Uber. It is not conceivable that one driver offers an extra service that a rider takes and subsequently enters another driver's car. See Nowag (2018) (n. 82 above) at 16.

privately-owned cars.[121] To guarantee its presence, Uber altered its business model from its model elsewhere in the world. Uber partnered with locally established taxi companies in major Japanese cities.[122] Thus, the Uber partners differ from city to city. In Fukuoka, the main city on the Southern island of Kyushu, about 15 local taxi companies have signed up with Uber.[123] The Uber platform allows users to book a ride in Fukuoka through the platform, after which a taxi from one of these 15 taxi companies picks the user up and brings them to their destination. Uber gives a price estimate for the ride, and this estimate applies across the 15 partnered taxi companies. In some cities, like Kyoto, riders can select a price estimate for all partnered taxi companies, except the MK Group, which applies another fare calculation. This new business model may not necessarily affect applying the unfair trade practice of trading on restrictive terms; however, assessing the pro-competitive effects may turn out differently. In the end, Uber is setting the price estimate for existing taxi companies as no ride-sharing drivers can access the market; hence, this model does not stimulate inter-brand competition. The availability of similar apps, such as Didi Taxi, may compensate for the loss of inter-brand competition. The strict regulation of prices in Japan may also weaken the double marginalization argument. In the end, if the algorithm would enable a differentiated price setting, the taxi companies would still be bound by the government regulation fixing basic prices for taxi rides.[124]

---

[121] On the difficult initial start of Uber in Japan, see Shigenori Matsui, 'Is Law Killing the Development of New Technology?: Uber and Airbnb in Japan' (2019) *B.U. J. Sci. & Tech. L.* 100. In an article in Reuters, it is mentioned that "Uber is not allowed to run its own ride-sharing fleet in Japan as it does in the United States and elsewhere since local regulations ban non-professional drivers from ferrying paying customers." Reuters Staff, 'Uber Widens Taxi App to Japan's Tokyo but Ride-Sharing Still Barred' (3 July 2020), available at www.reuters.com/article/us-uber-japan-idUSKBN24416F (accessed 30 June 2022). Ryosuke Hanada and Kento Urasaki, 'Rules leave Uber with Hard Road in Japan' (29 May 2016) *Nikkei Asia*, available at https://asia.nikkei.com/Business/Rules-leave-Uber-with-hard-road-in-Japan (30 June 2022).

[122] Reuters Staff, 'Uber Pulls Up in Japan with Taxi-Hailing Service' (22 May 2018) *Reuters*, available at www.reuters.com/article/us-uber-japan-idUSKCN1IN14O (accessed 30 June 2022).

[123] Currently, Uber is available in 15 cities in Japan. See Uber, 'Use Uber in Cities Around the World' (2022), available at www.uber.com/global/en/cities/?utm_campaign=CM2088583-affiliates-impactradius_85_-99_JP-National_r_all_acq_cpa_ja-JP_Forestone%20Co.%2CLtd_click-VKsX4DRgvxyITT8Q9kyPkU0OUkGRYkQIOREzXg0&utm_medium=impact&utm_source=affiliate-ir-Forestone%20Co.%2CLtd&utm_term=VKsX4DRgvxyITT8Q9kyPkU0OUkGRYkQIOREzXg0.

[124] David Flath, 'Taxicab Regulation in Japan' (2002), available at https://academiccommons.columbia.edu/download/fedora_content/download/ac:109357/content/WP_201.pdf (accessed 30 June 2022).

6   CONCLUSION

With the Algorithm Report, the JFTC received an expert opinion on the AMA's difficulties with algorithmic collusion. The conclusion of the Algorithmic Report is quite optimistic. Provided the algorithmic collusion can be linked to the conduct of a human representative of competing firms, it is understood that the provision dealing with collusion, the unreasonable restraint of trade prong of Article 3 of the AMA, can be applied. Human conduct does not require active communication, but it can be an understanding of implementing a single algorithm in the industry. When the collusion results from the independent behaviour of algorithms, the Algorithm Report implies that the AMA cannot apply. However, as this kind of algorithm operates only within an experimental context, there is no immediate threat to the market, and, therefore, no further suggestions are made.

These conclusions are not comprehensive enough, as not all algorithms can be linked to the human conduct of representatives of *competing* firms. Actors outside the competitive ring may facilitate collusion, and third-party cartel facilitators could run the algorithm. The Algorithm Report could have seized the opportunity for experts to clarify the most current view on the application of the AMA toward third-party cartel facilitators and indicate whether the reserved stance toward punishing such facilitators has finally been abandoned.

It has also been pointed out that the frequently cited example regarding an algorithmic third-party cartel facilitator – the Uber business model – may not be a good fit to describe algorithmic collusion. Without sharing sensitive information among the drivers and offering a matching service toward drivers for which it also calculates the price, it could be argued that the application of competition law should focus on the vertical relationship between Uber and its drivers. We have argued that the AMA could also apply to this scenario with a rich set of unfair trade practices. Specifically, we have demonstrated that dealing on restrictive terms, an unfair trade practice applying to the factual situation wherein a supplier imposed a price on a retailer without reselling a product could be applied. We also indicated that pro-competitive effects, including tremendous inter-brand competition or the avoidance of double marginalization, could outweigh the restrictive terms. Nevertheless, the question remains whether such pro-competitive effects could stand in the Japanese Uber business model, whereby the Uber service does not exist separate from the traditional taxi service.

8. Price-monitoring algorithms and resale price maintenance: an analysis of recent cases in Europe

Yoshiteru Uemura

1 INTRODUCTION

Resale price maintenance (RPM) has not been a regulatory priority for the European Commission for some time. Following the 2003 decision against the Japanese musical instrument maker Yamaha,[1] the Commission did not initiate any RPM enforcement action for about 15 years.[2] The circumstances changed in 2018, when the Commission fined four consumer electronics manufacturers for engaging in RPM. The difference from the Yamaha case is the use of algorithms. The manufacturers used complex and sophisticated algorithms to monitor and track their online distributors' resale prices. When their suggested prices were not met, the manufacturers intervened.

The Commission's concern may have been triggered by a report published in May 2017. As part of the European Union's digital single market strategy,[3]

---

[1] Commission Decision of 16 July 2003, *Case COMP/37.975 – PO/Yamaha*, available at https://ec.europa.eu/competition/antitrust/cases/dec_docs/37975/37975_91_5.pdf (accessed 30 June 2022).

[2] In the meantime, many resale price maintenance (RPM) cases were handled at the Member State level under domestic competition laws. Marc Israel, Jacquelyn MacLennan and Jan Jeram, 'Vertical Restraints in an Online World: Competition Authorities Gear up their Enforcement Approach in the Digital Economy' (2019) 18 *Competition Law Journal* 17, 18. For more discussion, see Peter Georg Picht and Gaspare Tazio Loderer, 'Framing Algorithms: Competition Law and (Other Regulatory Tools' (2019) 42(3) *World Competition* 391, at 401–02.

[3] Commission, 'Communication from the Commission to the European Parliament, the Council, The European Economic and Social Committee and the Committee of Regions: A Digital Single Market Strategy for Europe' (2015) *COM(2015) 192 final*, available at https://eur-lex.europa.eu/legal-content/EN/TXT/PDF/?uri=CELEX:52015DC0192&from=EN (accessed 30 June 2022).

the Commission published the Report on the E-commerce Sector Inquiry,[4] revealing that e-commerce in the EU had grown steadily in recent years. According to the report on the inquiry, the proportion of individuals aged 16 to 74 who had ordered goods or services over the internet continuously grew, from 30 per cent in 2007 to 55 per cent in 2016.[5] The latest data from Eurostat reveals the percentage of online shoppers reached 63 per cent in 2019.[6] The e-commerce report also indicated that 53 per cent of respondent retailers track competitors' online prices, and 67 per cent of these retailers use price-monitoring algorithms for that purpose. Many of those retailers (78 per cent) subsequently adjust prices to those of their competitors, the report states. In this way, not humans, but automated computer programs monitor competing retailers' prices in contemporary online retailing. At the core of those computer programs are sophisticated price-monitoring algorithms that can monitor, track and adjust prices instantaneously.

Increased online price transparency through price-monitoring algorithms enables manufacturers to easily detect retailers who deviate from manufacturers' pricing recommendations. It could also allow manufacturers to retaliate against retailers who do not comply with pricing recommendations and ultimately limit retailers' incentives to deviate from such recommended prices. This chapter focuses on algorithms in a vertical context, analyzing the recent RPM cases in Europe.

Section 2 introduces price-monitoring algorithms in a vertical context. This is followed by a description of four RPM cases, Asus, Denon & Marantz, Pioneer and Phillips, in Section 3. Section 4 details the concerns of the European Commission regarding the use of algorithms in an RPM context. A conclusion is provided in Section 5.

2   PRICE-MONITORING ALGORITHMS

2.1   Price-Monitoring Algorithms in a Vertical Context

Price-monitoring algorithms have usually been investigated in a horizontal context in which competitors in a price-fixing agreement use algorithms

---

[4]   Commission, 'Report from the Commission to the Council and the European Parliament: Final Report on the E-commerce Sector Inquiry' (2017) *SWD (2017) 154 final*, available at https://ec.europa.eu/competition/antitrust/sector_inquiry_swd_en.pdf (accessed 30 June 2022).

[5]   ibid., para 7.

[6]   Eurostat, Statistics Explained, 'E-commerce Statistics for Individuals' (2022) available at https://ec.europa.eu/eurostat/statistics-explained/index.php?title=E -commerce_statistics_for_individuals (accessed 30 June 2022).

as a means of monitoring the prices of the other participants in an illegal, anti-competitive agreement.[7] Ariel Ezrachi and Maurice E. Stucke referred to such cases as the "messenger scenario"[8] while the OECD categorized them literally, as "monitoring algorithms."[9] The role of price-monitoring algorithms as facilitators of price-fixing collusion is in monitoring and collecting competitors' prices to enforce a collusive horizontal agreement. By using sophisticated algorithms, colluding companies are able to effectively monitor one another's pricing behavior to achieve illegal purposes.

In addition to the price-monitoring algorithms in a horizontal context, the European Commission also referred to price-monitoring algorithms in a vertical context at an OECD roundtable entitled "Algorithms and Collusion." The Commission raised the particular issue of price-monitoring algorithms in relation to RPM and expressed concerns.[10]

2.2 Price Monitoring in RPM

Article 101(1) of the Treaty on the Functioning of the European Union (TFEU) prohibits agreements between business undertakings for the purpose or with the effect of limiting competition in the internal EU market. This provision makes it possible to regulate not only horizontal agreements, such as price-fixing agreements between undertakings in competitive relationships, but also vertical agreements between undertakings that are active in different distribution stages.[11] Unlike horizontal agreements between competitors, many vertical agreements do not pose problems under EU competition law.[12] Nevertheless, in principle, some types of vertical agreements have been treated as illegal in the EU. RPM is one of such practices. RPM is the act of determining the

---

[7]   For example, OECD, 'Algorithms and Collision: Collaboration Policy in the Digital Age' (2017), available at www.oecd.org/daf/competition/Algorithms-and -colllusion-competition-policy-in-the-digital-age.pdf (accessed 30 June 2022). In addition to price-monitoring algorithms, the report introduces three types of algorithms that can be involved in pricing between competing parties, and presents the possible responses and limitations of current competition laws.

[8]   Ariel Ezrachi and Maurice M. Stucke, *Virtual Competition: The Promise and Perils of the Algorithm-Driven Economy* (Harvard University Press 2016) 39–45.

[9]   OECD (n. 7 above) 26–7.

[10]   OECD, 'Algorithms and Collusion – Note from the European Union' (2017) *DAF/COMP/WD(2017)* 12, available at https://one.oecd.org/document/DAF/COMP/ WD(2017)12/en/pdf (accessed 30 June 2022).

[11]   Joined cases 56 and 58/64, *Consten and Grundig v Commission* ECLI:EU:C:1966:41, 340.

[12]   Commission, 'Notice: Guidelines on Vertical Restraints' (2010/C, 130/01) para 6, available at https://eur-lex.europa.eu/LexUriServ/LexUriServ.do?uri=OJ:C:2010: 130:0001:0046:en:PDF (accessed 30 June 2022).

price (resale price) or minimum resale price when the purchaser of a product sells the product to a third party through an agreement between undertakings in a vertical business relationship.[13] Such restrictions in a buyer's ability to determine sales price generally constitute a restraint of competition by object, and the benefit of the block exemption by the Commission regulation shall not apply to such vertical agreement.[14] RPM falls under Article 101(1) and is usually presumed not to meet the requirements of Article 101(3).[15]

In the case of RPM, the seller's side must monitor whether the buyers, who are trading partners, are reliably following the level of resale price that the seller is seeking to maintain. For example, when a manufacturer asks multiple retailers in a business relationship to maintain specific resale prices, it is difficult to request different resale price levels for each retailer. That is because retailers are often exposed to fierce price competition at the retail level, and are likely to accept the resale prices manufacturers suggest on the condition that other retailers in the same retail network comply and adopt the same retail prices. Without this kind of assurance, retailers cannot easily join in on an RPM scheme; therefore, manufacturers are usually required to set products' resale prices at the same level throughout distribution networks. However, there is also a risk of cheating by retailers, as they can make a profit by secretly lowering retail prices below the agreed retail price level with which other retailers comply. To respond to this, manufacturers try to monitor each dealer's actual sales price in some way. Traditional approaches adopted by many manufacturers engaged in RPMs include price checking at offline bricks-and-mortar shops, collecting retail price information through advertisements, and purchasing price information from third parties, such as marketing research and analytics firms.

There is also an incentive for each retailer participating in RPM to monitor the prices of other retailers' offering the same products. They will monitor for deviations from the agreed manufacturer resale price. Resale price agreement does not imply a consensus regarding retail prices between retailers, as is the

---

[13]   ibid., para 48.

[14]   Commission Regulation (EU) No 330/2010 of 20 April 2010 on the application of Article 101(3) of the Treaty on the Functioning of the European Union to Categories of Vertical Agreements and Concerted Practices (*OJ* 2010, L102/1) Article 4(a). Commission, 'Guidance on Restrictions of Competition "by Object" for the Purpose of Defining Which Agreements May Benefit from the De Minimis Notice' *SWD(2014) 198 final*.

[15]   Commission (n. 12 above) para 223. However, if a business undertaking who is questioned for violation succeeds in insisting on a certain improvement of efficiency and the return of its result to consumers, such as enhancing pre-sale services by retailers and preventing freerides against them, they may be exempt from the application of Article 101(1). ibid., para 225.

case with horizontal price-fixing agreements; however, each retailer usually expects that compliance with the manufacturer's resale price will not result in an intra-brand competition. In fact, in the EU, RPM schemes often result in retailers' complaints that individual shops or stores are selling at lower prices. Based on such complaints, manufacturers usually take remedial actions that may lead to infringement of the EU competition law. The following RPM cases involving consumer electronics manufacturers have demonstrated this as well.

3   RELATED RPM CASES

On 24 July 2018, the European Commission imposed fines totalling more than 111 million euros on four major consumer electronics manufacturers based in Asia and Europe for violating Article 101(1) TFEU. In these cases, the four companies fully cooperated with the Commission's investigation, submitting significant value-added evidence before the issue of the Statement of Objections by the Commission, clearly acknowledging that they had violated the EU competition law. The Commission reduced the fines by 40 per cent (three companies) and 50 per cent (one company) according to the degree of cooperation of the violating companies in accordance with the relevant regulations.[16] The violation facts established by the Commission in each case are summarized as follows.

---

[16]   See Commission, 'Antitrust: Commission Fines Four Consumer Electronics Manufacturers for Fixing Online Resale Prices' (Press Release, July 24, 2018), available at https://ec.europa.eu/commission/presscorner/detail/en/IP_18_4601 (accessed 30 June 2022), for a list of the percentage reductions for each violator and the amount of fines ultimately imposed. It is notable that as a feature of the RPM cases discussed in this paper, the reduction of the fines was made despite the non-cartel circumstances; however, this paper does not address this issue. Refer to the following as papers that touch on this point. Alexandra Rudi, 'Consumer Electronics Case: The Butterfly Effect on RPM?' (2019) 3 *European Competition and Regulatory Law Review* 420; Aurelien Portuese, 'European Algorithmic Antitrust and Resale Price Maintenance: Asus, Denon & Marantz, Philips, and Pioneer Decisions' (Competition Policy International, 2018), available at www.competitionpolicyinternational.com/european-algorithmic-antitrust -and-resale-price-maintenance-asus-denon-marantz-philips-and-pioneer-decisions (accessed 30 June 2022).

3.1 *ASUS*[17]

Taiwan-based ASUS is a multinational company that manufactures computer equipment (hardware) and electronic products, producing and selling a wide range of related equipment and products, such as notebook PCs, tablet terminals, desktop PCs and electronic displays.[18] ASUS established wholly-owned subsidiaries in Germany and France to provide marketing, sales and repair services. In both countries, ASUS sold its products to retailers through independent wholesalers and not directly to end-users.[19] The wholesalers primarily controlled the delivery of ASUS products and retailers' payment, and ASUS employees negotiated directly with the retailers regarding the terms of product purchase. In this way, ASUS substantially controlled many retailers, although it had no direct business relationships.[20]

For sales in Germany and France, ASUS sought to ensure that its products' selling prices remained stable at the recommended price level. For that reason, ASUS continuously and systematically monitored its products' retail prices and endeavoured to identify retailers selling below recommended prices. If a low-pricing retailer was discovered, ASUS employees contacted the retailer and requested that they raise the retail price. To maintain retail prices at the recommended price level, ASUS not only asked low-pricing retailers to raise prices, but also reacted through robust means when a request was refused. For example, the company imposed sanctions on retailers that repeatedly did not to follow recommended prices in Germany by halting product shipments, reducing shipment volumes, excluding them from partner programs that allow preferential purchase prices, and banning the online use of logos.[21] In France, the company also threatened to curtail conventionally granted financial support from ASUS to low-pricing retailers, tangentially generating a rise in retail prices.[22]

---

[17] Commission Decision of 24 July 2018, *Case AT. 40465 – Asus*, available at https://ec.europa.eu/competition/antitrust/cases/dec_docs/40465/40465_337_3.pdf (accessed 30 June 2022).

[18] ibid., para 4.

[19] ibid., para 10. ASUS also sold directly to a limited number of retailers.

[20] ibid., para 11.

[21] ibid., para 68.

[22] ibid., para 93.

3.2   *Denon & Marantz*[23]

Japan-based Denon & Marantz (D&M) is an international manufacturer of audio equipment, video equipment, and home entertainment equipment that has three brands under its business holding company: Denon, Marantz and Boston Acoustics.[24] D&M established wholly-owned subsidiaries in Germany and the Netherlands to sell related products. In both countries, D&M sold its products to end-users through independent retailers but adopted a selective distribution system, selecting retailers based on specific objective qualitative criteria.[25]

For sales in Germany and the Netherlands, D&M adopted a sales strategy to stabilize products' retail price. As a result, D&M monitored retail prices and sought to identify retailers in its sales network selling at lower prices or below recommended prices. If a retailer was found to be selling at a lower price, sales contractors in Germany, and D&M employees in the Netherlands, contacted the retailer to request an increase in retail prices. D&M was tough on retailers selling at low prices to stabilize their products' retail prices and to prevent sharp price declines. In Germany, for example, the company pressured retailers through sales contractors and threatened to stop supplying D&M products if they sold below the level of the retail prices indicated.[26] Moreover, information on sanctions, such as suspension of shipments, leveraged against individual low-pricing retailers was communicated to other retailers in the sales network, using threats to maintain the retail prices sought by D&M.[27] In the Netherlands, D&M sent an email to retailers explaining that if they did not sell at the recommended price, the company would remove the Marantz-approved logo from the price comparison site and stop delivering D&M products until the situation improved.[28] The company took steps to suspend supply to specific retailers who continued to set retail prices below D&M's recommended prices, although they had since readjusted retail prices to the recommended price level.[29]

---

[23]   Commission Decision of 24 July 2018, *Case AT. 40469 – Denon & Marantz,* available at https://ec.europa.eu/competition/antitrust/cases/dec_docs/40469/40469 _329_3.pdf (accessed 30 June 2022).
[24]   ibid., paras 4 and 5. For example, D&M provided AV receivers, Blu-ray players, etc. under the Denon and Marantz brand names and various speaker products under the Boston Acoustics brand name. ibid., paras 8 and 9.
[25]   ibid., para 12.
[26]   ibid., para 54.
[27]   ibid., para 58.
[28]   ibid., para 76.
[29]   ibid., para 77.

3.3   *Philips*[30]

Based in the Netherlands, Philips is a multinational technology giant that manufactures and sells medical and healthcare products, and a wide range of consumer products in France, including electric shavers for men, home communications equipment, electric toothbrushes and coffee makers.[31] Retailers selling Philips' consumer products in France were primarily online shops and stores selling both offline and online.[32] For sales in France, Philips established a system to thoroughly monitor retail prices by collecting daily retail price information for each retailer and sharing that information among the employees involved.[33] When contacted regarding retailers selling at prices below the recommended price, Philips immediately contacted employees to ask such retailers to increase retail prices. In this way, Philips closely monitored its products' retail prices to stabilize the resale prices across the entire market.[34]

Philips also took a tough stand against low-pricing retailers by imposing certain sanctions against them to maintain the retail prices in its sales network.[35]

3.4   *Pioneer*[36]

Japan-based Pioneer established a wholly-owned subsidiary to oversee Europe and operated a home appliance business across Europe. The presiding company sold home appliances, such as audio equipment and video playback equipment, through subsidiaries or branches located in 12 European countries (Germany, France, Italy, the United Kingdom, Spain, Portugal, Sweden, Finland, Denmark, Belgium, the Netherlands and Norway).[37] Pioneer's European headquarters adopted a Europe-wide strategy to monitor the retail prices of its product. This strategy required subsidiaries or branch offices responsible for sales in the 12 European countries to regularly report retail prices.[38] Pioneer specifically asked low-pricing online retailers to increase

---

[30]   Commission Decision of 24 July 2018, *Case AT. 40181 – Philips*, available at   https://ec.europa.eu/competition/antitrust/cases/dec_docs/40181/40181_417_3.pdf (accessed 30 June 2022).

[31]   ibid., paras 4–11.

[32]   ibid., para 12.

[33]   ibid., para 30.

[34]   ibid., paras 34–45.

[35]   ibid., paras 24 and 32.

[36]   Commission Decision of 24 July 2018, *Case AT. 40182 – Pioneer*, available at   https://ec.europa.eu/competition/antitrust/cases/dec_docs/40182/40182_370_3.pdf (accessed 30 June 2022).

[37]   ibid., paras 7–10.

[38]   ibid., paras 22 and 24.

retail prices to prevent their home appliances from being sold cheaply online,[39] and closely monitored retail prices by country or region to maintain retail prices.[40] The company also took a tough stand against some low-pricing retailers who did not respond to requests to raise retail prices to maintain the selling price; for example, by threatening not to cooperate with sales promotion campaigns,[41] not responding to additional requests[42] and reducing rebates.[43]

4 CHALLENGE OF ALGORITHMIC RPM

4.1 Concerns Expressed by the European Commission

As noted previously, the European Commission emphasized the role of price-monitoring algorithms in RPM and expressed concerns regarding such algorithms in the RPM context during a discussion on "Algorithms and Collusion" at the OECD's competition committee.

As they are far more sophisticated than traditional means of price monitoring, these algorithms can effectively detect deviations from fixed or minimum resale prices. The Commission noted that while the algorithmic price monitoring action itself is not a violation of RPM, it constitutes part of the violation if it contributes to improving the effectiveness of an actual RPM offense.[44]

Second, regarding manufacturers' recommended prices, price-monitoring algorithms improve price transparency in the market, making it easier to identify retailers pricing in a way that differs from the manufacturer's recommended price. It allows manufacturers to retaliate against retailers that do not comply with recommended prices, depriving retailers of incentives to deviate from the manufacturer's suggested prices. If manufacturers' use of price-monitoring algorithms pressures retailers to maintain recommended prices, the Commission asserts that manufacturers are essentially converting recommended prices into fixed resale prices.[45] In the OECD discussions, the Commission also confirmed that manufacturers' suggested prices for retail sales to retailers is not an issue under EU competition law;[46] however, manufacturers should continuously monitor whether this suggested price is

---

[39] ibid., para 27. At the same time, it also stopped online retailers from selling Pioneer products across borders to other European Economic Area countries.
[40] ibid., paras 48–98.
[41] ibid., para 69.
[42] ibid., para 72.
[43] ibid., para 74.
[44] OECD (n. 10 above) at para 14.
[45] ibid., para 15.
[46] ibid., para 12.

fixed against a background of various pressures and inducements and is not functioning as an RPM.[47]

Third, the Commission contended that the danger of RPM's price-stabilizing effects will spread rapidly across the entire market due to retailers' use of price-monitoring algorithms to monitor competitors' retail prices.[48] For example, if retailer A complied with the resale price sought by a manufacturer and retailer B, which was not involved in the RPM, used algorithms to monitor retailer A's retail price, retailer B could match its price to that of retailer A. In this case, RPM's relatively high price will propagate to other retailers that are not involved in the RPM scheme, affecting the overall market price. This trend will strengthen, especially if retailer A functions as a price leader in a particular market.

The Commission cited three scenarios representing the adverse effects of price-monitoring algorithms used in RPM considering the characteristics of online transactions. How do such concerns transpire in actual RPM cases involving algorithms? The possibility of the three scenarios will next be examined along with the RPM cases in Europe mentioned in Section 3.

4.2   Improved Effectiveness of RPM

Of the four RPM cases above, ASUS explicitly stated that trading partners' retail prices were monitored using an algorithm. In this case, in addition to monitoring retail prices through price comparison sites in Germany, ASUS used in-house price-monitoring algorithms to identify retailers selling ASUS products below the recommended price.[49] ASUS launched a Premium Partner Program to sell network-related products, paying incentives to premium partner retailers on the condition that they comply with the company's recommended prices. An internal watchlist monitored the sales prices of retailers participating in the programme, with a mechanism in which online retailers who set retail prices below the recommended price were instantly displayed in red.[50] The watchlist allowed ASUS to quickly detect retailers selling at low prices and swiftly request retail price increases through individual contacts, with a complete view of the market's retailing prices.[51] The watchlist identified at least two suppliers selling at retail prices below ASUS's recommended prices, and ASUS requested that they raise their prices.[52] The European

---

[47]   Commission (n. 12 above) at paras 48 and 227.
[48]   OECD (n. 10 above) at para 16.
[49]   *Case AT. 40465 – Asus*, para 27.
[50]   ibid., para 37.
[51]   ibid., para 39.
[52]   ibid., para 63.

Commission's decision states that ASUS's business partners participating in the programme were immediately contacted by ASUS and requested to raise prices if they had priced below the recommended price, suggesting that the watchlist had a significant role in improving the effectiveness of the RPM.[53]

4.3   Fixed Recommended Prices

As *ASUS* demonstrates, price-monitoring algorithms make it extremely easy to detect retailers who do not follow manufacturers' recommended prices. The manufacturers also succeeded in inducing retailers to sell products at recommended prices with the threat of retaliation for noncompliance with recommended prices.[54] That is precisely the circumstances in which manufacturers pressured retailers to comply with recommended prices, and the recommended prices functioned as substantially fixed resale prices.

In addition to price-monitoring algorithms, manufacturers have several other approaches to monitor whether retailers are complying with recommended prices. For example, price comparison sites were used to monitor retail prices in *D&M, Pioneer* and *ASUS*.[55] In *Pioneer*, the products' serial number tracking system was reasonably effective in identifying low-pricing retailers.[56] These monitoring methods contribute to efficient detection of low-pricing retailers, and this effectiveness is expected to significantly increase due to manufacturers' establishment of comprehensive and continuous monitoring systems.[57]

As noted, if price-monitoring algorithms and other efficient monitoring methods are used effectively, and pressure is applied via threat of retaliation and sanctions, with which the European Commission is concerned, it would be exceedingly difficult for retailers to set lower retail prices that differ from recommended prices. That is essentially equal to manufacturers maintaining retail

---

[53]   ibid., para 40.

[54]   ibid., paras 28 and 75.

[55]   ibid., paras 27 and 33; *Case AT. 40469 – Denon & Marantz,* paras 45, 49, 56, 76 and 77; *Case AT. 40182 – Pioneer,* paras 70 and 97.

[56]   *Case AT. 40182 – Pioneer,* paras 28, 38 and 126.

[57]   For example, in *Philips,* a system was established to comprehensively monitor retail prices within the company, and the information regarding each retailer's daily retail prices was collected and shared internally. More generally, these can be achieved by closely monitoring each retailer's website manually and by receiving information about low-pricing retailers from other retailers. In fact, according to the European Commission's fact-finding report, the most common way for manufacturers to monitor recommended prices (rather than retailers' monitoring one another's retail prices) is not via software that tracks prices (price-monitoring algorithms), but by manual tracking websites. Commission (n. 4 above) at para 577.

prices at a recommended price level. The RPM cases in Section 3 represent circumstances in which the fixing of the recommended prices became a reality.

4.4   Impact on the Entire Market

The European Commission emphasizes the implementation of RPM, such as improving the effectiveness of RPM by significantly enhancing detection capabilities and fixing recommended prices, as an adverse effects of price-monitoring algorithms in RPM. The Commission also points out an issue of retailers' pricing behaviour in online transactions. The problem is that the price maintenance effect of a particular RPM spreads to retailers that are not directly bound by the RPM, and the impact of the RPM spreads to the entire market. In this regard, *Philips* and *Pioneer* demonstrate that many retailers closely monitor the retail prices in online transactions and quickly respond to low-price competition. In particular, *Pioneer* revealed that many retailers use software called "spiders" that track other companies' retail prices, automatically adapting retail prices to the lowest prices.[58] *Philips* illustrated the price movement of retail prices in online transactions, revealing that many retailers adjusted retail prices in response to competitive price cuts.[59] *D&M* shows that software that automatically monitors and adjusts prices increases price movement in the market.[60] Similar judgment is clearly shown in *Philips* and *Pioneer*.[61] In online trading, it can be understood that retail prices are easily the same when retailers use price-monitoring algorithms. The European Commission notes that manufacturers can closely monitor retailers' prices, target the lowest-priced retailers, and intervene in reference to low prices to avoid price declines and price erosion across their online sales networks.[62] The Commission suggests that if retail prices are maintained through RPM, the effect will spread widely throughout the market. It is fair to say that the concerns expressed by the Commission at the OECD roundtable have been realized in the actual RPM cases above.

---

[58]   *Case AT. 40182 – Pioneer*, para 136.
[59]   *Case AT. 40181 – Philips*, para 47. Simultaneously, a graph in the decision indicates that specific retailers' price levels have significantly impacted other retailers' pricing behaviour.
[60]   *Case AT. 40469 – Denon & Marantz*, para 95.
[61]   *Philips* (n. 30) para 64; *Pioneer* (n. 36) para 155.
[62]   *Case AT. 40465 – Asus*, para 103; *Case AT. 40469 - Denon & Marantz*, para 95; *Case AT. 40181 – Philips*, para 64; *Case AT. 40182 – Pioneer*, para 155.

5   CONCLUSIONS

The European Commission's E-commerce Sector Inquiry states that of the various contractual restrictions retailers receive from manufacturers in online transactions, the most common is pricing restrictions, at 42 per cent of the total.[63] In second place is the limitation on sales in online trading platforms, at 18 per cent. Overwhelmingly, many retailers indicate that manufacturers have restricted retail prices in some way.[64] Among other things, manufacturers often establish recommended prices, and about 38 per cent of retailers acknowledge this.[65] Likewise, manufacturers recognize that recommended prices are more common, with 80 per cent of manufacturers responding that they have established recommended prices for retailers and other distributors.[66] Of course, manufacturers' establishment of recommended prices does will not violate EU competition law unless it constrains retailers' free pricing. However, as observed in Section 4.3, by closely monitoring retail prices using a price-monitoring algorithm or similar method, manufacturers can effectively fix the recommended price. After publishing the report on E-commerce, the European Commission launched an investigation into vertical price restrictions that had not been formally investigated for a long time, which seems to be predominantly due to the reality of online transactions revealed by the report.

The four RPM cases discussed in this chapter suggest the following insights. The use of price-monitoring algorithms in RPM can undoubtedly strengthen the effectiveness of RPM by making the detection of low-pricing retailers easier, quicker and less expensive for manufacturers. Moreover, given retailers' prevalent use of software programs that track prices online and automatically adjust to match competitors' prices, there is a risk that high pricing generated by RPM could immediately spread across the entire online market. Some commentators contend that this is why the Commission has turned its limited investigative resources toward RPM cases.[67] In any case, the Commission's first RPM case in almost 15 years was a decision made in a much more dramatically altered business environment than before. By the end of 2020, the size of online transactions in the EU was expected to be

---

[63]   Commission (n. 4 above) at para 334. However, the 'retail price limit' here includes RPM that violates EU competition law and the presentation of a true recommended price and the setting of a maximum resale price that is not treated as illegal in principle. ibid., para 335.

[64]   ibid., para 334.

[65]   ibid., para 557.

[66]   ibid., para 559.

[67]   Israel, MacLennan and Jeram (n. 2 above) 19.

around €717 billion annually.[68] More attention should be paid to the European Commission's response to vertical price restrictions in the future.[69]

---

[68] Ecommerce News, 'Ecommerce in Europe: €717 Billion in 2020' (2020), available at https://ecommercenews.eu/ecommerce-in-europe-e717-billion-in-2020/ (accessed 30 June 2022).

[69] On 17 December 2018, the European Commission imposed a fine of approximately 40 million euros on the European affiliate of the US apparel manufacturer Guess for banning retailers from advertising and selling online goods across borders. The case further called into question Guess's practice of maintaining the resale prices of the retailers involved. Commission Decision of 17 December 2018, *Case AT.40428 – Guess*, available at https://ec.europa.eu/competition/antitrust/cases/dec_docs/40428/40428_1205_3.pdf (accessed 30 June 2022).

9. Pricing in online grocery markets: challenges in monitoring competition

Cassey Lee and Gloria Lin[1]

1 INTRODUCTION

E-commerce has become an integral component of the economy in many countries. Major e-commerce platforms today sell hundreds and in some cases, thousands of products. For such platforms, the use of computers to set prices – algorithmic pricing – has become inevitable. Major e-commerce platforms today use algorithmic pricing to set their prices dynamically. The use of algorithmic pricing has raised concerns about tacit collusion. Research using computer simulations has shown that the application of machine learning to algorithmic pricing can result in tacit collusion.[2] Despite such concerns, there is a relative lack of empirical studies that have attempted to investigate how prices are being set in online markets, including the extent to which algorithmic pricing is being used, as well as whether there is evidence of tacit collusion in pricing in these markets.

In a sense, the paucity of research on pricing in online markets is not surprising. Whilst it is increasingly feasible to scrap price data from websites, it is likely to be very difficult to detect tacit collusion driven by algorithmic pricing. Automated dynamic pricing algorithms change prices very frequently for a high number of products. Amazon.com is reported to change the prices of its products 2.5 million times a day, or an average of once every ten minutes for each product. The high frequency of price change together with a large number of products (more than 12 million), implies that large computational capability

[1]   The authors thank the Ministry of Education for providing funding for this study under the Social Science Research Thematic Grant.

[2]   Emilio Calvano, Giacomo Calzolari, Vincenzo Denicolò, and Sergio Pastorello, 'Artificial Intelligence, Algorithmic Pricing, and Collusion' (2019) 110(10) *American Economic Review* 3267; Emilio Calvano, Giacomo Calzolari, Vincenzo Denicolò, and Sergio Pastorello, 'Algorithmic Pricing: What Implications for Competition Policy?' (2019) 55(1) *Review of Industrial Organization* 155.

is required to apply statistical methods to detect tacit collusion amongst large e-commerce platforms.

Even though it might be very challenging to detect tacit collusion in e-commerce, some attempt should be made with the view to understanding the nature and limitations of the methods that can be used to detect tacit collusion. Furthermore, not all sellers in online markets use algorithmic pricing. Some investigation on whether online markets exhibit hybrid pricing – where fixed pricing co-exists with algorithmic pricing – would yield valuable insights on how pricing actually works in markets that are still transitioning to more extensive adoption of algorithmic pricing.

With the above issues at hand, the goal of this study is to explore the nature of pricing in the online grocery market using data from Singapore. This entails an analysis of whether sellers use algorithmic pricing and if so, how useful are the different methods of detecting collusion. The data used in this study were collected during different phases of the COVID-19 pandemic in Singapore. This provides the opportunity to examine whether collusion detection can be carried out by comparing pricing during normal periods (low number of daily COVID-19 cases) and periods of market shocks (associated with a high number of daily COVID-19 cases).

The outline of this chapter is as follows. Section 2 will review the literature on collusion detection. Section 3 discusses the collusion screening methodology used in this study. The results are discussed in Section 4. The issue of price correlation and algorithmic pricing is discussed in Section 5. Section 6 concludes.

2   LITERATURE REVIEW

The detection of collusion is a key activity in competition law enforcement. It is the initial activity that leads to verification/investigation, followed by prosecution and sanctions. For explicit collusion, such as cartel activities, the focus of detection has primarily been on uncovering direct evidence of communications between colluders.[3] The leniency programme has been an important mechanism to incentivize defection by colluders. In the absence of direct evidence of collusion, competition authorities can use data analysis to detect collusion. There are a number of data analytic approaches to detecting

---

[3]   Robert H. Porter, 'Detecting Collusion' (2005) 26 *Review of Industrial Organization* 147.

collusion. Joseph E. Harrington has classified these approaches into four categories, namely:

A. Investigate firm behaviour whether it is consistent with competition e.g. price correlation, and price response to cost and demand shocks.
B. Test for a structural break in firm behaviour e.g. changes in average prices, variance of prices, price relationship among firms, and market shares of firms.
C. Compare the behaviour of suspected colluding firms with that of competitive firms e.g. comparison of competitive prices and collusive prices.
D. Estimate collusive and competitive models to see which one fits the data better.[4]

Historically, the data analytic approach to detecting collusion began with pioneering work in the 1980s and 1990s using data from cartel cases, mostly in the United States. In terms of method, these entailed approaches (C) and (D) above. Even though the United States Department of Justice began exploring the use of approaches (A) and (B) as early as the 1970s, the application of approaches (C) and (D) have only become a focus of intensive research since the mid-2000s. These approaches are known as collusion screens or markers in the literature.

John M. Connor provides an early discussion of the use of price variance and skewness.[5] The study's review of the existing empirical studies suggests that collusion is associated with less dispersed prices (lower variance) and more negatively skewed prices.

Using data from collusion in the supply of seafood to military installations in the United States, Rosa Abrantes-Metz, Luke Froeb, John Geweke and Christopher T. Taylor found evidence of higher mean price and lower price variance in periods of bid-rigging collusion.[6] Prices are also less responsive to cost shocks during these periods. Abrantes-Metz and Bajari further suggested the use of market share as collusion screen.[7] The market shares of colluding firms tend to be more stable and are negatively correlated over time.

---

[4] Joseph E. Harrington, 'Detecting Cartels', in Paolo Buccirossi (ed.), *Handbook of Antitrust Economics* (MIT Press, 2008), at 213.
[5] John M. Connor, 'Collusion and Price Dispersion' (2005) 12(6) *Applied Economics Letters* 335.
[6] Rosa Abrantes-Metz, Luke Froeb, John Geweke and Christopher T. Taylor, 'A Variance Screen for Collusion' (2006) 24(3) *International Journal of Industrial Organization* 467.
[7] Rosa Abrantes-Metz and Patrick Bajari, 'Screens for Conspiracies and Their Multiple Applications' (2009) 24(1) *Antitrust* 66.

Yuliya Bolotova, John Connor and Douglas J. Miller applied two-time series estimation methods – autoregressive conditional heteroscedasticity (ARCH) and generalized ARCH (GARCH) – to investigate the simultaneous impact of collusion on the first two moments of prices (mean and variance) in two markets with proven collusion (citric acid and lysine).[8] The study found the two moments – mean and variance – to be useful indicators of the beginning or collapse of collusion.

von Blanckenburg and Geist proposed a concept (the Coordination Failure Diagnostics Concept) which captures the multi-dimensional aspect of market adjustment dynamics.[9] This leads to a proposal of using a system of cartel markers (SCM) comprising a number of variables, namely, capacity utilization, rate of return, capacity growth and price changes. Using data with proven collusion in the German cement industry, the study showed collusion is associated with a low level of capacity utilization, unresponsive prices to exogenous shocks, excess rate of return, nearly constant capacities, lower price variance and lower variance of capacity growth rate. The SCM was further refined by von Blanckenburg and Geist by adding cost efficiency (which declines under collusion) as another collusion marker.[10] The study used wage ratio (total wage paid divided by gross value added) as a proxy for cost efficiency.

Using data from 11 cartel cases in Germany, von Blanckenburg et al. compared the four moments of prices (mean, variance, skewness and kurtosis).[11] The study found some evidence of collusion being associated with higher mean price, lower variance, more skewed distribution and leptokurtic distributions. However, these findings are not robust across all of the cases. The study also showed that the Kolgomorov-Smirnov test (a non-parametric test) is a more robust test that can be used to differentiate price distributions under collusion and non-collusion.

To sum up, much of the literature on the detection of collusion using data analytics have relied on the application of collusion screening methods on known cases of cartel in markets involving relatively homogenous goods. The research interest in this topic has waned in recent years, probably due to

---

[8]   Yuliya Bolotova, John Connor and Douglas J. Miller, 'The Impact of Collusion on Price Behavior: Empirical Results from Two Recent Cases' (2008) 26(6) *International Journal of Industrial Organization* 1290.

[9]   Korbinian von Blanckenburg and Alexander Geist, 'How Can a Cartel Be Detected?' (2009) 15(4) *International Advances in Economic Research* 421.

[10]   Korbinian von Blanckenburg and Alexander Geist, 'Detecting Illegal Activities: The Case of Cartels' (2011) 32(1) *European Journal of Law and Economics* 15.

[11]   Korbinian von Blanckenburg, Alexander Geist and Konstantin Kholodilin, 'The Influence of Collusion on Price Changes: New Evidence from Major Cartel Cases' (2012) 13(3) *German Economic Review* 245.

data availability. The explosion of e-commerce powered by digital platforms should reinvigorate interest in the use of collusion screening. However, this too is constrained by data availability. This is overcome in this study by using high frequency price data from major online grocery retailers in Singapore.

3   METHODOLOGY

Studies on collusion screening have typically used data from verified collusion cases that contain prices from collusion and non-collusion periods. This type of data does not exist for online markets as there are no known cases of collusion in online markets powered by digital platforms. To overcome this problem, this study proposes to study the challenge of detecting collusion using selected collusion screening methods review earlier. As this study cannot separate the data into collusion and non-collusion subsets, it examines how collusion screen tests perform in online markets that experience demand shocks. This approach is not novel as many of the studies on collusion and price wars have examined the role of demand shocks (boom). This study differs from the existing literature as the demand shock incorporated is different from those discussed in the literature. More specifically, this study incorporates demand shocks arising from the COVID-19 pandemic.

3.1   Market Shocks and COVID-19 Pandemic

The COVID-19 pandemic generated demand shocks in online grocery markets in a number of ways. First, during lockdowns, consumers are constrained from buying groceries from physical stores. Second, when the infection rates were high, consumers were afraid to venture out to buy their groceries from physical stores lest they became infected by the COVID-19 virus. These two factors are likely to have increased demand in online markets. Aside from demand shocks, the COVID-19 pandemic has also resulted in supply shocks arising from lock-downs and border closures (affecting both production and distribution). Recent studies have considered COVID-19 as both demand and supply shocks to the world economy.[12] There are in fact concerns that the supply chain disruptions

---

[12]   Mitsuyo Ando, 'Demand and Supply Shocks of COVID-19 and International Production Networks: Evidence from Japan's Machinery Trade' (ERIA Discussion Paper Series No. 366, 2021), available at www.eria.org/research/demand-and-supply-shocks-of-covid-19-and-international-production-networks-evidence-from-japans-machinery-trade/ (accessed 30 June 2022).

and demand shocks experienced during the COVID-19 crisis may make it easier for online retailers to influence prices and supplies of groceries.[13]

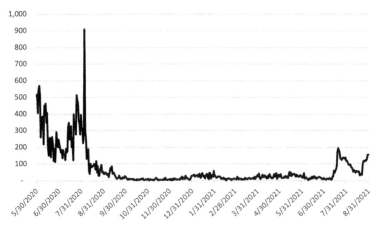

Source: MOH, Singapore

Figure 9.1   *COVID-19 new cases in Singapore, 30/5/2020–31/8/2021*

The data used in this study comes from Singapore. The data covers the period from 30 May 2020 to February 2022. During this period, there are four distinct time periods during which Singapore experienced varying degrees of COVID-19 infection levels. The first shock period – which is associated with the first and second waves of the COVID-19 pandemic – began in early 2020 and subsided in mid-August 2020 (Figure 9.1). The second shock period is associated with the third wave of the pandemic which covered the period from late August 2021 to mid-December 2021 (Figure 9.2). The third shock period covers the period from mid-December 2021 to late February 2021, during which the number of COVID-19 cases experienced a significant increase.

Based on these trends in COVID-19 cases, this study categorizes the time period in the data set in two ways/groups (Table 9.1). In Group 1, the three periods with a high number of COVID-19 cases (shock period) are pooled together and compared to the normal period. In Group 2, the three shock periods are not pooled to allow for comparison between the different shock periods.

---

[13]   OECD, 'Exploitative Pricing in the Time of COVID-19' (26 May 2020), available at www.oecd.org/competition/Exploitative-pricing-in-the-time-of-COVID-19.pdf (accessed 30 June 2022).

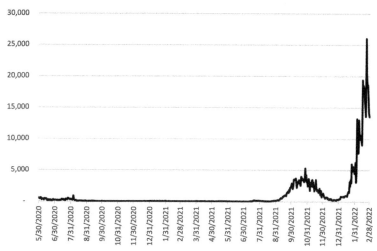

Source: MOH, Singapore

Figure 9.2   COVID-19 new cases in Singapore, 30/5/2020–28/2/2022

Table 9.1   Classification of time period in data set

Time Period	Group 1 (Pooled)	Group 2 (Unpooled)
30 May 2020–14 August 2020 (77 days)	Shock Period (SP)	Shock Period 1 (SP1)
15 August 2020–23 August 2021 (375 days)	Normal Period (NP)	Competitive (NP)
24 August 2021–19 December 2021 (118 days)	Shock Period (SP)	Shock Period 2 (SP2)
20 December 2021–28 February 2022 (71 days)	Shock Period (SP)	Shock Period 3 (SP3)

3.2   Collusion Screening Methods

Following Connor and von Blanckenburg et al.,[14] this study uses the four moments of price distribution (mean, variance, skewness and kurtosis) and the Kolgomorov-Smirnov test as collusion screening methods. These are reviewed next.

---

[14]   See Connor (n. 5 above) and von Blanckenburg, Geist and Kholodilin (n. 11 above).

3.2.1 Comparisons of means

Evidence from the literature suggests that mean prices of goods are higher during periods of decreased competition. In this study, shock periods associated with high COVID-19 cases could be periods with less competition. Following this interpretation, the following hypothesis could be established to compare the mean price (P_{SP}) in the pooled shock periods (Group 1) with the mean price in the normal period (P_{NP}):

$$H_0 : P_{SP} \leq P_{NP}$$

$$H_1 : P_{SP} > P_{NP}$$

Using the standard F-test, H_1 could be true if H_0 is rejected at the 95 per cent significance level.

The same test is applied for Group 2 (at the 95 per cent significance level) to compare the different shock periods with the normal period:

$$H_0 : P_{SP1}, P_{SP2}, P_{SP3} \leq P_{NP} \quad H_0 : P_{SP1} \geq P_{SP2} \geq P_{SP3}$$

$$H_1 : P_{SP1}, P_{SP2}, P_{SP3} > P_{NP} \quad H_1 : P_{SP1} < P_{SP2} < P_{SP3}$$

In the above hypothesis, the one-way ANOVA test is used to verify if H_0 can be rejected at the 95 per cent significance level.

3.2.2 Comparisons of variance

Another screening method to detect collusion entails a comparison of the variance or standard deviations of prices between the different time periods. The literature suggests that the variance of prices of goods (σ^2) during periods of decreased competition is lower than in periods of heightened competition. Applying this concept to the study for the time periods in Group 1, the following hypothesis could also be established:

$$H_0 : \sigma^2_{SP} \geq \sigma^2_{NP}$$

$$H_1 : \sigma^2_{SP} < \sigma^2_{NP}$$

Using the Welch T-Test, H_1 could be true if H_0 is rejected at the 95 per cent significance level. The same test is carried out for Group 2 at the 95 per cent significance level:

$$H_0 : \sigma^2_{SP1}, \sigma^2_{SP2}, \sigma^2_{SP3} \geq \sigma^2_{NP} \quad H_0 : \sigma^2_{SP1} \leq \sigma^2_{SP2} \leq \sigma^2_{SP3}$$

$$H_1 : \sigma^2_{SP1}, \sigma^2_{SP2}, \sigma^2_{SP3} < \sigma^2_{NP} \quad H_1 : \sigma^2_{SP1} > \sigma^2_{SP2} > \sigma^2_{SP3}$$

In the above hypothesis, the Levene's test centred at the median is used to verify if H_0 can be rejected at the 95 per cent significance level.

3.2.3 Comparisons of skewness

The literature on collusion screening suggests that the skewness of price distributions during periods of decreased competition is more negative as compared to that during increased competition. The skewness of distributions during the shock period should be more positive as compared to the normal period in Group 1. For Group 2, the value of skewness during the three shock periods (SP1, SP2, and SP3) should exhibit an increasing order.

3.2.4 Comparisons of kurtosis

A comparison of the kurtosis of price distributions can also be undertaken by observing the peaks of the density plots of each period or by comparing its respective value of kurtosis. The literature proposed that the distributions of prices during periods of less competition have a higher peak or are more leptokurtic as compared to that of those during more periods of competition. Thus, the value of kurtosis during the shock period (SP) period is expected to be more positive compared to that of during the normal period (NP) in the Group 1 categorization. A similar approach is used for the time periods in Group 2 where the value of kurtosis during the three shock periods (SP1, SP2, and SP3) should be found in an increasing order.

3.2.5   Comparisons of distributions

The Kolmogorov-Smirnoff test (a non-parametric test) can also be applied to compare two distributions of different time periods. The hypothesis and test statistic (D) of the test are as follows:

H_0: The samples are from the same distribution.

H_1: The sample is from different distributions.

$$D = \sup_x \left| F_0(x) - F_1(x) \right|$$

where $F_0(x)$ and $F_1(x)$ are the two cumulative distribution functions being compared. The largest absolute difference between the two distributions is used for the Kolmogorov-Smirnoff test statistic which is then compared to a certain critical level. In this study, the test statistic is compared to the critical value at the 95 per cent confidence level and if the former value exceeds the latter, the null hypothesis can be rejected.

3.3   Data

The price data used in this study comprises the daily prices of online groceries from four major online grocery retailers in Singapore, namely, Amazon, Cold Storage, FairPrice and Lazada. These prices were recorded and updated weekly. The list of 64 products in the data set is summarized in Table 9A.1 in the Appendix. The products in the data set are identical (brand-wise) for all sellers. For some products, there are less than four sellers. The data set covers the period from 30 May 2020 to 28 February 2022. The price data is extracted through the use of a commercial service that specializes in online price comparisons.

4   ANALYSIS USING COLLUSION SCREENING METHODS

4.1   The Results of the Collusion Screenings Tests

The results for the four tests are summarized in Tables 9.2 to 9.6.

4.1.1   Mean

The mean prices during the shock periods (pooled – in Group 1) are higher than in the normal period for 30 out of the 66 products monitored (Table 9.2). The mean price test is less robust when it is applied to compare each shock period (Group 2) to the normal period. However, the mean price is higher for 19 products for comparison of mean prices in the different shock periods.

4.1.2 Variance

A total of 30 products exhibited higher price variance during the shock periods (pooled – Group 1) compared to the normal period (Table 9.3). Interestingly, many of these products are different from those with higher mean prices. This is consistent with observations of higher mean prices and lower price variance in markets with less competition. A comparison of price variance amongst the three shock periods yielded weaker results.

4.1.3 Skewness

Close to half (32) of the products monitored have greater price skewness during shock periods compared to the normal period (Table 9.4). The pooled sub-sample for shock periods (Group 1) appears to give stronger results. However, the results for individual comparisons involving each shock period (Group 2) with the normal period are much weaker. A comparison amongst the three shock periods yielded only slightly stronger results.

4.1.4 Kurtosis

There is evidence of leptokurtic price distributions for some products (Table 9.5). However, these results are not as strong as those observed in the mean and variance tests. Similar to the skewness test, the comparisons between each shock period distribution against the normal period distribution yielded very few affirmative results. Interestingly, the comparison between the different shock periods yielded stronger results (more affirmative cases).

4.1.5 Kolgomorov-Smirnov test

The results from the Kolgomorov-Smirnov test consistently show that each of the distributions is different. This is a very strong result – perhaps even too strong. This is similar to the robustness claim for the test made by von Blankenburg.[15]

4.2 Remarks on the Collusion Screening Tests

The results from the application of the five different types of collusion screening tests provide some insights into the usefulness of these tests for monitoring pricing in online grocery markets. First, there are significant variations in pricing behaviour across products even though these products are sold by the

---

[15] von Blanckenburg, Geist and Kholodilin (n. 11 above).

Table 9.2   Results for price mean test (✓ indicates reject Null Hypothesis, ✗ otherwise)

Product	Mean (SP>NP)	Mean (SP1,SP2,SP3>NP)	Mean (SP3>SP2>SP1)	Product	Mean (SP>NP)	Mean (SP1,SP2,SP3>NP)	Mean (SP3>SP2>SP1)
Agar Agar	✗	✗	✗	Dishwashing Liquid	✗	✗	✓
Alcohol	✗	✗	✗	Eggs	✓	✓	✓
Almonds	✗	✗	✗	Floor Cleaner	✗	✗	✗
Aluminium Foil	✓	✗	✗	Flour (Flying Man)	✓	✗	✓
Baby Wipes	✓	✓	✓	Flour (Prima)	✓	✗	✓
Baking Soda (Arm&Hammer)	✗	✗	✗	Frozen Chicken	✗	✗	✗
Baking Soda (BakeKing)	✓	✓	✗	Hand Soap (KireiKirei)	✗	✓	✓
Biscuits (Chipsmore)	✗	✓	✗	Hand Soap (Walch)	✗	✗	✗
Biscuits (Julie's)	✓	✓	✗	Hazelnut Spread	✓	✗	✓
Biscuits (Khong Guan)	✓	✗	✗	Hot Pot Seasoning	✗	✗	✗
Biscuits (Meiji)	✗	✗	✗	Ketchup	✓	✗	✗
Biscuits (Oreo)	✓	✗	✓	Liquid Detergent	✓	✗	✓
Body Wash	✗	✗	✓	Malt Drink	✗	✗	✗
Bread	✓	✗	✗	Milk	✗	✗	✗
Butter	✓	✓	✗	Noodles	✓	✗	✓
Cake	✗	✗	✗	Pasta	✓	✗	✓

Product	Mean (SP>NP)	Mean (SP1,SP2,SP3>NP)	Mean (SP3>SP2>SP1)	Product	Mean (SP>NP)	Mean (SP1,SP2,SP3>NP)	Mean (SP3>SP2>SP1)
Canned Soup (Baxter's Asparagus)	✓	✓	✗	Peanut Butter	✗	✗	✗
Canned Soup (Campbell's Mushroom)	NA	NA	NA	Potato Chips	✓	✗	✓
Canned Soup (Heinz Tomato)	✓	✓	✗	Rice	✗	✗	✗
Canned Soup (Swanson's Chicken)	✗	✗	✗	Salt	✓	✗	✓
Canned Tuna	✓	✗	✗	Shampoo	✗	✗	✗
Carrots	✗	✓	✗	Soft Drinks	✗	✗	✗
Cereal	✓	✗	✗	Soy Sauce	✗	✗	✗
Cheese	✗	✗	✗	Sugar (Fine Grain)	✓	✗	✗
Chilli Sauce	✗	✗	✗	Sugar (Flying Man)	✗	✗	✓
Chocolate	✗	✗	✗	Tea	✗	✗	✗
Cocoa Powder	✗	✗	✗	Tissue (Beautex)	✓	✓	✗
Coconut Milk	✓	✓	✓	Tissue (Kleenex)	✗	✗	✗
Coffee	✗	✗	✗	Tissue (PurSoft)	✗	✗	✗
Cooking Oil	✓	✓	✗	Tissue (Scott)	✗	✗	✗
Detergent	✓	✓	✗	Toothpaste	✓	✗	✓
Diapers	✓	✗	✗	Water	✓	✓	✗
Dishwashing Liquid	✗	✗	✓	Yeast	✓	✓	✓

Table 9.3　　Results for price variance test (✓ indicates reject Null Hypothesis, ✗ otherwise)

Product	Variance (NP>SP)	Variance (NP>SP1,SP2,SP3)	Variance (SP1>SP2>SP3)	Product	Variance (NP>SP)	Variance (NP>SP1,SP2,SP3)	Variance (SP1>SP2>SP3)
Agar Agar	✗	✗	✗	Eggs	✗	✗	✓
Alcohol	✓	✓	✗	Floor Cleaner	✗	✗	✓
Almonds	✗	✗	✗	Flour (Flying Man)	✗	✗	✗
Aluminium Foil	✗	✗	✗	Flour (Prima)	✗	✗	✗
Baby Wipes	✗	✗	✓	Frozen Chicken	✗	✗	✗
Baking Soda (Arm&Hammer)	✓	✓	✓	Hand Soap (KireiKirei)	✗	✗	✓
Baking Soda (BakeKing)	✗	✗	✗	Hand Soap (Walch)	✗	✗	✗
Biscuits (Chipsmore)	✗	✗	✗	Hazelnut Spread	✗	✗	✗
Biscuits (Julie's)	✓	✓	✗	Hot Pot Seasoning	✗	✗	✗
Biscuits (Khong Guan)	✓	✗	✗	Ketchup	✓	✓	✗
Biscuits (Meiji)	✗	✗	✗	Liquid Detergent	✓	✓	✓
Biscuits (Oreo)	✓	✓	✗	Malt Drink	✓	✗	✗
Body Wash	✗	✗	✗	Milk	✓	✓	✗
Bread	✓	✓	✗	Noodles	✗	✗	✗
Butter	✗	✗	✗	Pasta	✗	✗	✗
Cake	✓	✗	✗	Peanut Butter	✓	✗	✓

Product	Variance (NP>SP)	Variance (NP>SP1,SP2,SP3)	Variance (SP1>SP2>SP3)
Canned Soup (Baxter's Asparagus)	✗	✗	✗
Canned Soup (Campbell's Mushroom)	NA	NA	NA
Canned Soup (Heinz Tomato)	✓	✓	✗
Canned Soup (Swanson's Chicken)	✗	✗	✗
Canned Tuna	✓	✓	✓
Carrots	✓	✗	✗
Cereal	✗	✗	✗
Cheese	✓	✓	✗
Chilli Sauce	✓	✓	✗
Chocolate	✗	✗	✗
Cocoa Powder	✗	✗	✗
Coconut Milk	✗	✗	✗
Coffee	✗	✗	✗
Cooking Oil	✗	✗	✓
Detergent	✓	✗	✗
Diapers	✗	✗	✗

Product	Variance (NP>SP)	Variance (NP>SP1,SP2,SP3)	Variance (SP1>SP2>SP3)
Potato Chips	✓	✗	✗
Rice	✓	✗	✗
Salt	✓	✗	✗
Shampoo	✓	✗	✓
Soft Drinks	✓	✓	✗
Soy Sauce	✗	✗	✗
Sugar (Fine Grain)	✓	✗	✗
Sugar (Flying Man)	✓	✓	✗
Tea	✓	✓	✗
Tissue (Beautex)	✓	✓	✗
Tissue (Kleenex)	✗	✗	✗
Tissue (PurSoft)	✓	✗	✓
Tissue (Scott)	✗	✗	✗
Toothpaste	✓	✗	✗
Water	✓	✗	✗
Yeast	✓	✗	✗

Table 9.4   Results for price skewness test (✓ indicates greater skewness, ✗ otherwise)

Product	Skewness (SP>NP)	Skewness (SP1,SP2,SP3>NP)	Skewness (SP3>SP2>SP1)	Product	Skewness (SP>NP)	Skewness (SP1,SP2,SP3>NP)	Skewness (SP3>SP2>SP1)
Agar Agar	✗	✗	✗	Eggs	✓	✗	✗
Alcohol	✓	✓	✗	Floor Cleaner	✓	✗	✗
Almonds	✓	✗	✗	Flour (Flying Man)	✗	✗	✓
Aluminium Foil	✗	✗	✗	Flour (Prima)	✗	✗	✗
Baby Wipes	✓	✗	✓	Frozen Chicken	✓	✗	✗
Baking Soda (Arm&Hammer)	✗	✗	✗	Hand Soap (KireiKirei)	✓	✗	✓
Baking Soda (BakeKing)	✗	✗	✗	Hand Soap (Walch)	✓	✗	✗
Biscuits (Chipsmore)	NA	NA	NA	Hazelnut Spread	✓	✓	✓
Biscuits (Julie's)	✗	✗	NA	Hot Pot Seasoning	✓	✓	✗
Biscuits (Khong Guan)	✗	✗	✗	Ketchup	✗	✗	✗
Biscuits (Meiji)	✗	✗	✗	Liquid Detergent	✗	✗	✗
Biscuits (Oreo)	✗	✗	✗	Malt Drink	✗	✗	✗
Body Wash	✓	✓	✓	Milk	✓	✓	✗
Bread	✗	✗	✓	Noodles	✓	✗	✓
Butter	✓	✗	✗	Pasta	✗	✗	✗
Cake	✓	✗	✗	Peanut Butter	✗	✗	✗
Canned Soup (Baxter's Asparagus)	✗	✗	✗	Potato Chips	✓	✗	✗

Product	Skewness (SP>NP)	Skewness (SP1,SP2,SP3>NP)	Skewness (SP3>SP2>SP1)	Product	Skewness (SP>NP)	Skewness (SP1,SP2,SP3>NP)	Skewness (SP3>SP2>SP1)
Canned Soup (Campbell's Mushroom)	NA	NA	NA	Rice	✓	✗	✗
Canned Soup (Heinz Tomato)	✓	✗	✗	Salt	✗	✗	✓
Canned Soup (Swanson's Chicken)	✓	✓	✓	Shampoo	✓	✗	✗
Canned Tuna	✗	✗	✗	Soft Drinks	✓	✗	✗
Carrots	✗	✗	✗	Soy Sauce	✗	✗	✓
Cereal	✓	✓	✓	Sugar (Fine Grain)	✓	✗	✗
Cheese	✓	✓	✗	Sugar (Flying Man)	✓	✗	✓
Chilli Sauce	✗	✗	✓	Tea	✗	✗	✗
Chocolate	✓	✓	✗	Tissue (Beautex)	✗	✗	✗
Cocoa Powder	✓	✗	✓	Tissue (Kleenex)	✗	✗	✗
Coconut Milk	✗	✗	✗	Tissue (PurSoft)	✓	✗	✓
Coffee	✓	✓	✗	Tissue (Scott)	✓	✗	✗
Cooking Oil	✗	✗	✓	Toothpaste	✓	✗	✗
Detergent	✗	✗	✗	Water	✗	✗	✗
Diapers	✗	✗	✗	Yeast	✓	✗	✗

Table 9.5   Results for price kurtosis test (✓ indicates leptokurtic distribution, ✗ otherwise)

Product	Kurtosis (SP>NP)	Kurtosis (SP1,SP2,SP3>NP)	Kurtosis (SP3>SP2>SP1)	Product	Kurtosis (SP>NP)	Kurtosis (SP1,SP2,SP3>NP)	Kurtosis (SP3>SP2>SP1)
Agar Agar	✗	✗	✗	Dishwashing Liquid	✗	✗	✗
Alcohol	✗	✗	✓	Eggs	✓	✗	✗
Almonds	✓	✓	✗	Floor Cleaner	✓	✗	✗
Aluminium Foil	✗	✗	✗	Flour (Flying Man)	✗	✗	✓
Baby Wipes	✓	✗	✗	Flour (Prima)	✗	✗	✓
Baking Soda (Arm&Hammer)	✗	✗	✗	Frozen Chicken	✗	✗	✗
Baking Soda (BakeKing)	✗	✗	✗	Hand Soap (KireiKirei)	✓	✗	✓
Biscuits (Chipsmore)	NA	NA	NA	Hand Soap (Walch)	✗	✗	✓
Biscuits (Julie's)	✓	✓	✗	Hazelnut Spread	✗	✗	✓
Biscuits (Khong Guan)	✓	✗	✗	Hot Pot Seasoning	✗	✗	✗
Biscuits (Meiji)	✗	✗	✗	Ketchup	✗	✗	✗
Biscuits (Oreo)	✗	✓	✓	Liquid Detergent	✗	✗	✗
Body Wash	✓	✗	✓	Malt Drink	✗	✗	✗
Bread	✓	✓	✗	Milk	✗	✗	✗
Butter	✓	✗	✗	Noodles	✗	✗	✓
Cake	✗	✗	✗	Pasta	✗	✗	✗

Product	Kurtosis (SP>NP)	Kurtosis (SP1,SP2,SP3>NP)	Kurtosis (SP3>SP2>SP1)	Product	Kurtosis (SP>NP)	Kurtosis (SP1,SP2,SP3>NP)	Kurtosis (SP3>SP2>SP1)
Canned Soup (Baxter's Asparagus)	✗	✗	✗	Peanut Butter	✓	✗	✗
Canned Soup (Campbell's Mushroom)	NA	NA	NA	Potato Chips	✓	✗	✓
Canned Soup (Heinz Tomato)	✗	✗	✗	Rice	✓	✗	✓
Canned Soup (Swanson's Chicken)	✗	✗	✗	Salt	✗	✗	✓
Canned Tuna	✗	✗	✗	Shampoo	✗	✗	✓
Carrots	✗	✗	✗	Soft Drinks	✓	✗	✗
Cereal	✓	✗	✗	Soy Sauce	✗	✗	✓
Cheese	✓	✓	✗	Sugar (Fine Grain)	✓	✗	✗
Chilli Sauce	✗	✗	✗	Sugar (Flying Man)	✓	✓	✓
Chocolate	✗	✗	✗	Tea	✗	✗	✓
Cocoa Powder	✗	✗	✗	Tissue (Beautex)	✓	✗	✓
Coconut Milk	✗	✗	✗	Tissue (Kleenex)	✗	✗	✓
Coffee	✗	✗	✓	Tissue (PurSoft)	✓	✗	✓
Cooking Oil	✗	✗	✓	Tissue (Scott)	✗	✗	✗
Detergent	✓	✗	✗	Toothpaste	✓	✓	✓
Diapers	✗	✗	✗	Water	✗	✗	✗
Dishwashing Liquid	✗	✗	✗	Yeast	✗	✗	✓

Table 9.6   Results for Kolgomorov-Smirnov test (✓ indicates difference, ✗ otherwise)

Product	KS Test (SP>NP)	KS Test (SP1,SP2,SP3>NP)	Product	KS Test (SP>NP)	KS Test (SP1,SP2,SP3>NP)
Agar Agar	✓	✓	Dishwashing Liquid	✓	✓
Alcohol	✓	✓	Eggs	✓	✓
Almonds	✓	✓	Floor Cleaner	✓	✓
Aluminium Foil	✓	✓	Flour (Flying Man)	✓	✓
Baby Wipes	✓	✓	Flour (Prima)	✓	✓
Baking Soda (Arm&Hammer)	✓	✓	Frozen Chicken	✓	✓
Baking Soda (BakeKing)	✓	✓	Hand Soap (KireiKirei)	✓	✓
Biscuits (Chipsmore)	✗	✓	Hand Soap (Walch)	✓	✓
Biscuits (Julie's)	✗	✗	Hazelnut Spread	✓	✓
Biscuits (Khong Guan)	✓	✓	Hot Pot Seasoning	✓	✓
Biscuits (Meiji)	✓	✓	Ketchup	✓	✓
Biscuits (Oreo)	✓	✓	Liquid Detergent	✓	✓
Body Wash	✓	✓	Malt Drink	✓	✓
Bread	✓	✓	Milk	✗	✓
Butter	✗	✓	Noodles	✓	✓
Cake	✓	✓	Pasta	✓	✓
Canned Soup (Baxter's Asparagus)	✓	✓	Peanut Butter	✗	✓

Product	KS Test (SP>NP)	KS Test (SP1,SP2,SP3>NP)	Product	KS Test (SP>NP)	KS Test (SP1,SP2,SP3>NP)
Canned Soup (Campbell's Mushroom)	NA	✓	Potato Chips	✓	✓
Canned Soup (Heinz Tomato)	✓	✓	Rice	✓	✓
Canned Soup (Swanson's Chicken)	✓	✓	Salt	✓	✓
Canned Tuna	✓	✓	Shampoo	✓	✓
Carrots	✓	✓	Soft Drinks	✓	✓
Cereal	✓	✓	Soy Sauce	✓	✓
Cheese	✓	✓	Sugar (Fine Grain)	✓	✓
Chilli Sauce	✓	✓	Sugar (Flying Man)	✓	✓
Chocolate	✓	✓	Tea	✓	✓
Cocoa Powder	✓	✓	Tissue (Beautex)	✓	✓
Coconut Milk	✓	✓	Tissue (Kleenex)	✓	✓
Coffee	✓	✓	Tissue (PurSoft)	✓	✓
Cooking Oil	✓	✓	Tissue (Scott)	✓	✓
Detergent	✓	✓	Toothpaste	✓	✓
Diapers	✗	✓	Water	✓	✓
Dishwashing Liquid	✓	✓	Yeast	✓	✓

same (four) seller platforms. This warrants further investigation especially on whether platforms use the same pricing approaches including pricing algorithms. Of course, the broad proxy used for market shocks does not capture how individual products are affected by shocks. This could also explain the heterogeneity in pricing behaviour observed.

Second, the performance of the collusion screening tests differs. There is greater consistency across the different tests when the data sets (shock periods) are pooled. This seems to suggest that the t-dimension (length of the period) of observations matters, which presents a quandary to regulators. Collusive mechanisms that take effect for a short period are likely to be undetected. This temporal dimension of collusion detection merits further investigations in terms of alternative dynamic detection methods. The Kolgomorov-Smirnov test yields strong affirmative results easily and as such is perhaps too strong a screening test.

Third, a key weakness of this study is the use of COVID-19 daily cases as proxy for market shocks. Future studies can explore alternative proxies such as Google mobility data which tracks the extent of mobility in various activities including retail and recreation (Figure 9.3). Another possible proxy would be the Stringency Index which measures the degree of restrictiveness of control measures in response to the COVID-19 pandemic (Figure 9.4).

Fourth, another limitation is the periodization of the shock and normal periods. This study has classified these periods based on the number of daily COVID-19 infections. Obviously, the periodization will affect the results obtained. One alternative approach could be to undertake an econometric analysis to uncover parameter instability and structural breaks in proxy variables.

A deeper understanding of the state of competition in the online grocery market will require a more detailed examination of pricing trends across the different products. This includes an investigation of whether and how prices are correlated across the different sellers. This is examined further next.

5   PRICE DYNAMICS, ALGORITHMIC PRICING AND PRICE CORRELATIONS

The five collusion screening tests discussed earlier are based on comparisons of price distributions. Such tests do not shed light on price dynamics directly even though price distributions are generated by price dynamics. To get a clearer picture of any observed changes in price distributions, it is useful to examine price dynamics in detail. This can begin with an examination of graphical plots of prices over time for each product. The patterns of price dynamics are summarized in Appendix Table 9A.1.

Price change dynamics can be classified into three types of patterns – fixed price (no change in price over time), staggered price change (infrequent dis-

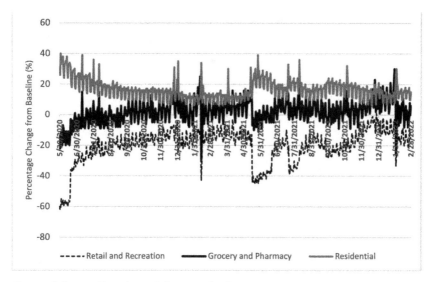

Figure 9.3   Google mobility trends, Singapore

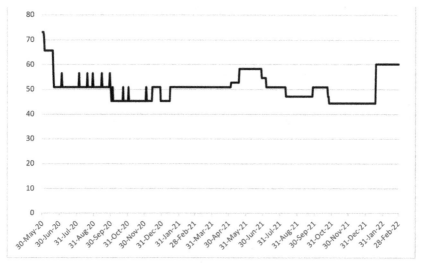

Figure 9.4   Stringency index for Singapore

crete change in price) and frequent price change. Examples of graphs depicting these three types of price dynamics can be seen in the case of three products – Magnolia Fresh Milk 1 Litre (fixed price – Figure 9.5), Cooking Oil Sunflower Nature (staggered price change – Figure 9.6) and Rice Song He (Frequent price change – Figure 9.7 and Figure 9.8).

These different patterns of price dynamics across different products and sellers show that price dynamics for a given seller can vary across products in its product portfolio. Whether this is constrained by the supplier/wholesaler through pricing agreements/contracts similar to resale price maintenance (RPM) requires further investigation. Clearly, sellers have full flexibility in setting the price of products for some products. For such products, differences in pricing mechanisms used are also evident. In particular, the use of algorithmic pricing by some sellers is evident for some products that exhibit large and frequent variations in price, for example Seller 1 in Figure 9.7 and Figure 9.8. In addition, the price patterns observed suggest that algorithmic pricing is adopted by firms that do not own physical stores (such as Amazon). Retailers who operate physical stores (FairPrice) are less likely to use algorithmic pricing.

One challenge in interpreting price dynamics driven by algorithmic pricing is accounting for the role of personalized pricing. Sophisticated algorithmic pricing based on machine learning can set unique prices for each individual buyer based on information collected about the buyer such as age, gender, past purchase, intensity of search etc. Price dynamics in such cases are also often driven by the group of identified potential buyers for their product i.e. how many other buyers are interested in the product. In addition, information about the price and availability of the product at other sellers' website can also be extracted and fed into the pricing algorithm for the product.

Finally, the interpretation of the collusion screening tests in markets with diverse pricing mechanisms can be challenging. For example, if one seller uses algorithmic pricing while the other three do not, will the use of algorithmic pricing result in greater or lesser price correlation? Personalized pricing algorithms may shift prices away from rivals' prices.

The above observations imply that price correlations will have to be carried out product-by-product. An econometric analysis of pricing for a sample of products can be used to demonstrate this. The following specification is employed for such analysis whereby the price of seller 1 at time t (P_{1t}) is a function of the prices of other sellers (2, 3 and 4) at time t (P_{2t}, P_{3t} and P_{4t}):

$$P_{1t} = \beta_0 + \beta_1 P_{2t} + \beta_2 P_{3t} + \beta_3 P_{4t} + \varepsilon_t$$

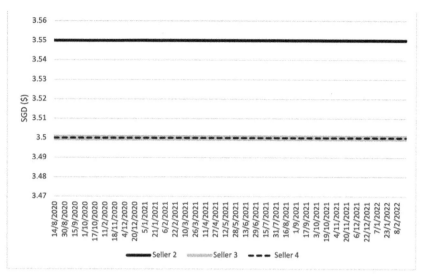

Figure 9.5   Price of Magnolia Fresh Milk 1L

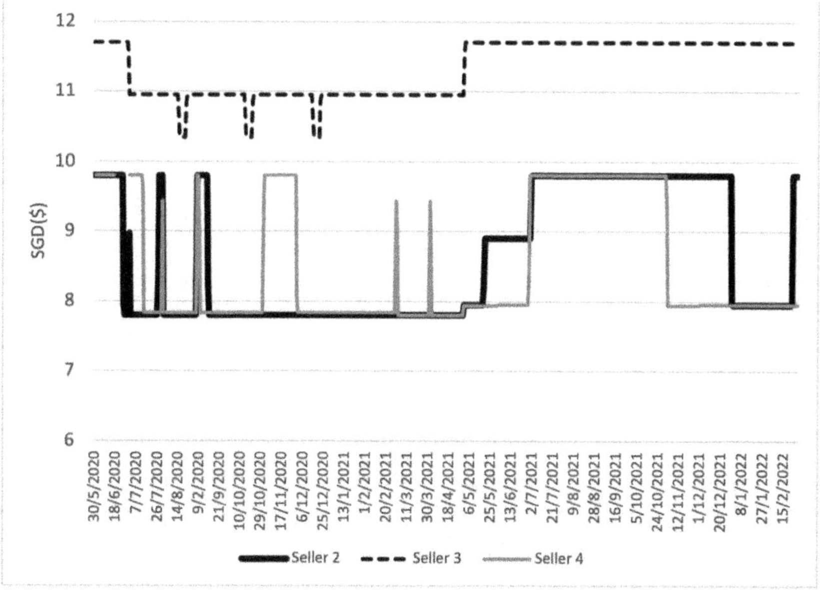

Source: Google mobility trends, Singapore.

Figure 9.6   Price of cooking oil – Sunflower Nature

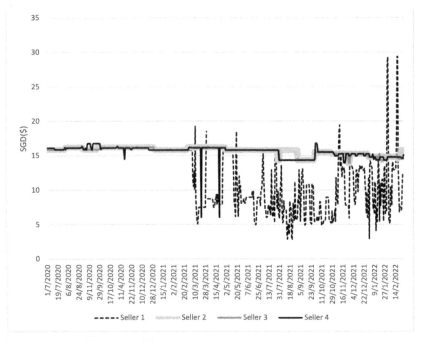

Source: Google mobility trends, Singapore

Figure 9.7   Price of Royal Umbrella Rice

Table 9.7 summarizes the ordinary least squares (OLS) regression results for two different brands of rice products. The results indicate that the relationships between the prices of sellers can vary across different products. This is also borne out by examining the correlation matrix for the sellers' prices (Table 9.8). Price correlations are weaker for the Song He rice compared to the Royal Umbrella rice.

For many products, prices adjust in discrete and staggered manner (see Appendix Table 9A.1). A visual depiction of this is in Figure 9.6 (Cooking Oil – Sunflower Nature). The staggered manner of price adjustments suggests that prices are not set using algorithms. The timing of the price change appears to be coordinated. This is confirmed by the very high correlations in the prices of the three sellers. It is plausible that the parallel nature of such price changes is driven by the pricing arrangements between the sellers and their suppliers (wholesalers or factories). Thus, supplier-seller pricing arrangement is still an important area of investigation in online markets.

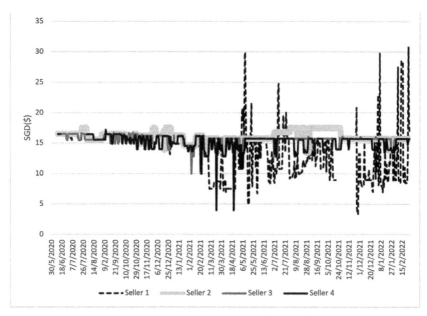

Source: Google mobility trends, Singapore

Figure 9.8   Price of Song He Rice

5   CONCLUSIONS

E-commerce platforms offering a large number of products are important features of today's digital economy. The scale of these platforms and the use of
algorithmic pricing driven by machine learning have raised concerns about the
potential harm from tacit collusion. Our current understanding and concerns
are mostly informed by computer simulations today. Not much is known about
pricing practices and price dynamics in actual online markets where platforms
sell a large number of products. There is also a lack of empirical study on the
possibility of collusion in such markets.

This study attempts to fill this research gap by investigating the potential use
of collusion screening tests in online grocery markets in Singapore. This study
shows that it is challenging to use collusion screening tests to monitor competition in online markets. Such tests should be supplemented by more detailed
examinations of the price dynamics of the many products sold. This can also
help identify pricing practices of online grocery platforms. This study finds
that not all firms use algorithmic pricing. Firms that operate physical stores
are less likely (compared to fully online stores) to use algorithmic pricing to
set prices online. There is evidence of parallel pricing for some products but

Table 9.7   OLS estimates of price correlations

	Royal Umbrella Rice	Song He Rice
Variables	Price 1	Price 1
Price 2	-0.404	0.226
	0.512	0.171
Price 3	3.071***	0.0775
	0.492	0.178
Price 4	0.659***	0.608***
	0.247	0.133
Covid	0.000130**	4.87E-05
	5.43E-05	4.70E-05
Constant	-39.73***	-0.615
	4.975	3.431
Observations	624	611
R-squared	0.221	0.053

Notes: Standard errors in parentheses. *** $p<0.01$, ** $p<0.05$, * $p<0.1$.

Table 9.8   Correlation matrix for prices of rice products

	Royal Umbrella Rice			
	Price 1	Price 2	Price 3	Price 4
Price 1	1			
Price 2	0.3515	1		
Price 3	0.4508	0.8264	1	
Price 4	0.3744	0.5631	0.6743	1
	Song He Rice			
	Price 1	Price 2	Price 3	Price 4
Price 1	1			
Price 2	0.0924	1		
Price 3	0.1163	0.1684	1	
Price 4	0.2205	0.1881	0.4337	1

this could be driven by pricing arrangements between sellers and suppliers/ wholesalers.

The scale and scope of e-commerce platforms make it extremely challenging to monitor competition in such markets. Even though the use of collusion screening tests can be problematic, further improvements of such methods by augmenting them with structural break mechanisms could be the way forward. The only reasonable way for regulators to do this is to automate the competition monitoring process. In other words, there is a need to explore the possibility of using robo-regulators to monitor the robo-sellers.

APPENDIX

Table 9A.1   List of products and price change pattern

Type of Good	Brand	Price Change Pattern
Agar Agar	Swallow Agar Agar Powder – White 10g	Mixed – staggered, fixed
Alcohol	Tiger Lager Beer Can, 320ml (Pack of 24)	Frequent
Almonds	Nature's Wonder Baked Almonds, 380g	Mixed – fixed, frequent
Aluminium Foil	Diamond Heavy Duty Aluminium Foil, 37.5 Sq Ft	Mixed – staggered, frequent
Baby Wipes	Huggies Clean Care Baby Wipes 3x80s	Mixed – staggered, frequent
Baby Wipes	Pigeon Baby Wipes - 100% Pure Water 3 x 80 per pack	Mixed – staggered, fixed
Baking Soda	Arm & Hammer Pure Baking Soda 454g	Fixed
Baking Soda	Bake King Baking Soda 100g	Staggered
Biscuits (A)	Chipsmore Cookies - Original 163.2g	Fixed
Biscuits (B)	Julie's Butter Crackers 10sX25g	Fixed
Biscuits (C)	Khong Guan Crackers - Cream 300g (12 per pack)	Mixed – staggered, fixed
Biscuits (D)	Meiji Plain Crackers 832g	Mixed – staggered, frequent
Biscuits (E)	Oreo Cookie Sandwich Biscuit – Original 9 x 29.4g	Mixed – staggered, fixed
Body Wash	Dove Beauty Nourishing Body Wash, 1L	Mixed – staggered, frequent
Body Wash	Lifebuoy Total 10 Anti-Bacterial Body Wash, 950mL	Mixed – staggered, frequent
Body Wash	Shokubutsu Anti-bacterial Body Foam, 900ml	Mixed – staggered, frequent
Body Wash	Dettol Anti-Bacterial Body Wash, Fresh, 950ml	Mixed – staggered, frequent
Body Wash	Ginvera Natural Bath Roya Jelly Milk Shower Foam, 1000 g	Mixed – staggered, frequent
Body Wash	LUX Soft Touch Body Wash, 950ml	Mixed – staggered, frequent

Type of Good	Brand	Price Change Pattern
Body Wash	Johnson's PH 5.5 2 in 1 Body Wash with Moisturizers, 1L	Mixed – staggered, frequent
Body Wash	Kirei Kirei Anti-bacterial Foaming Body Wash, Moisturizing Peach, 900ml	Mixed – staggered, frequent
Body Wash	EverSoft Beauty Shower Foam – Refresh and Energise 800ml	Mixed – staggered, frequent
Bread	Gardenia Enriched White Bread 600g	Constant
Bread	Sunshine Bread	Staggered adjustment
Butter	SCS Pure Creamery Butter Portion – Salted 12 x 10g	Fixed
Cake	Sara Lee Chocolate Pound Cake 300g	Mixed – staggered, fixed
Canned Soup	Baxters Cream Of Asparagus Soup 400g	Fixed
Canned Soup	Campbell's Cream of Mushroom Condensed Soup 290g	Mixed – fixed
Canned Soup	Heinz Tomato Ketchup	Staggered
Canned Soup	Swanson 99% Fat Free Clear Chicken Broth 1L	Mixed – staggered, fixed
Canned Tuna	Ayam Brand Tuna Light Flakes in Water 150g	Mixed – staggered, fixed
Carrots	Carrots 500g	Fixed
Cereal	Nestle Cereal – Koko Krunch 330g	Mixed – staggered, frequent
Cheese	Kraft Singles Hi-Calcium 60% Less Fat Cheese Slices – 12 Slices	Staggered
Chilli Sauce	Maggi Chilli Sauce, 500g	Mixed – staggered, frequent
Chocolate	Ferrero Rocher Chocolate – T24	Mixed – staggered, fixed
Cocoa Powder	Now Foods Real Food Cocoa Lovers Organic Cocoa Powder 12 Oz (340 G)	Mixed – staggered, frequent
Coconut Milk	Kara UHT Coconut Milk – Light 200ml	Staggered
Coconut Milk	Ayam Brand Coconut Milk 200ml	Staggered
Coffee	Nescafe Instant Soluble Coffee Jar – Classic 200g	Mixed – constant and frequent
Cooking Oil	Naturel Sunflower Cooking Oil 2L	Staggered adjustment
Cooking Oil	Knife Brand Cooking Oil (2L)	Staggered adjustment

Type of Good	Brand	Price Change Pattern
Detergent	Top Detergent Powder – Anti-Bacterial (5.5kg)	Mixed – staggered, frequent
Diapers	MamyPoko Air Fit Diapers M 64s 6-11kg	Mixed – staggered, frequent
Dishwashing Liquid	Mama Lemon Dishwashing Liquid, Lemon Gold, 1L Banded with 1L Refill	Staggered
Eggs	Seng Choon Farm 3 Eggs	Mixed – fixed, staggered
Floor Cleaner	Mr Muscle Marble and Terrazzo 3-in-1 Floor Cleaner, 2L	Mixed – staggered, frequent
Flour (A)	Flying Man Corn Flour, 400g	Mixed – fixed, frequent
Flour (B)	Prima Self Raising Flour, 1kg	Mixed – staggered, frequent
Frozen Chicken	Sadia Frozen Whole Chicken Griller 1kg	Staggered
Hand Soap	Kirei Kirei Anti-bacterial Hand Soap – Moisturizing Peach 250ml	Mixed – staggered, frequent
Hand Soap	Dettol Anti-Bacterial Hand Wash, Original, 250ml	Mixed – staggered, frequent
Hand Soap	Lifebuoy Antibacterial Hand Wash – Mild Care 200ml	Mixed – fixed, frequent
Hand Soap	Simple Gentle Care Anti-Bacterial Hand Wash 250ml	Fixed
Hand Soap (B)	Walch Anti-Bacterial Hand Wash – Moisturizing 525ml	Staggered
Hazelnut Spread	Nutella Hazelnut Spread 350g	Staggered
Hot Pot Seasoning	Hai Di Lao Hot Pot Seasoning Broth 110g	Staggered
Ketchup	Heinz Tomato Ketchup	Staggered
Ketchup	Del Monte 100% Natural Tomato Ketchup 340g	Staggered
Liquid Detergent	Attack Liquid Detergent – Plus Softener 3.6kg	Staggered
Liquid Detergent	Persil Concentrated Liquid Detergent – Front Load 3L	Staggered
Liquid Detergent	UIC Big Value Liquid Detergent – Anti-Bacterial 4kg	Staggered
Liquid Detergent	Dynamo Power Gel Laundry Detergent – Regular 3kg	Mixed – staggered, frequent
Liquid Detergent	Breeze Liquid Detergent – Anti-Bacterial & Colour Protect 3.8kg	Staggered
Malt Drink	Milo Instant Chocolate Malt Drink Powder – Regular 1.4kg	Mixed – constant, frequent

Type of Good	Brand	Price Change Pattern
Milk	Farmhouse Milk – Fresh 1L	Constant
Milk	Marigold HL Milk 1L	Constant
Milk	Magnolia Fresh Milk 1L	Constant
Noodles	Maggi 2Min Curry Noodles 5 Pack	Mixed – staggered, frequent
Pasta	San Remo Instant Spaghetti 500g	Mixed – fixed, frequent
Pasta	Barrilla Pasta Spaghetti No.5 500g	Staggered
Peanut Butter	Skippy Creamy Peanut Butter 500g	Mixed – staggered, frequent
Potato Chips	Lays Classic Potato Chips 184.2g	Staggered
Potato Chips	Ruffles Original Potato Chips 184.2g	Mixed – staggered, frequent
Rice	Royal Umbrella Rice 5kg	Staggered
Rice	SongHe AAA Thai Hom Mali Rice – New Crop 5kg	Frequent
Salt	Pagoda Fine Salt 500g	Mixed – staggered, fixed
Salt	Flying Man Table Box Salt, 500gm	Mixed – staggered, fixed
Shampoo	Dove Shampoo – Daily Shine (680ml)	Mixed – staggered, frequent
Shampoo	Pantene Pro-V Shampoo – Anti Dandruff 750ml	Mixed – staggered, frequent
Shampoo	Clear Anti-Hairfall and Anti-Dandruff Shampoo, 650ml	Mixed – staggered, frequent
Shampoo	Head & Shoulders Anti-Dandruff Shampoo, Cool Menthol, 720ml	Mixed – staggered, frequent
Shampoo	Sunsilk Smooth and Manageable Shampoo, 650ml	Mixed – staggered, frequent
Soft Drinks	Coca-Cola Light, 320ml, (Pack of 12)	Mixed – staggered, frequent
Soft Drinks	Pepsi Can Drink (24sX320ml)	Mixed – staggered, fixed
Soy Sauce	Tai Hua Standard Light Soy Sauce, 640ml	Mixed – staggered, frequent
Sugar (A)	Flying Man Fine Sugar, 1kg	Mixed – constant and frequent
Tea	Lipton Yellow Label Tea, 100 x 2g	Frequent

Type of Good	Brand	Price Change Pattern
Tissue (A)	Kleenex Ultra Soft Toilet Tissue Rolls – Cottony Clean (20 per pack)	Frequent
Tissue (B)	PurSoft Bathroom Tissue Roll – Unscented (4ply)	Staggered
Tissue (C)	Scott Extra Toilet Tissue Rolls – Regular (2 Ply)	Mixed – staggered, frequent
Tissue (D)	Beautex Bathroom Tissue Rolls – Premium	Staggered
Toothpaste	Colgate Total Toothpaste, Professional Clean Gel, 150g (Pack of 2)	Staggered
Drinking Water	Dasani Drinking Water, 1.5L, (Pack of 12)	Mixed – staggered, frequent
Drinking Water	Ice Mountain Pure Drinking Water, 1.5L (Pack of 12)	Mixed – fixed, frequent
Yeast	Saf-Instant Dry Baker Yeast, 55g	Mixed – fixed, frequent
Yeast	Bake King Instant Yeast 50g	Mixed – fixed, frequent

10. Algorithms unravelled: observations on the audit of Uber and Amazon marketplace algorithms

Steven Van Uytsel

1   INTRODUCTION

Competition law scholarship received a warning in 2015. Collusion would soon no longer only be the result of meetings on golf courses or in airport lobbies; computers would replace this process. Algorithms, a "set of rules to be followed in problem solving,"[1] would enable computers to collude in price setting, "free from any direct human control."[2] These predictions were made without empirical evidence on the full capacity of algorithms. In the wake of these predictions, computer scientists also shed light on the issue. While establishing that some self-learning algorithms may have the capacity to collude without human intervention, they acknowledged that real-world settings would likely still be too complex for these algorithms to collude.[3]

Parallel to these discussions, scholarship began to focus on how actually applied pricing algorithms operate. In this respect, two studies of Le Chen, Alan Mislove, and Christo Wilson (Chen et al.) are worth mentioning. *Peeking Beneath the Hood of Uber* explains the operation of the pricing algorithm of Uber Technologies, Inc. (Uber) in the United States (Uber study),[4] and *An*

---

[1]   Philip Sales, 'Algorithms, Artificial Intelligence, and the Law' (2021) 105(1) *Judicature* 23, 24, available at https://judicature.duke.edu/articles/algorithms-artificial -intelligence-and-the-law/ (accessed June 30, 2022).

[2]   ibid., at 23.

[3]   Q-learning algorithms as a specific class of reinforcement learning algorithms may be able to achieve collusion. For a more detailed discussion, see Van Uytsel, 'The Algorithmic Collusion Debate: A Focus on (Autonomous) Tacit Collusion', this volume.

[4]   Le Chen, Alan Mislove, and Christo Wilson, 'Peeking Beneath the Hood of Uber' (Internet Measurement Conference, Tokyo, October 28–29 2015), available at www.ccs.neu.edu/home/amislove/publications/Uber-IMC.pdf (accessed June 30, 2022).

Empirical Analysis of Algorithmic Pricing on Amazon Marketplace details the interaction of the different algorithms operating on Amazon Marketplace (Amazon study).[5] Though these studies are frequently referenced in competition law scholarship,[6] it is primarily done to indicate the complexity of algorithms, rather than to discuss implications for competition law.[7] Indeed, to understand how algorithms function, Chen et al. had to engage in reverse engineering, emulate web applications, or intercept algorithmic output.[8]

If the identity of such algorithms cannot be uncovered without intrusive research methods, one can imagine how difficult it will be for a competition law enforcement agency to take appropriate steps toward the regulation of pricing algorithms. Competition law scholars praise the auditing of algorithms, particularly those undertaken by Chen at al.[9] This is not to say that Chen et al.

---

[5]   Le Chen, Alan Mislove, and Christo Wilson, 'An Empirical Analysis of Algorithmic Pricing on Amazon Marketplace' (25th International Conference on World Wide Web, Montréal, April 1–5 2016), available at https://dl.acm.org/doi/10.1145/2872427.2883089 (accessed June 30, 2022).

[6]   See, e.g., Friso Bostoen, 'Competition Law in the Peer-to-Peer Economy' in Bram Devolder (ed), *The Platform Economy* (Intersentia 2019) 143, 161; Rob Nicholls, 'Algorithm-driven Collusive Conduct', in Deborah Healey, Michael Jacobs, and Rhonda L. Smith (eds), *Research Handbook on Methods and Models of Competition Law* (Edward Elgar 2020) 142; Colm Hawkes, 'A Market Investigation Tool to Tackle Algorithmic Tacit Collusion: An Approach for the (Near) Future' (Research Papers in Law – College of Europe, 2021) 10, available at www.coleurope.eu/sites/default/files/research-paper/ResearchPaper_3_2021_Colm_Hawkes.pdf (accessed June 30, 2022); Cheska Tolentino, Artificial Surge Pricing as Price-Fixing: Why and How to Avoid It' (2021) 4, available at https://scholarship.shu.edu/cgi/viewcontent.cgi?article=2234&context=student_scholarship (accessed June 30, 2022); Anne-Sophie Thoby, 'Pricing Algorithms & Competition Law: How to Think Optimally the European Competition Law Framework for Pricing Algorithms?' (2020) *Competition Forum, Art. n. 0009*, n. 79, available at www.competition-forum.cfom/ (accessed June 30, 2022); Keyawana Griffith, 'The Uber Loophole that Protects Surge Pricing' (2019) 26 (1) *Virginia Journal l of Social Policy & the Law* 34, 36 and 40; Mark Anderson and Max Huffman, 'The Sharing Economy Meets the Sherman Act: Is Uber a Firm, a Cartel, or Something in Between?' (2017) *Columbia Business Law Review* 859, 910.

[7]   Bostoen (n. 6 above) at 161.

[8]   Le Chen et al. (n. 4 above).

[9]   See, e.g., Autorité de la concurrence and the Bundeskartellamt, 'Algorithms and Competition' (2019) 68, available at www.autoritedelaconcurrence.fr/sites/default/files/algorithms-and-competition.pdf (accessed June 30, 2022). Auditing in general is welcomed, but they point out that with current auditing studies not all competition law issues are addressed. An indirect praise for auditing can be read in determining auditing as one of the best enforcement practices, see Cary Coglianese and Alicia Lai, 'Antitrust by Algorithm' (2022) 11 *Stanford Computational Antitrust* 1, 22. Others have put some notes next to auditing as being next to impossible. Algorithms are prone to technolog-

are the only academics doing this kind of research.[10] Despite this positive note, the Chen et al.'s Uber and Amazon studies have barely been referenced in discussions of possible competition law implications.[11] This chapter endeavours to do so, examining these works from the perspective of algorithmic collusion. Two elements in the competition law literature on algorithmic collusion warrant this approach. First, Uber has been described as a textbook example of algorithmic collusion.[12] Second, transparency has been identified as a driver of algorithmic collusion.[13] The research question is whether both issues are confirmed by the studies undertaken by Chen et al.

The chapter will begin by introducing the Uber and Amazon studies (Section 2). This section will conclude with observations regarding the infor-

---

ical evolution. See Aurelien Portuese, 'Prologue: Algorithmic Antitrust – A Primer' in Aurelien Portuese (ed), *Algorithmic Antitrust* (Springer 2022) at 22.

[10] Similar to the Amazon study, see Marcel Wieting and Geza Sapi, 'Algorithms in the Marketplace: An Empirical Analysis of Automated Pricing in E-Commerce' (NET Institute Working Paper #21-06, 2021), available at https://papers.ssrn.com/sol3/papers.cfm?abstract_id=3945137 (accessed June 30, 2022). A study in relation to algorithmic pricing and the German retail gasoline market, see Stephanie Assad, Robert Clark, Daniel Ershov, and Lei Xu, 'Algorithmic Pricing and Competition: Empirical Evidence from the German Retail Gasoline Market' (CESifo Working Paper No. 8521, August 2020), available at https://papers.ssrn.com/sol3/papers.cfm?abstract_id=3682021 (accessed June 30, 2022). Christo Wilson provides a wealth of information on auditing and auditing studies in Christo Wilson, 'The Promise and Peril of Algorithm Audits for Increasing Transparency and Accountability of Donated Datasets' (2019), available at https://securelysharingdata.com/wilson.html (accessed June 30, 2022). Annie Lee accounts that auditors are mainly academics, computer scientists and journalists. See Annie Lee, 'Algorithmic Auditing and Competition under the CFAA: The Revocation Paradigm of Interpreting Access and Authorization' (2018) (33) *Berkeley Technology Law Journal* 1307, 1309.

[11] Current debates sometimes examine the competition effects of the use of algorithms, particularly since the use of algorithms is expected to increase exponentially. This increase could be attributed to the fact that algorithms render positive business and become progressively easier to implement. Nicholls (n. 6 above), at 142. Regarding market impact, "algorithmic price-setting opens the door to a series of intentional and unintentional market distortions." Coglianese and Lai (n. 9 above) at 6. For example, non-algorithmic sellers could face difficulties competing with algorithmic sellers. It is also asserted that the use of algorithms does not necessarily result in lower prices for consumers. Prices could be in a constant state of flux, making it more difficult for consumers to decide on purchases. Algorithms could also be implemented to collude; however, it should not be deducted from these insights that a price-setting algorithm "will or should not inherently be suspect." ibid., 6.

[12] Ariel Ezrachi and Maurice E. Stucke, *Virtual Competition: The Promise and Perils of the Algorithm-Driven Economy* (Harvard University Press 2016), 50–5.

[13] ibid., at 64, 73, and 229–30. See also Fransisco Beneke and Mark-Oliver Mackenrodt, 'Artificial Intelligence and Collusion' (2019) 50 *IIC – International Review of Intellectual Property and Competition Law* 109, 126–7.

mation that is collected to allow algorithmic operation in Uber and Amazon business settings. Next, competition law concerns will be formulated based on the analysis of the algorithm(s) operating on Uber and Amazon platforms (Section 3), with a focus on collusion and possible alternatives to collusion. The chapter concludes by asserting that additional auditing is required, no matter how difficult and time-consuming it may be, to generate appropriate competition law conclusions (Section 4).

2   ALGORITHMS USED BY UBER AND AMAZON EXPLAINED BY CHEN ET AL.

2.1   Chen et al.'s Engagement with the Uber Algorithm

Uber, one of the firms that understood the usefulness of algorithms for developing a business plan early on, was the subject of a Chen et al. study.

Uber is active in the sharing economy and seeks to match "willing drivers with customers looking for riders."[14] Uber does this by providing different smartphone applications for riders and drivers. Chen et al. indicate that at the time of the study,

> [d]rivers use the Uber *Partner app* on their smartphone to indicate their willingness to accept fares. Passengers use the Uber *Client app* to determine the availability of rides and get estimated prices. Uber's system routes passenger requests to the nearest driver, and automatically charges passengers' credit cards at the conclusion of each trip.[15]

The calculation of the price is made dependent on local transportations laws, but always includes "a minimum base fare, cost per mile, cost per minute, and fees, tolls, and taxes."[16] The base fare may differ depending on the type of vehicle; however, in general, the exact calculation base was once opaque. Uber introduced a surge multiplier in 2012 that allowed Uber to adjust pricing to real-time supply and demand, making rides more expensive in times of high demand and low supply. It has been contended that the surge multiplier enabled Uber to manipulate the price.[17] It was also asserted that the surge multiplier did

---

[14]   Chen et al. (n. 4 above) at 1.
[15]   ibid., 2.
[16]   ibid.
[17]   Ben Popper, 'Uber Kept New Drivers Off the Road to Encourage Surge Pricing and Increase Fares' (26 February 2014) *The Verge*, available at http://bit.ly/1hoPgU8 (accessed June 30, 2022).

not allow for a fair market response in times of crisis, an issue that was brought under scrutiny after Hurricane Sandy and the Sydney hostage crisis.[18]

The contention of price manipulation and accusations of unfairness inspired Chen et al. to devote a study on Uber's price-setting algorithm, aiming to investigate the claim of whether the opaqueness of the algorithm allowed Uber to "artificially manipulate prices"[19] and whether the dynamics of price setting was fair to customers and drivers. To answer these questions, Chen et al. initiated field studies of downtown San Francisco and midtown Manhattan to collect data on Uber and its price setting.[20] These areas were chosen for three reasons. First, each had a relatively large population of Uber drivers. Second, Uber accounted for a high proportion of all taxi rides in San Francisco and a substantial amount of the rides in New York City. Third, differences in terms of culture and access to public transportation between these two cities were another motivation for choosing these two cities, as it may reveal different dynamics in the use of Uber.[21]

Chen at al. report that collecting relevant data from Uber at these two locations was not possible through the publicly available Uber Application Program Interface (API).[22] This API only rendered information regarding the estimated price and waiting time, whereas the study required information on car supply and passenger demand. To address this, Chen et al. designed a script to replicate the information shown on Uber's Client app. The Client app displayed "a map with the eight closest cars to the user (based on the smart-phone's geolocation), and the Estimated Wait Time (EWT) for a car ... Users [were] not shown the surge multiplier until they attempt[ed] to request a car."[23] None of this information could be retrieved by a driver through the Partner app; however, this app was useful for determining areas with high demand.[24]

Regarding the special script, Chen et al. share that the script logged into Uber's Client app and sent client messages to Uber's server every five seconds. In response to these messages, the server provided a

JSON-encoded list of information about all available car types at the user's location. For each car type, the information of the nearest eight cars, EWT, and surge multi-

---

[18]   Chen et al. (n. 4 above) at 1.
[19]   ibid.
[20]   ibid., 3
[21]   ibid. Chen et al. also note that Manhattan is useful because data are also available on all taxi rides in New York City.
[22]   Chen et al. (n. 4 above) at 3.
[23]   ibid.
[24]   ibid.

plier [were] given. Each car [was] represented by a unique ID, its current geolocation, and a path vector that trace[d] the recent movement of the car.[25]

As the available information was limited to eight cars, Chen et al. could not
rely on just one Client app clone. To cover a broader geographical area in the
two cities, 43 Client app clones (Uber accounts) were created.[26]

Determining how the 43 Uber accounts should be spread within San
Francisco and Manhattan was subject to experimentation. Once the optimal
positions were identified, Chen et al. began to collect data between April 3–17,
2013, and April 18–May 2, 2013, in midtown Manhattan and downtown San
Francisco respectively.[27] The data collected allowed for the measurement of
supply and demand. Chen et al. describe this process as follows:[28]

> To measure supply, we can simply count the total number of unique cars observed
> across all measurement points; each of these cars represents a driver who is looking
> to provide a ride. To measure demand, we can measure the aggregate number of
> cars that go offline (disappear) between responses; one of the reasons a car may go
> offline is because it picked up a rider.[29]

Chen at al. convey a warning that the measurement of supply and demand
was an approximation. The method of measurement made it impossible to
distinguish between cars picking up a passenger and cars simply going offline.
Furthermore, a car that frequently went on- and offline in a short period of
time, would be assigned a unique ID each time; thus, it was possible for the
same cars to be counted twice or more.[30]

Based on the collected data, Chen et al. conclude that four trends can be
detected.[31] The first trend was that the use of Uber peaked during the day and
use was remarkably higher around the morning and afternoon rush hour. The
second trend was that one specific type of Uber, UberX,[32] was the most preva-
lently used. The third trend was that San Francisco had about 60 per cent more

---

[25]   ibid.

[26]   ibid., 3–4.

[27]   ibid., 6. The paper also indicates that client data was collected between December
27, 2014 and March 1, 2015.

[28]   The authors acknowledge that this way of operating has remaining limitations,
including measuring only fulfilled demand (passengers that are effectively picked up by
an Uber driver), the danger of overestimating demand, as cars may go offline without
picking up a customer or may move outside the measurement area, and the inability to
identify individual Uber drivers to avoid multiple IDs.

[29]   Chen et al. (n. 4 above) at 3.

[30]   ibid., 4.

[31]   ibid., 3.

[32]   UberX is the standard Uber service seating up to four passengers.

Uber drivers than Manhattan. The fourth trend was a difference in the surge multipliers in both cities, wherein prices were surged more often in downtown San Francisco than in Manhattan, as "86% of the time there is no surge in Manhattan, versus 43% of the time in S[an Francisco]."[33]

In addition to these trends, the data enabled Chen et al. to reveal aspects of the conceptualization of the pricing algorithm. First, the Uber algorithm was set to change the prices about every five minutes. The changes often showed "a high correlation with supply, demand, and EWT over the previous 5-minute interval."[34] Second, it was evident that Uber had intentionally divided cities into smaller areas for the purpose of the surge multiplier; hence, a small change in location could result in a substantially different estimated price.[35] Third, it is not possible to predict when a price will surge unless one understands the algorithm's operation.[36]

It is also notable that Chen et al. did not compare the data retrieved in the Uber experiment with data from other ride-sharing services. Although the authors indicate that they attempted to collect data elsewhere, collecting data on Lyft was not possible on ethical grounds, as prices are only available after a user requests a ride. Another ride-sharing platform, Sidecar, allows its drivers to set their own rate depending on time and distance, making it impossible to collect data.[37]

2.2   Amazon Marketplace Algorithms Analyzed by Chen et al.

The Amazon Marketplace is another example of a space that "unlocked practical applications for *algorithmic pricing* (also called dynamic pricing algorithms), where sellers set prices using computer algorithms."[38] Lack of regulatory and public knowledge regarding the operation and performance of these algorithms inspired Chen et al. to "empirically analyse deployed algorithmic pricing strategies on Amazon Marketplace."[39]

---

[33]   Chen et al. (n. 4 above) at 8.

[34]   ibid., 2.

[35]   ibid., 2 and 13.

[36]   ibid., 12.

[37]   ibid., 4.

[38]   Chen et al. (n. 5 above). A similar study on the e-commerce platform Bol.com has been undertaken by Wieting and Sapi (n. 10 above).

[39]   Chen et al., in their Amazon study, emphasize two examples of unexpected results in the use of the algorithms that demonstrate the need for more broad understanding. The first example was the rise in the price of a genetics textbook, *The Making of a Fly*, authored by Peter Lawrence. Flawed implementation of the pricing algorithm drove up the price to the absurd amount of more than $23 million. The second example is the Topkins case, in which several executives of competing poster firms were suc-

The aim of the Amazon study was manifold, including uncovering how the algorithm behind the Buy Box[40] operated, how sellers, who were likely using algorithmic pricing, were setting their prices, and the differences that the pricing algorithms generated between algorithmic and non-algorithmic sellers.[41] To formulate an answer, the study focused on two different algorithms active on Amazon Marketplace: the algorithm facilitating the display of price and shipping information of the different sellers offering the same product on Amazon Marketplace, and the algorithm that aids price determination for third-party sellers (i.e., merchants other than Amazon) and Amazon.[42] Though both algorithms influence the business on Amazon Marketplace, for the purpose of this chapter, only the pricing algorithm will be subject of further exploration.

To gather data on the pricing algorithms, Chen et al. engaged in web crawling focused on the best-selling products[43] featured on Amazon's New Offers page because this gave them information on all active third-party sellers, their prices, and their shipping costs.[44] The New Offers page was crawled every 25 minutes[45] between September 15, 2014 and December 8, 2014 and between August 11, 2015 and September 21, 2015.[46] In the first period, the authors followed 837 best-selling products, while during the second period,

---

cessfully prosecuted for price fixing assisted by algorithms implemented on Amazon Marketplace. Chen et al. (n. 5 above) at 1.

   [40]   The 'Amazon Buy Box'
         is a box on the product's details page, where customers begin the purchasing process. Often, the same product is offered by multiple sellers (i.e., several Merchants, including in some instances Amazon itself). Thus, these sellers compete to be in the Buy Box. Amazon may select one seller among the eligible sellers based on algorithms and then grant that seller the Buy Box.
See Thomas Hoppner and Philipp Westerhoff, 'The EU's Competition Investigation into Amazon's Marketplace' (2021) 7 n. 3, available at https://papers.ssrn.com/sol3/papers.cfm?abstract_id=3495203 (accessed June 30, 2022).
   [41]   Chen et al. (n. 5 above) at 1339–40.
   [42]   ibid., 1340.
   [43]   Chen et al., in their Amazon study, acknowledge that a focus on best-selling products could be a limitation; however, the research team randomly compared selected products with the best-selling products, concluding that best-selling products had more competitors than the randomly selected products. Chen et al. (n. 5 above). at 1343.
   [44]   The focus of Amazon study was on the total price, referencing the price including the lowest-cost shipping option. Chen et al. (n. 5 above) at 1343.
   [45]   Short timescales of changes in less than one minute are neglected, as these are considered to be Amazon inconsistencies; therefore, the crawling frequency is aligned with longer timescale price adjustments of more than 30 minutes. Chen et al. (n. 5 above) at 1343.
   [46]   Chen et al. (n. 5 above) at 1342.

1,000 best-selling products were followed.[47] Chen et al. indicate that these best-selling products were not necessarily identical, as the first and second crawl only had 196 products in common.[48] It is also noteworthy that the data crawled were visible to the majority of Amazon users, and exclude information that was visible only to Amazon Prime users.[49]

Chen et al. further clarify that they built a detection system that allowed them to estimate which sellers behaved "like 'bots', i.e., sellers where the prices they set and the timing of changes suggest algorithmic control."[50] This system was constructed on the presumption that algorithmic pricing usually operates with target prices,[51] whereby the price is determined by prices set by competitors.

Chen et al. conclude their study with four notable findings.[52] First, the active algorithms on Amazon tended to take the lowest price as the target price. This was apparent across all sellers, indicating that even if non-algorithmic sellers had the lowest price, it was quickly met by the algorithms of the algorithmic seller. Second, algorithmic sellers always matched other sellers' prices and usually followed the lowest price; however, most of the time, the algorithmic sellers were able to sell products at a price that was 40 per cent higher than the lowest price. Third, Amazon itself often used a pricing algorithm that would seldom adjust to exactly the lowest price. The Amazon algorithm almost always charged a premium, because of which the Amazon price was slightly higher than the lowest price. Fourth, although the premium of the Amazon pricing algorithm did not always apply, it appeared to be different once the lowest price drops under $US 9.

---

[47] ibid.
[48] ibid.
[49] ibid.
[50] ibid., 1344.
[51] Three target prices are considered in the study: the lowest price, the Amazon price, and the second lowest price. Ibid.
[52] Chen et al. (n. 5 above) at 1346. The conclusions drawn by Wieting and Sapi are quite similar. The majority of the pricing algorithms on Bol.com follow a target pricing strategy, whereby the algorithms follow the price as it goes up or down. Jitters seem to drive the price up or down. Another major similarity is that the pricing of algorithmic sellers is higher and offers bigger margins. Their study does not allow to conclude whether the higher prices are the result of a failure to learn or an ability to learn to coordinate. Wieting and Sapi (n. 9 above) at 19–21 and 40. A study in relation to the retail gasoline market also indicated that the use of algorithms in areas where the retailer was facing competition, the margins have increased by 9 per cent. This was unlike in areas in which the retailer was already a monopolist. In those areas, there was no change of the margins after the retailer started to use pricing algorithms. This study has further concluded that, if all retailers shifted to algorithms, there was even a margin increase of about 30 per cent. See Assad, Clark, Ershov, and Xu (n. 10 above) at 42–3.

2.3   Transparency of the Algorithms' Sources of Information

Chen et al. clarify that understanding the operation of Uber's and Amazon's algorithms requires knowledge of the data upon which the algorithm functions. The Uber study reveals that this was not easy, as no publicly available information sources indicate how the price is calculated.[53] In contrast, the Amazon study indicates that such information can be readily available.[54]

The different nature of information access not only has implications for the chosen information gathering methodology, but it also has an impact on how competing firms are able to interact with Uber or Amazon Marketplace. It is logical that if the information necessary to run an algorithm is opaque, competing firms must then actively interact with one another to reach any kind of price agreement. This could also be accomplished indirectly if a competing firm releases information, creating an artificial information dump that causes competing firms to adjust pricing according to the information released.[55] Alternatively, establishing transparency could be achieved by reverse engineering a competing firm's algorithm of, as Chen et al. did, to adjust their prices. The opposite is also true. If the useful information to operate an algorithm is transparent and accessible, competing firms can use it without having to engage with the competitor in any way.

Scenarios in which there is direct communication between competitors are not controversial for competition law. If the required evidence can be obtained, competition law can easily apply. It should thus not be a surprise that such uncontroversial issue is less discussed in the literature.[56] Conversely, if new technology creates circumstances in which consumers tend to be more financially disadvantaged, and these situations are potentially or currently outside the scope of competition law, there will be a need to reconsider the scope of competition law intervention. Transparency is one of the elements highlighted by Chen et al. that is given a central place in the competition law literature regarding algorithmic collusion; however, this discussion is not linked to

---

[53]   Chen et al. (n. 4 above).

[54]   Chen et al. (n. 5 above).

[55]   Simon Martin and Alexander Rasch devote a study on how algorithms need to be designed in case no signals are being sent in order to still achieve collusion. See Simon Martin and Alexander Rasch, 'Collusion by Algorithm: The Role of Unobserved Actions' (CESifo Working Papers No. 9629, 2022), available at https://papers.ssrn.com/sol3/papers.cfm?abstract_id=4060524 (accessed June 30, 2022).

[56]   Despite being uncontroversial, some of the literature discusses this issue. See, e.g., Ina Fey, 'The Application of Current Antitrust Law to Explicit Collusion by Autonomously Acting Pricing Algorithms' (2019), available at https://papers.ssrn.com/sol3/papers.cfm?abstract_id=3526100 (accessed June 30, 2022).

Amazon Marketplace.[57] Competition law literature on algorithmic collusion has been less outspoken regarding the issue of information opaqueness. To get a sense of its impact, one must consider the discussion of business models that operate with information opaqueness. The most obvious example is the one examined by Chen et al.: Uber.

Transparency, and especially "greater transparency," assert Ariel Ezrachi and Maurice Stucke, "can … lead to a unique phenomenon known as tacit collusion."[58] To exemplify this, the authors reference, among others, the retail petrol market in Perth, Australia. The government in this city implemented a scheme in which the retail prices for petrol were fixed for 24 hours. To achieve this, firms operating in the oil retail market had to submit the price for the following day before 2 pm. The prices for the following day were made public at 2:30 pm. Through trial and error, for about 12 years, without any communication, petrol firms were able to achieve a pricing structure that reflected collusion, increasing their profit margins. An argument could be made that algorithms can accelerate this tacit collusion because they operate in a real-time price-setting environment.[59] Though not explicitly elaborated in the context of tacit collusion, Ezrachi and Stucke note that Amazon "'aggressively changes prices, sometimes altering them more than once per day in reaction to other retailers.' Its algorithms can adjust prices quickly to respond to changes in market conditions, including its competitors' prices."[60] This kind of action is not only to be expected from Amazon, as its competitors also engage algorithms. Each of these algorithms will "anticipate and respond to rival algorithms' actions."[61] Whether the response will eventually amount to tacit collusion, as, in the end, all these algorithms are connecting to transparent information, is not touched upon.[62]

---

[57] See, e.g., Ezrachi and Stucke (n. 12 above) at 229–30.

[58] ibid., at 56.

[59] Ariel Ezrachi and Maurice Stucke, 'Algorithmic Collusion: Problems and Counter-Measures' (Note submitted for OECD Roundtable on Algorithms and Collusion' *DAF/COMP/WD(2017)25* (2017), available at www.oecd.org/officialdocuments/publi cdisplaydocumentpdf/?cote=DAF/COMP/WD%282017%2925&docLanguage=En (accessed June 30, 2022). See also Ezrachi and Stucke (n. 12 above) at 212, stating that "[a]nother set of scenarios involve pricing algorithms tacitly colluding in a transparency-enhanced environment."

[60] Ezrachi and Stucke (n. 12 above) at 13.

[61] ibid., 14.

[62] But see, Weiting and Sapi (n. 10 above) at 41–2. They state that their research has focused on the result of the use of algorithms. However, they indicate that it is also necessary to see what kind of data is given to these algorithms. It could be, according to them, that "algorithms that take as input the prices of rivals may cause more harm in competitive markets than algorithms that merely experiment and observe the resulting demand." ibid., 42. If this were to be true, it is so much more important to further audit

If the introduction of algorithms aggregates opportunities for tacit collusion, in contrast to current contentions regarding transparency in the literature, it could be presumed that opaqueness actually offers less opportunity for tacit collusion. Investigating this presumption regarding information opaqueness is only possible by looking at examples of business models where an algorithm is operating based on opaque information. As mentioned above, Uber has a prominent spot. When elaborating their understanding of algorithmic collusion, Ezrachi and Stucke opined that Uber's algorithm could be a new expression of a hub-and-spoke conspiracy.[63] It is new because Uber's algorithm, the hub, is designed to tamper with competition without necessarily facilitating collusion. Several elements contribute to this tampering, one of which appears to be the opaqueness of Uber's algorithms.[64] This can be deducted from statements that Uber has full control over the operation of its algorithm.[65] Further, when Uber deems appropriate, either because of the data collected or the position it has obtained in the market, "one may wonder what effect its algorithm could have on the market price."[66] In the end, Uber makes us believe that we are being charged a competitive price. As Ezrachi and Stucke label it, we are left with "the illusion of a competitive price"[67] or are functioning "under the guise of a 'market-clearing' price."[68]

Of course, for the claim that Uber's algorithm, as a hub, has the ability to set a price that is potentially influenced by unfair factors to hold true, all spokes

---

this kind of unsophisticated algorithms and, especially, the nature of the data on which they operate.

[63]   Ezrachi and Stucke (n. 12 above) at 50–4.

[64]   ibid., 211, mentioning that "[c]onsumers do not know how Uber's pricing algorithm calculates the surge price or whether the surge price is fair."

[65]   ibid., 51. This does not mean that all Uber drivers have no control over the price setting by the algorithm. Pinar Akman reported in her extensive study on online platforms that the control over the price may vary depending on the geographical area. She states that "[t]he figure provided by Uber is a 'recommended fare' and the driver can agree a lesser (but not greater) sum with the passenger" and "Uber drivers can also request different fares than that recommended by Uber's algorithm in that they can accept a lower sum from the rider." See Pinar Akman, 'Online Platforms, Agency, and Competition Law: Mind the Gap' (2019) 43 (2) *Fordham International Law Journal* 209, 265 and 285 n. 314. Julian Nowag, however, indicates that BlaBlaCar uses a recommended fare, while Uber "uses an algorithm to set a unified price for all sellers on its platform." See Julian Nowag, 'When Sharing Platforms Fix Sellers' Prices' (2018) 6(3) *Journal of Antitrust Enforcement* 382, 386.

[66]   Ariel Ezrachi and Maurice E. Stucke, 'Artificial Intelligence & Collusion: When Computers Inhibit Competition' (2017) 5 *University of Illinois Law Review* 1776, 1788.

[67]   Ezachi and Stucke (n. 12 above) at 208.

[68]   ibid., 211. For an elaborate study on how Uber can be connected to manipulation of market prices, see Ryan Calo and Alex Rosenblat, 'The Taking Economy: Uber, Information, and Power' (2017) 117(6) *Colum. Law Rev.* 1623.

must be situated within the closed ecosystem of Uber. It is only when Uber developed software to encroach upon the software of other ride-sharing firms that the competition law literature began to consider other pricing strategies,[69] such as exclusionary conduct.[70] Yet, this artificially created transparency could also potentially enable tacit collusion. The reason that the literature has not examined this is simply a lack of examples. Nevertheless, in line with Chen et al., one should understand that the transparency created can potentially transgress ethical and legal boundaries.[71] Furthermore, the software to monitor other ride-sharing platforms does not prove anything in relation to algorithms' ability to engage in other pricing strategies.

3   CHEN ET AL.'S STUDIES IN A COMPETITION LAW CONTEXT

3.1   Collusion in Terms of Information Transparency and Opaqueness

The Amazon study begins with the observation that "dynamic pricing algo-rithms can implement collusive strategies that harm consumers. For example, the US Justice Department successfully prosecuted several individuals who implemented a price-fixing scheme on Amazon using algorithms."[72] Although

---

[69]   For information on Uber's strategy encroaching upon Lyft, *see* O.C. Ferrel, John Fraedrich, Linda Ferrel, *Business Ethics: Ethical Decision Making and Cases* (13th edn, Cengage Learning 2021) 401 (providing this story in the framework of a case study called 'Uber Collides with Controversy'); Catherine Shu, 'Uber Reportely Tracked Lyft Using a Secret Software Program Named "Hell"' (2017) *Techcrunch*, available at https://techcrunch.com/2017/04/12/hell-o-uber/ (accessed June 30, 2022); Danielle Muoio, 'The FBI Is Investigating Whether Uber Used Secret Software Called "Hell" to Track Lyft Drivers' (2017) Insider, available at www.businessinsider.com/fbi-uber-investigation-hell-software-lyft-driver-tracking-2017-9#:~:text=Uber%20is%20said%20to%20have,how%20many%20drivers%20were%20nearby (accessed June 30, 2022). The strategy led to a court case, see *Michael Gonzales v. Uber Technologies, Inc,* Case 3:17-cv-02264-JSC, U.S. District Court for the Northern District of California.

[70]   See, e.g., Thomas K. Cheng and Julian Nowag, 'Algorithmic Predation and Exclusion' (University of Hong Kong Faculty of Law Research Paper No. 2022/05, 2022), available at https://papers.ssrn.com/sol3/papers.cfm?abstract_id=4003309 (accessed June 30, 2022); Ignacio Herrera Anchustegui and Julian Nowag, 'How the Uber & Lyft Case Provides an Impetus to Re-Examine Buyer Power in the World of Big Data and Algorithms' (Lund University Legal Research Paper Series Lund Comp. Working Paper 01/2017, 2017) 3, available at https://papers.ssrn.com/sol3/papers.cfm?abstract_id=2998688 (accessed June 30, 2022).

[71]   Chen et al. (n. 4 above) at 4.

[72]   Chen et al. (n. 5 above) at 1339.

collusion may be one of the "intentional or unintentional market distortions"[73] of the use of algorithms, Chen et al. demonstrate that their data did not reveal such an issue.[74] Chen et al. are probably correct within the limited scope of explicit collusion, whereby communication occurs between different active actors on Amazon Marketplace. A recent example is "Sold by Amazon," an exclusive program that enabled "the online retailer to agree on price with third-party sellers, rather than compete with them."[75] Amazon was ordered to close down this program because it constituted price-fixing under competition law and also had to pay a \$US 2.25 million fine to the Washington Attorney General's office.[76]

However, if collusion is extended to include its tacit version, referring to the freedom "to change … prices, taking into account in so doing the present or foreseeable conduct of his competitors,"[77] the story becomes different. The Amazon study demonstrates that it is fairly easy to collect data on products sold by online retailers, especially in relation to price; therefore, if sellers employ the right kind of technology on the platform, they should be able to change their price in relation to others' price. This will be especially so when the price setting algorithm uses a target price methodology. This is exactly what the Amazon study concluded.

Algorithms active on Amazon Marketplace primarily function on the principle of target pricing. According to the Amazon study, the target price of the majority of the algorithms was the lowest advertised price. This resulted in the algorithmic seller quickly matching the lowest price, whether that price decreased or increased. Regardless of whether the algorithmic seller was a third-party seller or Amazon itself, the result was the same. A decrease of the lowest price triggered a reduction of the algorithmically determined price, and the opposite was true as well. When the lowest price increased, the algorithmically determined price raised as well. As noted previously, though the algorithm of Amazon itself followed the price patterns of the lowest price setters,

---

[73]   ibid., 1348.

[74]   ibid.

[75]   Washington State, Office of the Attorney General, 'AG Ferguson Investigation Shuts Down Amazon Price-Fixing Program Nationwide' (26 January 2022), available at www.atg.wa.gov/news/news-releases/ag-ferguson-investigation-shuts-down -amazon-price-fixing-program-nationwide#:~:text=The%20%E2%80%9CSold%20by %20Amazon%E2%80%9D%20program%20allowed%20the%20online%20retailer %20to,profits%20off%20third%2Dparty%20sales (accessed June 30, 2022).

[76]   Hannah Brem, 'Amazon to Pay \$2.25M, Shut Down Price-Fixing Program after Washington State AG Investigation' (28 January 2022) *Jurist*, available at www .jurist.org/news/2022/01/amazon-to-pay-2-25m-shut-down-price-fixing-program-after -washington-state-ag-investigation/ (accessed June 30, 2022).

[77]   Case 48/69 *Imperial Chemical Industries*, ECLI:EU:C:1972:70, para 118.

it did not always set its price at the exact same level as the lowest price.[78] The Amazon study seems to confirm the proposition that tacit collusion is a likely outcome of increased price transparency.[79] Moreover, the study demonstrates that this algorithmic tacit collusion does not necessarily require extremely large data sets, or Big Data.[80]

It is for sure that an increased use of the above-mentioned pricing algorithms coupled with transparency of information may lead to more tacit collusion. The question is whether this kind of collusion could ever be considered illegal. Rosa M. Abrantes-Metz and Albert D. Metz seem to suggest that we may need further information on how algorithms function together as a set to answer that question. By looking at a single pricing algorithm that is set to replicate the price of a competitor, it is difficult to discern an algorithm reflecting a rational business decision and an algorithm implementing illegal collusion.[81] It is not possible to say something valuable in this regard based upon the Amazon study of Chen et al. No detailed information is provided on how the different algorithms operate in relation to each other.

When the information source is opaque, explicit communication may be required to achieve collusion. Such accusations have emerged in the context

---

[78] By lowering their price, they can force the other party to increase the price, even if they do not go entirely to the lowest price, reflecting the non-profitability of price lowering.

[79] Similar, Wieting and Sapi (n. 10 above) at 21. This conclusion is reached after pointing out that unexpected cost shocks are unlikely to occur this fast. Moreover, the authors point to the release of jitters, either up or down, which could be considered as signaling to competitors the intent to raise or lower the price. ibid., at 20.

[80] But see, Ezrachi and Stucke (n. 12 above) at 11–21 and 233, implying that Big Data is one of the aspects to facilitate algorithmic collusion. Wieting and Sapi further state that the drive towards pricing that looks similar to collusion may even not require complex algorithms. When investigating Bol.com, a Dutch e-commerce platform similar to Amazon, these authors share their impression that the "re-pricer software is relatively unsophisticated. We see little trace of complex learning behind the documented pricing patterns." Wieting and Sapi (n. 10 above) at 9. They further argue that unsophisticated algorithms are not less dangerous and opine that "[a] secret to successful collusion may lie in managers' ability to commit to simple strategies, such as leader-follower prices … via the simple *if-then* formulae in off-the-shelf re-pricer software." Wieting and Sapi (n. 10 above) at 41. The study of Assad, Clark, Ershov, and Xu further indicates that there is information on the mass availability of algorithms, but not whether the same or different algorithms are used. See Assad, Clark, Ershov, and Xu (n. 10 above) at 43.

[81] Rosa M. Abrantes-Metz and Albert D. Metz, 'Pricing Algorithms and Collusion: Is there Clarity on What Corporations May be on the Hook For?' (2020) *CPI Antitrust Chronicle* 5–6, available at www.brattle.com/wp-content/uploads/2021/05/20513 _pricing_algorithms_and_collusion_-_is_there_clarity_on_what_corporations_may _be_on_the_hook_for.pdf (accessed June 30, 2022).

of Uber.[82] Spencer Meyer alleged that Travis Kalanick, the CEO of Uber, had "orchestrated and facilitated an illegal price-fixing conspiracy in violation of Section 1 of the federal Sherman Antitrust Act."[83] A class action lawsuit was filed against Uber's CEO. Thanks to Judge Jed S. Rakoff, we know some of the arguments to support such an allegation. Meyer's claim began with the observation that the price is determined by an algorithm, and despite Uber's claim of the opposite, there was no possibility for a driver to lower that price.[84] If given the opportunity, Meyer claimed drivers would have competed on the price and prices would have been substantially lower.[85] Furthermore, Uber had created a surge multiplier, allowing its algorithm to multiply the price "ten times the standard fare during times of high demand."[86] Making the surge multiplier dependent on supply and demand, Meyer argued, could generate a "common motive to conspire."[87] Frequent meetings, organized by Uber itself, in the form of picnics or partner appreciation events, offered an excellent venue to implement this common motive.[88]

The courts did not decide the case based on merits. Kalanick was able to compel arbitration, and the award was not favourable for Meyer.[89] This arbi-

---

[82] See *Meyer v. Kalanick*, 174 F. Supp. 3d 817, 819–820 (S.D.N.Y. 2016). For a discussion of the Uber competition cases, see Ezrachi and Stucke (n. 12 above) at 54; Daniel Bitton, David Pearl, and Patrick Shaw, 'Let Me Ride: No Short-Cuts in the Antitrust Analysis of Ride Hailing' (2019) 29(2) *The Journal of the CLA Antitrust, UCL and Privacy Section* 20; Herbert Hovenkamp, 'Platforms and the Rule of Reason: The *American Express* Case' (2019) *Columbia Business Law Review* 35, 73–4; Nicholas Andrew Passaro, 'How *Meyer v. Uber* Could Demonstrate that Uber and the Sharing Economy Fit into Antitrust Law' (2018) 7 *Mich. Bus. & Entrepreneurial L. Rev.* 259, 265; Johannes Safron, 'The Application of EU Competition Law to the Sharing Economy' (European Union Law Working Papers No. 27, 2018) 28–9; Ahmore Burger-Smidt and Graeme Wickins, 'The Uber Price-Fixing Ride: What are the Antitrust Co-ordinates'(2016), available at www.werksmans.com/wp-content/uploads/2018/10/061416-Uber-Pricing-Fixing.pdf (accessed June 30, 2022).
[83] *Meyer v. Kalanick*, 200 F. Supp. 3d 408, 411 (S.D.N.Y. 2016).
[84] *Meyer v. Kalanick*, 174 F. Supp. 3d 817, 819–21 (S.D.N.Y. 2016).
[85] ibid., 821.
[86] ibid.
[87] ibid., 821, 823, 824, 827.
[88] ibid., 821.
[89] For a possible reasoning on why outcome may not have been favorable, see Bitton, Pearl, and Shaw (n. 82 above) at 22–6. The arbitration issues are covered in the press, see, e.g., Jonathan Stempel, 'Uber Wins U.S. Court Appeal to Push Price-Fixing Case to Arbitration' (18 August 2017) *Reuters*, available at www.reuters.com/article/us-uber-decision-idUSKCN1AX1MU (accessed June 30, 2022). The arbitration award was contested, claiming partiality of the arbitrator who stated on the record that he would not dare to declare Uber's practices illegal for his own security. No matter how controversial, Judge Rakoff did not overturn the award for this reason. See Tina

tration award may satisfy economists.[90] It is argued that as the operator of the platform, Uber "needs to seek out the equilibrium spot that will bring in the optimal number of drivers and riders. Setting fares too high discourages riders, while setting them too low discourages drivers."[91] The surge multiplier enables Uber to find the equilibrium. However, Meyer was not necessarily disagreeing with this. His claim centred around the idea that there was collusion between Uber's CEO, who often functioned as a driver himself, and the other Uber drivers to artificially increase prices. The evidence? Uber organized meetings for its drivers and their families.[92] No details were given regarding what was discussed during those meetings; however, Meyer implied that these meetings could have been a forum for communication about how to influence ride prices.[93]

Despite the absence of direct evidence of communication during meetings organized by Uber, Minda Zetlin has reported attempts to manipulate the surge multiplier through communication.[94] Zetlin conveyed that a group of 50 Uber drivers at Reagan National Airport near Washington DC agreed to turn off their apps when they expected a huge increase in demand.[95] Every time several airplanes were to land, these drivers artificially decreased the supply, driving ride prices up. Two members of the group would monitor the Uber app to see when the prices began to surge. At that point, the other drivers would switch on their app again. Zetlin reported that this increased fares by about $US 13.[96]

Uber contested the ability of drivers to manipulate the surge multiplier. According to Zetlin, Uber's best argument was a newspaper article in the Washington Post.[97] Despite Chen et al.'s acknowledgment that drivers could

---

Bellon, 'U.S. Judge Denies Claims Uber Won Price-Fixing Suit Because Arbitrator Was Scared' (August 4, 2020) *Reuters*, available at www.reuters.com/article/us-uber -lawsuit-idUSKCN24Z2RL (accessed June 30, 2022).

[90] Hovenkamp (n. 82 above) at 39.

[91] ibid., 73.

[92] See *Meyer v. Kalanick*, 174 F. Supp. 3d 817, 821 (S.D.N.Y. 2016). For a study on the operation of the surge price mechanism, see Jonathan Hall, Cory Kendrick, and Chris Nosko, 'The Effects of Uber's Surge Pricing: A Case Study' (2016), available at https://economicsforlife.ca/wp-content/uploads/2015/10/effects_of_ubers_surge _pricing.pdf (accessed June 30, 2022).

[93] See *Meyer v. Kalanick*, 174 F. Supp. 3d 817, 821 (S.D.N.Y. 2016).

[94] Minda Zetlin, 'Here's Why Uber and Lyft Drivers Are Artificially Creating Surge Prices: Really, it's hard to Blame Them' (May 23, 2019) *Inc.*, available at www.inc.com/minda-zetlin/uber-lyft-drivers-artificial-surge-pricing-reagan-national -washington-arlington-drive-united.html (accessed June 30, 2022).

[95] ibid. See also Bitton, Pearl, and Shaw (n. 82 above) at 26.

[96] Zetlin (n. 94 above).

[97] Abby Phillip, 'No, Uber Drivers Can't Game the 'Surge Pricing' System the Way One Driver Claims Image Without a Caption' (May 19, 2015) *The Washington*

manipulate Uber's algorithm and that their operation had limitations in detecting this kind of manipulation, a few findings in relation to the surge multiplier allow for some interesting observations. Chen et al. found that the surge multiplier operated in the smaller geographical areas delineated by Uber caused the effects of a price surge in limited spaces.[98] Within these areas, it was difficult to predict when the surge multiplier would apply. None of the collected data, whether related to supply, demand, or EWT, revealed a correlation with the surge price. Chen et al. subsequently suggested that other, non-public information may also be used to calculate price surges.[99] The study also found that Uber recalculated the surge multiplier every five minutes.[100] Therefore, if collectively turning off the Uber app led to a price surge, it could be expected that such collusion would only be effective for a limited amount of time. The difficulty for drivers to put the decision to collude into practice, of course, does not detract from the fact that collusion is an infringement of competition law that, in principle, does not depend on the effect of an agreement.

The above explanation elaborates on a circumstance in which the spokes are in direct communication. The other scenario of collusion, as described in the early competition law literature on algorithmic collusion, would be one in which the hub, Uber's algorithm, is steering equitable price calculation for all the spokes.[101] Although this kind of scenario may be feasible, there is one notable observation in the Uber study. Chen et al. reveal that Uber manually divided the map of cities and made price calculations based on this division; hence, it was possible to be presented with an entirely different price, either higher or lower, by moving a few feet or crossing the street.[102] This makes it more difficult to sustain the claim that Uber aims to provide the same price across its drivers.

Of course, the geographical price differentiation could trigger the question of whether this is happening on fair grounds. Chen et al. explicitly did not think so,[103] but it should be noted that they only came to this conclusion after an extensive audit of Uber's algorithm. In other words, the algorithm's opaqueness forces consumers to believe that they are offered a service for market

---

Post, available at www.washingtonpost.com/news/the-switch/wp/2015/05/19/no-uber -drivers-cant-game-the-surge-pricing-system-the-way-one-driver-claims/   (accessed June 30, 2022).

[98]   Chen et al. (n. 4 above) at 10.
[99]   ibid., 11.
[100] ibid., 1.
[101] Ezrachi and Stucke (n. 12 above) at 53.
[102] Chen et al. (n. 4 above) at 3.
[103] ibid., 13.

value, while in reality this may not be the case.[104] However, this is impossible for them to know. This issue relates to Ezrachi and Stucke's other warning in relation to hub-and-spoke collusion in which circumstances may enable Uber to manipulate the price at its discretion.[105] Whether such conduct can be linked to a theory of harm will be difficult to ascertain. This will require a competition authority "to delve into the heart of an algorithm to establish whether it is designed in a way that would lead to, or may lead to, exploitation."[106] This may prove extremely cumbersome,[107] as made obvious in Chen et al.'s Uber study.

3.2 Little Signs of Pricing Strategies Alternative to Collusion

From the outset of the algorithmic collusion debate, there has been an understanding that algorithms are "programmed to monitor price changes and swiftly react to any competitor's price reduction."[108] The idea behind this understanding is that each algorithm will eventually move toward the same price. Nicolas Petit attributes the concept "algorithmic homogeneity" to this understanding.[109] Maurice Dolmans does not agree, and is one of the first to posit that a pricing algorithm could develop different pricing strategies, claiming that a pricing algorithm may eventually choose predatory pricing or any other exclusionary conduct as the optimal strategy to realize a long-term profit.[110]

---

[104] Chen et al. demonstrate that price is not necessarily a reflection of market forces. They assert that there was no conclusive evidence on whether a price surge attracts new drivers. It seemed that the supply side did not correct the market and unlike the demand side, Chen et al find price surges to have a considerably negative effect on demand, leading to speculation that customers are aware they have to wait for a few minutes for the surge multiplier to disappear. Chen et al. also suggest that potential customers, if possible, will move around if they are confronted with a price surge. As indicated in the main text, cities are divided into "surge areas" and moving into a different area could lead to a different price calculation. ibid.

[105] Ezrachi and Stucke (n. 12 above) at 54.

[106] ibid.

[107] Bostoen (n. 6 above) at 161, indicating that auditing is very complex.

[108] Damien Geradin, 'Algorithmic Tacit Collusion and Individualized Pricing: Are Antitrust Concerns Justified?' (Copenhagen Economics Conference, 2017) 2, available at www.copenhageneconomics.com/dyn/resources/Filelibrary/file/6/66/1498204706/geradin.pdf (accessed June 30, 2022).

[109] Nicholas Petit, 'Editorial: Antitrust and Artificial Intelligence: A Research Agenda' (2017) 8(6) *Journal of European Competition Law and Practice* 361, at 362.

[110] The information may include "rivals' market share, assets, capital reserves, employee count, variable and fixed costs, etc." See Maurice Dolmans, 'Artificial Intelligence and the Future of Competition Law – Further Thoughts (Reaction to Prof. Ariel Ezrachi)' (GCLC Lunch Talk: Algorithms and Markets: Virtual or Virtuous

To focus this discussion to the subject of one of the Chen et al. studies, Amazon has been accused of predatory pricing. The current chairperson of the Federal Trade Commission, Lina Khan, claimed in her student-written paper of 2017, titled *Amazon's Antitrust Paradox*, that Amazon is guilty of predatory pricing. She writes in the abstract to this note, "[a]lthough Amazon has clocked staggering growth, it generates meager profits, choosing to price below-cost and expand widely instead."[111] A later paper by Shaoul Sussman, sided with Khan's claim and developed new insight on how Amazon could successfully engage in predatory pricing without raising its prices to recoup losses.[112] Sussman expands on how Amazon aims to continue this low price setting by divesting its costs to suppliers and partners.

The Amazon study does not produce evidence that Amazon has engaged in predatory pricing. The study is an empirical analysis of existing algorithms active on Amazon Marketplace.[113] Nevertheless, by studying these algorithms, interesting observations can be made. One may be relevant to the predatory pricing argument. The use of algorithms, by third-party sellers and Amazon itself, on average, resulted in a price that was 40 per cent higher than the lowest price. The price efficiency generated by the algorithms could, but this requires a further investigation, reveal a predatory pricing strategy rationale.[114] The efficiency could contribute to recouping the losses sustained for products on which Amazon is the loss leader.[115]

Considering the overall price setting on Amazon Marketplace could also suggest that the algorithms do not demonstrate a downward price-setting

---

Competition, 2017), available at www.coleurope.eu/sites/default/files/uploads/event/dolmans.pdf. (accessed June 30, 2022).

[111] Lina M. Khan, 'Note: Amazon's Antitrust Paradox' (2018) 126(3) *The Yale Law Journal* 564. For a critic, see John A. Fortin, 'Predatory Pricing and the Flaws in Brandesian Economics Challenging Recoupment Theory' (2020), available at https://papers.ssrn.com/sol3/papers.cfm?abstract_id=3676799 (accessed June 30, 2022).

[112] Shaoul Sussman, 'Prime Predator: Amazon and the Rationale of Below Average Variable Cost Pricing Strategies Among Negative-Cash Flow Firms Get Access Arrow' (2019) 7(2) *Journal of Antitrust Enforcement* 203.

[113] Chen et al. (n. 5 above) at 1339.

[114] The Amazon study also asserts that the algorithm helps third-party sellers to compete with Amazon, only ranking in the top five sellers 88 per cent of the time when third-party sellers use algorithms, while this occurs 96 per cent of the time in markets without such sellers. ibid., 1347.

[115] A counter argument could be that efficiency cannot sustain a theory of harm. A similar critic is delivered to Sussman's point of view. See Kristian Stout and Alec Stapp, 'Is Amazon Guilty of Predatory Pricing?' (7 May 2019) *Truth on the Market: Scholarly Commentary on Law, Economics, and More*, available at https://truthonthemarket.com/2019/05/07/is-amazon-guilty-of-predatory-pricing/ (accessed June 30, 2022).

spiral. There is more of a tendency to collude on the lowest price, after which the prices rise again. In this regard, the Amazon study indicates that the majority of the algorithmic third-party sellers set their price within $US 1 of the lowest price. Other algorithmic third-party sellers match Amazon's price; however, they tended to have a higher price than Amazon's. The study estimated that these sellers' algorithms would set their new price 15 to 30 per cent higher than Amazon's price, which could be linked to the commission fee that third-party sellers are obligated to pay Amazon. Chen et al. further observed that Amazon itself was using an algorithm in its price-setting policy.[116] The Amazon algorithm tended to set its prices at a premium. The prices on Amazon were always slightly higher than the lowest price of all other sellers. The Amazon algorithm also appeared "to have a ceiling at around $[US] 9, above which they match the lowest price, but below which they sell the product with a small premium relative to the lowest price."[117]

The assertion that the algorithm did not engage in a downward price spiral is further supported by the observation that low price setting of algorithmic sellers occurred for a relatively short time. The Amazon study revealed that once algorithms adjusted their price to the lowest one, prices rise again relatively quickly.[118] The overall observation that the low price setting is relatively short may prevent the development of the exclusionary effect indicative of predatory pricing.[119] However, this statement should not lead to the conclusion that Amazon did not engage in overall predatory pricing strategy.

To understand whether pricing strategies leading to other anti-competitive tactics than collusion, in case of Uber, it is important to start from the opaqueness of its algorithm. The Uber study demonstrated that the opaqueness requires reverse engineering to obtain information; otherwise, the price-setting information would not have been available to Chen et al. Similar issues exist with other ride-sharing firms. In general, this complicates access to pricing information within this industry. In principle, Uber's pricing algorithm may not be able to do anything more than it has been trained to do. This changed

---

[116] Chen et al. (n. 5 above) at 1339.

[117] ibid., 1346..

[118] ibid., 1345. Figures 14 and 17 in the Amazon study of Chen et al. exemplify the speed with which prices go up and down.

[119] In order to speak about predatory pricing, a firm has to reduce "its prices to a loss-making level for a short-term to discipline its existing competitors or foreclose the market to new entrants with a view to strengthening or maintaining its market power later." The time element needs to show a "deliberate sacrifice." See Gönenç Gürkaynak and Onur Özgümüş, 'Predatory Pricing' in Deborah Healey, William Kovacic, Pablo Trevisán, Richard Whish (eds), *Global Dictionary of Competition Law, Concurrences,* Art. No. 12336, available at www.concurrences.com/en/dictionary/predatory-pricing (accessed June 30, 2022).

with the implementation by Uber of another piece of software, called "Hell."[120] Hell was a piece of software allowing Uber to track which drivers were also working for Lyft. The software's aim was to determine which drivers were multi-homing to then treat them more favourably on Uber. The favourable treatment included offering multi-homing drivers more passengers and awarding them special bonuses if they reached a certain number of rides per week. The hope was that this strategy would entice drivers to exclusively drive for Uber, weakening Lyft's market position.[121]

Underlying the implementation of Hell was an explicit decision of Uber's executives. It was not a turn made by the algorithm used to determine price setting. The reason for this could once again be found in the opaqueness of the information necessary to determine the prices within a ride-sharing sector. Due to the opaqueness, a system needs to be built, as Chen et al. did to obtain information on Uber that emulates the operation on a specific ride-sharing platform. This is exactly what Uber did. The company indicated that Hell software allowed the creation of fake rider accounts on Lyft,[122] something that Chen et al. refused to do for ethical reasons.[123] These

> fake riders were positioned in a grid to give Uber the entire view of a city and all of Lyft's drivers within it. ... While keeping an eye on its rivals' cars, though, Uber noticed that Lyft's drivers are identified by special numbered IDs that never change like its own tokens do. That allowed the team running Hell to learn of each driver's habits, which, in turn, helped them to figure out which drivers practice "double-apping".[124]

In terms of the Uber ecosystem, Chen et al. indicated that when they conducted the experiment, Uber did not give its drivers control over price. Despite this observation, it has been reported that drivers are able to adopt a common strategy to steer one element of the price-setting algorithm: the surge multiplier. The example suggests that this result could only be achieved because the drivers began to understand the operation of the algorithm, after which they communicated to collectively achieve a higher price. Chen et al. seem to confirm this when noting that the pricing algorithm itself could not temporarily shut down driver accounts to increase the price. If communication is essential to achieve a specific price setting, it is questionable that drivers would consider

---

[120] Cheng and Nowag (n. 70 above) at 5–6.
[121] ibid.
[122] Bostoen (n. 6 above) at 163–4. See also Mariella Moon, 'Uber's 'Hell' Program Tracked and Targeted Lyft Drivers' (13 April 2017), available at www.engadget.com/2017-04-13-uber-hell-program-lyft-drivers.html (accessed June 30, 2022).
[123] Chen et al. (n. 4 above) at 4.
[124] Moon (n. 122 above).

any other outcome rational than the one that will increase their income. The low entry barrier for other car owners to join the Uber network may prevent any attempt to exclude drivers from the Uber network as a rational strategy. It is thus questionable whether any strategy other than collusion, either on the price or on the division of the market, would be preferred by drivers.

4   CONCLUSION

Algorithms have opened new opportunities for the business community, whether for optimization of price setting (Amazon) or the creation of new business models (Uber). Despite these new opportunities, little is known about how these algorithms behave. This is problematic for regulatory authorities, among others. It is only through a better understanding of these algorithms that appropriate enforcement policies can be developed. Chen et al. contribute to this better understanding by auditing the algorithms of Uber and Amazon Marketplace.

Chen et al.'s auditing leads to the conclusion that there are at least two kinds of information sources: transparent and opaque.

Transparent information allows for competitors to easily engage in tacit collusion, triggering the question of whether some additional regulatory intervention on algorithms is needed to temper the transparency. Chen et al.'s auditing also reveals that transparent algorithms increase efficiency, enabling higher price setting, which may not be problematic; however, this efficiency may be leveraged to cross-finance an overall predatory strategy.

Tacit collusion is less likely in the case of opaque information. A circumstance of opaque information would be different if transparency is artificially created. Then, other pricing strategies are possible, even exclusionary ones. In business models operating on opaque information, algorithm auditing has revealed that even explicit collusion may be difficult, as it requires group agreement and a full understanding of how the algorithm operates. Furthermore, even with an understanding of the algorithm, the effect of such collusion is only short lived.

Index